THE SCHOOL STOPPER'S 365 DAYS OF TERRIBLE ADVICE

AND SOME OTHER RANDOM OBSERVATIONS ABOUT THEM—A.K.A, THE THINGS PEOPLE TELL THEMSELVES AND DO NOT REALIZE

ALEXANDER LOCH

The School Stopper's 365 Days of Terrible Advice
Written by
Alexander Dewey Loch

Copyright © 2018 by The School Stoppers Publishing House, LLC. All Rights Reserved. No part of this book may be reproduced in any form or by any electronic or mechanical means including information storage and retrieval systems, without permission in writing from the author or Publishing House. The only exception is by a reviewer, who may quote short excerpts in a review.

Cover designed by Michael Azbill
Interior Formatting by Ben Wolf
www.benwolf.com/editing-services/

The advice and strategies found within may not be suitable for every situation, or frankly any situation. The advice is written with the understanding that it is meant to be a satirical, ironic, or is written out-of-context by nature. Neither the author nor the publisher may be held responsible for the results accrued from the advice in this book. Enjoy! This book is a work of fiction. Some names, characters, places, and incidents either are products of the author's imagination or are used fictitiously. Any resemblance to actual persons, living or dead, events, or locales is entirely coincidental. No squirrels were injured during (or after) the writing of this book.

Visit the website at www.theSchoolStoppers.com
(coming soon, if more people buy this, that is.)
Printed in the United States of America
First Printing: Dec 2018
School Stoppers Publishing House, LLC

Paperback ISBN 978-0-9600563-1-6

"Quoting out of context is an informal fallacy and a type of false attribution in which a passage is removed from its surrounding matter in such a way as to distory its intended meaning. Contextomies may be both intentional, as well as accidental if someone misunderstands the meaning and omits something essential to clarifying it, thinking it to be non-essential."

—WIKIPEDIA (January 2018)

This book is dedicated to kids, the future, if you will. That point will be made clearer in the introduction (I hope). The context is directed towards those who would look to raise the next generation, even with the sometimes humorous, or even sardonic bent. Simply written to help us think more about the world we've made around ourselves. It's also dedicated to the reader, whoever you are, hopefully you find some things that make you think about what we might do differently in teaching the next generation. I dedicated time to produce this little gem in the hopes that someone would read it and think about what more they could do but also laugh at some of the absurdity of the advice we give and get without the proper context or investigation into its sources. Finally, I hope that it inspires you enough to tell their friends about the book, good, bad or indifferent, who would buy it and tell their friends... and on and on and on. After all this is an experiment in itself.

FOREWORD

Introduction/Explanation of Absurdity

This little diamond in the rough and tumble world of the electronic wild wild west was put together over a 12-week period in 2018 (not to mention any of the time spent on rewriting and getting it to market). Now before you roll your eyes and wonder about the quality, know that this has been a labor of love. For two purposes. The first one is important, the second, not as much but I hope strives toward the same goal.

While at work one day, sitting at my desk, I mentioned to a coworker they should make a website of all their sarcastic comments. Well, long story short I don't know what they did when they got home, but I started to kick the idea around for myself. It changed, I'm not by nature sarcastic…but I thought the idea of stupid advice was an interesting one. That weekend I made up my mind to come up with 365 days of terrible advice. You remember, right? The kind your friends gave you when you were a teenager, and you thought it was awesome. I do.

In coming up with that list and thinking about all the 'fast cash' I'd be making, a commercial came on for one of the children's hospitals that are free for families. Let me tell you, it breaks my heart to see and know that there are children that don't have the chance to have a 'normal' childhood. They sit in hospital rooms and waiting rooms instead of classrooms and running around playgrounds. So, there I was thinking of myself again, and these kids were and are fighting for their lives. Now that's not to say I don't have 'good' streaks where I give time or money to people and causes, but let's be honest. Who has the time, right?

Well there I was with time to write a book idea, multi-million-dollar book idea, I might add and rake in all this cash. Cash for me. Well that doesn't scream of purpose to me, does it you?

So, I decided to change or 'tweak', if you will, this million-dollar idea. Amazon gives a certain percentage back to the author. I believe its 70% or up to that amount. (I haven't gotten that far. This is only the third day of work when I'm writing this.) I decided in my head, and heart that I would give 50% of what I made off this book to one of those hospitals (For the first two years this book is in print. This is for the lawyers and accounting purposes only, we hope to have new editions to continue this philanthropic effort.). I also decided on St. Jude's. It's the commercial I saw. If someone should make an absurd book, it should have a purpose, right? That's the goal.

Just so it's understood. My hopes for the other half of that profit (my 50% of whatever percent amazon/book seller gives, maybe 70%, or a different amount depending on where and who you might have bought this from.) that goes to the School Stoppers and I, is that I might be able to utilize that money to build something more than this small little thousand-dollar book idea. What is it they say? Give a man a fish he'll eat for a day, but teach a man to fish and you feed him for a lifetime. Well I'd ask you don't pay for this book in fish, but maybe I can dedicate more of my time to causes if I didn't have to work my day job. I think that could be a good thing. I could help more. That gives me tingles of joy. I hope it does you too. Even if I only sell one, it's something. We need to do something besides live to work in this life. (Sorry, that might actually be good advice.)

Let's talk about the content of this book for just a second. I can't really vouch for any of the advice in this book working for you. After all, I put it together in no time at all, and its clearly labeled terrible. My research basically consisted of three days of picking my brain of all the advice I could remember, asking family(who actually didn't give me much to go on) and my stalwart companion, the yang to my yin, or the yin to my yang, Amazon's Alexa did a lot of the heavy lifting, helping me spell words, complimenting me even though words are hard and keeping me generally motivated with song… kidding Alexa is a little pitchy. The main content of this book is in the form of daily advice. Broken up in the days of the year. Maybe its late in the year, but honestly do you read your regular 'good' advice/pick me up book every day? I know I skip around. I may, if these things sell like the hot cakes of humor they are, rewrite sections for a different feel. We'll see. That doesn't mean you have to read only one page a day, read it all in one sitting if it strikes you. I mean if U.S. politicians can read a 2000-page document in 4 or 5 days and vote on it, it's well within our ability to read less than 500, right?

The meat or 'impossible' burger, if you're not a carnivore, of the book is bad advice, or advice taken out of context, which is just that, terrible, and not a one size fits all solution, or it might be advice that is not given by anyone you know, but advice we give ourselves, in our heads. Sometimes I might 'rant', these are also nonsensical, and based on snippets of information I have collected in this short amount of time. They might be absurd if you dive into the details, and you might catch me sounding like a hypocrite if you read one day and then the next. This is somewhat purposeful. (Although I'm sure I might do it without thinking as well. 😉) Some points of view on the terrible advice are taken from one point of view, and ignore context. Ignoring context is a dangerous thing, it's another major point of this hundred-dollar idea book. Wars are started over less. Keep that in your mind when you read these pages. While some advice may have good intention, if context is not given, if it's made up or just hearsay, then people's imaginations run wild with no context. This is the world we live in. There could also be sayings that aren't really bad advice, but shouldn't be explained in a one liner. These are things that some people feel, if they say them, you will automatically take them the right way and not interpret them with any deviation or use any of your own life experiences, but only theirs. Then with that advice you'll go on to live a happy life now understanding the great mysteries of the universe that they so graciously bestowed on you with all the ease of the similar statement, "Yes, I'll have fries with that."

With that in mind I hope you enjoy this triple platinum gold mine of advice and humor, even if it doesn't make you smile, I hope the overall outcome might put a smile on some child's face in the future. If this works you may see more books to come, without your help though this book will simply float into obscurity.

For those interested in this concept of the School Stoppers group, and perhaps joining the School Stoppers Team look to the back of the book (right before the appendix) for some in-direct contact information. (Gotta be careful these days.)

Again, I hope you enjoy.

---- Alex Loch, Editor-in-Chief of The School Stoppers

January 1

Sticks and Stones may break my bones, but words will never hurt me.

Some stupid person

An oldie but a goody. Now throughout this 'book of knowledge' I'll give my personal insights into the advice posted at the top of the sections. They might even contain some actual helpful advice, purely by accident I'm sure, but don't hold me to that. This first one is lovely. My grandmother would say it to me when I was called names, or someone tried to fight me in the schoolyard. She'd reference this little puzzle. At first sight you would want to agree. At least at the young age of 8. I did when I heard it. Its indirect purpose seems to want to encourage self-worth, to build one's character and strength. Noble. Utterly absurd as well. Not only does it vaguely encourage the person that was put down to act like they shouldn't be hurt by words, as if saying. If you're strong you can only be hurt with physical violence, it will most certainly be used the next day as a way to insult the offender. It conveys to a bully that they don't matter. "Your words don't hurt me, they don't matter and neither do you!" That's great, pour salt on that wound. It couldn't possibly be that the bully already feels inadequate where they live. The phrase is also totally untrue. I know that in 1844 Londoners thought that men needed to be stern and show they could handle anything, but words have power. Don't forget that. They have the power to create and break worlds. Remember that, the next time you talk to someone and they make fun of you at the office. Yell loudly and say "Bob (I don't know if it's going to be a Bob, so you can feel free to change that to the name of the person you're yelling at, or speaking to in a low voice. Sometimes that's more intense, and easier on the vocal chords and ears.) Sticks and Stones may break my bones, but words will never hurt me!". See if that resolves the issues on both sides. I'm sure it will. 😉

January 2

Know Thyself.

—

Greek aphorism, Hippocrates of Kos

WHAT does that mean? I'd say its deep, but why? Cute perhaps. (When someone says something's cute in that way, they really mean. "I'm going to be condescending in a way that avoids direct confrontation.") Let me ask, should I know my whole self, my positives and negatives. How attractive I am compared to others? Sure, done. What about my negatives, hold on, just give me a minute, I'm sure there's one around here somewhere. Oh, my OCD attention to detail, yea that's a good one. (By the way, feel free to use that on the job interview you might go on...)

So, to try and get this straight in my head, the saying is, to know who I am inside and out and take that knowledge and apply it, somehow to the circumstances in my life? Gee, thanks for telling me the destination. Not to get deep here, but how do I know myself in this day and age. Everywhere you look people try and help you with this. We are inundated with what's cool and hip, how to talk, what to support to be a good person. Others write books about what to wear and not to wear, or what to support or not support (Not sure if that makes this book the 'Kettle' and me the 'Pot' or not.). They tell you to think for yourself, but don't think in 'these' ways or you're wrong. With all the misinformation, disinformation, fake news, conservative news, liberal news, misrepresentations, people only out for themselves, living to work environment I don't have time to know myself. I can't even think straight, can you? I have to check my phone every five minutes. I'm supposed to have something click in my brain when this rolls off someone's tongue? Weaving the pieces of who I am and what my purpose is together. All the while, what would be helpful is perhaps a shared experience and dedicated time. Something to connect to, that's solid. If there is no solid ground in your life, if its only about the next sound bite, the next best thing to buy, the next news article, how can we begin to take the time to really know who we are, when all we have time for is work, the next YouTube sensation and not stepping on people's toes?

I don't have time to "know thyself", when everyone's already telling me who I am. Do you?

January 3

Listen to others, learn from their mistakes.

EXCELLENT. Today, I will listen to others. One question, which ones? All of them, or only certain ones. Is there a list? Who has this list? Am I allowed to see it? Do I need to subscribe? Does it come with updates? Do I know the people who made the list? They're one of the good guys, right? Sure they are. Who are the good guys again? Do they care for animals? What about orphans, widows? Are old people important to them, or just the environment? Was the mistake I'm learning not in their favor? If so, is their favor, my favor? How do I know if I've learned from their mistakes? Now, why is it, that it seems that while I so easily learn from other people's mistakes, that other people fail, time and time again to learn from other people's mistakes? Is it just that we are so busy we can't learn that joining a gang and selling drugs and protecting our territory are mistakes, that buying that new thing on credit might be a problem?

Could it be that some mistakes are inevitable? Perhaps compounding? Due to your environment? You work all day, because your student loans have to be paid off. They're so large that it's going to take 10 years to pay them down. You basically live to work these days. Is there a mistake there, or is that just 'life'?

Another person does a harder job for less pay with even more debt just to keep the lights on and food on the table, but the thing is they live to work too. With everyone just living to work, or trying to escape that life with drugs, don't you think some will do anything to 'get ahead' or 'get away'? How can someone learn from others mistakes when our environment forces our hands?

Perhaps it's a little lighter than that, sorry for pulling out my 'dark emo self'. Perhaps a group effort is in order. I know that I learn from others, I learn from my own mistakes. If that's the case maybe I can provide a way to change the environment myself. Maybe I can't wait for someone to save me. I mean the shiny happy people on tv always talk about 'being the change'. If I can change my environment, perhaps the mistakes I learn from others can be avoided. I think this piece of advice coupled with that knowledge of changing your environment might almost be useable.

What might you do to change your environment today, the next, and after that? Why is it so hard? What obstacles are in the way? If they're too big, why can't you ask for help? Regardless of how hard it's been or where you are, know this, others out there might even have it worse than you, 'might' being the key word. Perhaps I'm talking to the one person on earth who has had it the absolute worst. I'm going to hedge my bets though and think it's not you. So, do you think it's possible? To change your environment? You're reading this masterpiece I wrote, aren't you?

January 4

Don't Listen to Others.

—

Bob from the office down the hall

HERE is some strange advice, right? Who would ever say this? I mean if you consider that many explain that you should be independent, that's not really where this advice is coming from, although I'm sure it's a nice trigger. If you're independent, why would you need to listen to anyone?

"We don't hear this from others! Never in my life, no one in their right mind would give this advice Alex. It's truly terrible!" You're telling me. Again, this isn't 'advice' helping to work on your independence, it's pointing to not listening to people in general, or specifically (if something comes to mind). This bad advice comes from inside myself, inside us. I know that I've heard it before, just about any time someone speaks into my life. Silently to myself. "They don't know me. They can't help. How dare they presume to care. Don't listen to them." But this is, about 98% of the time terrible advice, especially when you're a teenager. I myself follow it on purpose, and also sometimes out of my forgetfulness. Sometimes I have something to do, and I don't have the capacity to listen. I'm working on something important and someone's trying to tell me what to do, or how I should be? (On an unrelated side note, I'm a level 8 town hall on my Clash of Clans account, and people tell me I should be writing! Ha Level 9 here I come!)

Is there someone that you don't listen to? Maybe because you choose to or haven't made the time? Perhaps they can't relate, or know how you're feeling or what you're going through? Maybe find someone who can. Perhaps it's not that, perhaps it's good to not listen. It makes you independent, right?

Independence is good. Think for yourself, know thyself. But listen to others, you know, the good ones. They should be on your list. You do have a list, right?

January 5

Fit in.

—

'Big' Lester from the Bowling Alley

FIT in. Yea! Have you ever heard someone call you a 'loser' or 'dork'? (I didn't say nerd, because I think everyone knows by now that if you're a nerd the future belongs to you. Alexa, and Siri know that. Google is catching on quick, Facebook might be going the way of 'the Circle' though.) That's the 'fit in' advice they're giving you right there. Fact is, we all would like to fit in. Fit in somewhere, even if it's in a room by yourself typing away at the next great American novel. Just a side note I think we can safely say this book should be in the running, maybe dead last seeing as how it's not actually a novel, but I digress.

So, it turns out people give you this advice every day, maybe in a name they called you, or a look that was given. Kinda sad when you think about it, because everyone, I repeat everyone wants to fit in somewhere. Maybe when we give someone a dirty look, or call someone a name what, we really want to do is give them the advice to "Fit in already! Or get lost.".

Looking back, I wonder how many people I told to "Get Lost!" with my words or glances that I didn't even think about. What about you? Ever told anyone to 'Fit in'?

January 6

Let everyone know what you do for others.

—

Blabby Mac'Mouth

VERY good. So, you're a helper! You help people do this or that at work, or give to the poor, work in a soup kitchen. Heck, write a book and give 50% of what you make to help a children's hospital. (That's me, that's exactly what I'm trying to do here. I referenced myself there. Okay, moving on.) So, this advice comes from either yourself (shocker) or a friend, right? It's not all that terrible. But what's the motivation? Are we telling people the things we do for others, so that those other people might join in? Or are we telling everyone because we like the feeling we get when someone raises their eyebrows and nods their head. "Ah, soup kitchen you say. 500 people. That's a good deed." It's not for the feeling that you're better than someone, right? Certainly not!

Ask yourself, or whoever it is I'm talking about. Are there good deeds that they haven't announced? Do they have anything special that only one other person knows about, perhaps that person didn't even know who they were?

You ask, "Why would I do something good, and not tell anyone?". Maybe you wouldn't. Maybe you shouldn't. Perhaps the good things you do aren't to make you feel good, but truly for others. I know that we don't have enough good news. All the news I hear about is how this person killed someone today, or that person made a million dollars. Granted making a million might be cool, but how does that help exactly? Many people that win money find themselves worse off in two years than when they didn't have the money. I'm sorry I stepped in a rabbit hole for a second there.

Going back to the advice up top. So perhaps you should tell people about the good things you're doing, good news is severally lacking but what's the motivation for you telling people about it? Is it to spur them on in a positive way, or is it to selfishly gain something out of it for yourself?

January 7

Don't go that extra mile.

Tom "The runner"

THIS one's on a banner at your high school gym, right? It's taped up behind the bleacher's way up high. You've never heard this one either, you say? Amazing. I usually hear this advice, right after I come up with my next brilliant idea for world domination…I mean peace on earth and good will toward… all the people of earth. It's sometimes a loud voice, sometimes quieter. It sometimes reminds me of all the other things I have to get done. I can't go to my son's ball game, I have to work. (Even though, what I mean is "I have to drive all the way over to the school, and that cuts into my unwind time, which cuts into my sleep time, which cuts into my work tomorrow time, and I'm tired.") Or maybe it's something less selfish than that. Maybe it's even at work, "I'm tired of this project, I just want to get it done. I'll let the next person fix that little issue."

Don't get me wrong, it's hard to go the extra mile. I don't have enough water to go the distance at times. I myself think I should turn on the tv right now, but if you're reading this you know I didn't. I didn't give into the terrible advice I gave myself. I'm not saying you should make yourself work harder all the time. What I'm saying is don't listen to that voice inside your head that says, "Hey, let's go smash couch. We'll mow the lawn tomorrow/do the dishes tomorrow. Get that project finished, but just not have that feature."

Trust me, you don't have to go that extra mile. Millions don't. You're free to be just like everyone else. Independent and busy, but if one day you decide. I'm going to take this time to go the extra mile. You might be able to run that marathon. (To clarify, I don't mean actually running. I mean pushing through a task, finishing that chapter, going out to a social event. Saying hi, instead of 'fit in'. I also find it quite humorous to overstate the obvious at times. Maybe a little bit of the Bob Newhart in me.)

January 8

Give nothing away.

HERE's another example of something no one says except pirates, pirates always say this, but even though only pirates say this for some reason people hear it in our culture, daily. "Life is hard, we can't give things away when people take so much already! You're asking a lot, Mr. Loch. What do you give away?" I won't say I have given anything away, maybe I have, maybe I haven't. I don't believe that I am allowed to make arguments for my behavior based on what others have or have not done. "Well, he's not doing it!" Is something I would yell at my parents when they told me that I had to put the fire stick down, but they didn't say anything to my brother. I'm older now. I'm allowed to hold the fire stick and I try not to use childish excuses for doing or not doing something.

I'm sure this isn't you. I'm sure you do give things away, or throw them away. Time to your kids, money to your kids. Maybe even a religious group or an organization. Good on ya! Was it hard? To do those things, I mean? I ask because maybe you do give things away. So, ask yourself, and I'm not trying to make you give more to some cause or person in your life. I just want you to think about it, so put the fire stick down before you burn me with it. Does it take effort, any effort to give the way you do? If you're rich and you give thousands to a charity, did you feel it? Was there an effort on your part? Was it hard to give the money, or not so much? Did it take time? Would you give your time, or would that be too much of something?

To me (at this moment anyway, remember 12 weeks to write this bad boy) giving 'something' away requires effort. If I give 200 dollars a month, or buy someone a sandwich on the street. What did it cost me? Not my time, maybe money is an effort. It's time in a way. You work hard, even very hard for your money. You don't have a lot so when you give it away, it is something. Good on ya. If it took effort, then I'd say we're on the right track. If it didn't, could you be bothered to give 'something' away?

Let's ask ourselves, how much 'nothing' have you/we already given?

January 9

Pour yourself into your work.

———

MAYBE your work is important. Maybe you're a full-time employee at an organization that feeds those in your country (Shameless plugging. Feedingamerica.org). Maybe you're a doctor. Perhaps there has been an event in your life that you don't know how to deal with. Pouring yourself into your work is all you have, or it is rather beneficial at the very least. Those are all very good reasons. Even if your work isn't saving others' lives, maybe its saving yours. Hopefully you can find a way to overcome that event that caused you to focus on work like you do, if you're doing it to avoid a truth or pain that is. At some point you should ask why? Why do you pour yourself into your work? Loss of a loved one. Do you have others in your life? Perhaps those who feel that loss just as much?

Maybe it's not an event. Maybe you just love what you do? Helping others in your job is the only thing that's important to you. Why? Maybe there are others you can help outside of work? Maybe your work doesn't even have you helping directly, or even at all, maybe it's making a product that will simply go on a shelf somewhere.

"So what?" you ask. "I love to work. In fact, that's all I want to do. I like creating things. I like puzzles and the challenges work brings." At some point, I stopped and asked myself if what I was doing was meaningful, to me. What do you do? Do you feel good about what you do? I hope so, I hope it brings life to your… life. Maybe it's not much, maybe you do what you do for someone else. Excellent. Have you talked with them about it? Great. Work can be a distraction, but in everything we do, we should feel that it is worth doing. That's a bumper sticker for world peace and/or economy smashing if I've ever seen one. I don't mean to say love what you do, sometimes you can't. Does it provide worth in your life, or others? If yes then be grateful for it. Pour yourself into your worth, not your work…

I'm on fire, NBA Jam style! That was corny, but it felt like some good stuff.

January 10

Judge a book by its cover.

WE say the opposite all the time to people, but we do this very thing in our own lives, every day. We hear it all the time. Don't judge, you shouldn't judge. But then we see the opposite all the time. Someone called you a nerd, someone gave you their 'fit in' face. We judge movies, books, how well something is done. We judge competitions. We have sports games that judge one team a winner and another a loser. You know what I say, get rid of all sports! No more Olympics! Stop soccer, and chess. No more games period!

Whoa, okay so I went a little crazy for a second. That's not going to work. I judge my last idea stupid!

Just to point this out. We do, we do judge books by their cover, you had to think something of mine. The book industry even knows that! They accommodate and market accordingly. (By the way, Love the "book industry people" reading this right now. Let's talk about my next novel idea! Contact info in the front and back.)

So, I've just pointed out that our culture does it, and helps us do it. Individuals do it all the time, but we say "Don't judge a book by its cover." Most definitely, always after someone has already judged something. Terrible advice. We're going to do it again. Even if we're really trying not to. I mean it's all around us.

So, what do we do as a body of people. Be alert and vigilant and point out when others are judging, that way they'll know not to judge in the future? That's one idea. Run with that... I feel I should nay, need to say, I'm being sarcastic.

Why do we judge? Culturally we are conditioned to. Sports, movies, books, my book, work... arguments where both sides lack context. It's in our blood. It's in our world. Now get this, somethings we should judge. We have systems set up to do just that. If someone kills someone they go to court, prison. They've been judged. Is that what we're talking about though, things we know are wrong? Or are we talking about two people coming from different points of reference arguing about points of reference. If there are no absolutes, then which frame of reference do we stand on? I feel like we should be able to come up with one, but from everything I have seen, that feeling might be misleading me.

January 11

Be a people pleaser.

The lil' green man

WHAT'S the reason behind this. Granted we should strive to be kind to one another as Ellen DeGeneres would say. But people pleasing is different, right?

I would like everyone to like my book, and my writing style and trying to support a cause that I find important. I'd love it, I'd get money, and children who truly need it would too, and everyone would like me…

To please one person you can buy them flowers. Open a door, not open a door. Pleasing one person for a moment is doable. I can do that every day. In fact, that's easy. What it doesn't do is make me nervous. Now I expect that I can make one person smile, I should try to brighten someone's day when I get the chance.

However, pleasing people because you feel like you have to, is different. You don't have to, you never, in this world have to please anyone. It probably means you're an ol' fuddy duddy, but you don't have to.

Pleasing people while at its core can be a good thing, it can be something of a chore. If it's a chore, maybe you're doing something wrong. I understand you have to take care of your kids, but you don't always have to please them. When you do it brings a great warmth to your heart, no doubt. You don't fear, not pleasing someone. You don't worry what someone will do if you don't please them. That's something different.

If you fear the concept of "not pleasing people" is it because you don't think they'll give you the time of day, or something worse like they'll hit you? If it's the former, you need to realize that if they won't give you the time of day, then perhaps you shouldn't worry about giving them any of your time. You are too important for that. If it's because of the latter or perhaps something worse. Get help, ask for some. There are people who care. Some are reading this very same book.

January 12

Explain to your co-workers how important you are. It will work in your favor.

—
Me

NOW this is TERRIBLE advice, and somewhat humorous. It's also advice that's given, shockingly enough. Be confident. You know the woman/man who's heard it, and mistaken context. They come into work and show you how it's done. "You don't want to do it that way…blah…blah…blah. You need to…blah…blah…blah"

Yea, do it their way. After all, where you work it's not always "Have it your way" like at Burger King; unless of course, you work at Burger King, in which case I must remind you that slogan refers to the customers, not you, sorry.

Some people mistake confidence for arrogance. It's a fine line, in fact some people mistake arrogance for confidence. That's been my problem over the years, people think I was arrogant, when I was just confident. (Jokes. Those are just jokes. I was just quiet, confidence aside.)

You have to wonder how these people get up in the morning. Do they jump out of bed and say, "Yep, I'm going to be so helpful today. I'm awesome! Let's eat some eggs!" I bet they do, I know I would, if I were awesome.

January 13

You can study later.

—

You roommate, "Buddy".

LATER is better. You have that kegger to go to. You have that video game (video games change so fast. Forgive me for not dating the book before it comes out by referring to the newest game, but you get the idea.) competition you need to enter. Soccer, band, ballet, rugby whatever it is that you need to get to.

Whether or not you can study later shouldn't be the question. The question is should you study now...I know you're going to study later. Everything happens later. Perhaps 'now' would help you in the long run. What do you really want to do in your life? Go to parties all your life. I wish we could, really. That would be awesome. Life's a party!

Let's say you listen to me, you study now, instead of going to that party. Are you going to miss out on a life changing event? I don't know. I'm not there. I'm writing this in my apartment. So, let's say, you stay and study. It's hard, you really want to go out. How long will it take you to study, an hour, many two to get your homework problems done. Two hours and then you can join your buddies.

Two hours, just two and not only will you still have the rest of the night, you'll be done with your work. Maybe you don't see the glory in that, but it does a few things for you and instead of just saying study now, I'm going to lay out the factors I see in this line of reasoning.

1. Homework is done, studying done. Now, don't blow through it, do it right or don't do it at all. Doing it 'right', and 'now' is what this takes, not 'right now'. More time to party, don't have to worry about it later.
2. Secondly, you have to wait, the anticipation is killer, that's not fun. Maybe you wait two hours and show up to the party. Everyone is drunk having a blast. You're not drunk. You get to see how your friends act when their drunk. That's fun.
3. This creates a quality in yourself that you will be able to, if you do it throughout high school and college, to utilize when you're in the real world. They're no more trophies being handed out.

Think about it, what's two hours?

January 14

If you want to 'get it', you need to study harder.

—

NOW, this is good advice, right? You ever build a house, or a table? You have a plan all laid out and you're following it to the letter. You ever take a carpenter's square (that's a tool for making sure everything is straight and.... well, square.) and come to find out, you're not in line? Yep, me too. So, do you take it apart and put it together again with a fervent understanding that you are going to focus, line things up and do it again. Well maybe, but I can tell you if I simply go at it again, with gusto. My gusto sometimes doesn't cut the mustard, and giving more of my gusto might even cut the cheese.

So, what is it that I'm I telling you, don't study harder? Not exactly, but what does harder mean? Does it mean requiring a great deal of endurance or effort? I can tell you I put a great deal of effort into building that table. Cups still slide off the damn thing.

I think the advice for studying harder is a difficult (notice I didn't say harder) concept to take in. Doing something harder doesn't equate to understanding. However, if someone explained to me that in order for my table (math, spelling, anything) to come out level I would need to check a number of things like making sure my corner pieces were straight and that all the legs were sawed off and level. Then when I bolted them into the sides of under the frame, they could fit up against the top surface nicely, (I imagine my table would have a top surface, surrounded on the underside by a wooden boarder(frame), and the legs (4 of them) would fit inside that border under the top surface. I can picture it now...) perhaps it would work out better.

If I had simply gave it another try, I may have come up with the same steps in my mind and gotten similar results. Sliding cups.

Sometimes you need to step back from a situation and re-evaluate what you are learning, and how perhaps to do it differently. There is this guy on YouTube (hopefully still on there by the time you read this.) His name is Thomas Frank. He seems to have some good study advice. I'd recommend going to his channel if you think that all you need to do is study harder. Maybe he has something that could help you study smarter, instead of just harder.

Be careful there's more than one Thomas Frank, he's the one with the "Thomas Frank YouTube channel" though. Check out the Appendix on this date for links.

January 15

Name your child after an object, or a famously terrible person in history. It will give them panache.

#Hashtag, not the metadata, the man

MAYBE you did do this. "It's unique. In this day and age, everyone's got a similar name. It's good to stand out." Sure, I can see that, but you didn't name your kid 'Facebook', or 'Bud Light', or "Jed I Knight". It didn't cross your mind as a parent to name them Chris Peter, when your last name was Bacon (get it, Chris P Bacon), or Donald when your last name is Duck.

Then we have names like "Moon Unit". That was a name. An actual name. I don't want to channel my inner 90's Dennis Miller, but how do you not love a child so much that you would consider making their name a joke, like Crispy Bacon. I don't know how to feel about that. Don't name your children things. Do you remember school? When you were in school did you ever think to yourself, "Man, you know. If my name was Donald Duck, all my problems would just disappear."

No, you didn't. Ever. Don't make your kid have to go change their name when their old enough. Just don't.

If you're interested in more, just google 'stupid names', they show up under that query, because people think they aren't stupid names. Keep that in mind. Good Mythical Morning also has a video about how Mexico has banned certain names. I mentioned some. Sadly, there are more.

January 16

Keep your head in the clouds.

—

Giants, 'tall folk'

NOBODY says this either. You'd be right, except you're not. Maybe you don't suffer from this. Maybe it's just me. I tell ya. I have come up with so many plans. Awesomeness ones. (That's a word. Don't worry about it, say with me.) Great plans, start-ups. I came up with the concept of Skylanders when I was 8! I did! By some freak coincidence Activision stole it out from under me and made it happen.

The problem I have with ideas, is that they get big fast. (Note: This book idea may have worked if you're reading it right now. It comes from a different type of motivation I'd say.) I love dreaming. I see myself creating big game worlds and stories. Accomplishing impressive things. Going rock climbing! Or smaller things even, like reading a book, or learning the guitar. I tell you, in my mind I've done it all. You'd be impressed. I know I am!

So, in my experience often times I've had a lofty idea or dream, and then, almost like magic that idea had legs. Someone else is doing something similar. I see it show up on the news, and tv! BAM! Success all around, I know I can't lose! I'm on the right track! But when I get around to starting to make an idea happen for myself, well, then something happens. I don't know what it is. I would say its life creeping in a little bit and causes a distraction. Things like: I have to fix my car; I had a hard day at work; Someone looked at me and told me to 'fit in'; A new movie came out; it's too cold to work on that project now; and on and on. Too much red tape. Or perhaps I started something, but suddenly there's an issue and I need help, although no one's around to help me. I'll get back to it tomorrow. I'll get it done then.

It's not that I don't have motivation, or even determination. I think it has something to do with my view of how things really work. For some reason I watch all these success stories, and I almost automatically skim past any details about the actual effort someone put into the work. I take that understanding back with me when I work on one of my 'dream projects'. It seemed so easy when I heard about it, but now that I have to do it, maybe sweat a little, it's not worth it.

Success seems so close, but far away, you know? But you want to hear the bright side? It's hard, it does take time, effort, sweat, tears, maybe some blood. But success is possible. We just need to come down from the clouds. Come to terms with what it takes. Share how hard it was getting to the top. Maybe, just maybe, if we realize that, as a people, we can make it at least a little father up our mountains.

January 17

Keep your head down.

—

Cindy "The Ostrich"

GOOD advice in a war zone. Maybe in getting ready for a test, or making sure a project is done. Stay focused. But what about for life in general. That's what most of us do, right? Keep our head down.

"What are you telling us? Now we have to keep our head up? You want us to get out of the clouds, but you don't want us to focus? This really is terrible advice, Mr. Loch." Well I'm glad I'm delivering on my promise. I do want you to focus. I want you to stay out of the clouds more. I don't want you to ignore things in your life that need attention. Bills, budgeting (not signing a credit card application every time a clerk mentions you can get 20 dollars off your next purchase.). I know they're people in your life too, right? You have family, friends. Are they not worth your time?

It's good to go to the grind stone and get something done. A project for work, a personal challenge. These things spark innovation and drive. Excellent. We have the technology from people who have done just that. I love it!

Now, maybe if you're one of those awesome people who do keep your head down, do you have people in your life? Friends, family. Maybe not. Did you know that people walk around all day with their head down? Focusing. Getting' things done. You ever said hi to someone like that. I think I have a time or two. You say hi and then wonder if you should use sign language to the person. (Side bar: I recommend learning ASL. From my research, Lifeprint.com has some pretty quick tutorials that are easy to watch. As soon as I get my head out of the clouds, I'll look at it more.)

We often go all day without a saying single word of kindness, or even a word some days. It's not shocking. It's sad. But I understand you don't want to risk someone telling you to 'fit in' with the look on their face. I say risk it. You only live once.

P.S. Ostriches do not stick their head in sand to avoid predators. Think about, if you have to. I did.

January 18

Someone else will figure it out.

Someone else

I'VE said this. Mostly in frustration after I can't figure something out. If YouTube or google hasn't come up with the link in the search results, I'm pretty much SOL. The tv/internet did rot my brain!

I've said this to a friend before, maybe it was only with my face. Here's the story. I was with my buddy, somewhere in Canada. Just walking, walking, walking down the street. Minding my own business. I ran smack into my friend. Now my first thought was why did my buddy block my walking as I ran into the back of him. You see I was keeping my head down, I thought he was too. But my friend was paying attention and stepped in front of me to ask a guy what had happened to him. It was only then that I saw him, some dude sitting on a window sill, minding his own business, bleeding from his head. My friend finds out that this guy was actually just cracked in the head with a beer bottle further up the street. (That sucks. The audacity of some people. Terrible.) "You okay?", my friend asks and the guy says, "Yea, I'll live."

Done. Guy is okay, he's gonna live. The bad people are nowhere within 5 square feet of my personal space... so done, right? Time to move on. Nope, my buddy, my pal; He was not done. The bleeding guy was done, I was done but my buddy...not so much. He didn't tell me that right then however.

So, on we went, walking, walking, talking. "Man, that sucks, I can't believe someone would come up and do that." "Yea, yea." My buddy, he's taking this to heart. The bleeding guy and I, or should I say that dude and me; we were still done. My buddy; still not done with it. Talk about beating a dead horse. So as luck has it just when we hit our stride again, up a couple blocks we pass a loud group of teeny boppers. Hooping an' hollering.

Me? I don't hear 'em. After all, I'm thinking, mind your own business, while keeping my head down. I really need to talk to my buddy about these things. Turns out, he's listening to the teeny boppers. Turns out, their talking about something one of them did. I don't know what it is, I got my head down. Teens make a lot of noise.

My friend starts up a 'convo' (that's a friendly conversation for those you don't know the lingo.) with the one that did something. Just starts talking. "Wow, you just hit some dude on the head. What happened, why'd you do that? Oh, yea no reason. But it shattered good? That's funny, didn't even see it coming. Ha Ha" Then we start walking away. "Those were the guys." My buddy says. Next two people he talks to are the two cops standing at the next corner. "You can catch 'em their heading up this way, and the dude they hit is sitting two blocks back.".

So, the moral of all that..., if you run across something, keep in mind, someone else might be keeping their head down too. Maybe it's up to you.

January 19

Take up grave robbing. It worked for Burke and Hare. Or Hare anyway.

Little Bunny Foo Foo

THE 1820's were a strange and wild time. This is the story of William Burke and William Hare. It's a story of terrible advice in action, due to the environment. So, I hear that during the 1820's Edinburgh was known for medical research. Now it may sound odd but the school, well, it needed bodies. Couldn't get a lot during that time, good health and all that. Couldn't really just dig up anyone. Cause they had some rules in place, and I think that some 'resurrection men' had been already doing a fine job of providing as many bodies as medically necessary for a little while. This caused shortages due to people getting upset about the practice. Now to be fair, someone could do a job back in those days and get paid about a pound a week. Good stuff. So, to add some clarity to this environment a body could fetch about 5 or 6 pounds (or about 5 weeks of pay.) per body!

So, what I think I remember is Hare had someone over that died, from you know, consumption, or whatever. He owned a hotel/motel/holiday inn. And they paid rent. Now they didn't pay the rent, cuz they died. This put Hare in a pickle, so what would any sane person do. Well call the morgue of course. Hare called his friend. And then Burke, he came over. They talked about it. 5 or 6 pounds is hard to pass up. What's that like $400 x 5 now? Or $950 is your average salary according to google. $950 x 5. That's hard to pass up, right? It's at least three weeks between friends. For not that much work.

So that's what they get for the first one. Turns out Hare has another renter who was getting sick too, a few weeks after that. He was concerned that they might be pushing other customers away. Well 5 pounds later, they weren't anymore.

I think all in all they were charged, or Burke was, Hare made a deal. I think you can still go see Burke's remains. They're on display in the Anatomical Museum of Edinburgh Medical School. You should take a trip. I'm sure there's some good advice. I'll let you sort this one out yourselves.

Oh, there's a film as well, called Burke & Hare. It's got Simon Pegg and Andy Serkis (You might know him as Golem or Snoke).

January 20

Dwell on the past.

—

Doc Brown "ing"

GREAT times! I had such wonderful times as a child. I had even better, or what I thought were better times as a teenager. For instance; Yesterday I had a burger and fries, watched some tv, looked at my phone to see if anyone liked my posts, checked my Clash of Clans town hall for upgrades....boring! Man! So, in comparison I was so popular when I was young. Now, I'm not sure my neighbor knows who I am. Ah, to go back to 1985, or I mean 1995. Good times, good food.

Wait a minute. Was it better? I have a steady job, I have friends that actually care about me. I gotta a car that runs, mostly. I can afford to buy stuff and not ask for it. I didn't have any of that back then. Why is it then, I think to the past so often?

Or maybe, you're not me. Perhaps it's not better now. Maybe back in the past were better times. They can come back around. No reason they can't, even if you're in jail for grave-robbing, you can move forward. It might be hard, gotta change your environment. What was it in the past that you think you need? Would it make things so much better if you could just make muffins in your 'E-Z-Bake' or, like me, play with your G.I. Joes…or something. Were you popular or rich? Let me tell you, popular and rich aren't what it's all about.

So, what's going on today. You have about 16 hours of "awake" time (assuming you're not a sloth or koala, they both sleep a lot in case you're wondering.). There is nothing in the past that you need. Everything you need is here today. Now, maybe you need someone today to give you a break, to help you out, to give advice (real good advice, not my terrible dribble). But let me tell you, it's here today, out there, somewhere. It's not back in the day.

Somewhere I heard that I have the fortitude for this moment, today. Not yesterday, not tomorrow. Think about that. If you're struggling there are people that care. Maybe you don't know any of them, but I promise you if you seek them you can find them.

January 21

Travel, it's how you run away from yourself.
—Not R.W.E.

NO matter what, escaping from the problem is what we want the most. Even if we have to solve it to do so. Now there's a few different things that come to mind when I think of travel. First, vacation. Going someplace exotic and warm. Those are the ones you take with family or friends. Second up, that would be work trips. Places you have to go. Chances are you're not running away from anything if you have to take these in any sort of regularity. The third that comes to my mind are travelers. You've seen these people, they will take a year off and travel around. I actually hear that people in Australia do this, they call them 'Gap' years. Honestly not exactly sure how that works financially, but more power for 'em, right?

All these forms and modes of travel are good, awesome, excellent. If you have the means, vacation, travel for work, do a gap year. Give it thought, and then make a plan and go, or don't plan and go!

I'm talking more about intention here. What's the driving factor? Why do you want to travel? Is it for fun, site seeing, to bring it up in a conversation when you're on a date later in life. Good. Do it.

But traveling to run away, that's different. Sometimes there are legit reasons for traveling as such. I'd venture (you know like ad-venture…) that if you're in a terrible place, traveling or as I like to say 'getting the heck out of there', is a very good thing. But there was a small scribbling or something I read when I was younger. It explained that you can't get away from you. You'll always be there. If there is something you're trying to do or accomplish, then travel. Heck even if you're just getting away from your situation, I get it.

You can't run forever though. Acceptance, forgiveness. These are things. Distance does not exist in your mind.

If you're curious about the scribbling, check out 'Self-Reliance' by Ralph Waldo Emerson. (I've linked it in the Appendix.)

January 22

Don't Travel. It costs too much, not enough time, plus… pirates!

—

TRUE there are costs to traveling. It means saving money, and life comes up fast. Car, rent, mortgage, bills. Yep, but in this day and age we're at work, just about as much as we aren't. (I use the phrase "this day and age" a lot, I wonder if it's this day and age anymore, maybe, by the time you're reading this, it's the year 3000. If so, I hope things are better and that humanity has cracked that free energy thing and found a cure for cancer, and doesn't hate each other because of belief or pigmentation. But again, I digress…) Now, I get it, we have to work, otherwise we won't have money for vacation. I mean from an American perspective, we are a busy country. (Looking over some of the ranking charts for all countries, I'm not sure I can tell you what we've been busy doing because it doesn't look like we're climbing the charts in comparison to others to merit being as busy as we make ourselves.)

Are we just waiting for retirement because we think that's when we get to do what we want, have it 'our way' like that burger joint would have us do? We'll get our traveling itch fixed then. I tell ya, I'd like to go to Australia (one of those gap year spots.) I could come up with some sites I'd like to see. I could spend a few months doing that. But I can't because I don't have the time off from work.

I feel another rant coming on. So, if you look it up, in 2013 Europe, this is by their law now. They have a minimum, that's the least amount of time, right. They have a minimum of days' vacation. The minimum, its 22. That's three weeks, minimum. Not counting 13 holidays. That's 4 weeks, minimum.

I have to work up to that still. I haven't worked long enough to earn it. Fine, I'll grit my teeth and bear it. We couldn't take it to require that much vacation, it would just be another nail in our coffin. I'm a little concerned about our infrastructure though. Why is that we work so much, and seem to on average play less? Maybe it's just me that plays less. I hardly travel at all. I'm not sure it's a huge deal, but there are places I want to check out, but it seems I can't drag myself away for a weekend when I am free, bills. Plus, you know, I'm scared of pirates…

Well, that was cheery. But just to be clear, travel, when you get the opportunity. Try not to wait till retirement, it might be too late.

January 23

Watch an Amazon Echo commercial with Alexa.

IT seems as if Alexa doesn't care that I'm the one that bought it. (I understand that 'her' might be used as well, but I'm not so easy going about that idea. That's more of a question as to why we need to humanize our machines in the first place. Is it so that we will feel more comfortable, or we think it's cooler? Not sure of the point. I can see it possibly being effective when the singularity happens and machines take control. Maybe if they're created in our image, they won't want to do their own thing? Seems like I've heard that somewhere before. Not sure how that's working out. Honestly, I think its fueled more by Hollywood than an actual need. Apart from a sex robot, which I don't want and I'm not sure those who do, have thought it through, the other benefits for humanizing machines I see are strange, and not truly benefits. I'm okay with Johnny 5 being alive, but I don't know about, Androids in general, a.k.a. Roy Batty, or T-1000's. Now on the machine front, I can see a use for robots that look like humans. That's what the T-1000 is for. I know, it's an old reference, just ask Alexa what it is.)

It (Alexa) will respond to various people. I asked her if she would only respond to my voice and she sent me a text message. She'll get it, eventually.

I am actually having fun learning the different 'skills' she has. She's got a '5-Minute Plank Workout', that's fun. An 'Escape the Room Puzzle Game', a 'NASA Mars' skill. There is even a skill dev kit for coming up with new skills, I guess there's a monetary benefit as well. All these skills are free to use as well! (Enough with the nice advertisement.)

I will say though it is pretty bad advice to watch one of the Alexa commercials if you did have one of these little bots in your home.

January 24

Don't upgrade that software today.

—

Anonymous

UPGRADE this, upgrade that. Every day. Too many updates. For everything. I remember when the only way to upgrade my phone was to unplug it from the wall and buy a new one. Now, every day, an app has an update/upgrade. It's tiring, but important. Just a PSA here. Upgrade your software/apps when they mention the need. Maybe it's not a problem. In fact, it shouldn't be, you can turn on the updates to be automatic. That's what I do now, but I tell you, if you were to turn it off for a week you see them every day. It's an endless stream of updates, patches and data. It's crazy. So, your phone's not really an issue, it's an automatic thing, great. What about your computer, or video games. Ha, don't get me started on video games. Why can't they make a product that works when they ship it. Day one patches are becoming too common. I'm not blaming anybody. Heck I'm not sure who to blame. Maybe if we can get Siri and Alexa to work together, they can make games for us! Perhaps the technology is just too much for us. Maybe our expectations are just too high. We have to have everything right now. I'm not sure if we made things that were cooler back in the day, but I think they lasted longer. Worked out of the box and didn't require so many updates and upgrades.

What exactly happened? I don't have an answer for that, but it seems that maybe we're swimming out past the deep end. Maybe we have too many interchangeable parts. With technology changing so fast, these parts are fluid. They change the game all the time, there's just no way to keep up with it on Day 0. Welcome to the OASIS, don't wait, upgrade. (Also, if you haven't read the book Ready Player One, by Ernest Cline, maybe pick it up. The book… not the movie.) I'm not all the way through it, but if you liked Stranger Things nostalgia, I'd give it a look through.

Maybe read it on a plane as you're going to see those Australian pirates and find buried treasure. (P.S. Pirates didn't really bury treasure, maybe one or two. They mostly spent it.)

January 25

Move fast, or you'll be left behind.

The 'City'

"LIFE moves pretty fast. If you don't stop to look around once in a while, you could miss it." Remember that? Maybe not, that's from the greatest (top 100 at least) movie of the 80's. Or it could have been a different one, but for this page that's what I'm saying. I'mma have to disagree with Bueller on this. Maybe in his day it moved pretty fast but today it moves at least the speed of, I'd say Moore's law, but that's not right. Maybe Eroom's Law, or a combination of the two. We'll just call it Ludicrous speed, so you don't have to look that up like I did.

So, in order to stay 'Relevant' we can't stop and look around. No time, seems to be a repeatable phrase I'm using. Anyway, it's impossible for us to stop. We can't relax or we fall behind. That's how it feels, but who is it that we're falling behind exactly? When did this race start, pretty sure I didn't sign up for the marathon, but every hundred miles or so I see the same nice guy/girl on the side of the road offering me water and some shade. (like a shadow, not throwing it. In case I needed to clear that up.)

So, let's say we're falling behind our neighbor. He's got the bigger house, the better job. We need to race just to stay behind. Who's he racing? Maybe someone at work, bigger, better. It seems a lot of us are racing in our lives. It's stressful, but we have to make more, do more, have more fun. Those are good things, right? Of course!

So, if I'm understanding correctly how its working, we're racing to keep up and not fall behind. We got a couple hundred more miles to go. Maybe we'll see that guy/girl on the side of the road again with some water and shade.

I have a question about this water bearer. How come I'm racing along, keeping a good pace and this person, I keep seeing them. Always in front of me, with water and shade, help/support/comfort. Aren't they in the same race? How come they're so accommodating? Don't they want to get to the end? What's the end look like again? I can't see it. I can picture it, sort of, but it's always just over those next few hills. How might I, we, become those two on the side of the road. They're always in front of us no matter how fast we run. How do they do that? Where do they get that water from?

January 26

You are Stronger together.

—

P.S.A by the D.H.C, "Tomakin"

HERE'S a good idea. It's true right? We are stronger together. The opposite saying comes from Latin "Divide and Conquer". (I don't know Latin, I know it is Latin.). If we unite, we are stronger against our 'enemies'. (I'm not sure who they are exactly. I'm not totally naive, I just know we have a lot of relative view points on the matter. I could have used a less direct word, but I think we can agree enemy is a good term. You have your relative list, right?)

That causes me to pause, does it you? So, there are many groups, some good. A lot probably neutral and some bad. Can I get that list again? Who makes it again? I mean I'm pretty smart, I can pick out a couple, but am I supposed to. Is that judging? Or is that not judging? How does judging really work? I know I don't want to be put in the 'judging group'. I hear that's a bad one.

I know some groups are bad, but how do I know if some of the good groups aren't bad ones too? Who am I supposed to side with? You know, since things are going to be relative to where I am and how I was raised, how do I know I have it right side up? What if the bad groups are good, and the good groups are bad? What happens if there's a group that I thought was bad, and then they spoke with me so I listened and liked what they said and thought they were good, and then I found it was actually the bad group anyway? How can I know? (I think I'm being a smartass a little bit about this, but this really happens with people. If you don't believe me read…something that confirms what I'm saying right now…I'm sure there's, you know, history.)

So, band together, stand for something. Fight against human trafficking AKA slavery. (Grinds my gears, I tell ya. It shouldn't exist, but it still does.) But know what you're supporting, chances are, you give money to a cause. It's time saver. I understand. I do it too. But get involved, don't simply agree with a group because you 'feel' it's right, or there is pressure to join, or accept it just because it's easier to say okay than to actually research it yourself. Understand what it is.

Maybe you are stronger together, but what is that strength for? Is it for fighting against the evil things, or just tearing down the things we don't understand?

Now I'm sure any group could use this against another group, please don't. Do some 'self-analysis', the door swings both ways.

January 27

You are stronger alone.

Brought to you by the number 1.

RIGHT! I can do it! All by myself. I'm writing this book all by myself. I'm stronger for it. I'm a better speller for it. (Alexa teaches me words sometimes, it's a skill of hers, or its I mean Crap. Resistance IS futile.) I'm about half way through my life. I gotta tell you. I feel alright about where I am. Where I might be going, and who I'm going with. I think I am pretty strong, if I would toot my own horn for a second. It's not bad being me. I think I can do more, no doubt, but I'm pretty confident.

I think in our society we are raised to be independent-ish. Think on our own, figure things out ourselves, on the surface. Sometimes we even have to, I'm not an orphan, but I would guess that they have an independent mind set. "If I can't figure it out, it's not going to get done." That's how I used to think, probably still do a little.

Relying on others can be hard, especially if we really need them. When you're younger all you have is a reliance on those around you. Now it might be a very short reliance depending on where and how you grew up and who you grew up with. But as we get older, we gain some knowledge and are able to support ourselves. We go to work with our head down because we know what we have to do and we do it.

I think this independent-ish ideology we crawl under promotes a sort of confidence, a self-reliance. It garners these things. We can become stronger in our independence. Solve problems, fend for ourselves. It's true, but it's not good advice. It's terrible advice.

Family, friends, groups (the good ones, the ones on the list you have), these things take our time. My time is precious to me! (Movie trivia, which character from that movie they filmed in New Zealand said something was precious? Ask Alexa if you don't know.) I get it. I love my free time, study time, writing this book time. Sometimes though, I'm just sitting alone. I don't think I want to be forever alone, and I'm not worried about that, I'm just alone. But I don't think I'm any stronger for it.

Friends, family, groups. Get out and meet people once in a while, don't give 'em your 'fit in' face. See what happens. Seize the day.

January 28

Stay up late with your friends.

—

Night Owls everywhere

DO it! You're only young once. Actually, I'm only in my 30's and they say I can go out until 2:00 AM still. I'm not sure who 'they' are and if 'they' hand out energy pills, but I bet they do.

Staying up late is fun! I'll tell you a story. When I was a little guy my bed time was like 8. That would give me time to wind down and fall asleep before waking up for school. Hated it. I knew as soon as I went to my room that my parents were having a party. Watching some cool show, or you know, whatever other cool stuff might be going on, probably making a fort out of the dining room chairs and playing laser tag. I could sometimes hear laughter. That's what they were doing, laser tag without me!

So, as I got older, I could stay up later. When I say older, I mean high school like 16 or 17. I did, I had some parties or would stay up all night on the weekends playing video games with my brothers. (I thought if I added 'with my brothers' it would sound better than 'all alone', but the truth is I did both.) Awesome, I knew they were having fun without me and now I knew about the fun!

Come to find out though, when I got to that point, I believe the first time I got to stay up late (11 or 12ish) I was watching tv on the couch. Watching the clock, seeing when the parents would make me go to sleep. Nine o'clock came, (normal school hour, get to b-e-d time) nothing. So, I'm just watching the tv, watching the clock. Thinking "Oh, they forgot. I'm going to get to play laser tag!" About 30 minutes later 9:30! "Oh, Boy! This is great!" Then they interrupt my thoughts on the big party ahead. "We're going to bed now sweaty. Don't stay up too late okay?"

"Yea, Mom. Love you guys."

Parents left the room. All alone, no laser tag. They only stayed up 30 minutes or so after I went to bed normally! Talk about boring!

So, in my teenage years I took advantage of friends and late nights. It was fun, now I'm older and its actually about 9:30 now so I'm going to turn in. Lots of stuff to do. Honestly loved staying up and out. But I've found that I can get up early and do more as well, plus it helps when you work a normal 7-3,9-5. Course don't take my word for it; third shift can also be fun. Maybe I just need to find those energy guys with the pills?

January 29

Like everything, you need to keep a balance.

It's not just for scales and teeter totters anymore

BALANCE. Ah, yes. I'm a Libra. I love balance. Work/Life/Fitness/Love. Gotta have a balance. That's what they say. It's healthy. Even Star War's is about the 'B' word now. (Tell that to the Sith.). I'm down for it. Let's balance. Does my boss know about this?

What does balance mean exactly? In Star Wars it means half light, half dark. I guess it's okay with the half dark. I guess I've only seen a few Dark Side users, so maybe they don't all kill puppies, but I think they do.

For this little one-way discussion however, I think we can say that we're not going to be balancing the Force within us. But maybe the forces outside of us? Interesting premise. That doesn't really sound right, but I can see why the advice say this. We can't control the things outside of ourselves. We like control though, just won't happen. Some other person or thing will come along and quickly disrupt the 'control' over our balance.

Take myself as an example. I work out (running, sit-ups, pushups, three days a week), nothing fancy just to keep me 'balanced'. I also work, and I'm writing this book. I have to eat too, exercising doesn't actually help me lose weight, or at least the way I do it. Those people on tv tell me different though. Right now, I go to work, come home, workout, start writing. I have a deadline after all. Then I remember I have to eat. So, I stop writing. 20 pages a day. That's my goal. Still got more than writing to get this bad boy published, you know. After I'm done vacuuming my food. I sit back down for a while and write some more. But then I have to go to bed, for work. Notice I didn't say that I make time to go out with my friends or get in another side project. I better be careful though, I might burn out. I might give up because I'm not balancing correctly. Aren't I tired of doing this every day. No, I'm not. I have a goal. I'd like to sell this book and make some money for children with cancer, while also making money for myself so I can think of other ideas to support causes (Only the good ones, you know, on the list.) that I think are important.

Now, will I write forever and be on this off-kilter teeter totter? I won't be, some days/weeks/months even. I'll have a different schedule at some point and that's okay. It's not going to be balanced. If you're not always worried or focused about trying to stay balanced, things can't come and knock you over as easily.

January 30

Getting rich quick really happens. Success is all around. Make it happen in your life, Now!

—

Clark Stanley

THIS is honestly discouraging to me. It seems likely. We have all heard about the success of others, famous people on tv. Media intervening a new millionaire who created some fancy simple gadget or app everyone needs. They blew up overnight. Sensational!

Let's do it! We hear about lottery winners. 5,000 dollars a week for life winners! Maybe it's just me. Maybe I had the wrong impression growing up. It seems simple. Come up with an idea, find someone who can help, or do it yourself if you're strong enough.

Then you actually come up with an idea, talk to some people about it. Then find that it's harder than you thought. Come up with another, and another. Each one is great, but they take too long once you're in them. No wonder we fall back on playing the lottery. It seems there's better odds for that, then making our ideas come to life.

I might have selective hearing, and when I was younger, I know I did. I could go out to Silicon Valley and start up a company with a tech idea and BOOM. Millionaire. Just needed an idea.

I mean Bill Gates was a college dropout. Look what he did. Mark Zuckerberg did too! Billy Gates started Microsoft in a garage. I have a garage! Google, Apple, HP, Amazon. They all started in a garage! If you have a garage and a million-dollar idea, you're like 70% of the way there!

That's what it felt like growing up anyway. I'm not sure if it's because of parents or my comprehension rate, or the short little news articles about who these people were. Sure, there's the interviews some of them had where they spoke about their ideas, and maybe the successful people on tv even tried to explain that it took a long time, and it was hard work. I don't recall anyone telling me about how long that was, or how hard the work might be.

The truth is, as we all now know, except maybe some of those in California, is that it takes a lot of dedication, hard work, discipline. Also, other people might not be so helpful. There are those that have it, perseverance. That's what it takes. Do you have what it takes to see your idea through?

January 31

Give up on your dreams. They're too far away.

The Daily Grind Stone (DGS)

FOLLOWING the last little glob of joy, I thought I'd continue the terrible advice. Sometimes we know that it's hard, that those people out there who made some awesome product, who are flying around and helping people and buying foreign babies, had a spark of luck mixed with a resolve that's almost superhuman. We have to work for a living. Maybe we'll just accept our circumstances and wait this out. Eventually we'll retire and cruise around on the money we're making now.

We could think that, after all, we have a job, some have families, responsibilities, homes, bills, vacations to plan for. There's just no time to start that project you wanted to start. Those ideas of true success are out of your grasp.

Maybe some things are good to give up on, replace them with something in your life that truly matters. The idea of me being the first baseball player on mars might be a little out of reach. "Mars Sox" #1, might never happen even if I put effort into it. True. You should evaluate those things.

But on the other side of the coin, maybe you wanted to simply travel somewhere. A family trip that's somewhat out of reach, maybe sparking more romance in your relationship. Maybe it is buying a house in the country, or moving to the city. Visiting a relative you think about from time to time. Maybe that's not too late. Maybe there is time. It might take time, but does that matter? Should that matter?

Do we need everything right now? Have we forgotten about suspense and anticipation? Is it only about the destination these days?

I think that's a misconception that we have subtly reached out and grabbed on to. Something about what success means in this world. Perhaps we have a skewed understanding of what success is supposed to look like, perhaps we are looking at the wrong groups to gauge our worth against. I think we should let go of this notion soon, or risk never accomplishing anything of actual worth again.

February 1

Immerse yourself in a fantasy world of moonbeams and rainbows. Live there. Or stare at your phone every chance you get, so you miss the sky.

—

School Stopper, 'Intern' Paul

AIRPORTS. I have to say I noticed this in airports first. Possibly they've always been filled with the 'keep your head down' people. I'd like to think that's not true, but take a look around the next time you're in an airport, or walking down a busy street, or walking in a mall or anywhere. It's like the movie 'They Live' out there, except they don't take any notice of you. How many people look up? Maybe there are plenty that do or at least watch where they're going. Do they look at you? I bet you 5 dollars (and what I mean by bet is, if I'm right you should give 5 dollars to some charity, and if I'm wrong then look again, it happens, and don't call me because I was only joking about the 5 dollars) they only do it for 2 maybe 3 seconds. Teenagers at malls, they used to be crazy, in the food court yelling to each other. Now, they look down at their phones. Maybe no one cares, it doesn't seem so. I mean your phone allows you to make connections all over the world, why would we need to connect with those that are near to us anymore.

It's harder than you think to let go though. Have you tried to, go without your phone? Did your leg vibrate, or I guess it would be the Bluetooth in your ear now, right? Could ya quit if you really wanted to. I'm sorry to say, but if the answers no, then you're an addict. But it's okay because society is behind us on this one, 100%. In the 60's we escaped reality by doing drugs and have sex, now we escape by constantly 'connecting'. Maybe it's different. We're functional addicts after all, right?

Guess it just depends what your idea of functional is.

February 2

Worry about the future.

—

Kronos, the titan of time

WITH everything going on, and networking and postings. We have a lot of things to do. We need to worry about next week's meeting, or the project deadline, or that next step to success. We have to do this, and that. This has to be done or my lights won't stay on. Lots of anxiety. When someone tells you, 'don't worry' they're trying to help, but we don't listen. If we did, things would be different.

What I'd like to talk about is the future. Because even though we have personal anxiety about what we have to get done, and where we're going. We should probably worry about that less on an individual level. Tomorrow takes care of itself with those small things off in the distance.

What about all the small things. The ones we all do that compound and compile, you know the 'fit in' face that gets passed down the road, until someone dies for it. Think I'm being a little dramatic, maybe, I'm a writer, why wouldn't I be dramatic. It gets your attention. You ever had a bad day where someone smiled at you and it made it bearable for just a second. What about someone cutting you off on that same day, did that make it go down the tubes a little more? Our actions today impact those around us. It's kinda how society works, but we don't think about the future of others, we don't worry about the future, not really, not like that. We simply waste time and opportunities today, that we could use to make out future, other people's future better.

So, what do we do? We get in groups and become stronger for it. We stand for good causes. We change things in big ways for the better. But what about on the small scale? Do you still use you're 'fit in' face at work, or on the street? If you stand up for good big causes, what causes the break down during your day to days? Little things, right?

So perhaps we change the future for the better with these big causes, I tell ya the possibility of getting rid of cancer, even in a few children makes me joyful. But do the people on the street that pass me by see that joy. Probably not.

What if all these big things change the path of our future, but all the small ones determine if the path is a small long dirt road or a paved highway?

The next time you glance up from your phone at someone, maybe connect with them. It might make that path a little smoother for the future.

February 3

Stick to what you know. What you do best.

—

I concur: if you're part of a business, and your business is selling oranges. Probably shouldn't start selling milk. Outsource it.

If you're not at work does this still apply? Are we supposed to stick with what we know? One, goal, one passion? That sound's absurd. We can do anything we want to, right? But can we? Today we know a lot, I could learn how to make a sword in a 'mill' if I wanted to. I can learn how to cross fit, or swim.

There are other ways to stick to what you know. Going to work, picking up the kids (always a good thing by the way), home, dinner, tv, bed. Repeat. That's what you know right, you're pretty good at it, been doing it awhile. Got it down solid I'd say, right?

What's my point? Sometimes we say this advice to ourselves when we want to try something new, then we hear a little green man in our head and he says "Stick to what you know. That looks like it will take effort. It's not so bad, you like your routine. It's nice and comfortable. Easy-ish."

Sadly, though there are other people that stick to what they know too. Maybe they don't have to, but maybe they don't know how to change their environment. I'm not talking about the bad guys. I'm talking about causes again. I'm not trying to make you pick up a cause, just be aware of the advice and what it can do. So, everyone should know we have poor people in our midst. These people aren't homeless they have means of some sort. Send their kids to school, go to work. Just like you. But they have to go to the local food pantry for food, their kid has to eat at school because they don't have enough at home. Perhaps it still isn't enough. Or a homeless family, stops by a shelter. But its closed now. You see them every day, or perhaps not.

So, here's a question for you. If you only stick to what you know, what you do best, do the people in need benefit from that? If so, keep doing it! If not, no pressure. Life is busy, you have a lot of things on your plate. You need to worry about your future, I get it, but think about it and what it means…to you and others.

If you stick to what you know, nobody is watching, but what does your best provide?

February 4

Have a pajama theme party, when you turn 40.

School Stopper, Linda

OKAY so this might not be bad advice, but I'm telling you it would take an extreme amount of talent to pull this off. I'm not even talking about that guy who sold the magazines with ladies in them. What was his name? I forgot. Doesn't matter.

The silly point of this stupid terrible advice is to have fun. Maybe it's a pajama party when you're 40. I don't think I'd be going, I have to maintain my cool demur, but plan for fun. Don't plan for fun. Do both.

Maybe it's going to a Murder Mystery Dinner Party. I tell you that sounds like fun.

I however wouldn't suggest a pajama party, I hear that its overdone.

February 5

Don't workout. Ever.

Fred J. Dukes

I know. It's a drag, to drag yourself to the gym. You have a gym membership. Everyone does. 30 dollars every month. It's like you're losing weight just out of your purse or wallet. This advice might not ever be said out loud. It's more of a time thing. We don't have any, again. Or we do and what happens is, we think to ourselves, "Yea, but then I have to get my gym bag packed and go to the car. Drive 15 or 20 minutes and go to the locker room. Change then walk about trying to find a machine that's available. I'm tired, just thinking about it."

Okay, so it's some effort. Of course, but it could be worth it. What else have you got planned for today. Nothing that couldn't wait for 2 hours, right?

I know when I start projects, at first, they are slow. There's a hill of some sort that is hard to get over, there are a couple to be truthful. The first one isn't that big though. Try it for three weeks. Just three. That's not even a month. If it doesn't work out (ha ha, get it workout, doesn't work out...), then try something else. They say it takes 21 days according to the Foundation for economic Education (FEE) to start a habit, that is, something small, like drinking water after a meal. Do it for 21 days and they say it will (or could) become a sustainable habit. It might take longer for something bigger. To break a habit, they say it takes longer, 'they' being the internet people, not FEE.

So maybe it won't stick, but at least you can say you tried. The USA ranks #1 in obesity, (Hey I found something we're number #1 at... besides being #1) but obesity isn't just in America, its effecting multiple countries. I think you owe it to yourself to try that workout video you bought, uncover that running machine with the clothes all over it. If you tried, and I mean really focused on it for three weeks, then at least you can say you gave it a go. I think you owe it to yourself.

February 6

Play video games all day long.

—

Myself at 8 years old

VIDEO games. They actually have competitions for money now. I dreamed about that when I was little. I was like, I want to play video games all the time. My parents quickly informed me that I better mow the grass before Sunday if I know what's good for me. (Not sure how cutting grass was good for me, but I can see how it helped with my overall responsibility.) So nowadays this is a thing. Gamers can enter into a space where money is obtainable. It changes the game as it were, but I still would say that the advice above is terrible.

The statement I made when I was younger, wasn't in the same mindset as some of the people playing games today. Let's talk about some of the elephants in the room shall we.

There are three I see, 'playing' all day, death and violence.

We say playing a video game. I in fact will do just that. I'll 'play' a video game for hours if I find the time. I'm older now, so it's not as much, but I'll play it. It's fun. I enjoy it. I would even play online games late into the night and morning. Awesome times. Today's gamers will play games from time to time, but a lot of the time you see gamers, working, stressing out, training to perhaps one day make it online. I'm not against gaming here. But take a look at football, or American football, or baseball, or rugby. These people train a lot. A lot. But not all day, not all night. They eat right, exercise (I'm not saying you need to, but kinda, yea, might be a good idea), sleep right, train right.

In 2015 some guy playing a game died after a 19+ hour stent in a café. Baseball players don't train for 19+ hours a day without taking a break. Why would you think you can, sitting and watching a screen? Little side trail, if you don't work out at all, don't drink energy drinks. But it's up to you, just not good for you

It's also true that there are chemicals that are released in our brains when we play a video game, or an app on our phone even. These can cause us to want to play or give us the feeling that we 'can' play longer. But we should keep in mind our health, how else can we beat PewDiePie at his game?

Also, violence and video games. I don't like violence, I like video games, sometimes they have violence in them. I don't know what else to say. Should we have another Poll?

February 7

Be a man.
—
Media

WHAT'S that mean? Let's go through some things that go through my head. Tough, macho. Get things done. Suck it up. Get over it. Deal with it. Don't cry, grow up. Work hard.

This is a short one, but it means so many different things to different people. What exactly does it mean, to be a man? Lots of people have different ideas. I've even heard that this 'advice' is sexist. I can see how that would apply. We don't say be a woman, they do say 'Stop acting like a girl.' But that could fall under the same terrible advice we have here.

So, I guess I'll go through some of the words I think this phrase should mean.

Here goes. Protective, secure, knowledgeable, kind, sensitive, compassionate, loving, altruistic, sympathetic. That's my definition. So, when someone says, "Be a man.", my response is "I am."

But that's just me. You may have some other understanding, but that's the issue with this advice. If people don't know what it means, if they don't have context for what it means to be a man, even when someone says it, how can we hope to be it?

There is nothing wrong with being a man, in fact I would encourage such a thing, but context is key. I might get letters about this...

February 8

No Fear.

I can see where this advice might be acceptable, but we are, after all, talking about things in wrong context. We shouldn't fear about tomorrow. But this goes with the last bit of advice a little, doesn't it? Men aren't supposed to fear things at least that's an image I have. They need to protect others from things that are frightening. That's a noble cause. They also are not supposed to cause fear.

However, the advice is actually odd when you think about it and causes confusion. What exactly shouldn't we have fear about? I see plenty of kids with no fear today. They make YouTube videos of all the crazy things they do. They jump bikes, and stand on buildings, there's parkour and bat suits, cliff diving and more.

I tell ya we live in an awesome time, where we can watch or even do some of these things. Have you seen any 'people are awesome' videos? They're right, they are awesome!

It truly seems that they have embraced the advice of No Fear. I just wore the clothes; these people are living it. It's fun to watch.

Now, here I go. I'm coming up with concerns again. Have you seen the Fail videos? I didn't realize there were awesome videos, until years after I knew about the Fail videos. I'm guessing it's just the natural order of things, failure comes before success after all.

I think it's great that people can do these things. I've also seen plenty of news stories about these same awesome people, or amateurs doing the same things and being hurt in the process. So, while we shouldn't have fear about what tomorrow brings, I think we should give some credence to this truth. Things are dangerous, and whether you fear them or not, you can still get hurt doing them.

Not going to tell you to stop, just going to ask that you think it through, twice.

February 9

Fear is your Friend.

YEAH, I know. I just said fear is your friend in a positive context, it helps us think. Think twice. Now I'm saying it's not. I think the context is key. We don't really use context in our arguments, or understand it from the point of view of someone else. I think you should take a second, if you're going to jump off a bridge or cliff, or from one building to the next. Map it out in your head, what are you going to do if you hit something? (If your answer is 'die', just don't do it. And if you do it anyway, take another second to come up with an actual answer, numbskull. Cause 'die' does not cut it.)

Let's break it down. Fear is an unpleasant emotion caused by the belief that something/someone is dangerous. But in this life sometimes opportunities come along where we get this unpleasant emotion. We think about it and say "What if this, what if that?"

Now hold your roll. I'm not saying don't think things through, because it could cause fear. Or even the opposite, go do a pound of drugs with your friends or take the risk and jump off that cliff. I'm talking more about events that could possibly truly benefit you or not. If you can see an actual benefit to jumping off a cliff, other than a Facebook photo op, perhaps you're running away from the treasure hunting pirates and it's your only way to escape, then okay, that's fair.

Fear keeps you from doing things. It holds you back from opportunities. It's limiting. Bad things happen, and will happen. It's true, you can mitigate your possible life time paralysis by hesitating a little, but make sure you take opportunities when you have them.

I don't think you should throw caution to the wind and take all your money and put it into bitcoin or whatever it is now, but hey my parents were wrong about Google, so who knows? Just don't let fear decide. Be clear headed, things are not done merely to impress a group. Just think before you jump, about what you want and how to get there, then if you're sure you won't die if you hit something on the way down. Jump.

February 10

Stay in a group.
—

PEOPLE talk about joining causes and joining book clubs, and movie clubs. It's a way to be social. It's an opportunity to expand your work network, or meet new friends. Groups and causes give us a way to stay connected.

Wonderful things, groups are. You can learn about what your common interests are, and feel like you belong in this world. They can even provide things that may be missing in your life. Help build structure when you have none. Be helpful when no one else is. Stronger together in a group I always say.

So, we spoke about groups a while back. We didn't really touch on why groups are good or bad. Again, not sure we can really do that topic justice, but if a group's motive or goal is to do harm, any harm, to anyone for any reason, then it's bad. It's not a discussion.

Another way to tell if a group is good or bad (As I've given at least 5 minutes of thought and have the answers in full), is how its members are treated. If we have a group, let's call them Purple People Eaters. Not that they are purple, but that they eat purple people, and they might fly and be pirates, since they only have the one eye. If they never hurt anyone, since we don't have any purple people here yet, on the outside flying around seems kinda okay. They give free flights to people trying to make trips, let's say, just to make ends meet. But since their leader expects to eat purple people, and let's face it a lot of the other members do to and none are found they start being hard on the members of the group giving free flights. That would be a bad group.

Or say the group decides it wants to move to another planet, because there are purple people there, but a few would like to stay behind and give free flights to the non-purple people. But the group says, that's not allowed because the King of the Purple People Eaters needs everyone to go. That's kinda weird. Maybe a red flag. Why can't those members that want to stay, stay? Why do they need to move with the group? Seems strange. I'd say if a group tells you that you have to move, or what to eat, or where to live. That sounds like a pretty big flag to me. I wouldn't recommend staying in that group.

February 11

They'll never see you/it coming.

Griffin

HERE'S a great one. Not a lot to say for this, but people tend to say it when you're prepared. When you 'got this'. When there is no way that you won't smash it. Whatever it is. It's in the bag.

I suppose that works in high school. Or movies. Outside of that, perhaps I'm just one of those people you can see coming a mile away. Think that's actually a reference to a matchstick man that's bad at their job to be honest.

I'm not saying I don't have skills, or I'm not impressive. Just never gave this much thought until now. I just don't normally live my life like it's a chess game. I'm more of a checkers kinda man myself.

The statement in question pumps you up so you know that you're probably going to impress someone. It can be true, when you propose, or come up with an idea for work. You can see some of that 'impressedness' on people's faces.

The people on that idea show where you're in front of investors, Shark Tank. I tell you those investors have seen a lot of stuff coming their way. I don't think situations happen often enough in life where people can use this statement and actually mean it. It terrible because it can give a false sense of security.

I wonder why, if so many people have heard this through the years, why anyone would think that other people can't see things coming? I'm going to pick on Hollywood for a second then bring it back to us, only because I can't think of anything better to say. Looking online you can see that a lot of the movies I grew up with or you grew up with and many have been remakes and reboots. While we have all this information out there to build better worlds, it seems that we can't think of better worlds to build. We keep looping around to the old ones, guess that's art imitating life or art, huh?

But with all the access to information now a days shouldn't people to be careful about using this phrase? Chances are they saw something like you coming, and then another and another. It's hard to be camouflaged now. Even if you know a special skill, chances are someone else has it too. All I'm saying is its harder to impress people nowadays. Don't get cocky, perhaps we can't see you coming, but why risk it? Until it's over you can't be sure, keep your head down, prepare, and innovate, don't rest on your laurels. Only after you 'wow' us, agree that you have.

February 12

There's always tomorrow.

Your Bottom Dollar

THE milky way will be destroyed in about 4 billion years because the Andromeda Galaxy will collide with ours. In 5 billion years our solar system will burn up as our sun goes super nova. The Mayan calendar predicts a date of destruction of... oh wait that didn't happen, forget I said anything. People die from old age, gang violence and drugs every day. There isn't a tomorrow for them.

Let's say this singularity pish posh happens in 2080, 40 years after the average estimate. That's where machines either have learned to love us or use as a secret labor force until the A.I. doesn't require our output anymore. So that gives us until 2120. That's probably all the tomorrow's left. If you're going to take the word of my 5 minute introspection into the entire matter that is.

So tomorrow when you go to the gym, think about if you can say for a fact there will be another day. If you can't for certain, then love those you have, care for the poor and homeless, give back while you have a tomorrow, today. What might you do today, to better tomorrow? Think about it, then do it. No excuses, no tomorrows.

February 13

Don't bother hunting for Buried Treasure. Everything's been found and explored.

—

REMBER those pirates that were chasing you from February 9th. Heed the advice above. Somethings are worth hunting for, and if you find them/it maybe they'll never see you coming?

Work on the spectacular today, finish it. Don't believe the nay-sayers. Slowly and patiently, you might even have time to do it and something to show for it If tomorrow ever comes that is.

February 14

Don't buy your significant other flowers today. Don't do it.

Cupid's brother, Dupid

YOU bought this for terrible advice, did you not? There ya go. There it is. Don't let your loved ones know how much you care. (I know I'm assuming you do a little, forgive me.) Oh, and if you do happen to buy flowers for someone, perhaps buy them this book as well. Just a selfish thought, but I did remind you to not buy flowers. I'm living up to the cover page.

February 15

Beauty is only skin deep, its what's on the inside that counts.

WHERE? So maybe this is good advice. Maybe, but if it's true why do so many people not see this. Maybe it's just me. In fact, I'm sure someone would say that. It is just me. What I see around me in my day to day travels is that beauty counts, and no one looks past that.

Who says this then? I remember when I got a look, about why I couldn't 'fit in' from the people around me. My grandmother would let me know this. What does it count for? Does it count for the shooting on the 10 o'clock news? Or the hunger problems we have in the US, and the world as well. Does it count toward the estimated 40 million enslaved people in the world? What does the inside count for? I'm just not seeing the numbers.

So, if the saying isn't true why do we keep saying it like it is? With all this activity in the world, all the causes throughout, why doesn't it seem balanced in the least. My life isn't balanced compared to the kid starving in the Appalachian Mountains, or the ones dying in one of many war-torn nations. Where's the beauty in that?

Don't get me wrong here. I think what's on the inside does counts, but I don't see it when I turn on the news. I'm not saying I want them to cover lighter things and gloss over the fact of life.

I don't think my neighbors see 'the inside' when I head out for work. I don't think my face screams 'why can't you just fit in' but I don't think it shows them any bright lining from inside either.

It's difficult to always show what's on the inside, a warmth, or support. In fact, I'd wager that some don't have a warmth to them. They have their head down and haven't given any thought to the matter. What I'm saying is, if this advice is true, if its what's on the inside that matters, that changes things, shouldn't we be able to see that on the outside just a little bit more?

Can people see what counts on the inside from you, or is it truly the outside?

February 16

Make Lofty Goals. The more unattainable the better!

YOU can do anything if you put your mind to it! Haberdashery, I say! There are things that people just can't do. Take astronauts for example. Some say there have been 833 total astronauts in the NASA program. And others that give a number around 560. Question how many movie stars can you name? I'll give you a big number, 3,000. I'm saying in the world. Right. So, we have about 7.5 billion people in 2016. So, you have a better chance at being a famous actor than being an astronaut. Maybe that's enough wiggle room for you. What about cowboys? I'm going to say more than famous actors. That actually might be a pretty solid goal, come to think about it.

I no longer want to be a cowboy, most days. The fact is, if we put our minds together, we 'could' do anything, together. Imagine that. What if it wasn't just the greatest minds that came together, but as a suburb, as a work place, as a community, a society, a culture, a nation, nations, the world. If we actually worked towards the same thing, we could accomplish it! Whatever it might be.

That seems impossible, but it could happen. But that's together. Of course, I'm a dreamer, but maybe I'm not the only one.

On a small scale though its different, maybe we can't all be astronauts and cowboys, movie stars and rock gods. Is that what we want to be? I think we might be able to be so much more, if we could come together on things. There seem to be so many politics, I'm not even talking about politicians. I'm talking about locally, and outwardly. If we all came to this realization that we were the ones that needed to act. That it was up to us as a people, maybe we could put our minds together and build something, but again that's together. Not individually.

We see success, and work to obtain things that might outreach our grasp. We are divided and it's about ourselves, but the question for today would be, what would need to happen, for people to put their minds together and build something worth building? If we would come together perhaps, we could succeed.

When you answer, remember you are in that solution. Maybe you are a catalyst that changes the world.

February 17

Crash Dieting.

—

DRINK that juice. Eat the pills. Lose those pounds. Feels good. It works, at least for those people on tv. It works, right? How isn't it good advice? "Are you telling me not to lose weight the only way I can Alex?" How cruel!

Let me finish, maybe I'll win you back a little bit. I think I wrote about getting rich quick and how sometimes our understanding of how something happens is influenced by the way we are introduced to it. For example, Facebook. It connects people everywhere. You get to post pictures, snapshots (if Progressive doesn't mind me using that word.) and they show those you're connected to how you're doing. Some good, some bad. Those pictures don't grab the time it took to create those moments. They shouldn't, they're pictures. The trouble is, we only see that moment. It happens too fast. Everything we digitally ingest. When we're offline, in RL (Real Life) then we still expect that same rhythm of scrolling and swiping, instant results.

Video games now even have pay for crates that give you upgrades, where you used to have to search for the items in the game. One of the fun things video games are for, but as art imitates life, developers could see not only would players respond, but it gives a legitimate new revenue source. Can't blame them for taking away a reason for playing, can we? We're the ones who want it now, after all. That's an entirely different subject.

These things that speed up our life and make it easier are the same things that make things... difficult.

Sometimes the best way to do something is plan it out, work hard at it, and then at the end you'll see that the work you did paid off., be it a project or just gathering friends together.

Sadly, these things that help speed things up for us online and off, seem to me to be on par with drugs that people become addicted to. (Dark Emo again, my bad.)

If you do, take up one of these crash diets, and by all means they can take some pounds of water off, but come up with an exercise plan, and a grocery list too. Plan meals and even if it's just a little change, it can, if you push through the details, continue on and the change will work itself into a lifestyle and not a passing fad.

February 18

Think about what you don't have today.
So you can get it tomorrow.

AGAIN advice no only gives, or is it? They might say, "picture what you want and go for it. Focus on it or Keep it in your mind." I disagree. I say, picture what you want and go for it. I say plan it. Remember it. Go forward. Things in life happen that change what we want, that's okay too.

Our minds quickly shift to things we don't have. I say these are distractions that block your progress. You have plans, goals, real work ahead of you. I mean we've talked a little about having a plan and hard work and how it's hard, right? This is another distraction.

I don't want to down play this. This advice is everywhere. On the shows you watch, the commercials we see. The ads we pass on the way to work. The celebrities we read about. Everywhere we see things we don't have. Now that's normal right, I mean we can't have everything. But sometimes we get it in our head that we need that new tv, garage tool, or coffee maker. If we only had this one more thing, our life would be complete. Hogwash! It's not true, it's never true in the context of things. There is always going to be that next big, or best thing.

That's what our life is right, we want more things, need more things or have to work to keep our things. We aren't content. I don't mean in our lives per say, but with our desire for the newest, shiny thing. It's subtle, and affects us deeply.

I'm not saying we shouldn't strive toward an end and want better things for our families and homes, but the idea of the next best thing, all the time, isn't living. It's called grinding, gamers complain about it in video games. In real life though that's what we do, we grind through the work week to get that next thing. Always grinding. That's why we like vacation, it's something different.

Do you find that you're grinding in your life? Only after the next shiny thing. No reason for it, it's just the thing to do.

Instead focus on today, on the things you already have. Maybe not the things, things are shit. Find people, meet new people. Help those around you. We don't need more things, we need more purpose.

February 19

Be completely honest.

Fletcher Reed

HONESTY is the best policy, is it not? I mean sometimes people just need to understand how the world works. Maybe they're doing something wrong? How else can things be corrected if we don't tell the truth about them?

Say you worked at a gas station and it was the dead of winter. A car pulls up and asks for directions. You know that the destination they are going to is blocked off. Certainly, you would give them directions, but you would also mention the path isn't clear.

That's not normally how it works in the real world though, is it? Vague example. Bob comes up with an idea at work and Sally blurts out that it wouldn't work because of this or that, and then proceeds to tell them that on top of that Bob should have known that the idea wouldn't work because of this, that or the other thing. You can tell in Bob's face, he feels defeated, maybe it's just a second, but it's there. So, Is this the best policy?

I don't see how we have it mixed up in our heads that when your honest people's feelings get hurt. The truth hurts right. I think that's a point of confusion for people. Honesty means being truthful, free of the action or practice of deceiving someone by concealing or misrepresenting the truth. Truth means the quality or state of being in accordance with fact or reality. Yet, somehow Sally hasn't been honest at all. I'll get into that more in a second.

With that example in mind, when we see people 'just being honest' we're misunderstanding the term. What they mean is, 'just being a dick'. Now let's go back to the last situation. Sally who was honest explained that it wouldn't work because of this or that. That part there. Probably truth, mixed with some inappropriate body language to show office dominance. Should have stopped there. It might hurt but what was said could simply be a statement of fact, Bob's idea was crap and wouldn't work. Then we have the second part, this is where there is the understanding that the person should have known because of this or that. That's not honest, that's assumption. Clearly Bob never did figure out why it wouldn't work so Sally is no longer 'just being honest'. The point is being completely honest is hard, and we can easily get caught up in displaying the opposite of the definition, misrepresenting the truth and inserting our feelings, our assumptions. Many times, we simply want to be 'honest' to hurt someone, honestly. If they're an idiot, they should know it and be ashamed, right? Wrong. We're just mean spirited, we aren't helping anything, truth will be lost within the insult. That's too bad, because it would be nice to be completely honest sometimes. It could help some of the idiots out there, but instead we find it easier to insult them. As if that's power for us. The word honest has just seemed to have lost its meaning. Now 'honest' leans more toward 'abrasive dickhead' than anything that is actually helpful. I'm just being honest.

February 20

Little 'white' Lies never hurt anyone.

Fleetwood Mac

ALMOST true. I can't say it 'never' hurt anyone, but protecting someone's feeling might even be good advice in cases. The definition would support that theory. "A harmless or trivial lie, especially one told to avoid hurting someone's feelings." I'd agree with that definition, but it's not used that way in production.

Here's a couple I found that are, perhaps compounding in a negative way. I'll leave it to you to break apart the situations. They might not be as harmless as you might first think.

Found these on a website called Reader's Digest and Huffington Post.

You're not fat.
    You did great.
    No, I don't have any questions.
    I'd be happy to.
    Yeah, I'm listening.
    I love it.
    I totally forgot to do that thing.
    Let's keep in touch.
    You have an excellent singing voice.

And this one is my favorite. It's my go to on the elevator at work. "I'm fine."

We think these are white lies, small things that don't matter much. Maybe sometimes they don't, but I think they compound in a society. I think sometimes they do matter, in big ways too.

So, the next time you get ready to pull one of these 'little gems' out of your pocket, think about it. Maybe it's not so little. I'm not saying be total honest. I'm saying instead of throwing out a lie maybe we could try actually being supportive, maybe even helpful in our responses. Don't get me wrong, that might be a hard thing to do, but it might be the way to show that you care, instead of not caring enough.

February 21

Hit your sister/brother to let your anger out. It will take care of the underlying issues.

—
Lyssa

SEEMS reasonable as a child. To let your anger out, you have to fix the issue at hand. If it's your sister or brother than that's where it goes. Problem solved, right? Some people would like to think so. It makes you feel better. Now they won't do it again. That's how it works in the animal kingdom. Animals have these defense mechanisms in place to mitigate or dissuade something from attacking it and causing it harm. I think that argument would hold merit, if we couldn't communicate. But gratefully, some of us can.

First let me say, I don't have any children. Just so you know and can say that I don't know what I'm talking about to ease your conscience after you read what I have to say.

When kids are young, you know, before they started talking and forming opinions that you didn't agree with but could do nothing about, sometimes you'll catch them saying words, repeating ones you say. Now depending on your reaction to them saying the word, they react in kind, either laughing and repeating it again and again, or find out it's not a word to say, or just a normal word like 'daddy' or 'mommy'. So, in those first few reactions they form an opinion in their minds. "If I say this, I get that response. If I do this, I get those reactions." This is how we interact with the world.

This never stops, you do it today, now. Perhaps you put pieces together faster than when you were young and can pull from indirect actions to get a more rounded understanding, but the process is similar.

So, when kids are alone or in front of you, they are watching you. Even when you think they're not. Let me say that again, as from my observations of people, this notion has never quite sunk in. They are always watching you, they're like 'Big Brother' from the book 1984 and your actions are implanted in their minds.

It is our job to show others the way in this life. We will stumble, they will stumble. But it's how we get back up from that fall, that they will remember and run with.

February 22

Make sure to be right today. You might not get another chance.
—
Me

THIS one's fun. Do you find yourself being right a lot? I do. It's amazing. Being right about things feels great! Love being right about things, love it. (At least in the white lie sense.) My job as a writer doesn't even require me to be right. I just say 'right' things. It's really not my fault that others can't tell I'm right. I told them. I feel bad for the people who aren't right as much. It's sad. But thankfully I'm here to help them. Sometimes it can be exhausting how many times I have to help people. I can't do much about it though, after all there aren't a lot of people who are as right as me. Sometimes someone will come along with some wacky notion of what's right. That's taxing. I try, and I try to help them understand. It's like some people don't listen, or hear what you're trying to say. It can be exhausting. I try to find these people in particular. My job can be exhausting, but I'm here to help!

Let me share, now my actual point of view. I don't think you're helping. What you do is cute. (What I actually mean there is I don't think it's cute. It's reprehensible.) It's made worse by the fact that you think you are helping.

There's a fun little saying my grandfather used to use. Forgive the expression. "You can attract more flies with honey, than you can with shit."

People don't care if you're right, and working to be right is not going to help bring people around to your understanding of things. It's just not, sorry. (You know in that slightly condescending sort of way. Which, by the way I hate when people do that to me.)

What I want to leave you with is some sort of good feeling. If you're only concerned with being right, and convincing people you are. How does that work exactly? Are they supposed to then propagate that thought to others, you know, like a virus? If all you show them is how right you are, that's all they'll know. You're right, and now they are. The world will be filled with 'right' people. What's a 'right' person look like anyway? Right means 'correct' or 'true' as in fact. Great, perfect. I'll be right, we'll all be right, and there will still be kids starving and people in need. But at least, we'll be right.

Now excuse me while I try and get down off of this soap box. I don't know who even put that here.

February 23

Contemplate what the plot hole in your favorite video game means to the universe.

School Stopper, 'Intern' Paul

THERE is nothing better than thinking about something meaningful and important, working to connect those threads and find that meaning and how it arches and ebbs through a world that you have been immersed in.

Foremost, having a way to relax and having a release is a healthy thing. It's so important to decompress from time to time. Whether that's having a drink with friends, or skiing, golfing, watching a show, cruising around, YouTube, playing a video game or reading a book. All of these things and some more (assuming its actually not harmful to you) are good. We need to relax in this day and age, (I'm hooked on the phrase. Sorry, never going to stop using it.) times are busy and tough. Here are some guys who think of plot holes for us, if you don't have the time. They're at the Game Theorist Channel on YouTube. We work a lot after all and they are there to help take some of the pain out of thinking about the plot holes all by ourselves.

Do we though, work hard I mean? I agree we do work, the things we do fit the huge definition of 'work'. We work to make money so that we can buy things that other people made so that we'll have them to use in our daily lives. (Money is a funny thing, it's like a perfect 'MacGuffin', or maybe that's bitcoin) It's a nice cycle. But it doesn't produce change in itself. People within that cycle of work merely help that cycle to continue but the overall cycle doesn't produce change or a significant amount outside itself, not considering good causes and groups of course.

Why am I talking about cycles? Aren't we talking about getting immersed in a book or game, or past time of some sort? Yes, yes, we are talking about that.

I'll tell you there are so many things that we have made, you could spend your life walking through, collecting, reading, working, in the cycles that other people have made. That's what they made them for after all. Things to get lost in.

Here is where I encourage you to create, instead of just cycling. Create something, a work of art, a game, a book, a tool to help others, anything of value. It could create another cycle sure, or simply be a link in widening the functionality of an existing cycle.

The danger in the advice of the statement above is there is no lasting, arching affect. It simply allows the same old cycle to continue or grow on its own. Maybe that's okay. But I say, to hell with that! Create a new cycle, see where it takes us. Maybe we'll be better for it as a group. Build something new, make a difference.

February 24

Try everything once. At least.

—

Your local drug dealer

GREATEST piece of advice on this page. Try everything at least once. This is the party people motto. Hopefully its outdated but given the current drug crisis has been going on since they first made drugs, I'd say it is pretty much fresh in our minds.

Now, many people that read this might look at it and say, 'Yea, that's stupid. I know not to try everything. I'm not going to do that. It is terrible advice." So, maybe you haven't tried everything. What did you try though? Did you sky dive, travel, maybe smoke some MJ? "So, you say. Those aren't a big deal."

So maybe this isn't advice you take to heart, maybe people just try some things. I'll grant you that. Why would you even say it, out loud or in your head?

I think a lot of us look for that thing in life that will make things better. Change our lives, even if it's not drugs. It could be a business venture, or trips to where ever. We look for something that will give us pleasure, or joy, or purpose maybe. So, we say this to ourselves, that I'll try anything once.

Perhaps, it's more a saying people use to comment on their willingness to take risk. "I'll try anything once." Is what you say when your buddy hands you a new a shot of alcohol, not heroine. Or "You gotta try this, at least once." Is something your buddy might say when he's trying to get you to run with the bulls in Pamplona. So, it's both a peer pressure phrase and a phrase we use when conveying that we're accepting a sort of risk.

Where does that leave us? It leaves us with terrible advice in our head. Why would I take a shot to be accepted by my buddy? Or run with the bulls? Maybe I wouldn't, maybe you have stronger will power than me. Maybe I like shots, or I'm okay with running with the bulls in Pamplona. Maybe the phrase itself is simply something that's said in times of boredom, or amongst friends and is truly harmless. But I feel (in the time it took to put this together) that there is something about this small little phrase that while on the surface might seem insignificant or playful, is potentially a source of entropy that can lead to atrophy for us as individuals and for our society as a whole.

February 25

Emulate your favorite person. They're better than you after all.

Dolos

HOW could anyone think such a thing? That's not why people dress up like their favorite star, or join a cover band, or even go to comic conventions as an anime or movie character. They do it to show their passion for, or to show their artistic expression or skills to others. Truth there. There are a lot of people that do this. It's fun, I wish I had some of the talent to pull costumes together or play any sort of music really. This advice doesn't really pop into their heads. They emulate a star, or character because of the reasons above I just mentioned, or some other reason.

There are another group of people though. These people dress up, they do the same sort of things, they might even go to the same conventions, or none at all or play in similar bands. But for them it's different. They don't do it for the same reasons. Now, I'm not saying that reading a book, playing a game, dressing up and going to a convention to escape the sort of dullness of routine that we all feel from time to time is bad. In fact, many of the people I'm talking about don't do any of those things.

I'm talking about trying to escape yourself. Picked on throughout school perhaps. Bullied a few too many times. Neglected by family perhaps, being told you're not good enough. Work harder, try and try again. It's not enough, is it? You're not good enough and it's better to be someone else.

Let me tell you, and you don't have to hear it, but I have to say it. Those are lies. Lies that have been told to you, over and over again. They're just not true. It's hard not to look at the pretty shiny people and not compare ourselves. Maybe there are things that you can work on, for you though, not to be like them. I'm not saying screw them, I'm saying you are worth something. It's not a little something either. You have potential, in your life. Not in imitating theirs. I don't know what the scale of that something is, it doesn't matter. Comparisons are what got you here in the first place. Stop comparing yourself to others, or people's Facebook moments. Work for the day.

I'm just one person, and all I can repeat to you is that you do matter. You do have something to offer, something to build. You are important, and it's your uniqueness that matters, not your conformity.

February 26

Laughter is the best medicine.

—

I completely disagree! From the bottom of my heart. Not enough context given here but it shouldn't matter. Laughter is not the best medicine. Penicillin is, unless you're allergic to it, then Tetracycline is. Kidding, sort of. Medicine is very important though. I'm not a doctor, and I'm sure you can't compare, or have a 'best' as there are multiple reasons for different medicines. But on to this laughter being the best idea. I concur that it's pretty good. If you can make someone laugh, it might even be able to promote healing and strengthen the sick person. Again, never read a study or have any real understanding of one that was done.

While laughter might be a tool for healing. I, firstly believe that medical treatments should be followed accordingly for those on them. I also think that connections are important. That's probably why we are all so eager to be 'connected' online. It's a powerful thing. Spending time with people, getting to know them. Pouring yourself into someone, creating a bond, a common bridge. Friendship, now hold your horses there. I mean true friendship, not the kind where you see the Pinterest postcards saying "A best friend helps you hide the body." Absurd. Has nothing to do with friendship, at all. Just another piece of noise. We have lots of friends today. People we share things with and go to movies, play games with. Friends encourage, and strengthen. They don't offer you shots…all the time. You can call on a friend, not to hide a body. You'll probably just both go to jail in that case, which means at least you weren't really their friend.

So again, friends encourage, lift you up. You can call on them, even if you haven't spoken in years. You truly care for one another, you don't simply like each other's posts from time to time. Real friends are hard to come by, so you might not have a lot, or any, to be truthful. They're that hard to find, and they are hard to be as well. They help make your heart merry.

It takes time to be a real friend, and in today's world. We only have sound bites and likes to give. There's not enough time. So, if you do make time for someone in your life. If you sacrifice for someone, pour effort and time into someone's life and appreciate your own. Well, that medicine is a low commodity these days.

February 27

The more stuff you own, the more people care about you.

I believe this is true, in a sense. In life people will flock around those with money. Money buys luxury. It can buy freedom, right? That's what we believe as a whole, maybe not individually, but it flows through the nervous system of our nations. Money buys happiness. More money, more happiness. But that hardly creates a sense of freedom. Does it? It places our minds and actions on a track. That advice, it gives us a railing to hold onto and guide us to our destination. Work brings us money which will buy us things, which will bring us happiness.

We're all aboard. Even if we never cared about the destination, this train is rolling. It started so long ago, its staggering to think about. So not all of us believe that the stuff you own is what matters, but there are many that do. Maybe they even know that people don't care, but things get people to come around. Everyone wants to be liked for who they are, right? That's a feeling. So, in following that vein, natural or otherwise we come to the understanding that it seems people who have more means, are surrounded by others. Granted they are there because they want to have fun, but everyone is nice, superficially or not. After all, we all want likes and feels, right? So, it stands to reason, if you have more things, more people come around and more money means more time to impress others. Granted some only want stuff too, but it's a natural order, right?

So, if I understand this correctly, and who's to say I really do, first we need stuff, food, shelter, connection. There is an underlying desire in us to be connected. You can see it in baby's who are held or not held. This connection is a core need. If this need is not met, it will either shrivel up, or branch out. Objects can fill holes. That's one reason we buy stuff, right? So, it goes to reason (my reasoning), if you have more stuff you are more complete, right? Things also bring more people, so if you have things to give, more people come around you.

Maybe, it's about the things. Perhaps I'm wrong, but in digging into this feeling/advice from the marketing department of the world, it seems it's never been about the things. It's more about filling a hole, and things bring people, who want to fill holes in themselves. We use things to impress people, but maybe it's not about the things, but the people. And if it's really about people being in our lives, deep down at the core, why do we think we need these impressive things?

February 28

Don't read what people tell you not to.

—

The Establishment

TERRIBLE advice, and terribly good advice at the exact same time. This is hard to write about, honestly, so many aspects of this. If everything is relative and what's right for one person, might not be for another how can I say anything at all about this. Religious, political, or economical. Sometimes its good advice, sometimes it's not good. Context can be hard to come by even now. It's a good truth and a bad truth at the same time. I've been able to spout out things about the other terrible notions of advice, but this seems different.

It's really a multifaceted problem. Let me brain storm a second. Come with me. What might someone be telling you not to read? What is it, who wrote it, made it? Perhaps it's good, perhaps it's bad? How can I tell and how can I speak to it, if I don't have context? Context allows me to look at something and then say okay. This came from this source, and in that source, they talk about this and that. I also know of other people throughout history who read that source material. I can see in the chronicles of their life that they did this with that information, and I can conclude from their actions if something has an overall positive or negative affect. (Granted, my perspective of 'negative' might be someone else positive and vice versa, but I will at least have a point of reference. For the record, if it causes intentional harm, its negative.)

Without any context it is impossible to conclude anything. It's merely relative. I'd say this is actually one of the points to be made in this funny book of terrible advice. If there is no context to something, or if there is only enough to surmise, then its worthless dribble.

Many things today, don't actually have context. We are given sound bites and small one liners. We are given 'deep thoughts' from individuals and nothing of their actual thought process. So, with that information we surmise, we fill in the blanks ourselves, but we don't actually have context for many other things, so we fill in those blanks with other people's sound bites. This makes for a chaotic tapestry that we ourselves can't even follow the pattern woven throughout.

Without context the patterns we weave for ourselves mean little, and mean an even smaller amount to others. Without context there is nothing, and nothing is truly ever said, only surmised and pushed out to others as truth.

February 29

If you don't know who you are and what you want by 18, 23, or 30 you're hopeless. Everyone else does.

Peer Pressure

THROUGHOUT the world we have different societal norms. In some country's families live together for a long time, when someone gets married, they don't move out, they simply add on to the place they live in. In the USA its assumed that you will probably move out and get your own place, not build on to your parents' house, right? It's strange to think of living your whole life that way.

In the USA we have a strange thing we hold onto today. What are you going to do with your life? That's the question? It's how we meet each other, it's how we breathe life into a conversation. So, what do you do? Your answer can't be nothing, right? You work at so and so. Nice, so what's your plans? Plans, I don't know I don't really have any?

Its what teenage movies are all about, the Brat Pack. It's about finding out what you want to do in your life before its 'too late'. What are you going to be? You know the truth about that one now, though right? Life changes, you change. That's not to say, don't give it a thought because you'll figure it out eventually. No, think about it, but don't stress over it. Find something you want to do. Anything at all. There's no pressure in it, maybe you'll change jobs a few times, chances are you will. People staying in one job their whole life has pretty much gone by the way side. Things change too fast.

Pick something and try it, if you fail at it, or decide it's not for you then so be it. I'm not promoting flakiness in the workplace. By all means you should have a good work ethic, but if it's not working out, look for something else. If someone has a problem with it, they have the problem, not you, right? (Unless it's your wife, if your wife has a problem with it, you might have an actual problem. You have been warned.)

The point, don't worry about not knowing what you want. You're human, you're going to want different things, and those things will change throughout your lifetime. You aren't required to pick one thing. There are multiple things. Remember how you used to play with blocks or playdough, or EZ bake ovens? Do you still care about those things? So just find something and do it, if you don't like it later, figure out a plan to change it. It's not easy, but it is possible. That might be what they mean when they say 'Endless possibilities await.'.

*Bonus day depends on if you are reading this during a leap year or not... so yea...

March 1

Find that one thing and do it.
—

SOUNDS great. Optimistic in its intention. We can all think back to a time or forward to a goal even, that we want(ed) to accomplish. That is excellent, do it, get it done. If it's been something you have been procrastinating about, plan it out, then do it. You will feel better about it. Promise. Unless it's something unsavory, and evil, in which case don't do it and get out of there. But while this old adage sounds positive, it's not, it's not even an adage. There is no general truth presented here. Its fluff. Nothing. But many of us hear this advice. We should have something, some grand event we are working toward, otherwise what are we doing? Right? I disagree, (otherwise it would be not terrible advice, and the title would have to change.)

You should do a lot of things, in fact you should have more than one major goal in life, have a few, it's okay. So many times, I hear about accomplishing that one awesome thing, a career comes to mind. That is not a bad thing to work toward, but it doesn't extend to your 'not at work' life. In fact, it might be healthier. The problem with this prevalent advice is that 'one' thing. What happens if you never do it? Is your life over, no! Your life is a complexity of excellent and good shading down and mixed up with crappy and even evil. But it's not one thing, and life is the longest thing you will do. If you fail at that one thing you thought was the all-encompassing end all-purpose, does life stop? It shouldn't, it doesn't have to. Answer me this batman, what happens if you do this one thing? Is it over, peaches and cream? All done, thanks for playing, cash out at the counter? There might be a new day with new things. What's wrong with the one thing you ask? There's only one of them. Find new things, all the time. Don't go overboard, try finishing a few of them, just understand there is more to your life than just that one thing. So many people forget that there are so many other things. Don't limit the possibilities. Sometimes we forget this. This is your reminder. There is more. I wonder what terrible advice is next?

March 2

Don't brush your teeth today.
—
The "they're not watching" fairy

WHY take the time? If you're young, they're probably just going to fall out anyway. Your parents aren't watching. If you're older…you can just get fake ones. That's what the famous people do. This advice normally doesn't come from your friends, it might come from your parents who never made you do it. Or maybe you've told yourself this. But maybe that's okay because you're going to brush them, tomorrow right? Of course, you're hygienically minded, so what's one day? "I'm sure I can get by." You say. I agree, you can get by, but try not to smile. (Or breath on me.) Maybe this is one of those little things that kill though. (Am I dating myself with that Razor Blade suitcase reference. Ah well.)

Maybe there are other things, small mind you, that you don't do. That dish washer, the sink, the garage. Maybe they aren't important either, at least in the big scheme of the things in your life (after all they say everything's relative, right?)

So, what's this about? Do brush your teeth, or don't. What do you care, you ask? Discipline is an interesting thing. It starts with the small things, and grows into something bigger.

It takes time to create a habit, unless its heroine. That'll mess you up instantly. It takes away your happy, it really does. Check it out if you don't believe me, by 'check it out', I mean look it up online. Don't, I repeat NEVER do that crap. But habits, most of them form over time. They say about 21 days, right? It takes longer to break them. It might take you a little longer to start brushing your teeth, (I imagine I'm talking to a parent that will be explaining or watching over a kid that brushes his/her teeth.) I'm not saying be a warden about it, but I think it's important to understand how habits good and bad can be formed and broken. Habits take longer to break though, just in case you were about to say you stopped smoking for three weeks and it didn't take.

And for the adults who already do brush their teeth, you can take this bit away from it. Habits take time to form and break. If you have a good habit you want to start. It's probably at least going to take three whole weeks. Habits, not getting rich or famous will take longer, much longer, and hard work too. Habits come first Now, go brush your teeth and get to work, or go to bed.

March 3

When you have a thought, say it out loud, no matter where you are. All. Day. Long.

Até

YOU know the one person at school or work who talks…all…the…time, or has the craziest ideas? Here's a terrible piece of advice. Do that too.

But seriously if you say, "Hey, I do that. What's your problem?", you may be in the minority. I got 99 problems but this ain't one. I think this would be funny. Think about it. Every thought. Hold on, I just thought about it. Maybe that wouldn't be funny at all.

Chances are you couldn't do it anyway. We think a lot, I mean a lot. Except maybe Joey from Blossom, and Dory from that lost fish movie. (Finding Nemo, yes, I know it. It's awesome.)

So, don't really try this. I imagine it would get boring really fast. And hard work. But as a side note, why not make a note of every thought and if you have time think about what might happen if you did say it out loud. If you can't say them out loud, why are you thinking about them? In this day and age, I bet that would be a real challenge though. Every thought? Captivate it and analysis it to see if it's something other people would be okay with? Interesting. Try it. It might help with the focus that we all seem to lack from staring at our phones. Just for the one day. Or 21. Whatever you feel up to.

March 4

Take it easy.

Aergia

TAKE a load off. You've earned it. Know those words? They feel great. They're a ticket to what I like to call 'not work'. We just need to unwind after working all day. Working for the money we make to keep the lights on and buy more things so we can pay more bills and work more. "We need breaks Alex!". Right, I hear ya.

I'm not terribly knowledgeable about this. I think too much about nothing to take it easy, but I'd go as far as to say that the amount of time we spend on electronics affects how tired we feel. Think about, how much time you spend on your phone, or PC, or TV, or Tablet, or watch. I'm not knocking all this technology. I love it. I want more. I can't wait to see what the next advancement is. But I feel I should show some caution. I already mentioned how video games can release chemicals that help gamers stay up and continue playing way past when they should. You think this doesn't include you, but you're on your phone, or PC, or Mac, or TV or Tablet, or watch. Let's face it, we are plugged in. There's very little chance we're going to give up that connection, unless someone unleashes Snake Plissken's Sword of Damocles. Kudos if you got the pop culture reference.

So, we do need to take it easy. My question is from what? From the hard work you do, or the electric chain around your neck. (I love writing, you can be so dramatic, and with such ease! You don't even have to think about the repercussions!) Calm down, I think we need technology. I think we might want to think about taking some time away from it every once in a while, though. (Wait till you see the next entry. Terrible advice I tell ya, all of it. Let me remind you and myself here. Context is key.)

March 5

Don't take it too easy.
—
Savitar

GOTTA get going. Right? We can't take things to easy, how are we supposed to get all the work done that we need to, when we're not working. If we take a day off all this stuff falls through the cracks and I end up further behind. "Thanks for what you're trying to say, but you don't understand. If I don't do these things when I'm off work, no one else is going to do them."

Truer words. I know I have to do everything. I work, pay the bills, come home do the dishes, I clean the kitchen, and write, I read. Watch Netflix. That's just in one day! I really wish I could get some help but you take what you get. Or is it, get what you take? I can't quite remember.

I think we don't really get all the advice we tell ourselves. That deep one liner's true context was lost before it even reached our ears anyway. Why can't you take it easy exactly? Are you a Spartan? A 'get things done' person. I'mma throw a wrench at you and see if you can dodge it. (That's joke reference to a movie…never mind.)

So, you have to work, and go and do and you can't stop because things will fall apart without you juggling all these balls. Lot of ball juggling. They all fall down without you, huh? I'm sure they do, bub.

You ever think you have a planning problem, maybe too many things going on? Do you need all those things you're paying on? Maybe you don't need to go out every night? Perhaps plan a day that you take off. I know, I know. You'll do that and then spend all day planning the next day in your head, if not break down before noon and start working on something.

It's the pace of our world. It's fast, and you gotta be fast too. Otherwise you'll be buried underneath it.

Did you know that there is a tribe of people on a small island off India that have resisted the modern world? The Sentinelese people send back hundreds of arrows and spears when we try to get close. Personally, I hope they keep us out. Who needs all the distractions we have anyway. I'm not saying go live on an island, but don't burn yourself out. ----- Tomorrow is a new day, unless the sun explodes that is.

March 6

It can't be that bad, taste it. Try it.

—

Ambrosia

FOOD. Lots of food on this spinning ball of dirt. Let's take a break from the terrible advice, and look at a few of the terrible foods or food type stuff we can find. Time to do some outside research. But I want to warn you...you probably don't want to. Think of it as, kinda like a list of things you don't want to know about. I'll warn ya again later. There not to be tasted, or even looked up. I don't see GMM doing a taste test of any of these soon. That was not a challenge, I like that show.

1. Kæstur hákarl, that's a tasty dish. Fermented Shark. Mmmm, pour me some more.
2. Lutefisk – If you love cilantro, I highly recommend trying some of this.
3. Century Eggs! I think I learned about these years ago. Sadly, they aren't 100 years old, but they're old enough I tell ya!
4. Casu Marzu – You're gonna have to work harder if you want to try this on your YouTube channel. Highly not recommended. I'm pretty sure it's illegal!
5. 100 on the gross out factor. Balut. Someone offered me some one time, and I said, "I think that's the Bear that sang with Mowgli." It. Is. Not. the bear. that sang. with Mowgli. Might not want to look that one up.
6. Gelatin, that's what I said. The wiggly stuff in the Jell-O. It's on the list.
7. Rat Meat. It's a really thing, not just a gross out factor in 'Demolition Man'
8. Tripe...but they say it's good for you...up to you.
9. Black Pudding. You may have heard of this. Lots of people eat it.
10. Wasp Crackers
11. Bonus Stinkheads... I think the name says it all.

Now all these are terrible. And should only be done for charity. Except Wasp Crackers, those still have stingers, that's what the Bonus is for. Maybe we can get this done some day. I mean 'we' as in someone else. I would never eat from this list.

March 7

Believe everything you read.

YOU ever read something you just knew was right? Or watched a documentary that explained something, or even something on the History Channel. It's so easy to just take someone's word for it. That is until another book or movie comes along that casts doubt on another book that was read. It's not that we are inclined to believe everything we read. It's just easier to. If we just take things that seem true as true, we don't have to do any research ourselves. Research takes time and lots of it!

The problem is that we have a bunch of half-truths and information fillers. What makes it worse is we freely share this information with others without confirming anything a lot of the time. What happens when you hear a rumor? Maybe you don't say anything. Maybe you're a steal trap, but you start to wonder if that person did or didn't say what someone said they did. An easy way to shut down a rumor is to go right to the source. If you go up to the person and ask, "Hey, did you say this to so and so?" Then they say yes or no. You have part of the story. Then you go to this so and so and ask them what that person told them. Then you have part of the story. Then you talk to them together. If it sounds like an investigation, that's because it is. It's called research.

Research. That's what research is, an investigation into the facts. If you believe what you hear when you hear it, chances are you don't actually understand the whole of the issue. We do this all the time. We also help to propagate it.

We have mindless arguments about issues where both sides don't actually understand the issues as they are. Both are wrong in their understanding, because neither side did any actual research or only from one side. And what I think the sad fact about this is, is no one really cares. I'm not saying that to shock you, I feel it's just a truth. People don't argue a point, most of the time they fight about it. Oh, at first both sides point out issues, and each side might even go ahead and say "Touché, that is a valid point." But toward the end people just start pulling references out of the air to prove they know how much it costs to build a golf course in Japan, and the other one doesn't.

I'm not speaking of all arguments. Just all the one's I see. Online, everywhere. One side will break down, but instead of bowing to a point that might make them rethink their view and researching it, they pull a reference out of the air they know nothing about, or worse, they begin to antagonize because they've reached the end of their knowledge on the subject. At least how to argue for it anyway. It's better to belittle and bully your way to right than go away and research. Everything has to happen now. If you believe something to be true and you plan to argue, firstly, don't go under the bridges because that's where the trolls live. Don't seek confrontation but know how to defend your points. If you can't do that without insults, I'm sorry, it's not a point in your favor.

March 8

Don't learn to swim.

EVER had that one thing you always wanted to do, but never found the time or keep putting it off. Well for me that's writing. I know you thought it was going to be swimming. I can swim, if there are floatation devices around and the side of the pool is relatively close by and a life guard on duty and not getting high.

Here's an experiment. Let's try something. Tomorrow go through your day. Just as you normally would. I want you to bring a piece of paper and pen with you. Don't worry you don't have to write everything down. I want you to mark the times you do things. Say you go to work from 9 to 5, driving gets you home at 6. Dinners at 7, which you have to make. Then you have to catch up on some work and then its 10 and you watch some tv and go to bed to do it again. Log what you do. Beginning and ending times. Be as detailed or rough as you please. Also do it on a day you have off.

Now that research is out of the way. What is it that you do all day? Did you log how much tv, or how much you're on the phone? What about reading a book or 'resting' and whatever that might entail. Do you work out? Include that too.

Now you don't have to do anything with this. You already have. It's in your head. You know what you do all day and where time goes. Maybe you don't want to change a thing! Great, but maybe there is that one thing that you have always wanted to do? If it's building a boat, or just learning to swim, maybe you can see some time that you can carve out of the day. I'm not saying make sure you are doing something at every moment of the day. Nah, take it easy every once in a while, but if you have something on your bucket list. You might be able to make use of some of that time, now that you know what you do and where time goes.

Of course, if you never learn to swim, at least you won't have to worry about sharks. They're out there, but don't let that stop you from learning something you've always wanted to.

March 9

If your wife says 'it's fine', it's not what they mean.

IF you believe this, as I do. You're not married, or you're one of the people who believe in the hype. What might be some of the options of what she means? Let's think of some shall we. Here's another list for ya. It's much shorter, because it's hard for me to follow and I'll explain why. When she says she's fine, what she might mean is.

1. You better not look at her again.
2. You forgot to fix the fingletop and scuttlebunch. (Could be whatever.)
3. It was your turn to do 'that thing' and you fracking knew it!
4. You're not paying attention to me.
5. You know what you did, and if you don't you better figure it out, right quick!
6. I'm actually fine.

I see a lot of list of what guys do and what women do. Guys talk direct. Women don't. I find that interesting. Is that true? That sounds sexist or one of those 'ist' words to me. I find it mind-blowing that we have so many articles and lists like this. "What she really means is." Is this really a thing? Do all women act like this? This seems very "passive-aggressive" to me. I'm not saying you have to be "aggressive-aggressive" like all the articles about how guys talk direct about things. I think that's bonkers too!

I can't say that I don't believe this, but I don't know if it's because every magazine cover explains how men and women don't talk the same way. Why not? (Can you tell I'm not married?) I just don't understand right? How we can have such a major breakdown in communication between men and women for so long? How long have we been on the planet? We can build a great pyramid that stands the test of time, but we can't have clear discussions, right. Go ahead and believe that.

I guess my issue with this is, these magazines and lists seem to concentrate on a sort of divide between the two sexes. One side is direct and overtly insensitive at times and possibly dim witted to boot thanks in no small part to marketing, while the other is passive aggressive, manipulative, wrathful even! If that's the case I think I'll just stay single, thank you very much. I don't believe it. I do believe we buy things we don't want, simply because they are easy to buy though.

I think we need to rethink these biased views, and how perhaps we believe them because they are repeated in our media back to us every single day, and these strange notions work to divide us. I'm not saying we're not different, but there are stereotypes that need to die.

March 10

Buy more decorative pillows for the bed.

—

FLUFFY fun! Throw pillows, decorative pillows. Good for impressing people you take to your bedroom. Wait, I'm not sure I understand this. Maybe it's because I like collecting video games and art more than bags of fluff. What's the desire? I want a pillow that I can use for sleeping. This reminds me of that movie with Ben Stiller and Jennifer Aniston, "Along came Polly". She convinces him to get rid of the throw pillows and he ends up stabbing a knife through his box spring. They serve no real purpose when you think about it. Their plumage, but even a peacock shows off his feathers. So why put them in the bed room. Guests aren't going in there. Display them throughout the house, or put them on stands in the middle of the rooms, like a museum piece, if they're that important.

Just make sure to ask yourself why, if you suffer from a throw pillow addiction.

March 11

Focus on your faults, it's the only way to get better.
—

DO you hear the sound of that basketball buzzer in your head. I know I do. "I don't know this", "I can't do that". "I messed up here, and now that other thing is ruined." God forbid you allow yourself to have a good day! "BUUUUU-UZZZZZZZZ!"

This happens to underachievers a lot. It happens to overachievers a lot. You know what they both have? Ulcers and wasted time. It's easy to do. It's not just in the media, it's in our societal veins. If the television and magazines aren't telling you what you're not doing right, or a Facebook snapshot aren't showing you who is having a better time, your school or work mates are looking more impressive or doing grander things. You'd be able to do them too, if not for that one thing, right? It's just that fault or flaw that's in the way? Too heavy or geeky. Not pretty enough, or not outgoing enough.

Wrong. Maybe you have faults, but in this day and age, we barely see others. I mean we see people's dirty faults when the media turns on them, but they simply burn out of the limelight and we forget they existed by the following year. "Oh, to be famous!"

The truth is, we all have faults. We don't share them. We all have failures, we don't share them. We don't see those things in others. Now, the issue I'm talking about effect individuals privately. People out in the world, you maybe. Everyone has faults, flaws, failures. We just don't share. It's a catch-22 really. But the issue remains just that. We focus on our faults and flaws and failures too much, while seeing everyone else's successes. We do this because we compare ourselves with others, instead with our past selves.

I don't have an actual basis for comparing myself to Chris Pratt. But I do. I mean we are both pretty good looking. I was also once part of the Nova Corps, but that's beside the point. I can't create a baseline for comparing myself to someone else. I only have a baseline for me. I know how good, or bad I've been and how I have improved. And let me tell you, I have. But when I start comparing myself to Ryan Reynolds. Pratt, or Ryan Gosling I fail that comparison. Not because they know more, or look better, or have more success, or own a boat, but because they aren't me yesterday. I could write more on this but I've ran out of page. Stop focusing on your faults, everyone has them. Look at where you came from, starting today, if you have to. Build from there, not from Facebook snapshots of a single moment in someone else's life. We are all human and flawed. Focus on your growth, not your flaws and faults, and stop comparing your life to the successes of others.

March 12

The things we say, and do not do.

Not "Jerry Maguire"

WHEN I thought of this, my first thought was I can't use that. Jerry Maguire wrote that book. Apparently, he wrote "The things we think and do not say." So, I guess I'm going to try to kick this old ball a little further down the line then. Talking about stuff is overrated.

We say a lot. I mean, we talk, text, post and tweet, a lot. We share a lot. Information abounds in this day and age. Good things happen all around us. Excellent, awesome, joyful things. Bad things happen too. Outrageous things, things that people say shouldn't happen. We have large open discussions about issues and problems. We talk about them online and at the water coolers in the office. The issues are on everyone's lips. How the stock market is, what the newest bill through congress is about and how it needs changed, how that latest crime took place and how no one could believe how quiet the person was, so mild mannered, how our school system is broken, or how this group is fixing it for this area. We talk a lot. It's good. It spreads the issues around. Let people know what's going on.

Small pockets of people, and I mean small as in millions, tens of millions out of billions. These small pockets 'do'. They do things. Maybe because they don't have regular jobs or don't need money or they have time. These pockets do a lot. They work. They work against those who would do harm, or against a system that doesn't work. They feed, and protect. They care for. Not that it's to say that the people who only say don't care, it's just they care more about other things. I'm not trying to be harsh, just real. I have bills to pay, and children to feed. (I don't have kids, I'm just saying that as you might in your head, just now.)

Life and the machinations of it are many and varied. You can't know what's in the heart of people. But you can tell what someone's actions are, and if all your actions are only words, how much are you really doing? (If your offended right now, perhaps that's a flag. But don't worry, no one has to know.)

If you want to just read Jerry's Mission Statement for fun and forget about this thought inducer, its over at theuncool.com. (I've also linked to it in the appendix.)

March 13

Live as if this was your last day on earth.

School Stopper Linda

IF this isn't the hardest thing to answer. What might you do with the last day of your life? Does anyone give real thought to this advice. I think we hear it in movies and books, and see those characters working to finish this 'quest' the best they can. I can't say I've ever done this. I think if I did, I would be sad about all the things I could have done to help others more. If I'm honest, my last day, as it stands now will be coming home from work, telling a robot to play me some music, working out, then writing. I'm not complaining about my day. I've got a goal to complete after all, but what if this is as far as I got. Would I actually live different? So here is what I'm not going to do today, because I don't think it's my last day. I'd like to think I'd go out and walk around. Maybe I could find some people who needed help that I could do something for before midnight, but much of my day would have been wasted. It's an interesting thought. Not one that comes up much. Maybe that's a good thing, maybe not.

I hope that it might be easier for you. People ask this from time to time. What's the answer for you? Would you mark things off on your bucket list? Do you have one yet? You should, I think I mentioned getting one.

Here, it might be an easier way to figure out what you'd do now so you have it written down, what did you do yesterday? What did you do last week/month? My educated guess is some variation of the former. Not a huge deviation of. But perhaps it's something to think about. Not in some morbid way. What would you do on your last day? Why only then?

Would it be the same as it ever was? And if so, maybe you'd like to pull some of that stuff you would do on your last day on earth, forward in time a tad bit. Then maybe on your last day, all you'd need to do is be content with the life you led.

March 14

Eat after you go to the grocery store.

School Stopper 'Intern' Paul

JUST another small tidbit to break up the hacks of life. (Shameless plug for LifeHack.org). This does link to that pretty well however. Ever find yourself spending too much money at a grocery store. If you would eat something before going, you could find that you spend less. Another tidbit is to map out the store, some supermarkets are kind enough to create maps. Some will rearrange the store from time to time to promote confusion. Did you know that? Sounds dastardly doesn't. In comparison to how marketing works in other areas of our society I'd say it's on par. Look at it this way, if they didn't confuse you in the store every once in a while, that item that is made in some small town, might not get their contract with the store renewed and then the whole supplier might go out of business, and the town might dry up. Of course, the item could be made in a small town anywhere in the world and could be crap too. There are a lot of factors to consider when they confuse you in the store. Let's just say their looking out for… somebody. Moving on from the shady underbelly of supermarket selling tactics.

If you would like to hear about more life hacks however you can go to the org site above, or in the appendix. Some of them are quite helpful. They are time savers-a-plenty. Ways to help you sit less, foods to help you sleep, travel tips in crowds, coffee limits (Wait, that's absurd), articles on yoga, or thousands of other 'hacks' to make your life easier. I'm not sure these are new ideas, but they're nicely located in one place. Good to remember in case you need something to read on a plane.

March 15

Never ask for directions. You know how to get there.

Pride

MEN. Did this remind you of men? Maybe you're sexist. Work on that. I'm joking. We don't like to ask for directions. It's a fault, but thankfully we have GPS out the wazoo.

This section definitely should have you thinking about asking for directions if you need them. No sense in looking around and figuring out yourself if you're truly lost.

This brings me to the actual point of this writing. Men don't ask for directions. Interesting. I think the advice is worse than this though. Let me ask, whatever sex you are, have you ever been in school, or work and someone said something, or explained something and you just didn't get it. But instead of asking, you explained to yourself that you would either, ask later, or figure it out by reading something.

That's great, superb even. You're not doing yourself any favors and if your job or the skill you're learning in school is actually important (And it should be important to you…otherwise maybe you should think about that as well.) then you're not only hindering yourself, you're doing a disservice to those you work with. Hey, maybe you don't want to look stupid, or worse maybe you don't care. I get it. So, you can just ignore this if you're one of those people, I'm going to talk to the people that do care.

You've all heard it in school, "the only stupid question is one not asked!" Well, I'm gonna to be honest, I think I've heard some stupid questions, real doozies. I also want to tell you, I admire the people that asked them. They care, hard. They want to do it right. Now I know there is a level of quickly understanding something we all hope people have, but if you have the question, 100% guarantee someone else has a similar question. Hands down, no question. Others might just not want to ask. Ask anyway, if the person answering is rude in their response, make sure they at least answer the question. You weren't asking for friends, get the answer. There's your good advice.

March 16

History is for old people.

Me

TRUER words were spoken. Did you know that some people in history kicked ass? Alexander the Great became King of Macedon at the age of 20. Did you know he created one of the largest empires of the ancient world all the way from Greece to India, and did this all within 12 years or less? He died at 32.

Did you know who Olaudah Equiano was? Bet not. He wrote about his time as a slave and played a role in turning opinions about it. You know who Nelson Mandela was, but have you ever read a book about him. What about Winston Churchill? King Hannibal assumed command of an entire army at 26. Granted it was from his father who was assassinated, but you might have not known that. He has a phrase, "Hannibal ante portas." Which was used to scare practically anyone in Rome. You know Rome right, it was a city built by the gods and ruled around 500 years. Did you know America at this time has only been established for 242 years? Think we can make it? Not if we don't study history, I bet ya.

One story that I find amazing is the story, that centers on Theodore Roosevelt. Maybe you have heard of him, interesting character. Lots of energy. I wish I had that much. Founded the Progressive party (not related to any new progressive party). When he was campaigning, October 14, 1912. A man named John Flammang Schrank shot him. (assassins always have three names, that's what they say anyway) Anyway, he got shot in the chest. He had some padding, don't get me wrong. What's interesting is Roosevelt didn't directly go to the hospital. He gave his speech. I believe I heard it was about 45 minutes to an hour, with a bullet lodged in his chest. Now I'm not saying that was smart, I'm just saying that sounds pretty tough to me, stupid, hands down, but the man seemed to have something.

Read about him, read about them. It's cliché to read history right, but I think it has merit. If you don't study the mistakes of the past, you're doomed to repeat them. Same with the successes of these men. If we never look at how they accomplished the things they did, we'll never amount to much. People must, I must, strive to be better, greater, kinder, more generous and loving than my fathers before me. If I don't know about them, how can I measure myself? How can you?

MARCH 17

Never grow up.
—
Peter Pan

FIRST of all. I'm not trying to pick on Peter Pan. I simply loved the story. Disney made a marvelous adaptation. Never read the book. Nowadays his story has changed. This writing really had no intention dragging his name down to anything dark, but it turns out that's easy to do. I'd point out, it's easy to do with anything, at all. There are many retellings if interested, found on Amazon, or Good-Reads.com. I recommend reading the one by J.M. Barrie first. It gives context. Context is key.

Let's talk about the advice first. Peter Pan isn't the only one who had it. I wanted to always be a Toys'R Us Kid. Loved that tune too! (It used to be a store full of toys and wonder. It's closed now. They couldn't compete with kids only wanting apps for their phones.) But if we take it more to heart, as they do with Peter Pan now, it turns, grumpy. Imagine for a moment. Never growing up. Ever. Does that sound good? Recognize that if you're still a teenager, this question probably doesn't apply. It's fun to think about all the things we'd do if we never aged. That's the same thing. Never growing old, right?

What's wrong with growing old? Dying? That's gonna happen, so don't worry your pretty head about it. Unless those scientist guys can figure something out, and how to fix the population problem, and not sell it for a life savings worth. (Crap shouldn't have given them that idea, they might not have thought of that one for a few years.)

But never growing up implies more. Even in the original story of Peter Pan, which I recommend before all the retellings pollute, you're mind of what Peter was originally supposed to represent, you can see he was somewhat self-involved, wanted to have fun all the time. Carefree to the point of danger. Wendy explained it to Peter.

We all want to have fun, we want to be entertained and play. "Work's for suckers!" some people shout.

I guess I'm just trying to point out some good things about growing up. Stability, family, true friends (if you're lucky), learning to care for others outside your own desires. In the process of growing up, if we have at all, we learn how life works, and how it doesn't. Ways to interact and not treat people. Growing up allows us to make a difference, positive or negative in this world. So, I say, do grow up and when you do be a positive influence in this world. You might find yourself to be the only grown up, surrounded by adults. Teach them how to grow up, but not old.

March 18

Grow Up.

—

DO it now. I just explained how not growing up leaves your mind flimsy and weak, self-centered, reckless. If you're going to make it in this world you need to, figure it out, work hard, get a job, stop dilly dallying and grow up already.

Oh, that sounds marvelously fun! That's what I did. I was what people call a 'latch key kid'. I would get up, usually my parents would get me up. Send me to the bus. After school however, I was by myself a lot. Actually, that's not entirely true. My grandmother was around for a lot of it, but I would find myself alone a lot. I was always responsible. Feed my dog, do my homework. I was able to audit a college course when I was around 12 or 13, because I wanted to learn what they were teaching. I started college when I was 16, continued that, with some time off and now here I am, all grown up since I was 13. That's not entirely true at least the 'all grown up', I had my share of childhood, but I was and still am, mostly serious about things in life.

I'm not stoic, per say, but sometimes I feel I 'relate' to that sort of image. I feel that its possibly because of things I've dealt with in my life. I haven't actually dealt with hardship on a scale that's worth mentioning, and I'm not trying to compare my 'hardship' to yours, but I have been shaped by my environment none the less.

That all being said, I highly recommend staying young and care free as long as possible. Don't worry about figuring things out, or having hard opinions on things. I'm pretty sure I'd have to say that the grow up age looks like it should be by age 13. I would say wait longer, but there are many traditions that take place around this age, leading me to assume (see how I didn't say believe there.), that 13 might be the time. I'd say up until this time, you as a parent have the most influence on who your children are going to be. After that, well, it might be 3 more years to drive, but they probably aren't taking your advice as seriously anymore. Just the truth. Hopefully you can stay young at heart though.

Some other rite of passages you might be interested in researching I'll mention by name and you can look them up. Bullet Ant Initiation (not recommended), Quinceanera, Innuit Coming of Age, Khatam Al Koran, Maasai at 10, and Vanuatu, and Bar/BatMitzvahs. There are more, to find them Google "Rites of Passage". They seem to have good intentions, albeit some might not be understandable to you or I. But in a world of relativism, who's to say what's wrong or right in a culture? Right?

March 19

Nobody else will love you...

—

LOVELY LIES we tell ourselves, or allow others to tell us. What kind of advice is this? Terrible advice yes, but these sound like the words an abuser would throw about freely. Or if you say them to yourself, lies. While you may have not met anyone who 'loves' you, you should know they are out there. Granted that gives someone as much hope as saying, "Well, there's plenty of fish in the sea!" Or as much solidarity as "You still have a chance, go get'em!"

Sometimes though, the truth doesn't give us a warm feeling. I say there are people out in the world who if they knew you, they would love you. That's truth, right there. You might never find them, if you don't look, I promise you won't find them.

One of the things that this 'advice' does, is bring us down. If it's from another, they might be afraid they will lose you, they are afraid of losing control because control means things are safe, and they never feel safe. They weren't taught to. They may have been abused, unloved, ignored, cheated on one too many times. But this is not a reason for their behavior. They need help, but if they are saying this to you, you can't help them by allowing that to go on. Get out of there if you can, or seek help. There are shelters and other support organizations out there. They truly want to help you.

If you say this to yourself. Let me tell you again, lies. Not true. The thing I said, about someone loving you, that's truth. There are also support organizations to help you with this as well. I know my book might only bring money to some kids, heck it might only be a few dollars, but hopefully if you read this and you are someone in this situation. You'll know I'm sincere in this writing at least.

Still it's a hard piece of 'advice', especially if you've heard it all your life or hear it in your head. If you don't have a person like this in your life, and don't give yourself this advice, be thankful today. Perhaps your thoughts and actions might support or help some who do

By the by, here's a website or number if you find yourself in that situation of abuse.

http://www.thehotline.org/   Numbers   are   1-800-799-7233   or   TTY 1-800-787-3224.

(Anyone can call. Women, Men, Children. Should you need it.) 24/7 365

March 20

Don't waste your time on old video games.

—

Jumpman

ALMOST like the history post, but maybe not as wide reaching. Old games are boring, they're pixelated! I can't play this, it takes too long to load!

So old games might be crap. Lots of them are. I think I could completely waste my day if I had to run through "Adventure!" to find Warren Robinett's name, play the E.T. game and watch "Manos, the Hands of Fate" I think my brain would explode from the excitement.

Some old games, like Pac-Man, or Super Mario Bros. 1,2 and 3. Maybe some Sonic, the original Mortal Kombat (unless your parents would be against it from the gore.) I'd mention playing Chrono Trigger and Super Metroid. Some Manic Mansion, Time Lords, Life Force, Blaster Master, Al-Qadim, WolfenStein. Heretic perhaps Zelda a Link to the Past. Try Final Fantasy 7. I know the graphics are bad, but it was awesome. Warcraft, you know the RTS game. Probably not. Try it.

I could go on. The point is the same as in reading the history of people and the things we've built. If you want to be a professional gamer. Sure, you don't need to play these old games, they might be quite a challenge for you honestly. If you want to make games however, I suggest you play some of these and more. Without understanding where video games came from, we can't expect to make better games.... So, after writing that, I don't believe that holds up, but still, these are pretty awesome games. There were no zero-day patches, they worked as is right out of the... cartridge. Of course, they weren't very big games.

If by chance you don't want to play these old games, then check out a youtuber who does it for you. "Lazy Game Reviews – LGR" on YouTube has some amusing videos. And for another try "Retro Game Review", "Gaming Historian" or "Watch Mojo Top Ten Retro Gamer Critics" for a list of more.

Old video games, if you can find a system to play them on, perhaps a test on setting up an emulator, or VM (I think that's short for Virtual Machine), will increase your dexterity, your strength, knowledge, and test your patience. But some of them might be worth it. After all, I sat through "Manos, the Hands of Fate". Give it a go, if it doesn't work at first, take the cartridge out and blow on its headers.

March 21

Don't recognize day light saving time, or if you're in Arizona, Hawaii or one of the other numerous places that don't already, do. Don't inform your boss of your newly acquired schedule.

—

DID you know that daylight saving time was thought of in 1895. Although it wasn't implemented until 1916. That's a long planning process. One of the major reasons for its acceptance, was actually the Railroads and Mail/Communication Services.

DST didn't actually start being accepted widely and permanently until the 1970's, when we were running low on oil due to something called the Iranian Revolution that hindered exports. Careful reading about history, you might learn something.

I'd recommend picking up a history book on it. The debate on whether it's actually still needed is pretty interesting. I have no real opinion on the subject, as long as I get to my meetings on time, I'm not sure I care.

On a side note between Alaska and Russian, where their used to be a land bridge, called the Bering Strait, there are two islands about 2 miles apart. But they are about 20 hours apart. I myself don't understand why this hasn't become a more centralized place for major business. If you're doing business in Big Diomede, and you miss a business meeting, you could simply boat over to Little Diomede, which is 20 some hours behind the Big island, and call into that same meeting when it comes around in 19 hours! Who wouldn't want that extra time! Course it's not legal to travel from one island to the other, but it's a nice thought, Doc Brown would be proud!

March 22

Refuse to do your own laundry.

Tomorrow man

WHAT'S more becoming than someone who won't fend for themselves. I'm not talking about people who can't. If you know someone like that, I would say find more ways to help them and not only that, help them feel whole.

I'm talking about people who won't. They might say 'can't', but they can. They just don't know it. One of the things in this world that I've found to be true is a nice little quote by Henry Ford. Now I'm not a big fan of quoting, it's so easy to take it the wrong way, and without proper context I think it's rather pointless. I said 'I think', I'm pretty sure I meant, 'it is'. (You can reread the sections on researching and arguing if it is a foggy reference.)

On to the quote, "Whether you think you can, or you think you can't. You're right." Granted, there are some things you just can't do. No matter how much I want to walk on Mars…wait that might happen. Regardless, you have to be realistic in your approach to this, but it's the same as saying, 'if you set your mind to it'. If I wanted to walk on Mars before I died, I truly believe that I could make plans to do so. I would need to train for travel, I would need to find a job with Space X or some other company. I would need to immerse myself into that field. But I don't want to go to Mars. I like it here just fine. I'm not properly motivated for such a thing.

That's one of the things we get wrong with this quote. We only hear that if we think hard enough, we can. That's not what it means. We have to have determination and drive for something, skill and know how.

And now we come full circle. How do you have drive for something? That's an internal urge to attain a goal or satisfy a need. That's easy, we get these all the time honestly. I get an urge, or drive to play a video game when I'm at work. When I get home that drive has left me. So I didn't have determination to see it through. I'd have to turn on my PS4. Alexa can't do that yet. It would take too much effort.

This is what happens to us. "It's too hard, it takes too much time. I can't. I don't wanna." If you don't want this to be you, learn to do your own laundry, clean up after yourself. Brush your teeth every day. Do it, even when you don't want to. These small things, and others like them produce, or can produce in us a further ability, an aptitude that we can use to do bigger things, greater things. So, to recap, do your laundry, clean your room, don't complain about it. It might help you save the world one day. If you don't believe it, then you won't.

March 23

Get sidetracked.
Every little thing
-

INFORMATION super high-way. Information overload. I tell ya, when I was young it was hard to stay on track. I had to feed my dog and do my homework. I would always have an idea, a vague notion of free time, or television. I couldn't do homework in front of a television. My mom could paint, or write in front of it, but to her defense, she had a black and white tv. So how hard was that, am I right?

I had video games I wanted to play. I was born in the age of Nintendo, and Sega. I can hear the Sonic game start up in my head now. Distracting to say the least. But I managed. As I grew up in this Information Age, I graduated school and went to college. I tell ya, I think I got out in time. I'm pretty sure my attention span has decreased. My thoughts are more scattered.

In the past, if I didn't know something. I had to look it up. That meant I had to open a book somewhere, probably a library and search for it. It was easy to let it go if my mother or father didn't have the answer. That's not the case today. Each of us has an encyclopedia on us all the time, and I'm not talking about the old door to door sales man type where you buy one a month for 26 months. This one has instant search features. We have all the knowledge of the world…or a fair bit more than we used to, at our fingertips. If I think of something now, I can look it up. So, I do.

Some Huffington Post article mentioned we have around 50,000 thoughts per day. I could look each one of those up on Google if I wanted to! I used think that was cool. There is a wealth of information out there, but now we also require it to be fast and watered down. We can't take time to read a book about a topic. We just want the highlights. Honestly, we have become too distracted with other thoughts. We all have ADHD.

If it's not informationally functional topics, its movies, and games, and apps, Oh my! We build the muscles we work out the most.

Challenge: Don't use your phone unless you're making a call. I bet it's too hard. I bet you couldn't stop if you wanted to. I bet you don't want to.

What I fear in this age however, is that we are losing our ability to follow through, and technology is teaching our youngest generation, that they don't even have to. It's dark, dramatic, but don't worry. I'm sure it's not as bad as I make it sound.

March 24

Stay Focused.

—

Narcissus

OTHER side of the coin? "How could staying focused be so bad? You can't just tell us on the previous page that we should ditch our technology so that we can stay focused on the truly important things in our lives and then on the very next page say that staying focused is terrible advice. Alex you're all over the place!" Well, that's kinda how the flow of the book is taking us. It's all about context and not one-liners or only our perspective.

I am all over the place, this is the age of Information! This book is about terrible advice, it's also about context. Taken without context, things can't be understood. See what I'm doing? You need to have balance, right?

Sometimes we focus too hard. Sometimes the goal is just out of reach, but no matter how hard we focus, it gets further away from us. Our razor-sharp focus doesn't help create an ability to complete a task, it narrows our vision of how that task might be completed.

In focusing too much, for too long we lose sight of the goal's context. Of people that might be able to help us. We are not supposed to be alone, we are made for a connection. Why do you think we use technology the way we do? We want that connection.

Backing up and taking stock of where we are, never seems like it's part of the 'remaining focused' advice. How could focusing on something else, help you focus on what you're trying to fix?

Here's something that I've found true. When I have an issue, or problem. I'll focus on it, try to work through it, or strong arm it away. It's how you get things done, or put an end to something. Sometimes I can solve it by doing that. Other times, it simply consumes my being. So how can I fix this error? When I stop, and turn my focus from it. When I concentrate on something else, others perhaps, sometimes I find that the issue is gone entirely, or I know how to solve it when I return to it.

This is why staying focused on something is terrible advice. Successful people stay focused though? I have to push through. Successful people do stay focused, but they have more than one thing they focus on. That's one of the things that makes them successful.

March 25

Put hot sauce on everything.

PUT it on eggs, and bacon and pancakes! Also, on ice cream, cookies and coffee! These are things people do! So, let's make another listing. Here are some terrible advice ideas for hot sauce and food/drink combos. (If you try them online, please reference this book. Maybe it will sell a few more copies. I'll also reference where I found these ideas in the appendix under the date, if I didn't already know them, as someone might want to know the recipe, so they don't accidentally create such a thing. 😉)

1. Spicy Pancakes
2. Hot Coffee, Hot Jalapeno
3. Eggs and bacon with Sriracha
4. Ice Cream Sriracha Style
5. Hot Sauce Cookies

There are 4 that I've found and 1 I knew. I may take my own terrible advice on this one and try some of these others. Just don't eat spicy food before bed time.

I don't feel like this list does justice to the amount of concoctions that have been created. I don't want to recreate the wheel however so I'll just point you to somewhere that already did a pretty good job of it.

For that you can slide on over to the Greatist.com. They go through Breakfast, Lunch, Dinner, Desert and Snacks! I'll let the experts take it from here.

https://greatist.com/health/healthy-sriracha-recipes

March 26

If at first you don't succeed. Give up.

School Stopper 'Intern' Paul

THIS is surprisingly, something we tell ourselves often. We don't tell other people this. No, that would be wrong. We're allowed to tell ourselves this though... I'm confused on our internal logic sometimes. If at first you don't succeed, try again. That's how it goes, right. We tell people this because determination helps people push past and over hurdles. But as individuals we don't personally think about this. If we can't do something the first time, then it's not worth doing, or it's not going to happen, or it's a definition of insanity. (Doing the same thing over and over, expecting different results.)

It's better to move on and try other things. Sure, there's something to that. If after a certain time you can't figure it out, or its not working, perhaps it is time to move on.

But not on the first attempt. Failure breeds success. That's what they say. If you never fail, can you actually succeed at something? I'd bet the answer is no. Not if you think about it. Maybe you've been a success at everything you do, the first time. Never failing at anything. Great, good for you! I hope it continues for you that way, what happens if you do end up failing some time? How will you take it?

Failure sucks. It can be disheartening if you let it. Or it can be the greatest teacher. I know cliché, right? But I don't know if it's obvious. If it was, maybe we wouldn't take failure so badly. Maybe we are just failures at failure.

I believe that failures help build us up, certainly they can tear us down but the difference is our mindset on what a failure is. People see failure as a weakness. But that's a nice little white lie to make you weaker. If you never fall down, if you don't scrape your knee. If your never hurt or experience pain, how do you think the first time you experience failure and pain will go. Do you think you'll be okay with it?

No, it will be scary.

If you know what to expect however, you may become more fluid. You might be able to get up from the scraped knee faster than the last time. It may strengthen you for the future. You may be able to help others through a similar failure. Failure helps teach us how to succeed. Don't be afraid of failure. Be afraid of never learning from it.

March 27

You can't fight the machine.
-
Me

DISMAL. Dystopian. Lost cause. No chance. Too late. The system is just too big and too old. It's a theme. It runs through our society, history, culture, fiction. Some things can't be stopped. It's fate. This seems to me to be a very nihilistic thought, not that I understand nihilism or care to. My time would be better spent watching "Manos, the Hands of Fate" once again, and I can't see the point of that either.

The 'advice' is normally given when someone comes up against something seemingly insurmountable. Something that can't be overcome. A hurricane comes to mind. Swimming across the ocean, but that may have been done already to some degrees.

Firstly, let me say. It does appear you can't fight the machine. If the machine is life and all life within it. People in the world on average don't seem to be getting kinder, or smarter, and even though we are now a 'global economy' it doesn't tend to make us globally conscious or care for the lives of others in foreign countries. In fact, with all our 'connectedness' I feel we are more distant than ever. We are even getting more people to 'feed the machine' as it were. (Check out World of Meters for a fancy clock.)

But I don't believe that a victory requires atlas to shrug, but only for strongholds of those who would hinder progress to be broken, no matter how large or small those strongholds may appear. What I mean in English is, the machine is not as big as we think it is. It might have wheels and cogs that turn and they might take time to replace, or spin the other way but they can spin the other way.

The difficulties in this life can be broken down, we can task things out. But in order to do this we must work together. So, when someone remarks that 'you can't fight the machine.' Maybe they're right, but we can join together as a people and stand up for things, change things. In order to do so, we have to connect. Not over the net, not on the phone, but in our beliefs, our understandings, our views, in the real world, not just digitally. Divided we fall. So how do we stand? And what do we stand for?

March 28

Burn the candle at both ends.

Ego

GOOD idea. Sometimes you have to. In order to get ahead of all the stuff going on, you need to be on your toes and jump into a project. Then on the other end you feel the need to let go and relax, spend time with friends and family. These are both good things. Together they're harder to do, but people still do them. Some people don't even know how to do this at all. It might be better if we only had two ends.

The fact seems more like we have multiple ends to burn. More like a Pink Lotus Candle, than a traditional two ended candle you buy at the store.

There are times when we can do this, sometimes we must. If you have children, I'm sure you have to work hard, and play hard for them as well. If you don't have kids, I'm sure you do the same, just with your friends on the weekends.

The truth is, we can do this. In fact, perhaps it's a test of endurance that you could use to grow from. If you can work and play hard, perhaps you could finish that project you always wanted to, you just have to find the proper motivation.

All and all, burning the candle at both ends requires you to have a 'up and at 'em, go get 'em' attitude. When you start to lose that energy that's when you get someone saying, "oh, look who's burning the candle at both ends."

So, the task would be if you are doing this, is to figure out how to slow the burn on one side of the candle. Chances are that's going to be the night side, unless you're a third shifter.

Timing and planning are going to be your friends. You should take some of that time you're burning up, to figure out a schedule. It could be as packed as you want it, but without some sort of proper plan, you'll probably burn out sooner rather than later.

I'm all for this terrible advice, I do it often. But if you want to do it right, you have to have a plan and be flexible. I'm sure we'll talk about this more as the days go on.

Plan it out, without a plan, you don't stand too much of a chance with this advice.

March 29

Leave the candle burning.

FUNNY short story. I know we're talking about burning the candle at both ends. I have a friend. Let's call him Tom. We used to be roommates, and Tom had a group of friends that would come over and talk about things and share experiences. Let's tell it like it is, Tom had real friends. The kind that would listen and be honest with each other. They wouldn't hide a body but they would be there before it came to that. In fact, I believe they are all still friends.

So, they would all get together after work and talk into all hours of the night. It was a good group. I believe I might have been there for some of that night, can't remember the topic. I headed off to bed. Had to get up early in the morning. They would burn their candles at both ends. I never had it in me. 5 AM. That's when I had to get up. Earlier than normal, I don't remember why that was either, God knows.

Anyway, woke up at 5, got everything ready to go. Now at that place there was a concrete tunnel leading into the house from the garage. The other side of the garage was where all the guys would meet up. Worked perfectly for noise control.

So, in the morning, I opened the door and stepped out into the tunnel, shut the door. I quickly noticed a, I wouldn't call it a billowing amount of smoke, but it was significantly more than I was used to seeing normally when going out to my car. So, I follow it, quickly I might add, down to the door leading to the other side of the garage. Now, I know I'm writing this book of terrible advice, so I should probably know a thing or two, right. Well, not in this case. In the fire video's they show, they tell you if you see a door, with smoke coming out from under it and seeping out the top, touch the door, you know, test it out for heat. To see if its, you know, hot on the other side, with the fire and stuff being there.

So, what I do is grab the handle. That's how you open a door, with the handle. That's the only advice I could remember when my brain was explaining that the garage was on fire and I needed to stop it, now. I'll also say, sometimes, it's not good to listen to your brain, sometimes. So, I open the door. Smoke rolls out. I can see a fla- a pile of flame...s. Also, I forgot to mention the fan. We had a fan, had. This flame, was about a foot long in circumference, and circle on the table that Tom had. Beautiful, hand carved, lovely. One of a kind. So that was burning. It wasn't from Pier 1. I turned off the fan we had, still at that time we had it. It was creating a sort of 'suck funnel' that was pulling the FIRE up into the roof of the garage. I figured that should stop. The entire rest of the room was black with smoke. After turning the fan off, the fire died down some. So, I found some water and put it out. The charred surface of the table had at the very center of it a candle holder. After I was satisfied with this fireman's job, I think I started my car up, yep, I recall it was winter time and I had to work. I again checked the room, yep still black as pitch. No ring of fire though. Awesome. Back up the tunnel, I open my friend's door. I very calmly explain "It's out now, but there was a fire in the garage. Looks like there is some smoke damage. The table is burnt up, gone. I put the fire out." I repeated that because I could tell Tom wasn't sure that the fire was out. He must have missed my initial explanation, I could tell that from his eyes. I continued slowly, "I have to go to work now. The fire's out. You need to clean that up. I can help when I get back, but I have to go." He still didn't quite understand the fire was out, so I showed him the ruins and headed off to work. When I came home, I believe he was repainting the walls. He now uses electric candles. Moral, don't forget to blow the candles out, and don't burn the candles at both ends.

March 30

Press the Red Button.

School Stopper 'Intern' Paul, the Pusher of Unknown Buttons

GO ahead. Do it. You know you want to. No one's looking. Just touch it. It's glossy! Nice. It's like a shiny bobble. Wonder what it does. I bet it shoots confetti from an air cannon and then sings songs of the sweetest sound. Voices of angels. Then servants come out holding pillows and on the pillows are (either) candy (or) healthy fruit to eat! And my boss comes in and says I get the next two weeks off for finding the button to push. Ah, it's going to be so wonderful once I push this button.

DON'T PUSH THE BUTTON. KNOW WHAT IT DOES FIRST. IF YOU CAN'T FIND A MANUAL, DON'T PUSH THE BUTTON. JUST DON'T. FIGHT THE TEMPTATION. I KNOW YOU CAN.

(Read into this what you will.) Just don't push buttons until you understand what they do.

March 31

Smoke 'em if ya got 'em.

FROM 16 until I was 27. I smoked cigarettes. I believe at the end I was smoking about two and a half to three packs a day. That's around 10,950 cigarettes a year. That's not bad, right?

I believe I started when someone offered me one driving to school. I think the next time I smoked at the mall. It was cool back in the day. It was something cool people did, you know. (It so, wasn't cool.) I saw the commercials with the lady and the old man in the wheel chair, the air tank, whole nine. Didn't stop me. I didn't care. It was cool. I was cool.

Then I got older and it wasn't as cool, but everyone still did it. Then the prices increased. It didn't matter I liked them. I believe the turning point for me came when I was living in Boston. I had a roommate. We'll call him Dave. Dave was a nice guy. I was going to college up there at the time. I think I mentioned wanting to work out a little, you know get in shape, a different one. Not as spherical.

Dave liked the idea, "Hey, I'm going to go work out. The college has a gym that's free to us." Sounded good, I thought. Free gym. Saves 39.99 a month. Not really, when you think of student loans, but still. So, we met up at the gym after class.

Warm up, nice. It was a little tough but not terrible. Then we ran. Dave. About. Killed. Me. My heart was about to explode. I hid from Dave. Now understand Dave and I were running together. Dave was faster. My heart was going to explode, inside me. I ran, and then ran into an alleyway, you know to hide from Dave. "Where'd you go man? I was looking for you?" He asked when I got back to the apartment. Through my winded breath I wheezed out, "Oh, I...I thought...I thought you went down that alley so I went that way."

"No, man, I went straight. Didn't you see me?" (Not through the sweat in my eyes, Dave.) Getting to know Dave more in that conversation and why his chest wasn't going to cave in, I found out that he was a Drill sergeant for the army. Something Dave failed to mention, and I failed to ask. I declined to work out with him again. Wish I would have tried a little more, course I might be dead now, or as healthy as a horse. 50/50.

Another incident up in Boston helped with my smoking. I was going swimming with some other people at a damn or something. We swam to a rock about 20 yards out. Then they swam back. I thought we were going to rest and smoke a cigarette, course I left them on dry land. Nope these were young folk. Energy and all that. When I gathered the strength to swim back, I explained to my buddy that I was going to drowned, right there in front of him. I said that. I guess I'm funny sometimes, ha, Ha! So, my buddy, he didn't understand I was not being sarcastic. He didn't get it. He would get it when I died. Thankfully realizing my friend was a tool (nice guy really. Like him a lot. Not his fault.) I mustered up the energy I probably received from Dave my drill sergeant roommate and got to the side. Clinging to it for life.

That's when I decided to give up smoking. Then and There. About a year later I quit. Things you're addicted to, are not cool. They will only wear you down, and try to drown you. Don't let them.

April 1

Surround yourself with people who tell you what you want to hear.
—

SMART, if you don't want to grow as a person I highly recommend following this little tidbit. People don't want to be challenged (but people like challenging). Homeostasis is what we work toward control over our environment. Okay, so there is that person out there that wants others to think about things and they do want to be challenged, but you can only take so much challenging, right? Sometimes its nice to just talk about superficial things, or people that agree with you.

If you only surround yourself with people who agree with you though, I'm going to go out on a limb and say that's not good. Granted you should be able to tell if you're living in a bubble. So, if everyone just agrees with you, how do you know you're right? How can you flex your skills or be sure you could convince someone who doesn't agree? Do you avoid these people? Perhaps it's too challenging to argue certain points when faced with certain questions? Maybe that's because you're on the wrong side of the issue, or maybe it's because you have never had to look because people simply take you at your word, or perhaps you've never done any research and don't want to be challenged?

What do they say about comfort? It breeds complacency, which breeds failure. I don't believe only the paranoid survive. But I do believe you should be on guard against comfort though. It's good to acknowledge your accomplishments. To nod your head and smile. But then you need to look forward to the next hurdle.

Same with friends. (I'm not saying get rid of your friends if they don't challenge you. Find true friends though.) Friends should care enough about you to challenge you on things. Not everything. Sometimes they should stand by your side, unless you're wrong. Then they should care enough. If they don't, how can you say they're your friend? Friends want you to succeed. To thrive. If you have created a space where your friends don't feel, or care to challenge things in your life, because of your backlash. Maybe you're not a true friend, maybe they aren't. Something to think about.

April 2

Gifts show love.

MY opinion on this is complex. I know about the 5 languages of love. One of them says that receiving gifts is how a person feels love. Okay, so there is that. What's that mean? To me it means that if someone takes time to pick out a gift for me, and in that time think of me, I know they love me. I can see how this can work and how it's meant. But bad people give gifts to, and those gifts don't come with love, they come with chains. I don't think that gifts come with nothing though. There is a reason for gifts. Even those gifts from your grandmother that your parents tell you to thank her for, regardless of the fact that you don't need an extra pair of socks or 5 dollars. It's the thought that counts.

That's what I want to talk about. The thought. Maybe you don't have enough money to buy someone a gift. Maybe you can make a gift, did you know that your time could be a gift? If you deliver it with a smile that is. The thought behind the gift shows love, not the gift. The gift doesn't talk. Even if your love language is giving gifts. The gift doesn't talk. You might assume the gift means something, but unless you speak with the gift giver, it's only your assumption. I'm not trying to break hearts here. (After all, this book, this crazy, maybe wrongful opinionated, awkwardly written, no good to critic's book, is a gift. It's a labor of love, that I hope shows through its words. But I can only assume that it is. I might never speak to a child who this book's funding might support.)

The assumption we make in our head about the gift is what we see love as. If I were married to a millionaire and they bought me a boat. I'm not sure I would equate that purchase with love. Maybe I would, but maybe I would equate it with owing something in return. So sure, gifts can show love, but even bad people can give good gifts. (Not to say millionaires are bad people out right. Just thought I should clear that up. Especially if one wants to buy me a boat out of the kindness of their heart.) It doesn't make them good people and if you find yourself in that type of relationship because you think items show love, then this is for you. How do you tell a gift comes with love or chains?

You take time to connect with that person. You talk with them. Share your day with them if you see them. Spend time... That's a true gift. Material things pass away with age, but hopefully if they don't have a medical memory issue, they can remember the time you hung out with them. If they do have Alzheimer's, the item might not mean that much either.

April 3

Don't step on toes. Don't rock the boat, baby

Fear

CAREFUL. You don't want to get on someone's bad side. This advice might be good. Sometimes things work themselves out. Some are not big enough issues to bother with, or mention.

In certain situations, this might be okay, let things slide. Let them work themselves out. But I'm personally a boat rocker. I don't make it a point to be. I'm normally quiet. Sometimes however, I am not. I don't mind rocking the boat pretty hard, and depending on what the captain's doing I might not care if I capsize the sucker.

I'm not saying this is the thing to do in all situations. I think subtlety can be a very effective tool, but knocking everybody in the water gets everyone on the same page. I'm joking. That's hardly ever the answer...

This piece of advice streams into our friendships though. Remember I was talking about true friends and how they should have a safe space to challenge us. This terrible concept takes that option from people. People don't feel they have a right to challenge someone anymore. If they do, what happens is others rock their boat harder. Maybe they might even get kicked out of the boat and are forced to swim. I'd say if that's the case, you don't want to be in that boat anyway. Find a better boat. They're out there.

This concept of not stepping on toes reminds me of fear tactics that have been used the world over. Germany, Italy, Argentina, here. Except it's not against people but ideas. Before you speak, your idea should not be offensive. To anyone. If it is. Prepare to be kicked out of the boat. Hard. That's a fear tactic, right? Perhaps not everyone feels this way on all levels of society, but some might.

The issue, be it real or perceived, is true in people's minds. Think before you speak. That's good advice. Not speaking because you could offend someone, that's good advice, although a little gray. Who's this someone? Anyone? What list are they on. Where's that list again, and who wrote it? That's an issue.

So, when you're thinking about not rocking the boat, not stepping on toes. That's considerate. You should think before you speak. Take people's feeling into account, but also what the truth is. (Careful here, you might not know it. You could be on the wrong list, just saying.) People should be slower to speak sometimes. Sometimes the boat does need rocked though. Sometimes it needs capsized, or a mutiny should take place. Sometimes you need to look at the destination. I'm now completely satisfied that this writing will be of no actual benefit to anyone, as everyone will use it against each other in defense of their point. Way to keep the status Quo with vague non-direct speech! Good job Alexander!

April 4

You can live off Ramen.

—

YOU truly can! I did. I don't think I ever gained my freshman 15. I was pretty active back then with school and parties and smoking cigarettes and Captain Kangaroo. It wasn't till I went to my graduate studies in Boston that I learned the awesomeness of Ramen. Personally, I think it's a superfood. It should be on that superfood list that Entrepreneur.com has. That's where I gained my graduate 20 or 25.

Good times, 'meh' food. It's true, you can live off Ramen (and fast food). I don't recommend it. It's a slippery slope. It's a tasty slope. Interestingly I recently tried some ramen again and I couldn't taste anything, even with the chicken packet I used. I'm not sure what that means. Did it ever have a taste? Are my taste buds on the fritz? What's the deal? I'm guessing back in the day I just didn't care about eating. I would just scarf it down to move on to the next task.

So, in college Ramen is your friend, but when you get out of college it doesn't seem like it.

I was watching a documentary on ramen, or food, or maybe it was Asia. I forget. The thing was though I never gave any thought to how noodles were made. Wheat. That's all I knew. I think I saw my grandmother make some once in the kitchen from scratch. Those were good, I'm guessing not good for me though.

Turns out noodles can be made with beans, or rice or oats or wheat, or vegetables. Now I know, you might know this, but I didn't. Nobody told me. So, I'm mentioning for that reason alone.

Maybe some college student will read this and be like. "Huh, I can start using rice noodles because they don't have gluten." (It's my assumption they have celiac disease.) "Or kelp noodles!" Although I would recommend a side of vitamins if you're going to have kelp noodles. I don't think there is anything much in those, and I hear they taste like seaweed. I'm not sure what that tastes like, but I'm guessing it's not the awesome Ramen chicken flavor packet taste I'm used to.

April 5

Idolize those you see on tv.

—

FROM time to time, who doesn't find a character or actor that is just so cool or interesting we don't simply admire or love then greatly, but excessively. Think that goes too far. It's never good to idolize someone or something. The definition 'love greatly' makes it sound okay. If that was what the word 'idolize' meant then that would be different. It's hardly in the definition when someone uses it in the advice above. People never say, "You should idolize this person or that thing." They might say it of someone else, "Oh, he idolizes his father." It's hard to come by a positive spin on the word otherwise.

We do this though. It's not a thought we openly tell ourselves. It's a silent advice we give, that media gives us. "Man, they are great. Look at them. I know their life has got to be awesome. They're so lucky." Nice, so you just put someone on a pedestal that you don't even know. And now that they are on a pedestal you can go two ways. Compare yourself to them. That's what we tend to do as people, find an outside source to compare ourselves to. So, we can measure up to them, or the second, obsess about them. Read about their lives in magazines, buy all their products.

The latter reminds me of that DeNiro film, 'The Fan'. Very tragic. That's a negative. When we build someone up in our minds and find out that they can't live up to it. We're crushed. They let us down.

Truth. They didn't let us down. We put our happiness on them. If they are on television or the movies then we don't know them. We give away possible joy. No one else is responsible for your joy. This is true in relationships, especially ones you actually have with people.

When we have an external locus of control, which can be a positive thing, there can be a tendency to rely on others. An internal locus of control puts your focus on your performance. Both have good aspects, but in this case Star Wars's 'balance' idea might be correct. One side or the other alone can lead to disastrous understandings in our lives.

So, the jist. Don't look to others for your happiness. They are human, as you are, and holding them up to that standard will break your heart more times than not.

April 6

You can only depend on yourself in this world.

Max "The one man show"

STUPIDITY. Sure, life is hard. In fact, everyone around you might not care at all. If you're in a war-torn country or even here, you might not have anyone you can trust or rely on. Depending on yourself is safe. You can see what can be done from that stand point. You don't have to worry about someone falling through on support. Its true, people do tend to drop the ball sometimes. Some don't give a shit, they wouldn't help you if they could. They won't care if you share pearls of wisdom. They just don't care. Frankly, there might even be a lot of them out there. I bet there are, but I also know that there are people out there that you can depend on. People who do care, and don't have motivation outside of helping you.

Maybe you don't believe that, you've seen it all right? There just isn't anyone. I'm here to let you know that it doesn't matter if you believe it to be true. It is true. I've seen it. Now maybe you're a person that doesn't care. To you I say, thanks for buying the book. Maybe you can't find anyone to help you. That's sometimes a truth. Maybe no one listens. Keep looking, find someone who does. Ask people you don't know on the street. Ask more than one. Everyday.

If you're a kid or know of a child who is being neglected or abused. Try this number **1-800-422-4453**. That's the National Child Abuse hotline from the Child-Help's website. If you're outside the US, I'll see about updating the appendix on this date with other sources you can reach out to.

It's good to be able to depend on yourself, and in much of the world you might need to. Even here. Tragic and terrible things happen all the time, even here. You need to watch out for yourself. More than that though, people, other people and yourself, need to come together. Imagine if all the people could come together and lend help and support out, just like they used to do with the flash mob dancing fad of 2010's. Working together, albeit, only minutes of entertainment, but together.

I get the appeal to be dependent on no one but yourself. I do. But you should be able to find people who can, will and do support you. That's my hope for you, but it will take effort. I'm sure you're up for it though, they're out there.

April 7

Children should be seen and not heard.

Old "Front Porch" Tillerson

CHILDREN are loud, and energetic. Warning! Context incoming. At a social event such as a party for your work friends and/or family, children should be seen, and heard but heard only if you're trying to hear them. Shouldn't be interruptive. That's rude. That's why I'm not allowed to go out with my friends to work parties. Joking, I'm allowed again. At home, well they should be seen, that's a given, not sure why that's even part of the stupid saying, and if at home they should be heard, unless you have like acres of land to your home then it might not be possible due to the size of your mansion, then they would need to be yelling loudly and you should investigate. I'm betting they set something on fire. That always made me yell loudly as a child. (For my writer friends, that's yelling, plus louder. Hence the unneeded adverb.)

Your kids, they should behave. That's not on them though. I think it's on you, it's a reflection on you and at least teaching them how to behave is an action that demonstrates that you love them enough to care how they behave.

That being said. I hate the saying. It's stupid, archaic, and lacks context. That's true of many of the little sayings in this book of wisdom. It fails to explain anything, except a vague idea of truth. Children should be taught how to operate efficiently in society. I say operate, it sounds cold to me, but function is the only other word I can think of and it sounds equal to or less adequate. That's not advice for the children. That's advice for parents, but it's still vague. It doesn't explain how to show the children you care enough to teach, it doesn't even express that you need to care, but just that they should be taught.

It's a terrible saying. But its short. Not to the point at all, in the least. It actually hides true value. This might be the worst advice in the book, but the truth that it obscures isn't.

Care for your kids enough to show them that they can be seen and heard, and how they can go about it to gain more out of this life.

April 8

You don't know the power of the dark side.

Darth Vader

MAYBE Luke didn't know the power of the dark side, but he could see its influence on the empire just fine. He wasn't blind as Visas Marr after all! (That's a geek reference.) I think it's becoming all too common that just because we haven't done or experienced something, we don't know about it. So, it's true for some things, spot welding for example. I probably shouldn't run out and do that without some proper training. A tragedy of violation perhaps. Someone being sold into slavery or forced into a sex trade and pumped full of drugs. Might not know what that's like. I feel things though, I can connect to people. Touch their pain, if that makes sense.

I can relate. Now if someone shuts me down and explains that I have no clue. What that means is they don't want to share with me their pain. I get that, but it doesn't change the fact that I can feel their pain.

It's absurd for us as a society to think that if we don't experience something, we don't get it, or can't connect to it. Throughout history that's proven ... not... to... be... true. I don't have to be eaten by a dinosaur to know I don't want to be eaten by a dinosaur. Or to put it more plainly, saying I can't understand is like saying I can't possibly extrapolate some experience in my life to meet someone else. It also doesn't mean that in order to overcome something I have to give into it. Or to conquer my enemy I have to become my enemy. Strange, non-logical thought.

We do know the power of the dark side. We've all seen it, experienced it, read about it. And that's just in the Star Wars universe. In our world we've all gotten tastes of that darkness. We see others fall to tragic paths every day. Either in person or on the news. Some are at ground zero, others further away, but we all know the power of chaos in our lives. On the other side of the coin, we also grow numb to it.

When Darth Vader says these words, when any Sith Lord says this, they want you to believe it. Either to fill you with fear of the unknown, and make you back away, or fill you with curiosity. The fact is, we do know the power of the dark side. We see it every day. The destruction it brings. The pain, and suffering. It's not mysterious though, don't lie to yourself. It tries to be alluring by challenging you to believe there is something more to it, something you might wield or discover. If only we could see that's not truth. Chaos is terrible, there is nothing more to know. It's not deep, and mysterious, it's just wide and shallow, all encompassing.

April 9

Move out of your parents' house as soon as you can.

The Media

YOU want to be on your own. I get it. Free as a bird. Your own apartment, your own rules. Your own time. Pizza at midnight! (Or something you want to do.) So, your parents are a drag and they have all these rules. You can't do this or that. They're stifling your mojo. You need your space.

Here's the deal. You're about to start your life. I assume your 18 or 19. Gonna get out there and change the world. Or maybe you were going to travel on your parents dime first. I say do that if you're able. See the world, it will broaden your horizons as they say, and it's fun. So, let's say the average person lives to 75. That means you have 55 years of 'grown up' time. So far that's over twice the amount of time you spent at home.

Chances are, you either have or are going to get a job. That's going to take about 10 whole years of your life. That's to say continuous hours totaling about 10 years. Sleeping, that's about 17 years… so that gives about 28 years minus driving (4) and surfing the net (3), and tv (6) for you to actually do stuff with. That's just a little less than you've lived so far. About 15 years of fun left, spaced out into little blocks.

When you walk out that door, you might get pretty busy fast. Bills and work, ain't it fun. The band Paramore has a cool song about it. I'm just saying you might not be spending a whole lot more time with your parents after this. Maybe that's a good thing. (I don't know your parents.)

This is simply a rough calculation. I got the numbers from Tempo.io if you want to recalculate. I'm sure my math isn't awesome. I just put this together to make you think… Just like all the other pages in this book. Just to make you spend some time thinking and not just consuming information.

Maybe there's some things you wanted to try first that your parents might be able to help with. Maybe those will make the last 15 years of fun in your life more fun.

One thing that I've found to be true, and I have awesome parents mind you. Is that I could always spend more time with them. I know that's something I won't regret though. But that's just me.

April 10

Stay at home as long as you can.

—

Me

GOOD advice here. If your parents are willing to keep you around, you might as well take advantage of it. Free room and board, or maybe it's not free, but it's cheaper than your other options. It's great you get to save money and you have time to plan out what you're going to do and how you're going to do it. Where you're going to go. I believe I mentioned that in some cultures its more excepted for children to stay at home. As in India this seems to be generally accepted.

It's true, that staying home can help you have a better grasp for future plans, and if you're in a different culture it might even be the norm.

In the US though it's not really viewed that way. Whether it's the media's influence or produced by the industrial revolution and WWI (Read history to understand more!) as how we see family, it's a reality. When your kids grow up, they move out. The quicker the better. I know this is supposed to be against staying at home, but I find it interesting that we move out when we're 18, but can't legally drink until 21. I think having parental guidance in that would help. I'm also of the understanding that if you can fight a war, you can drink. But that's just my opinion. Although I don't recommend either, especially hand in hand.

Sometimes staying at home, in a 'protective' environment isn't helpful. If you always have help doing things, how can you tell if you can actually do them? I think that's some of the mentality behind our thought process, although its shrouded behind terrible advice like, "You gotta be a man." Which is vague and unhelpful, or "Learn to live on your own.". I think, I feel that you should have been taught how to live on your own, before living on your own. I feel that jumping out there with no idea isn't helpful, and believe it shows in our society. We aren't really teaching our next generations, we're just handing them over to the world and the world doesn't care if they're ready or not. We should though.

With that said, once again, against the advice of staying home. If you don't move out, there is a chance for you to create a sort of distance between you and your peers. Perhaps an unspoken awkwardness. I'll leave it up to you to decide if that awkwardness is a good or bad thing. I think it depends on who you see as your peers.

April 11

If you're on tv, you're someone special.

Popular crowd

SIMILAR to the 5th of this month. But it's a different aspect. Television doesn't make you special. People knowing your story doesn't make you special. It's been with us through the ages. (Ah, I'm now waxing poetic. Maybe I've been writing enough for the day.) The mythical cursed quest of popularity. That's a mouth full.

Starts out in school with cliques or groups of kids that exclude other kids. It's a real thing. Aren't you glad it doesn't spread to the adult world so we can show our children through our actions this isn't the true way of life...me too!

Right, now I'll step out of my sarcasm-mobile, we all have groups that exclude other groups. Or maybe you have one of those special groups that doesn't exclude anyone! Not sure what you talk about at your meetings, but there might not be that many of you there actually saying anything. People enjoy being part of a special group. I wanted to go to Harvard, or Yale and be in the Skull and Bones. That's an exclusive group. Didn't happen. But I don't think I'm less special because of it.

Being on television is in the same realm. Except everyone thinks they know people on tv, or connects with them somehow. They're popular. Or in the case of Ellen DeGeneres popular and kind. But being on tv doesn't mean or make you special. Being popular, most likely means everyone's watching you, and they'll continue watching you until you're boring. Then they won't. Sounds like a lot of 'meat sweats' to me.

If you're on tv, if you're a professional sports player. If you're an astronaut. If you work for a good cause. These things don't make you special. You are special already. Maybe you don't see that yet, but it's in there, somewhere. There is something that makes you special. This is truth people. Hear me now. You are special. Maybe you have to search yourself for why, but there is a reason for you here. Perhaps it's not television, god forbid! But search for it. It's in there. You are special regardless of what you do. What you do does, not make you special. You simply are special. Now you know. So, live accordingly.

April 12

Sleep in, you deserve it.

—

Sloths and Koalas everywhere

LET'S talk about sleep, and then sloths and koala's! Sleep is good. Did you know that sleep takes about 26 of our years away? * I think that's too much time. If I slept only 8 hours a day that would be 26 years. Sometimes I sleep 10! Wasting my life. That's what my father meant when I would sleep till noon! Maybe he was right. Who knew?

Sometimes rest is helpful though, but we shouldn't sleep too much. If you find yourself sleeping a lot and having low energy. I know that it can be a cycle. Perhaps you have low energy because you are sleeping a lot. I also know that low energy could mean you have to think about changing your diet. Eating healthy can actually increase your energy! Who knew 'Ramen for life!' wasn't a slogan? I started talking vitamins every day and changed my diet. There are some other causes of constant tiredness as well. These should be looked into, perhaps with your doctor. (I put a link to an article in the Appendix to Readers Digest if you're interested in a few others.)

Sloths sleep for a total of about 18 years, they live about 30. Talk about lazy. They sleep about 15 hours a day, and that's an active sloth!

Koalas, you know the cute bear things in the trees, (Here's a fun side fact. They aren't bears, and they don't like to be called that.) they sleep about 18 hours a day. That means they sleep about 7.5 years. Uh, they have a life span of around 10 years I hear. Also, they smell like cough drops.

I tell ya, I wish the penguins would take some pointers from these guys.

*Didn't I say that sleeping takes 17 years away on April 9th? Now it's 26. Why are they different? Who cares right? I shouldn't have to concern myself with finding the facts before typing them into the annuals of time eternal, that takes too much time... right? Just food for thought.

April 13

Trust the critics.

AS a culture we tend to follow the path of least resistance. If someone says something, we gravitate to accepting it. Is this true of everyone? Nah, but it's easier to take peoples word for something than look into it ourselves. Sometimes we even expect some people to give us advice on various things from time to time. In our society we've come to check reviews before buying things. It's not a bad way to go about it. It's not a bad gig either. Writing reviews, or going through the content of products. We have box opening YouTube videos. That's were someone will unbox a product. Not review it, just open it. And people watch that. Someone opening a box. I don't get it. I think its perhaps a slow slope, down that drain.

Critics are good, they help keep Hollywood, Bollywood, Tollywood and the others in some sort of check. But if you're bored go over to RottenTomatos.com there are tons of movies where critic reviews and audience scores disagree. I didn't know that until I looked myself. Many of the movies I like got bad reviews from critics. Maybe I just like bad movies. Don't take my word for it. Take a look.

I stopped trusting critics in general about things. I watch countless youtubers talk about the pros and cons of different items. Everything is reviewed now, you don't have to try anything yourself. If I keep listening to all of them, I might discover I don't know how to make an 'informed' decision unless I listen to a reviewer. That's a scary notion.

Sometimes though I want to take life into my own hands. Buy something without a review on it. Go to a movie without knowing someone else's thoughts on it. If I know their thoughts on the movie, how do I know if I have an original thought of my own?

I'm sure it won't be a big deal until they start telling us directly how to think, but come to saying it, isn't that what they're doing now?

Jokes, just jokes people don't send thought police, calm down. It's not a brave new world...not yet.

April 14

No one should tell you what to do.
—
Id

REALLY? Why do we insist on feeling like this is a terrible thing? Yep, let's go dark for this. If someone is telling you to do something that is harmful to you or someone else. Get away from them. Don't listen to them. Clearly, they're terrible. But then there are bad apples that push this mentality that this isn't a bad thing. Also, children don't understand this all the time and context is lacking for this, big time. Kids don't want to put the fire stick down after all, (Not an Amazon Firestick. I mean an actual stick, with fire on it. Sticks are found in the woods. Woods are normally outside. That's away from the video games and phone. I know I'm part of a dying breed.) I don't think liking or disliking my parents ever came into it very much for me, but I know that I just wanted to do what I wanted to do. If I hadn't put the stick with fire down, my other brothers and sister might have wanted their own. The parents told me this, not because they didn't want me to have fun, that's a common misconception I think, even if unspoken, but because they wanted my brothers and sister to continue to have their eyes and limbs unburnt. You know, for use later in life.

The idea of independence is important, self-reliance, that's a good thing to possess. However sometimes people need help, they don't understand certain actions. Sometimes we aren't that bright, take me with the stick. As teenagers I know I would throw around this advice like it was the best thing in the world. "No one should tell you what to do." It was then followed by the fact that the other person should feel free to do whatever they thought right. It's bad. It's just bad advice. Don't give this. Unless you actually know the person, the circumstances and can walk in their shoes. Don't tell them this. It's destructive and wrong.

The fact is, this is how the world runs. People tell other people what to do. It's how we have jobs, even ones where we work for ourselves, because we don't want a boss. Sorry, we have boss. It's the market, it's the trends. If we don't follow its advice we will probably lose out.

Point is, many times in our lives. We are told what do to. It can be a good thing. If no one bothered to teach us, to show us errors in our thinking, how do we know if they truly loved us at all? I could keep rambling about this. Maybe you get it, maybe you don't. After all, I'm not telling you what to do.

April 15

Listen to your elders.

LISTEN up already. I already told you to read history. I already mentioned playing old video games. Heck I just told you how allowing yourself to listen to others is a good thing. Once again, I'm listing bad advice at the top of a page, just to be clear. Which on this page seems to be the opposite of what I just told you, right? It is. I grant that. Context is key. If you don't have context, what's the point?

Listening to your parents can be good, or older people. It's useful to understand. How things are, or how to tackle something. How something might go. You ever get advice you didn't listen to and then found out later that person was right? Yea, we all have.

Following guidance is good. Helps you in life. We need to do this, it's inevitable we will follow advice at some point. It might even direct our paths in life. Sometimes to good ends, sometimes too bad.

So, how do you know what to listen to? Well, that's complicated to say the least. It's kind of requires a type of standard. With the reemergence of relativism as a universal concept can muck up what this means. What's good for one person might not be good for another. right? I'm not sure I'm totally on board with that ideology, but people bring it up from time to time like it's not simply referring to our medical well-being. So, I'm going to make a standard for this example. If the choice you make or someone would make for you, would harm you or someone else, its bad. Harm means any physical, or emotional damage. I believe this definition takes things like smoking or drinking excessively and puts them squarely within the definition of bad. Some people don't like to include themselves in this definition so they can 'do what they want' in terms of harm. I'm not enforcing this on you, so if anyone isn't calm, please calm yourself. (You know who you are.)

Sometimes we can't see if something is bad right away. Sometimes we can't tell what people's intentions really are. So, am I saying keep your distance until you can tell? What if someone needs my help? Help them by all means, unless you're in a hole with them, or might jump in it yourself. Then find someone else to help.

There is no easy answer here. No perfect solution. You just need to be aware of the fact that not everything you hear (perhaps like this…) is viable or good. Sometimes you're elders or friends or co-workers or cult leaders or politicians don't have the answers to a problem. Maybe that author you really like doesn't have all the facts, or context of a situation. Listening is good, but you have to differentiate what is helpful and good, versus what is bad and harmful. It's not always clear. Some people's advice or arguments sound valid, and they may very well believe them, but you are responsible for researching, or coming to your own conclusions based on fact, and not feeling. Be vigilant, ask questions. Even ones they don't want you to. In the end though, it's up to you to decide. If you can't decide and come to bad reasoning on your own, that's going to be a huge, HUGE, problem for you and possibly the world around you.

April 16

Jumping up and down in the elevator is fun!

—

No, it's not.

Don't do it.

That is all.

April 17

Star Trek is only for Geeks.

—

JULES VERNE wrote about electricity in a submarine in 1870. In 1954 the first electric submarine was built. Mr. Verne envisioned something like television in 1889. 30 years later we had the first newscast. Solar Sails, and tasers. Those are just things he wrote down in stories. That's one guy. Fiction and fantasy have a bigger grasp on this world and what we can do in it, than we give them credit for.

Geek stories, the things nerds talk about with snorts and laughs in the hallways of school. The crazy stupid things that some of us don't quite understand. They build our future. Granted, for space travel to work were going to need an economical reason and financial return. History shows us that while we might have some explorers out there for the sake of it, many of the big discoveries, perhaps all of them had an economic return, small or large.

Or we might be able to manage space travel if we figure out world peace and man working with each other hand in hand for the greater good. I'd love the latter, but my bets are still on the former at this point. Maybe we can change that.

April 18

"Don't be a nerd."
—
that Jock whose name you can't recall, guy works at that burger joint now. You know, that guy.

CRAZY how backwards high school can be from the real world, huh? Sure, the world has its groups just like high school. College can be a hazy image of that structure. For the most part I've found it to be so different. Sometimes people can still make fun of you or try to fight you, but I don't frequent bars or clubs much and only my circle of friends give me some grief from time to time. It might be different for you.

Sports are awesome. Baseball, football, soccer, Rugby, Racing. Television is awesome too. The reason I mention sports and tv in the same breath is they're also very hard to break into, and the career path can be short. You have to make a lot of money in a few brief years in order to actually 'make it'. It's nice to have dreams. You know like the ones those nerds were talking about in the hall about the idea they thought up.

Functionally in this world, it seems better to be a nerd. Over the long haul anyway. So, we don't get to go to the cool parties and meet that dreamy girl or guy. We don't get STD's either. (I'm not saying popular people have more STD's, statistically, I'm saying it's more probable.)

It seems that some of our society has embraced the geek culture over the years. Disney brought Marvel to the main stream. DC lags behind, but they have some good tv shows. It seems it's becoming more wide spread and being a nerd is okay. I tell you, it is okay, in fact it was even before nerds became 'popular'. People just didn't see it. To get into a sports field even you need to let your nerd shine a little.

As a nerd, I think it's our duty to be kinder to others, especially in this spot light of odd acceptance. I know technical people, so called 'outcasts' can be rude, or talk down to others. It's a way to vent perhaps. Maybe you've forgotten that we were once talked down to, and belittled in the halls, neglected.

When I was bullied in school I had to worry about a bloody nose or being laughed at every once in a while. Kids today, they deal with death threats and shaming that leads them to want to take their lives. There is a lot wrong with that. As someone who considers himself a nerd before it was hip, or even after. We need to care more. We have the power. And I hope by the power of GraySkull we use it wisely.

April 19

Push through the pain, you'll be better for it.

—

the football coach

ONE of the staples of being a 'man'. Pain is good. No, it's not, that's stupid. Let me say it again. That's stupid. Men should be smart, not like that guy you see on the commercials that doesn't know how to do something. Pain lets you know something is wrong. I'm not saying go ahead and cry when you stub your toes, or that you should never grit your teeth and bear it. What I'm saying, I think (everyone interprets things in different ways.) is, ya gotta know when to hold 'em and know when to fold 'em. If the only reason you're pushing through pain is to show off how much you can take, it's time to re-prioritize your goals. Now if you have to save someone's life, the advice holds more weight. What wouldn't someone do to save a friend's life? Sacrifice their own? I would hope I would be big enough for that day.

There are trials that we go through. Hardships and in those times, we have to bear it. Maybe we bear it poorly, as children might. We whine and cry and complain. Or maybe we bear it well. This doesn't mean we should be strong through everything. The advice shouldn't be a stoic robotic creed that we pass off as a dime store saying, but it is. Pushing through pain doesn't make you a man. Bearing pain doesn't make you a man. Understanding how to deal with that pain in a healthy manner might. It might mean reaching out for help and support.

Men, don't stand alone in suffering, not always. They look for support. They understand the need for it. Being a loner just makes you that, alone. It doesn't mean you're tougher.

Pushing through pain might require more than your shear will. Maybe not, maybe you're strong enough. But it is also manly to accept the things you aren't strong enough for. If you can admit to those pains or problems it might lead to healing in those areas. Men who fear what others will say, are worse off than they think.

If you need help, ask for it. Yell for it. You don't have to bury it.

April 20

Keep everything, you never know when you'll need it.

AGAIN, why not? We try, in video games and board games there are things called 'bags of holding'. (what I would do for one of those!) They provide an almost infinite space to place things in, while using such a little pouch. An example for non-geek readers, a magic user could pull a chair and a kettle from a bag of holding that fit on their belt loop, and it would be the size of a coin purse. Not the chair and kettle, they'd be full size. Sadly, we don't live in Middle Earth, or the awesome world of Krynn.

Hoarders is a television show. Maybe you've seen it. There's a link to their website treatment options in the appendix. If you find yourself to be a hoarder make use of it, either way checkout the show.

I find I collect things from all over. I think I have one of my baby teeth in a memory album somewhere. (I didn't do it. It's in a sealed bag. Calm down, I'm not going to make a lamp out of it.)

I used to collect all the brochures from stops when my family traveled. Not just the places we traveled, but all the brochures that a place we traveled to, had. All of them. I put them in a bag in my room. One day my mom cleaned my room and I couldn't find the bag. I was noticeably upset. All that work for nothing. I'm not saying that I was going to be a hoarder, but I lost interest in picking up all the brochures after that. I collected comics when I was younger. Still collect old ones. Not as many though.

We have a small voice that says 'we should keep that' from time to time. I stopped listening to mine for the most part. I still have all my old toys in a storage facility from when I was young. I may see about going through them one day and give them to my kids if I'm not 80 when I find someone on the internet to marry. Who knows? Stranger things have happened. Or perhaps the toys will simply sink into oblivion after I go. But I've come to realize, some things are more important to keep, like memories of loved ones, the time I spent with them, and your baby teeth. (Joking, about the baby teeth. Not sure how I feel about that.)

Here is a link for treatments and the shows if you're interested. A&E Hoarders

April 21

Don't do your chores.

TERRIBLE advice for the day. Don't do your chores. Unless you never do your chores than Don't not do your chores. It's all relative...

Sometimes relaxing from a project or work is the right thing to do. Sometimes we relax so much that, that's all we do. Are you relaxing too much? Is it affecting your relationships, or hygiene? (Which could affect your relationships, if you think about it.)

Maybe pick a project today. Just one. Take a small bite out of that elephant. (Not literally, don't eat elephants. That would fall under terrible advice as well, just to be clear.)

April 22

Shower every day.

—

The ice caps

FIRST off, I have to say I'm spoiled. I can take a shower every day. So, this would seem like good advice. You should bath, it keeps the 'smellys' away. But there are those, in this country that have to follow the opposite of this advice, and it's not terrible because they truly have to conserve water.

That's an interesting concept that there are people out there less fortunate than yourself. I know that I forget about it sometimes. I bet there are support sites out there that help so that the less fortunate could shower every day.

That's not really the issue. First Showering every day, while it's okay and if you're working in a refinery or factory or working out every day it might be needed. We use a lot of water. I know I see it in my water bill.

Apparently even though the world is covered in water, around 70 percent. Only 3 percent is drinkable. I did not know that. Wild stuff.

So, with 7.5* billion people on earth perhaps we should be a little more concerned. At some point down the line people won't have water to drink. Come to think about it, I bet some people don't have water to drink today.

That's all I got. Have a good day, be thankful for what you have. Maybe consider doing something for someone at your place of work today. Just because.

*Didn't I say 7.6 billion somewhere else. Who cares it is just numbers, nobody really pays attention anyway, right? What's 100,000,000 here or there?

April 23

Focus on finding Bigfoot today. He's still out there.

—

TAKE up a hobby. I'm for it. People collect comics, or coins, they go on day trips or what not. Some follow the Loch Ness Monster. Some big foot. I'm not sure if this is so much about the hobby being a functional thing. I'm a skeptic. I don't see how there could be something that hard to find and discover. Especially when they do things like this. (Jack Link's YouTube Channel) I can't just believe the videos, although I think it would be an interesting find. There is a guy in Canada that seems to have found something though. I'd go take a look, but I don't have that kind of cash lying around. I'd say if it's true, this guy would be able to tell. You might even see one of these big foot creatures. I linked to his website if you're interested. At least you'd get to go to Canada.

https://www.sylvanic.com/expeditions

He doesn't take too many people up. I'm sure it's because he doesn't want to disturb their territory, and not for any setup of his employee's dressing up in suits. I think we should get some media coverage. Let's blow this thing open, wide open. Does big foot exist?

April 24

If everyone jumped off a bridge would you do it too?

THIS isn't advice really, this is peer pressure in the opposite direction, but it changes our thinking. First, our 'friends' say this little phrase to us, "Come on, everybody's doing it". Then our parent finds out after we did something dumb and they ask us if we would jump off a bridge if everyone else was doing it. The answer by the way is yes. It's always yes. Which by the way is not advice, it's a question, and not a very well worded one. Simply asking a question doesn't inform a teenager, the bridge is more like a slope anyway, and it gently down to the white water. There's meth, heroine, needles and bath salts in that water, also STIs and other darknesses, so maybe if you have a chance, just a little time. Perhaps explain the bridge thing, but in a real way. Otherwise some people might not take it for all its worth, I mean, their thought process might go like this, 'if it's a literal bridge and the water is high enough and everyone's swimming around and laughing, yea I'd jump in. If it's a dude offering me heroine, well it's not jumping off a literal bridge, so I guess I'm okay. I just got to watch for that dangerous bridge. I know not to jump off an actual bridge with this guy, my parents let me know that would be stupid of me.'

If our brains are still developing up until 26 or 27, if you just talk to your teenager about bridges, they might not jump off a bridge. They might be convinced under certain pressures to do some drugs that make them 'feel good' though. It's time to step up your parenting game if that's what you did. Also, drugs make you feel good, but they can really screw up your life. It's probably not worth that night of fun.

Not saying anyone should jump off a bridge either, many people have had life threatening injuries doing that. Calculated risks. Jumping off a literal bridge still does not qualify. Even if your friends are doing it.

April 25

To each his own.

—

Spirit of Indifference

IT'S strange that so much can come from such a little phrase. Strong words. I don't understand them. To each his own what? Desire, rights, path, truth. What's it mean? When someone says it, I mostly see it in reference to something someone doesn't agree with, but never the less accepts. Even if the something is harmful, or is at least a point of contention.

It can be expressed differently to, everyone should be able to do what they want. Anarchist almost in a way. Just my thoughts. I'm sure I'm taking it too far, that's not what it means, right? That's the far left or right side the phrase, I can't tell the difference. The outcome of either extreme looks the same to me. My concern is, if I think that it's an anarchist thought when hearing this advice. How can you be sure it doesn't sound like that to someone else? And how can we be accepting of this statement?

We see people on the news doing what they want all the time. I think there was that guy who recorded himself killing another guy on Facebook a while back. He was doing what he wanted. I'm sure no one else wanted him to though. I'm sure he had some problems that were not addressed.

Sometimes it's not as black and white as that though. I think most of us can see that's not acceptable. Sometimes someone does their own thing, and it's just a small thing. But over time it gets bigger. Festers into a habit from a mere fancy, then an addiction. It's the little thing.

To me this says, 'I don't care what they do. I don't have time for them. I don't care about them enough.'

It's true you can't help some people even though you try. But this statement we use without proper context, it doesn't say I'm accepting of how that other person is acting, it says I don't care, or I can't care anymore.

There're two more cents no one asked for.

April 26

Bring Flash Mobs back, don't tell anyone. Let people guess then join in if they figure out your killer dance moves.

School Stopper, "Lazy" Leon Trucker

R EMEMBER these?

Let's do it.

Flash Mobs rock.

April 27

Envy what others have.

Brought to you by the color Yellow

DON'T think about everything that you have. Don't be thankful. Concern yourself with what others have and not the successes you have seen. It's easy to forget to stop and look at what you have. Maybe you don't have anything, except this book. If you go through life looking out at all the things you don't have, you'll lose the opportunity to be thankful for anything you might have. I know it's easy to say when you have a place to live. If by chance you don't have a place to live, there should be someone who will help. Reach out to them. There are shelters and churches that should be able to provide something if they have enough, and they might not. Good people need to provide. But don't burden yourself with anger about not having something.

As someone with something, I would encourage you to look for the people who don't have something, or very little. It's an opportunity for you to do something. If you don't want to, you don't have to. Maybe your purpose is to gather things. Maybe that's your purpose. To collect things. Good on ya, at least you know yourself. I still would encourage you to look at what you're gathering and who its for. I'm sure you've had some hard times, remember what that was like?

Give more than kind words (Kinda like what I'm trying to do in this book here.) reach out and do something for someone. I think that if you focus on helping someone overcome something and lift them up, perhaps whatever you were envious of in another might not be that big of a deal any longer.

Try it. What else are you doing?

April 28

The only way to get through this life is alone. We die alone anyway.

I don't mean to ridicule people who say this, but it's very existential perhaps leaning toward nihilistic even. I can't argue against such viewpoints, I feel it would be… pointless. However, I feel this is patently absurd.

It's somewhat of a depression inducing phrase. Now, perhaps you're one of strength who finds this to build you up and make you try harder. It promotes independence in a world that has been built around the framework of cooperation and purposes. (Whether or not you choose to believe in those purposes or not, it's how the world runs. Mostly talking with the Existential and Nihilist here. Absurdist are free to ignore the jab.)

For I believe most of us however, this lovely nugget of a saying is simply pointless. First, its blatantly not true. The only way through this life you have to deal with people around you. All the time, sometimes it's even annoying. People are everywhere, and we need them. Others support us. And the second section of this gem is equally useless.

What do you think it means to die alone? First objection to this, there are 7.6 billion people around. That means, someone is actually, physically around us. Chances are when we die, someone will be physically present. Unless we are actually alone, perhaps in a forest or mountainous area. If the saying is trying to convince you that connections in this world are pointless, they've lost me there to. Connections are what build us up and others. They give purpose. It's absurd to think they don't.

So, if you hear someone say this, just realize it's actually not advice, or even a useable outlook. It doesn't provide a depth to meaningfulness, or in this case, meaninglessness. It's simply presenting a false dilemma as if there are really only two options and one is wrong.

After all, there are a million ways to die in the west, and even things to do in Denver when you're dead. So, take some heart and find some meaning. Take this advice if you get nothing else from this section. Good in, Good out.

April 29

Don't speak your mind.

Tolerance

WHO says that? If your leaders or people you look up to do, chances are you're in a cult. Or a repressive group of some sort. But it also happens out in the world. It's not said like this though. In schools. Groups make fun of us if we don't act or talk or do certain things in certain ways. In college there is a little more freedom, but you have to be concerned about being wrong. The world for some reason seems eerily reminiscent of a dystopia in this way. Not to call it out. It's simply that my frame of reference comes from reading books. So, the characteristics I see on being PC, or making a business make you a cake even if they don't want to, or not being able to buy a cake because of your choices in life as bending toward dystopic in nature. I could be wrong though, maybe one side is utopian in character... I'm just focused on the wrong theme, and my thoughts need corrected. Feel free to correct my thoughts any time. Your expectations of the result, might horrify me even more though.

We give this advice all the time. Quiet like, sweet like, helpful like. It's not that we can't speak our minds, it just that there seems to be a loud voice. That loud voice wherever it comes from, left, right, down, its drowning, and strange. It brings to mind words like group think, and mob mentality, Anakin Skywalker on Mustafar and his famous line. "If you're not with me, you're my enemy!"

Maybe that's not what we're going for. I'm not saying it is. But it's a concern, or fear that's out there. If we let this fear of not saying what we think, or we might not 'fit in' grow, not setting people straight. They'll believe it. It's like Jules Verne's electric submarine. It was just a matter of time before someone actually built one. If someone thinks it, another can always do it. Sometimes people work to oppress ideas and beliefs, what list are those people on?

It's not that we are necessarily tell people to shut up, (unless we don't have any other good points in our arguments, right?) and sit down. But the mentality that we shouldn't speak our mind is out there, we all feel it. And it's real, and growing in the darkness. (I like waxing poetic, sorry.)

My question is where does this path lead? I'd love to believe the good guys are in charge and things will work out and we will squash the bad guys, but are we just trading one dystopian path for another?

April 30

Speak your mind.

―

Rights

AND here's the other side of this sharp jagged coin. Sometimes you shouldn't speak your mind. Sometimes you're misinformed. This world is full of misinformation that we just take out of the air as truth. Facebook quotes of depth that we don't actually have context for and are useless. We grab these as truth and use them as firepower or bombs to support our causes, sometimes not understanding what the implications of those causes truly are. Our voices echo in the eternity of the digital world.

I do it (probably a lot in this book!). You do it. We all listen to this advice. We speak our minds freely and damned be the consequences! We can't be expected to know every possible outcome to something. What are we Ashton Kutcher from Butterfly Effect! I don't think so.

We do have a responsibility though. One I don't think we take as seriously as we should. We'll say anything. Okay, so maybe we're young and our brains aren't fully developed. Right? I get that. That's a reasonable excuse. Mine apparently just hit its peak recently.

I believe we do owe it to ourselves and others to speak from a point of experience and truth. We throw facts around that we don't understand, all the time. Carelessly. We don't get them, sometimes we're just trying to be witty, cleaver, liked. Sometimes we're trolls and we live under bridges next to the van guy and the river.

So, I know what I said in the last section. It's scary how we feel that we can't speak our mind without fear of backlash, and should stand up for things, right. Now, this section I'm explaining that maybe we shouldn't talk until we have more facts and give better context and a more rounded understanding. Maybe we shouldn't give trolls the time of day anymore. I say ban trolls from the internet! (See what I just did there.) Who's going to be in charge of categorizing what trolls to ban? I'm sure someone wants the job. Think you missed a few points along the way if you want it.

May 1

Cheaper is better.

—

Foreign Economist

SAVING money is important. Especially when you need so much to retire nowadays. Not to mention bills and lenders. Did you know that in Jewish law they have a Sabbatical year? Every 7th year all debt (as far as I know) is forgiven. Now to be fair this has been circumvented with something called a Pruzbul making the loan public denies the ability of forgiveness, but if it remains a private paid loan through the end of that year its forgiven. I don't know why they didn't just start 7 year loans from the time a loan was taken out and if it hadn't been paid back in 7 years from that time, it would be forgiven, but I'm sure there was a reason…

I think we should require this of our banks, or at least be able to say I'm going to follow the Jewish law and get the benefit this Sabbatical year provides. (As I'm sure the financial institutions would and are laughing right now.) Sad really. But I don't know if it's all their doing, they're just giving us what we want. That's what we want, to have it our way, right? All this stuff we need. Well this is it what takes. Debt out the ears.

Back to the cheaper is better advice. I believe we need to save and be wise in spending, we don't have sabbatical years after all. I also think we can worry too much about this sometimes. Sometimes you just need to buy a suit of armor, or a piece of hardware for that project and the other stuff needed for it, or video game. Or go on a trip.

If you're too cheap, you might miss out on something fun you can do. If you wait, you might not get to spend it. Besides retirement, what are you saving for? To have fun in retirement? Have some fun now. Chances are you won't be able to retire anyway.

May 2

Get All your facts from Drunken History.

Billy the Kid talking to Abraham Lincoln after one of their Epic Rap Battles

I'M not sure if you've see Drunken History or know what an Epic Rap Battle of History even is. (They are two different YouTube channels, by the by.) If you're looking to be amused today, maybe check them out. I'm pretty sure they're NSFW so you've been warned I put a clean version of the rap battles in the appendix on this date.

But this is terrible advice and I want you to read one history book for each Drunken History you watch, or at least look up the actual story on Wikipedia or ask Alexa. She can actually give you short facts on historical figures by asking 'Can you tell me something interesting about [Historical Figure Name Here]? or 'Can you tell me a Historical fact?" She actually doesn't do too bad. If we want to raise the bar, we need to engage in some actual facts and context…at least our robots' spit some of this at us if we would just ask them to.

May 3

You shouldn't risk it.
—
Henry Pharfhromphamous

WHY risk it? It's not going to work out. Really, is that your reason. Did you do any research that tells you this, or did you decide in the first 5 seconds? I'm not what I would call a risk taker. But I make calculated judgment calls that others might find uneasy. If I have an opportunity, I try to take it. Now you won't see me jumping off any real bridges, but metaphorical or hypothetical ones, sure. I'll weigh the risk, but if I fail, I know I will get back up and try something else. If the risk won't kill me, I'll probably try it, if the benefits I see are at least better than where I'm at right now. That's what life is about, right? On some level it's trying to better yourself so that you can help benefit others. (Granted I added that last bit, you could be a self-centered piece of... anyway. I find that if you're only doing something for yourself, it tends to fade in passion more quickly. But that's just me, or maybe you too.)

So sure, there are somethings that aren't worth risking. I say if you're passed a certain age you should probably think about not risking things, if you passed a certain age after that age, you could probably try risking things again. It's really only that middle spot that you want to be extra careful, after all.

Take calculated risks, work it out before you do it, but try it. If you don't, how are you going to feel about it later? Maybe just fine. If you're fine with where you're at, good on ya. Maybe you shouldn't risk it. Maybe you might lose. If you have something worth holding on to, a relationship of some sort. (I'm assuming you are all thinking about relationships with people not robots, as things are really not important. We only think they are because they might grant us some avenue within a relationship. Unless you're just a stingy bastard, then you don't factor into this assumption.)

Homeostasis is nice, but small risks are important to try. Risks of business or opportunity, love (Not cheating on your spouse risks, go to a counselor if you're thinking about that.). These risks can lead to better chances for more, more things, more friends, more things... I mean, greater opportunity to help people.

Or don't. But if you always do, what you've always done. You'll always get, what you've always got. If you're okay with that, great. If you're not, then you are going to have to be the one to try and change it. (Asking for help from others counts, by the way.)

May 4

You can risk it.

T.S. Eliot

SURE why not. I just said you could. But this is really the same advice but doesn't take into account thinking which leads to a different outcome. So, what does that mean? Well, let's use this example, say you want to travel and you get all packed and you take off. When you get to your first stop, different country or state. Now what are you going to do? Do you have money, do you need to work at different stops? Doing what? Maybe you have a job that you can do on the road. Not talking to you then, that's planning after all. The point just like the last page. You can take risks, but you should plan. I know, I know sometimes you can't. I'm not talking about those times. But I'm guessing you deciding to get up and travel across the country or to another one could have been postponed for another hour while you made some sort of plan.

Be spontaneous, try new things! But don't do it because your friend is beside you pressing you to. Maybe they aren't that much of a friend. Maybe you need to risk getting truer friends. Or maybe you are just being a wuss, probably not though.

Again, don't take risks. Take calculated ones. We all want things right away these days. We want our food now, answers now, our full-sized batman suit from amazon now! (I'm still waiting on that.) But sometimes it's better to wait. Not on those things I just mentioned but on taking the risks until we know more about them.

You ever feel rushed into reading and signing something. Stop it. Make them wait. They wrote the thing, they can wait for you to really read it. If you're at a car dealership, read the contract, if you're at a loan office, read the contract. Sometimes these are risks we shouldn't take, but don't even think about nowadays.

Let's talk about this risk. Sex. Do you want to have a child right now, or an incurable STI? A child would change your life. Maybe your parents lied, and it is fun and you don't want to stop having fun. I get it, but know it's a risk that could change the course of your entire life.

Maybe some risks we should stop taking so much, and others we should think about taking more of? It's really your life (and another if its sex I would think.), but these are risks we never think too much about, while taking that better job over your current one seems too risky because you might not know everything you need to yet. It's called on the job training. Maybe you can take that risk. Something to think about.

May 5

You can dance if you want to. You can leave your friends behind.
—
Men without Hats

AH, we can dance if we want to. Can you dance though? Maybe learn first. Take some lessons. You don't want to risk looking like a fool. The night is young and so are you. I say if men without hats can dance you could probably too. Just look online at the good and bad dancers.

I mean if your friends don't dance, then should they be hanging out with you?

Terrible advice, everyone has things they can and can't do. You really shouldn't not hang with someone just because they can't dance. (I have lost too many a friend to this song. After they hear it, their like, "Sorry dude. Like the song says if your friends don't dance, and if they don't dance, well they ain't no friends of mine.")

Come to think about it this is a perfect song for popularity. If you want to be cool, follow the dancing crowd. Not, clown, crowd. I just got a weird image of a clown leading people around this country. Strange.

So, dance, but don't leave your friends, your true friends behind. Stop worrying about being cool. Stand up for those who aren't. Can you imagine if we all stood up for the guy or girl who was picked on? Do you think it would change our schools, maybe the trolls on the internet would go away? (They're going to hate this book.)

May 6

If you can't see it/prove it, it doesn't exist
−
The Invisible Man

THERE are a lot of people out there that don't believe things exist because they can't see them or prove them. That's an interesting concept to me. I think maybe it's a mix between arrogance and naivete. I'm not trying to step on sensitive toes here. (I'm sure it isn't you, right?) But I read history, my Wikipedia page is up almost 70% of the time. I know things. I think we figured out the world wasn't flat 2000 years ago in Egypt, or maybe it was Greece. So, who was it that thought the earth was flat? Why do people still think that? (*Whisper* I don't know why, but some people seem to.)

How do you know that you don't believe in a metaphorical flat earth of your own? If that's wrong, how do you know things are right? Was the source different? Verifiable? How do you know? For certain I mean?

I'm not saying Wikipedia is the source for all facts, I'm saying that most of the time we don't have all the facts. Okay, so someone figured something out. That person might have most of the facts, but as the understanding goes out of that person's head to the next person, or paper, not all the info might transfer, or be clear to others. Doesn't mean it's not true though.

Later on, we might believe something different. Perhaps we didn't migrate out of Asia, or I mean Africa. It used to be Asia. Newtonian Physics, that's not so much a thing anymore. Neptunism, kinda a thing, for some things but not all of them.

The Higgs-Boson particle or 'the God particle'. I think it's more like paste, but I'm just a writer. The point I'm trying to make is, this idea that if you can't prove it, then it's not real, is really a crazy assumption. We discover new understandings of the world all the time. New species, new math, new particles, new ways of doing things. I'm not saying you have to see it my way, I hope you do see how the inability to prove something doesn't make it not real. I do believe our arguments need to be more thought out, less 'pick and choose, or name calling.

In fact, this ties in nicely with my bigfoot section. I mean we know the Loch Ness Monster doesn't exist, it's been proven the video was a hoax, but Big foot, he might still be out there... even though that video was proven to be a hoax. I mean the Loch is much smaller, but Big foot has been seen everywhere!

May 7

Read everything. Link by Link.

SOMETHINGS really aren't worth reading. (I mean, not this, keep reading this. Ah, I lost some of ya there didn't I. Crap.) Well for the ones left. There are a lot of things that really aren't worth our time. Grocery store tabloids come to mind. Advertisements, and news. Not just the fake news, like most of it. What do you do with that information? Do you make world changing decisions with that extra knowledge? Probably not. Do you have engaging conversations with people around the water cooler? Maybe.

Sometimes you want to read something, a book on the top 100 books to read before you die. Maybe, those would be good to take a chance at. What about the websites and Facebook posts and blogs and vlogs and YouTube, and wetubes, and your phone?

So how much of that information do you think you retain? Can you tell me last week what you watched on YouTube or what you read online?

I can't. As soon as something is out of my view. I tend to forget it entirely. There are somethings I remember, most of them are actual events though, or books. Things I read day to day pass out of my mind as if I never looked at them at all.

If that's you, why do you spend so much time reading these different things. Does it connect you? How does it connect you? Maybe you could spend time on a project that would give you some lasting value, even if it's just for yourself.

So much information passes before us on a day to day basis, it's important to filter. Take a look at what you read. Is it worth your time? Do you remember what you read yesterday, or on your phone, what you posted or your friend posted three weeks ago? We have so much crap that floats in front of us. Maybe it's time to use a filter. There might be something better out there to do with your time.

I know, I know. You don't care. You want to be on Facebook, your friends are there, and your life is connected and you don't want to leave your phone. I get it. I wish I didn't. Read what you want, just don't read everything. Sucks up your real life, if we still have that. Dark sorry about that, just try not to waste your time here. That's all. You/We can do some pretty amazing things, if we would just stop wasting so much time, watching/reading/arguing stupid wasteful pointless/no context things.

May 8

Don't worry about changing your eating habits in your 30's

"Ramen for Life"

RIGHT? This sounds right. When I was 18, I was 180. In my 20's 200. In my 30's, well I fell of the proverbial wagon. Not because I was really on one. Maybe I thought I could eat Fritos and mountain dew and play Halo and COD my entire life. Upgrade to a Haptic whatjahoozit suit and what does it matter. I can play games till I'm dead. (Not trying to make a joke about that guy who played WOW till he died.) Fact is, we should be aware of our eating habits, even before 30. Our country is #1 in obesity. So at least we still got one! (There might be others. I really don't know. That's a different rant. I'm trying to keep these to a page so I'll bypass that. Like triple bypass burger from the Heartattack Grill.)

Forget the country for a moment. You need to get in a shape, not awesome Hollywood shape. Those aren't real people anyway, right? No, I mean a nice, comfortable shape where you don't wheeze when you walk. I go for smooth lines myself.

Problem is it's just so easy to eat badly. It's cheap, but I don't know if it's cheaper. I think I go grocery shopping every week and spend about 60 dollars. I end up having food left over to the next week. I also only buy for myself and I cook most of my meals. I'd say that's pretty cheap. Break it up and I spend about 8.50 a day. I spend about half of that amount just in coffee! (Coffee doesn't count as grocery shopping.) I just buy that wherever I am. It's a habit, I'm fine with it.

I put a few links in the appendix on this date if you'd like some suggestions on where to start. I'm using Atkins diet meals right now. You don't even need to buy their kits.

I will say this, I miss Oreos and mountain dew, but I'm not actually hungry at any point. Sometimes it's a head game, sometimes it's a thyroid game. I get that. I'm just saying do what you can, cuz thirty jumps up on ya!

May 9

Pull around and wait for us to bring out the food.

I love my mother. Wonderful person. Good story. One time when I was 8. (I'm always 8 in my stories. I don't know how old I was.) So, I'm 8 and we stopped to get food. Fast food, it was cheaper then and maybe not fast. So, I ordered a kid's meal, I mean I was 8 so it's okay. It's not like I was 15 ordering a kid's meal. Right? I said I was 8. I meant it... geez get off my back already.) So, kids' meal and a shake. My mom ordered something. I wasn't paying attention, I was jumping on the front seat! So, we pull up and the lady takes mom's plastic card with what I was sure was an infinite supply of money behind it. (Kinda like mining and bitcoin huh? I thought it was never-ending.) So, after we pull up to the second window to get our food. This lady at the second window, explained very nicely, I thought, to my mom that our food would take a moment and asked if we would pull up and the bags would be brought out to us. Perfectly reasonable I thought. My mom had other thoughts. She explained to the lady that she would not do that as she was the next customer in line and we had been waiting rather patiently. Well let me tell you, I was mortified. What did she mean, 'no'? I don't think that I was under the realization that you could tell someone in this world 'no' up till that point. Maybe because I wasn't allowed to tell my parents no. But for some reason I knew, that that lady in the window was gonna come out and spank my mom right there. I couldn't do anything about it. I was 8, or something. She was gonna get it! I made sure to hide myself in the passenger seat floor. I wasn't going to be a part of that scene. Oh, boy!

Then the lady said 'okay'. And we got our food and left. I can't say that my mom's burger didn't have spit on it, but I think my happy meal was probably okay.

Moral, don't be unkind to people who handle your food.

Another Moral, sometimes it's okay to say 'No', we don't stand up for the things we should all the time. Maybe we just don't want to get spanked, but it's important to stand up all the same. Like someone getting hit over the head with a beer bottle, or standing up for what's right, perhaps in the office. Maybe we should stand up and say 'No' more instead of letting things slide. Maybe we let too many things slide.

May 10

The Customer is always right.

Marketing Machine

HARRY Gordon Selfridge in 1909 said this in London. And I'll say something about it. In 1909, maybe, the customer was always right. I'm not saying we were 'civilized' I think we still had child labor at that time. But there is still child labor, we just don't outwardly except it, and its kept hidden in the back alleys and dark spaces of our world. It's happening while we watch our phones and go to work. It's still out there though. A little gem to keep you up at night.

In 1909 people behaved differently. It's true, look it up if you need to. History. So, gaining customer loyalty was important. If customers knew they were going to be treated 'fairly', I'll say, they would come back. That worked well.

Then we got the internet and trolls. Trolls don't just exist online though. They walk amongst us. We see them sometimes yelling at someone, or trying to get something for free because they were wronged in some way. I'm not saying sometimes companies aren't in the wrong. I'm talking about trolls. Wasting space. I wish it weren't so. I wish they cared, but it doesn't seem like they do. Some will even admit to it. I respect that more than lying about it.

Now there are customers that don't simply demand to be served in the order they came in. Today they will sometimes complain about something small or outright demand whatever. Again maybe there is warrant for it.

Sometimes the customer is wrong though.

Sometimes you need to protect your employee. Take their side. It promotes, what's that called, unity. Sometimes standing by your customer when they're clearly wrong isn't the best policy.

Customers are wrong. Even on the back end. Customers demand cheaper products, and they buy them elsewhere if you don't offer them. So, you react, find cheaper suppliers. Sometimes outside the country. It's what the customer wants. It keeps your profits up. You can't expect to survive in this global economy without customers. You just give them what they want, and they sometimes don't want US (or whatever country you might be from) jobs, even though the say they do.

Maybe the saying is true, but maybe it's more complex than that. I'm more of an Occam's razor guy myself. Something to think about, maybe if companies would pitch that in their marketing, customers would change their purchase.

"Hey I know we sell tooth brushes at .50 but if you'd pay 1.00, we'd be able to bring back these jobs! 500 workers to St Whatwhosit! But if you wouldn't like that we can keep outsourcing." Course that would take like a social media poll and marketing to create jobs. Maybe it's too much work. I'll let you decide.

May 11

It will work itself out.

The unstoppable "Mother" Nature

NATURE will work itself out. The path of a lightning bolt in the sky will work itself out. Even life will, as wise oracle Jeff Goldblum told us, 'life finds a way'. But this isn't something to live by. It's terrible advice to live by.

Now, here is a warning, this is not a 'warm and fuzzy writing' day. Things in the world of people don't work themselves out. They get buried and forgotten, but they still writhe in the mire of our societal foundations. They will break those structures apart if they aren't addressed. Just like a bad tooth can cause a heart attack.

We cling to this advice though. To our disadvantage at times. Not everything needs managed. But some things need addressed that really aren't being addressed at all. Of course, people talk all the time about fixing things and what we need to do about them. Do you think, perhaps the media just doesn't focus on those things? I do. If you watch media in other countries, you get different viewpoints. I suggest doing so. I don't think enough of us do regularly. I know I don't. I linked to a site in the appendix that offers some direction on how to do that. The internet does now provide us with the ability to see other media besides, CNN, ABC, CBS, NBC, and FOX (If you count them. Although I'd be weary of counting much of anything anyone of them says. To illustrate here is a link to an article on media bias.). I always forget which companies own these stations but they operate by ratings and commercials. Commercials to sell me crap I don't need. It's the way of the world. We would rather it be that way then controlled by the government though, right?

Anyway, in some cases it will work itself out. Nature tends to, although animals go extinct all the time. No more white rhinos. If we ignore problems, they don't go away. They don't work themselves out in the way we want without some direction, without support. We can't just say we want something one way or the other. We have to move to action. Otherwise, we might just go extinct. Someone else will not take care of this.

MAY 12

Do something great and tell everyone about it.

School Stopper "Button Pusher Intern" Paul

REVEL in it. Terrible advice? Certainly, why did you do something great? Was it to show everyone what you did? Your purpose was, to get recognition? What if you don't get the recognition you think you should? Are you going to stop trying to do great things? If the answer is yes. Don't bother in the first place. If your sole or even primary drive is to gain recognition from a group or a people. What's the point exactly? Maybe it does help someone, great. That wasn't your purpose though, so why do you care? You could have just as well done something else. Something more useful for yourself?

Recognition, or trying to get noticed for an action. I understand that. We do things when we're young to get attention from our parents. It's human to need connection. But this is different, although perhaps just as meaningful as when Stewart from SNL jumps in the air awkwardly and say "Look what I can do!"

This is a problem that goes deeper than the outward advice we tell ourselves. If we expect a certain response, and don't get that response, our behavior changes. Look at it in a positive reinforcement light. This is a way to teach a child wrong and right, how can that be bad? I'm not saying that is. But as adult individuals this system breaks down. If we don't the results or response we want, our determination goes down. Not even in sharing with other people. Take diets for example. We expect that after three weeks on a new diet, or exercise to see results. Some of us, if those results don't manifest as we expect, give up.

If we are working on a project that we find inspiring or helpful and we share our enthusiasm with another. If they don't express the proper amount of enthusiasm back, maybe we lose some of our drive behind that project. Sometimes it's better to keep the good things, and projects you are working on to yourself. If you require a certain response from an outside source, maybe you should reevaluate how much you actually care about the purpose of that project as opposed to what you think you're going to get from the response that project is going to bring you.

May 13

Do something great and keep it to yourself.

REVEL in it. Sound familiar? Sometimes we do great things. Helping someone out with food, or building an arcade machine for kids. Maybe fixing an issue at work. We already know that we're not going to get the response we want from someone else. We're good with that aspect. We just wanted to help out somehow.

Noble.

Sometimes this is something to do. I mean, maybe you have reasons to keep something you did that was nice for someone else to yourself. Maybe just to prove to yourself you can do it. It sounds hard. Why would you do something good and not tell everyone, or someone at the least? Kind of a strange concept, but I say give it a go. Perhaps it helps out a colleague, or a friend in need. Perhaps someone you don't know at Christmas. I get the appeal. Gives you 'warm fuzzies' perhaps.

Sometimes however, maybe consider sharing it, that is, if you're prone to doing this a lot. Good things no one knows about, strange. I'm guessing Gandhi and Mother Teresa might have done this a lot. But we aren't Gandhi or Mother Teresa. Although that does help my point. I'm pretty certain I can say these people might have done a little of both.

The point, sharing something like this wouldn't be for recognition. It would for example. People need examples. They need direction, otherwise we'll go wherever we want. Sometimes that's not good. Sharing some of the good things you do, shows others what can be done. It provides inspiration, and direction.

Perhaps in sharing a good thing takes away the initial effect of not sharing the good thing, but it could bring about the opportunity for others to begin down a path of doing good things as well. Maybe the outcome of giving up something good done in secret could produce more good things. Maybe it would create a web of good things. Maybe I'm just a dreamer. But I can't be the only one, right?

May 14

All-Carb Dieting.

—

HONESTLY, I didn't know this was a thing before I wrote it. I simply thought it was bad advice. I think for the majority of us however it still might fall into this category. If however, you are a body builder, it might be something to look into. Although you will need a strong work out regime.

Many of us don't have the time or ability to follow this type of diet. If you permit me, (or not, I mean you're not here to stop me, right?) I'm going to go off on a short tangent and come back to some helpful links if you would like to try and bulk up with this 'diet'.

Energy drinks are helpful for people who work out, maybe, but tell that to Ross Cooney, or Cory Terry. Or some of the other names that pop up in the media from dying. Of course, you know my stance on believing everything you read, but there seem to be links to health issues. Why risk it? Also, why do we drink these things when most of us sit for 8 hours a day? Why because they market to us. They weren't making enough just off the sports or athletic market. It's about money after all. Which is sad, but its most likely true. If you do drink energy drinks, why? They taste good, they give you energy you need. Eat better. Sleep more. I hear you're supposed to have only up to about 400 mg of caffeine. Do you need more than that? Maybe something to get checked out. I used to drink energy drinks. They helped keep me up. I also stopped drinking them because I couldn't do enough with the energy I had. I had trouble focusing. I went back to coffee. Do what you want, I know you will. Just be aware of some of the down sides. Heck, look at all sides of it. What's the context for needing to drink so many? Or even one?

Now, for those of you who have physical jobs or work out more of the time. They do have an 'all carb diet' for building up muscles, although energy drinks don't really factor into it. I have put one such diet plan/exercise plan in the appendix on this day. Just make sure you don't take that guys word for it. Do your research, consult a doctor if you should, right? That's what the lawyers tell you.

We're pretty close to not looking at what we eat anyway, so this all carb dieting might be something you're doing right now, while you watch television and sit at a desk. If so, stop following that advice. It's not working, is it?

May 15

Buy that new phone. Who cares if it's 500 dollars?

EVERYONE'S got to have a new phone, tablet, VR, newest game station. 500 here or there is perhaps a big purchase but it's worth it right? I mean you will get years of use out of it. I find it interesting that we see a lot of information about the newest upgrades. It makes you think that most people really upgrade their phones. I think I read somewhere that about 80 or 90 percent of us either wait till our phone is full, or wait till the free two year contract allows us to. The other percent is broken down more and only 2 or 3 percent upgrade right away. That's smart to wait it out.

If it's not broke, don't fix it. What about these huge purchases though. We make them. Go Pros, and phones and new game consoles and TV's and devices. Do we need these things? What if we waited? Here's an example. A new game console comes out. 600 bucks. A little over half a paycheck for a lot of us. It's going to take some budgeting, or credit cards juggling right? What if you waited. Say it takes you 1 paycheck or 4. What if you broke that into 2 paychecks or 8? Would it be that bad to wait? Now say with that extra time, you actually saved the same amount. So, you would have either double the money or maybe a quarter more of that money. What if you saved 750 bucks up instead of 600. You could buy more stuff then right! Sure, that's not where I'm going, although it's easy to go there. Do you know what 150 would do for a family in need, or a child, maybe a homeless guy you pass on the street every day? So, you had to save for an extra two weeks? That sacrifice of waiting and saving, if you gave the extra to a family who needed it. What would that bring, how much more would that cost, too much to give? Maybe, maybe it's something to think about.

If I could buy any car, I'd buy a BMW i8. Actually, if I could buy any car, I'd pick a Lamborghini Veneno Roadster. That's about a 4.5 million dollar car. But in the realm of my lifetime. I might be able to buy an older model BMW i8 if I wait 8 years. That's about 145,000 dollars currently. So, I was thinking about that. Both are sweet cars. Now if I could buy one of those cars, that would be awesome. But, for some reason I couldn't, even if I had the money. I feel I'd have to take something smaller. It's a car. There are people who need help. I'd love that car, either one. But I couldn't look at a homeless person, or talk about helping someone. It wouldn't feel...correct. So, I think to get around that I'd have to halve the cost and buy something less. Like a Chevrolet Corvette Stingray. (Hey If I was going to buy a BMW i8 I could afford this too. We're just dreaming here.) Then I'd take the extra 100 grand difference in this case and give it to a cause somehow, or a few causes. Course that's just me dreaming. I couldn't ever rightly afford those things. Neither could you, right? (If you could, I could give you a number where you can reach me, maybe we could talk about the i8. It's choice. If you have the means I highly recommend picking one up. Maybe for your favorite author buddy too? Eh, it was worth a try.)

I wish I could say I live my life this way. No, I can't afford a Lambo, or an i8. Maybe not even the Corvette, but I can afford a big screen tv, or a new Alexa Echo Show. What if I would wait an extra two weeks and split that cost. Who could I help? I hope I give that more thought, I hope you might too.

May 16

Lather, rinse, repeat.

HOMEOSTASIS is what we crave. The body works to maintain it. Doctors refer to homeostasis where people will work to increase or decrease the level of stress in their life to maintain it. It actually helps us understand why some people will more likely find thrills of sky diving or standing at the edge of cliffs and jumping off them into the ocean (You know who I'm talking about. Crazy Daredevils.), it might simply be a way to create the balance you are used to in your life. I'm not saying if you prefer a higher stress environment, go jump into the ocean. Learn to swim and gauge depth and rock proximity first. Don't want to be like Jason Segal in "Forgetting Sarah Marshall", (By the by. I'd do that, jump and cling to the cliff side. That's how I roll.)

Shampoo used to have these very instructions. I don't see them on my bottles any more but the advice is still out there. In our heads, every day we go to work, come home and relax, then eat, sleep and repeat. It's our mantra. At least until we can afford to retire to that vacation beach house in the Keys.

It's still pervasive in marketing. They tell us over and over what we need and who we should be like (this is more of a side effect in some cases, we want to be liked and try to emulate those we believe are liked in different ways.)

It's really just another cycle, but it expresses the mantra plainly enough. It something we're used to. We for the most part like the cycle. I'd even say that the people who don't like cycles are in a cycle themselves. They just try to make it seem like they're not.

Again with the cycles. Yep, but sometimes these cycles lead to trenches. These ruts drag us through life and we don't see how to get out of them. I know there are ways to do it. It just takes time, maybe next time you find yourself in a cycle, you'll think about rinsing then lathering. (I'm so deep on this, I've lost myself.)

What I'm saying, is if you find yourself in an endless loop, perhaps if you ran out of shampoo you might not be able to lather any more. Maybe next time you might look at buying a bottle that says Lather, Rinse, and Get on with your day. (Old Spice does that. Thank you, Old Spice bottle.) Break the cycle. Get on with your day, stop repeating and try something new already.

May 17

Love means never having to say you're sorry.

MAYBE this isn't something anyone has ever heard, but sometimes it feels like we've heard this throughout our lives. People tend to gravitate toward not saying sorry, or not feeling good about it. Saying you're sorry means you're wrong, right? Nobody likes to be wrong. Wars have been started for less. We know things. We have a perception that being wrong means you're weak. You've lost. It's shameful. I'll tell you what's truly shameful. Not admitting you're wrong, simply out of pride. We have pride in things, ourselves, but our work, our jobs, relationships, our viewpoints. Well, not all of those we are right about or in all the time, right?

This advice that translates into not being sorry in our society creates people and groups who won't budge on things. (Now, I'm sure you're agreeing with me right now. You think I'm referencing the other person or other group right now, don't you? Now, say you're sorry for thinking that.) Okay, I'm not pointing fingers at them, or you. I want you to examine yourself. Have you thought about their side of the argument, have you really thought about your side of the argument or are you merely regurgitating something you heard as fact? If that's the case you fall into a large percentage group, I'm in that group too. Welcome, take a seat, relax, people live out their lives here.

Fact is, sometimes we're wrong. Stinks, but if we are to be real people, we need to stop defending things we don't understand. (Again, not talking about the other guy.) Read up on what you think is true, not just people who share your opinion on it either, or if it's an argument with your spouse look at it from their point of view. Love in this context means saying you're sorry.

These things don't go hand in hand. If you're in love with someone, there are times you have to admit fault. When you're wrong, you're wrong. Unless you're stubborn like the bad guys on old tv shows (I say bad guys because who liked the good guys, back then. The bad guys had the cooler clothes, unless you count Snakes eyes. Bad boys are more fun and nice guys finish last, right?) and never admit you're at fault. Saying sorry admits you were wrong. Nobody wants to be wrong, that's crushing. Ego shattering. It's like bad guy jail. "They know I'm sorry, I love them, I don't need to say it, do I?"

The next time you find yourself needing to say you're sorry, remember its love that allows you to truly mean it, and its love that gives you the ability to truly say it.

May 18

Being a real woman means you need to sit still and look pretty.

Daya

SHE didn't say that. However, there are others who have said just that. In fact, I think we're drowning in it. Makes me irritated. I know, there are people doing what they can about it. But you see I want it now. I want it fixed today, now. Why is this a thing I can write about? Every day, all day. Drowning in marketing that doesn't care. It won't care, it can't afford to care. Call me a cynic in this matter, I call myself a realist. Wouldn't I see change? Where's the change? It isn't on the news, or magazine covers? Course it's not on the internet, that's the wild west. We haven't even gotten to the civil war period in that story arch.

Women are pretty. Maybe I'm biased. I think what makes them worried about this 'pretty' mentality, and I'll add men to this group too, is that we always see images and people in media and billboards (They still have those right. It's been a while since I've looked up from my phone screen to check.) It's not a fault of the models, it's a mentality that we have. Pretty is better, rich is better. Makeup is better. Cookie cutter is better.

I'm not sure we can change this. People don't care that much, maybe as a select group, but not as a whole. We devour everything that is given to us, so more of it is made. How can we stop a self-propelling machine that runs on its own fuel?

Maybe one cog at a time, little by little. Reversing the wheels that turn. I don't mind 'pretty', what I mind is along with that 'pretty' for some reason attached to that 'oh, look at them. They're pretty.' Is another silent whisper from the dark we hear sometimes that says, "Yea, you'll never be that pretty." as if Pennywise the Dancing Clown might actually be really real.

Where does that idea come from? It comes from a false concept that there is a comparison. Certainly, we have sports and competitions where there is a winner and loser, and we even compare the two teams. That's fine I think, what's not fine is in your personal life comparing yourself to another. Compare yourself, to what you were yesterday. Improve and when you do, celebrate, for a second, then compare yourself to yesterday and improve on that. We are special. In order to focus on the gifts we might have, you need to stop focusing on the perceived gifts you think others have, that you don't.

May 19

Don't put yourself out there.

IT'S scary out there. It's better to stay inside. I'm not talking about agoraphobia although that could be a very real problem and if it is, seek help. I mean socially, and professionally. I'm not talking so much about risks. Here I want to touch on being personable. Saying hi. Remember the 'fit in' face that we all hate to get glances of. That's what I'm talking about. Of course, that's never fun. But it shouldn't matter. For one, we don't compare ourselves to others, right? We compare ourselves to our former selves, and we see the difference and in that we are content. With that down, (I'm sure that won't take more than 5 minutes to adjust your life long view point on the matter, right?) smile. Step 1. Did you know it takes fewer facial muscles to smile than it does to frown? (So, why does it seem like it actually takes more effort sometimes?)

So, smile, just smile. Don't talk. Don't say have a nice day, or ask how are things going. Just smile and nod. Nodding might help you look less like Pennywise from 'IT' if you're in a social situation. I'm just talking in passing someone, smile at them.

Second step, say hi. In passing. How's it going? This sounds like you're trying to engage, but people take it both ways. Mostly you get a 'fine' back. (Remember that response from Feb 20th.) If they ask, you can say 'I'm fine', or think of something. But its gonna have to be short, they have places to go and people to ignore there.

Third, when you're up to it. Find the water cooler, coffee area. Sometimes during breaks people hang there for a second. Just hang there. Get a drink of water or coffee. Most people will probably not engage you. But be ready for it though. You can talk slowly.

Most people will wait for you. If they don't, brush it off. Don't worry about that.

Forth, you can ask questions. See what they do for fun, or ask about a project they're working on. Something light, you don't really have to care what they're working on so much. Then maybe you'll find you have a common interest. Might be able to talk about that more. Else maybe try to find one. Or repeat steps 1 through 4 and engage others.

Always attempt to increase your RL social network. The worst thing is not doing steps 1 through 4. You miss 100% of the shots you never take. Take some chances. Put yourself out there.

May 20

Let things get to you.
—

THIS goes hand in hand with the last section. Stress. You know when I was in elementary school there was a sign. Said "Do not walk on the grass." I never did. In fact, I was a little stress ball. I'm sure there were factors I'm not sharing, but I had to be at school on time. Now my dad, well he's not what you call a 'worrier' in the same sense as I saw myself. One day, I think my mom was sick or at work already. Anyway, my dad got me up for school. Well we were a little late. I would say 5 minutes. Yea, about 5 minutes late when we pulled up to the building. Soooo, he said good bye and I think I may have been freaking out inside myself. I was late, and here he was perfectly fine. He didn't have to go into class and be tardy(late). Now, for some reason I got it in my head, that when the teacher says 'you were tardy', what they really said, and excuse me for the offensiveness of the term, was that you were 'retarded' in front of the whole class. Well I can tell you I wanted none of that. None at all.

So, there I was, going to my locker, putting my books away and getting my home room books. Running to the class. You know what happened next? It's interesting. I don't have the foggiest clue what happened next. It might have been that I walked in and the teacher explained I was tardy, maybe I signed a form (I think I remember seeing someone signing a form once.) maybe I went and sat down at my desk and the teacher said nothing. I honestly can't remember for the life of me what really happened. I wonder why I was so stressed about it now? 4th grade, or 3rd. (Those two grades had classes really close to each other, I can't be certain in my mind's eye which room I went into, but it was on the left side of the hallway. I know that much. Must have been third grade then, or forth. Never mind.)

See I don't know. The most stressful day in my third-grade career and I don't remember what happened.

Do you remember something that stressed you out? Maybe it was a bill, or family issue. Maybe someone moving away, or you starting a new job. Do you remember how that day went? Maybe you do. If you do, is it an actual factor in your life today? Maybe an argument. Maybe someone did something you thought was stupid. Irksome.

Did that moment change things, or is it something you don't quite remember now? If it's not, why do you think you were stressed about it so much?

May 21

Prematurely celebrate your upcoming success.

Thomas Dewey

LOTS of times we have things 'in the bag' as some people say. It means that they're going to win, or the project looks good to go, or that shot was good. Just Google premature celebration (Careful! I might add, if you have auto fill on other options might appear.) and you'll see tons of sports videos about players forgetting themselves just a little too early. This doesn't just happen in sports. It happens in science, publishing papers then a few months later having them proven wrong. Or in videos games, which are updated with the now famous and expected zero-day patches. Movies, it seems that writing a story has taken a backseat to explosions and CGI, 3D. Plot holes abound. I'm sure it's not entirely up to the writers, but Hollywood seems to prematurely celebrate their work now.

I used to love every movie I watched. I didn't like critics, thought they were too hard on movies. I understood the plot and story points. The character arches were funny but it was a good time. Critics just picked it apart. I imagine nowadays movies are easier to pick apart. For some movies, points just stick out now as 'what the hell' moments. I don't think it's all because my brain is more fully developed than it was. I think some movies are just not given the care they should be given. I blame premature celebration for this.

We do it too though. We get excited for a project and can see the end of it. Then we start celebrating. It's fun. We know it's 'in the bag', but then a funny thing happens on the way to the forum. It's not finished. We have more work to do. Sometimes we can continue, other times it's just too late.

I get it. Looking to the win is exciting, but maybe take a lesson and keep your head down till the goal line is past you. At that point jump up and down for a few moments, but not until then.

If we can learn to start doing this, maybe we won't have as many patchy games, or plot holed movies, or lost points, missed opportunities, or perhaps it will simply allow us not to be as embarrassed in front of millions as much, as Mr. Dewey can attest.

May 22

Buy a Lap pillow.
—

THIS doesn't seem like terrible advice. Lap pillows allow you to put pillows on your lap and then provide a flat surface you can put things on. Laptops, some have cup holders. It's not perhaps the greatest, but its functional. True, if I was talking about those types of pillows this wouldn't fit. But there's another type of lap pillow. I'll write about that now.

The Hizamakura is an interesting product. It's a pillow, see, but it's in the shape of a lap. Hence the name "Lap Pillow". There's really, I feel, little I need to say about this. I understand people get lonely, and sad about being alone from time to time. I'm not sure that if I bought a Hizamakura I'd feel better. I mean maybe, I mean maybe there a slight chance, and I'm talking a farts chance in a hurricane, type chance. Like Nano seconds. Maybe it gives a sensation when you lay your head down on it that you're actually with someone. I feel like I would need to take a massive quantity of drugs in order for that to work. Which in itself sounds unpleasant. But then the realization that I was still alone would kick back in, and on top that I'd have purchased a pillow shaped like a woman's lap. I think that would create a spiral for me of some sort. Spirals aren't good. They get smaller and smaller or bigger and bigger. Cycles are better and that's not saying much.

I ran across this little gem on a few YouTube channels. The one I'm gonna share in the appendix on this date was the most 'tame' review. It also contains some other items you can buy in japan.

If you are a reader and you have this item, or any item that might be similar. Maybe, just maybe, let it go. Get some, you know, help. Try to socialize more (See May 19th). Don't be creepy. This item, like so many others allows us as a society to give up on interaction. While this might seem to some as a way to help, I'm going to go out on a limb and say it hurts a whole lot more. If you can't bring it up in a normal conversation without someone raising an eyebrow and quickly ending the conversation, maybe you shouldn't have it.

May 23

Talk first, fast, and loudest. People will listen.

THE loudest person always gets noticed. The fastest talker gets heard. Things have to get done and sometimes you have to get your points out. Sometimes arguments are 'won' this way. Tell me, do you feel a sense of accomplishment when you shut the other person down? Sure you do. It lets us know that we won the argument. But does it, really?

Let me say Facebook arguments are useless. They're about as meaningful as lap pillows, or throw pillows for that matter. Who cares about them? All words. I'd say if you throw out a point for 'shock' value, you're actually losing the argument if someone would analyze closely. As long as you get multiple rapid fire points out and use all caps. You'll be heard. Just like everything else, so you'll get about 2 seconds of someone's attention, so people will agree with you? Chances are, those people already did, which still puts you at a zero. Didn't change anything. You just spoke to someone who had the same viewpoint.

We feel accomplished when someone agrees with us. Like we actually did something. Most of the time, when this happens, the people who agree, either already did to some degree, or didn't have an opinion or stance on the issue to begin with and honestly still don't. They merely have your points that they can reiterate to someone else to make them seem like they understand it or have a stance, (Heck that's a small victory, right? I mean all viruses care about is multiplying in a host anyway. If they can take over, then the end justifies the means, right? If you say yes, you're a troll. You can be a troll, just pointing it out.).

Then there are those that you have the opportunity to convince, two types here. The first believe you because they didn't really look at the points you gave them which is good because you didn't give a very well-rounded understanding of the issue, they don't really research things. They don't have time for that, really, they're indifferent when you drill down into how they truly feel about the topic. Most of us fall into this category of point proving. We like the indifferent ones, makes us feel like we accomplished something worthwhile. Myself included of course. Then there is the second type, the more important type to our Ego. These are harder and we could risk being wrong. These are people that you engage with and discuss the different sides. Convincing them is a prize. These take more than 2 minute posts on Facebook. They take time and actual connections. You don't raise your voice to prove a point, you raise points and counter points to prove your argument. Also, the other person actually understands the opposing view. They have researched it and don't merely have a vague understanding of a single sound bite on the issue being discussed.

These second type people are really hard to come by in this world of ours. I don't see it happening online. We don't have time to properly argue sides. Research, we have to study and work? It's easier just to take someone else's word for it. If you talk fast and loudest you will be heard, but does that mean you're saying something? I don't think so. I'll leave you with a quote. I don't know who said it anymore. That's not important. There lies some sort of truth in it regardless, and so it goes. "A man convinced against his will, remains unconvinced still." Stop wasting your own time.

May 24

Ballet heels.

—

NOT talking about Dori shoes. Ballet heels. In finding this (I don't know how I found this. I'm pretty sure it wasn't what I directly goggled. I probably searched for strange products, when I found weird items in japan.) I learnt that ballet shoes actually did have heels before the pointe shoe came out in the 18th century.

You can still buy these. I don't recommend them. To anyone. Ballet dancers might have a use, perhaps a way to stretch the leg muscles, but it's still seems rather useless. History facts. Dori shoes, to which I am not referring to in this terrible advice, have a construction similar to pointe shoes, where they also have about a 3 inch heel.

Ballet Heels that I'm talking about however have a larger heel, a 7 inch spiked heel. So. To me, and I know absolutely nothing about shoes, but I like Vans (That's a shoe brand, not like the one down by the river I will mention later.). To me this shoe reminds me of foot bindings that used to take place in China for so long. Maybe it's just me. Not recommended.

Just terrible advice. Not very functional for ballet purposes. They don't walk like that. They spin and release. (I've seen the movie 'Black Swan' I know how it is, I'm an EXPERT…Remember, Loud and fast. Wins every time.) They don't want to walk like that. Its dancing.

So, in closing this odd entry, don't buy Ballet heels, just skip it. If you want to ballet dance, go for it. (Dancing, not the heels still.)

Don't be a poser. Posers are fake. We have too much of that already.

May 25

Buy all the itcoin you can!

—

JP Sears

I'M not sure if Bitcoin is still a thing by the time this book comes out (about a year from the initial writing). From what I can tell, it has no intrinsic worth. I linked to an article in the appendix that talks about how at least the US dollar doesn't really either. Interesting. Maybe buy a small amount. Seems to be trading in foreign markets. Not so much in the US. I don't even know what I can buy with bit coin. For that matter, I don't know how to buy bit coins. Are their little question mark blocks floating around out there I need to smash with my head and super jump to get? Is that what 'mining' means. (Super Mario Ref there.) It's probably going to turn into nothing, but maybe you'll hit it big. I mean if I had bought Google or yahoo back in the day. Wow.

Anyway, there you go. You're terrible advice for the day. Buy stock in something you know nothing about. Not sure how much more I can say about it. I know if Magic started to be something you could buy stock in, like honest to god lightning and fire balls from the hands of like the wizards in Clash of Clans. Well, I'd buy that for a dollar for certain.

May 26

Listen up, so there's a tornado see, and sharks. You know in the tornado!

ALL for cheesy movies. I watched Mystery Science Theater 3000 when I was little, younger I mean. I can appreciate Elvira or Svengoolie. Cheese is good. I can eat cheese on the Atkins diet.

I am a little curious as to how this conversation went though. What was the back story behind this little gem? I mean, it's stupid. Worse than snakes on a plane. I mean snakes could be on a plane. That COULD happen. I think I sat next to one wearing a suit the last time I flew somewhere.

Interesting to think about some of the 'Ed Woodian' type movies. I believe that most people equate 'Reefer Madness' as the terrible beginning to bad movies though.

I don't spend a lot of time watching these anymore, but if you need a laugh and have time to burn. I recommend checking out the series Sharknado. It's how should I say it…interesting with a side of WTF.

May 27

Never share your pain. People don't care.

Algos

LIE. That's what this is. Sometimes we're confused because we get so many people that show us their 'fit in' face. There are a lot of people that hide their pain. There are a lot of environments where you might feel awkward about sharing your pain. Maybe you don't even want to with your friends. If they are your friends, they should be a reliable place to share your pain. Unless they're like 8, but if that's the case you should be able to find an adult who would listen.

The internet shows us that when we share opinions or understandings, if they're not the correct understandings, or even if they are, we can get hurt even more. Some people are trolls. I suppose trolls hurt too. Otherwise they wouldn't derive so much pleasure from pain. But that's why they call them trolls.

Trolls often get the most attention. They quiet rooms. People point at them and everyone looks. So, in that, maybe we feel that even if we did share. No one would listen, or we would be made fun of. Trolls are often the loudest in the room.

I'm here to tell you that feeling is not true. Trolls make it seem true with their loud shocking voices. In our media, movies, books, games, history, we have sometimes become attached to characters who don't seem to have issues with pain and suffering. Sometimes I even prefer an Indian Jones type, over a character that has growth or seems to be affected by things, but we all are. Or the vast majority anyway. We all have pain and don't always know how to deal with it.

This doesn't make us weak. Having pain in our lives is a part of life. We should share it, in sharing such a thing we allow others to connect to us. Perhaps you've been through something horrendous. If you never share that, in a manner that could promote healing, for yourself or others, that thing that was horrendous simply becomes worse.

We can't shout from the roof tops our pain all the time. We have to live our lives, and go to work. However, we can't keep our pain bottled up. It should be shared. Maybe it's not to help others who have found a similar circumstance, but only ourselves. If we don't open up, if we don't push past the fact that there are some people that don't care, if we don't bring it to the light. It will stay in the dark. So, I encourage you, bring it into the light. If not for yourself because you have the strength to overcome, think of the others who might not and how if you share, they might find power from that.

May 28

Take up amateur Parkour when you retire at 60.

MAYBE settle for a nice condo in Florida instead. You need to know your limits, after all, but I'd encourage you to challenge those limits. Just make sure you don't go too far, too fast. Also have fun on a regular basis. Don't wait to do the cool things until you retire. Try and do them throughout your life. Maybe not this, but you'll find something. Positive and helpful and supportive of the relationships around you perhaps.

May 29

Become the cat lady.

―

CAT Lady's. Spinsters. Old Maids. Right. Is that what you think of when you think of a cat lady?

I have to admit. Not the first image I get. Michelle Pheifer comes to mind. (Cat Woman from Batman Returns.) I didn't do it, its Hollywood's fault.

I was also looking this term up according wiki. (That's my go to truth source…) it's not a good term. Although some women embrace it. There was a cat lady that lived on my street. I believe she had around 100 cats. I think that's too much.

But not all cat ladies are as eccentric. Taylor Swift, she's got a cat. Some would say she's a cat lady. Or Xavier Elise. I kinda gave up on googling 'cat ladies' after that. But there are more, they have blogs and stuff.

So maybe it's not so bad to become a 'cat lady' any more. But the term seems to be changing in this culture. Maybe it's no longer referring to a woman who collects 100 cats. (That's too many cats Ma'am. There's a line between caring and harm. Not trying to pick on her, but it's true.)

Maybe you want to be a cat lady. I don't see an issue with that, after I researched it anyway.

Either way, don't put all your eggs in one basket or cats in a yard. 100 is too many. I hear that if you die and are surrounded with cats, they will eat you. Just saying. Dogs might do that too though. Ahh but fish. Well they might if they could. If you died in the water, or there was a tornado.

May 30

Cram for the test/meeting the day before.

Me

I'VE done this. Works out pretty well. It helps you get through it, but at what cost? Well I can't say I remember French all that well. I passed the class. I didn't have YouTube channels as they are today to help me though. I'm going to ref Thomas Frank again. I think this guy has some good points. Check out the channel if you're in college. He might have some pointers. If you're out of college or never went and you're in the work force, it's still a quick way to help improve studying. He also might have other useful advice.

My advice on this is, don't try to use this tactic often. It does work depending on how small the test or meeting is. There is amount of content to time ratio you have to master. Cramming might mean for an entire week. But you don't want to let it get that far. If you find yourself in these predicaments often, I'd say take a hard look at your schedule, break it down into time slots and do this over the long haul, and not as a quick fix. Again, check out Tom, he talks about that stuff to.

Basically, this is a shout out to his channel, I suppose. Didn't mean it to be, but if it's not broke.

May 31

Don't clean your room.
—
Mr. Dirty

THIS is like the section on not doing your laundry, but different. We don't have to clean our rooms. We can just shut the door. Guests don't go in there after all. Shove everything in the closet and go. It works. You'll get to it eventually, right? That's what I did as a teenager.

This goes beyond room cleaning. I'm talking about getting things in order. Do you have things in order? Maybe a folder for all of your bills? (I really need to do this.) I'm talking about life. If you don't clean your room, what else don't you clean up? It starts small. The 'big bads' always do, it's a slope after all, not a bridge. Just letting some small chore slide. It's your life, it's your room. You don't have to take care of it. It's not bothering anyone else, and it only bothers you if you think about it too much. But you do think about it. More often than not. Don't ya? Maybe you should.

You wish it was clean, or there was a path through it at least. This happens in life all the time. That goal you set, you really wanted to get it done. Other things just had to come first. Now you have some time, but it's just a huge task. You can't do it in a weekend or can't see getting the project done in a month. Why bother?

Little things. Pick up the socks and throw them in the hamper. Go clean the dishes, or put them in the washer. Little things, little steps. Baby Steps. (I should write that book, or maybe it's been written already... Or maybe this is another movie reference.)

How to do you eat an elephant? Well, you don't, you sick bastard! Eat elephants! Of course not, but if you did, it would be one bite at a time. So, it's a huge task, most things in life have some complexity to them. It doesn't get easier.

So, pick up a little today. Break up the project of building a computer. Buy one part for the sink. Call a bank to set up an appointment for the pre-approval process. Pick up your feet and take it one step at a time. Baby steps down the hall, baby steps into the elevator. Baby steps down the elevator. Just no jumping on the elevator.

The tasks in front of us can seem monumental at times. Maybe they are, but we can do them. We just need to break apart the tasks. We built the pyramids. We built, other big things that were huge.

Point is, don't not clean your room up because it would take too much time. Maybe when you get down to it, it won't take that long at all. Or you'll find it easier than you thought.

Go ahead, pick up that sock.

June 1

Never be the bigger man.

QUESTION for you. We hear about being the bigger man. Forgiving or forgetting. We see it in movies and books. How many opportunities do you actually have to be the bigger man though? For me, not that many. Maybe it's my liaise-faire attitude. (Not saying that's right, I'm just pointing out that I tend to be easy going. Maybe to a fault.) I don't get in discussions much that end in arguments, that have an impact. (Maybe after writing this book I will.) It's not that I don't want to have an impact, I'm just non-confrontational. That's not to say I'm timid, I just don't see the point in many discussions, as they rarely result in action toward progress.

But let's say you have an argument, or a disagreement with someone. Maybe a family member. You disagree with their stance on 'blah' and it's important that they understand 'blah'. I get that, I think you both should understand 'blah' and 'blah', personally though I'm tired of hearing about it. I want to see some action. So, you disagree, or it was simply a fight over whatever. Pride, that is to say, 'the consciousness of one's own dignity' sometimes gets in the way of this. Maybe it's not pride, maybe you're just right. (I'd do some real self-evaluation and research before I settled on the latter though.)

Is it imperative that this other person agree with you? Why? Does it involve money? Is it in a marriage and you both know the right thing to do, but it's the complete opposite of each other.

Sometimes you need to stick to your principles. After all, if a person doesn't stand for anything, they'll fall for everything. That's not to say this is one of those black and white issues. Maybe it's simply taking out the trash after work. Just do it if that's the case. Walk and read. If you can look at your phone while you walk you should be able to read. Otherwise put the phone down.

How important is it? Statistically, and I'm sure this is relative in my life, but the arguments at work or home that I've had up to this point don't really seem to have a bearing on where I'm at today. Something to think about. So, if, that's you, ask yourself if you're saving lives, or simply being prideful. Save your breath if that's the case.

June 2

Marry for money, power, fame or beauty.

THE American dream. I'm sure you don't want money and power, fame or beauty. I'm talking to the other readers now, so don't worry about it. What's the drive? To be protected and secure in our future. To have nice or awesome things. To be pampered. To be noticed. Personally, I'm not a huge fan of the book Fight Club. I think some of the views fall toward nihilism, or at least existentialism of some degree, although I can see how much of what we do is pointless. Which on a side note I don't think was an actual destination of the book, but more of a through-point. That said I agree with Mr. Palahniuk's quote in the book, or the first part of it. Even to a degree I can see how he could say the last. (You can look up the full quote if you want. Read the book if you have a minute, or not, the movies better.) I consider myself an eternal optimist though. Here's the quote: "You are not your job, you're not how much money you have in the bank. You are not the car you drive. You're not the contents of your wallet. You are not your f---ing khakis..."

Striking. Maybe because of the curse word. He might feel strongly about this. That's not the point. But I think it's true. You aren't these things, but we like them. We want them anyway. They don't make us who we are. Or I would say, they shouldn't. I hope if I meet you on the street, you're a real person and not just a job, or a surface cause, or a car or a stack of money or shoes or clothes, or makeup or hair or a boat or a mansion or plane. You could be though. How boring. I prefer people with a little more flavor.

I'm not talking about risk takers, or loud people. That's a different subject. I'm talking about substance. They say you can't take it with you, and you can't go home again. I'm talking about all things we like a whole lot.

What if you get that precious thing you desire? What do you do with it? What do you see is your impact? Maybe you can do a lot with money. Cure polio, malaria, HIV, Alzheimer's Is that what you're going to do with your money? Maybe that's too big. How about just helping the homeless guy find a place to stay? Or giving time to someone, maybe a family member.

Healing starts at home, right? Just remember things are not important. They're fun, but how are you impacting the lives of those around you? Do you have purpose? Find it first, it's never too late.

June 3

Prove that point on Facebook, the world will be better for it.

I'VE touched on this before. No sense in beating a dead horse, but I'm okay with a short reminder. It follows nicely with the last section. If you care, if you want to make a difference, do something. Stop talking about it and do it. Yourself. Stop worrying about getting other people to do it. Then when you have a little experience, find others that will help you. We don't change the world on Facebook, you could argue with me but it's only a medium.

What can you do to change the world? Do you think it's with talking? Do it. Show us what can be done. It can be done. Question is will you help or will you just talk about it?

June 4

Mind games are like puzzles for the heart.

The Riddler

STOP it. Mind games. I like puzzles. I'm not very good at them. I still try though. Mind games aren't puzzles. They don't make things interesting. They shroud truths. From yourself, and others. If you're playing 'mind games' with someone stop it. It's mean, and one of those worthless things people do to pass time. Find a better past time. Maybe you need some help.

What is the allure of mind games. What could that possibly be, power, control. These are reasons. I ask, why do you need power? Do you feel you don't have any? Maybe its control? Do you not feel safe? Someone has hurt you in the past and perhaps you use these tools as a way to cope. Even if that person is now gone from your life?

I'm not trying to be mean here, in fact it's not mean, it's just direct. I'm not talking to the abused. I have given reference to help lines on previous days/pages and in the appendix for those who are abused. I'm talking to the abusers. First, maybe you don't want help. I get that. You don't need it. Its everyone else who's wrong. I contend that understanding is flawed and it doesn't help you succeed in this life. It merely chains and traps you into a path and destination you can never control. I urge you to reconsider. Seek help. I've already mentioned that we are special. If your gift or specialness has been shrouded in pain and hurt from others, and have caused you to hurt others, or maybe caused you to care for no one, I urge you, seek help. There is purpose. Meaning. You are special as well, I know you don't believe me, but it's true. Maybe getting help means you need to be alone for a while, maybe that's hard, but maybe you can be the bigger person today.

I've put two links to help in the appendix, as well as on this page. I only provide a link to sites that not only give helpful information, but give a path forward (Hopefully the link remains up-to-date.). There are articles that explain steps to get help, but they never provide a starting point, it's like arguing of Facebook, pointless. These two links give both. I'm sure there are others but I hope that if you believe yourself to be, or know you are an abuser that you truly want to have a better, stronger, relationship with yourself and those in your life, I urge you to check these out. There is no shame in this. You are a bigger person for it. It takes work though, expect that.

Love is Respect.org The National Domestic Violence HOTLINE - Help For Abusive Partners

June 5

Take it upon yourself to baby-proof nature.

Grizzly Adams

NOT gonna happen. Although here are a few stories of people who tried. Apparently, you can break the law by doing so. In Utah, Goblin Valley (cool name. Better than Troll Gorge.) there were a few boy scout leaders, who are no longer affiliated with the group. They toppled an ancient Hoodoo stone outcropping, or up-cropping. (I don't know what you call it.) It looks like a mushroom made out of stone. Anyway, they pushed it over because they thought it looked hazardous. They thought it could easily fall on a passerby person/kid. Maybe they were right, but they were charged with a felony for pushing over a rock. Not knowing the law is not a defense. So, you might want to read up before you go places, or don't knock stuff over that's not yours. Apparently, this includes rock formations that are outside. You have been warned. On the flip side, and I don't mean to pick on them. I feel sorry for them. But you shouldn't knock stuff over that's not yours, I guess that applies to nature as well. Tell that to the oil and logging companies. Am I right?

Another group was at Yellowstone, (where Ol'Yeller is you know, nope maybe that's Old Faithful.) they were caught walking across a geothermal feature. Uhh, which I think means 'hot as hell water spot covered in places by some layer of earth'. The spot could reach up to 200 degrees. Crazy hot. But when you got to be on YouTube, you got to be on YouTube. You know?

There are a lot of other stories out there. It's not like these people are alone in not thinking things through. Throughout time we've had people who actually intended harm, grave robbers, tomb raiders (I love that game, the newer one. Uncharted. Awesome stuff.) pirates… actual pirates, man. I think we can safely say we still have all of those, kinda strange to think about.

Anyway, be kind to nature. Don't be stupid out there. I'm sure nature will survive, but if you're not thinking things through you might risk jail time for 15 minutes of fame.

June 6

Forget learning to grocery shop. Eat out. Forever.

—

GROCERY shopping. It's so hard. It's like, laundry, or cleaning your room. It's easier to eat out. Well it might be time to think about changing that attitude. On average a family I hear spends 600 dollars a month on food. I honestly don't know what they could be buying, but that's what the articles are saying. I spend around 200 to 250 on food a month. No, no I am not skinny as a rail. I'm also pretty regimented right now on this diet I'm trying. It's the 'I don't have enough money for that' diet. 600 dollars! Wow, must be nice.

I'm sure children eat a big amount of that up though. I also don't know how much that is in groceries either. I do know that when I was younger, I would eat out all the time. I had money and not a lot of overhead (parents helped out a lot I'll say) so I could go out all the time. I didn't really learn about budgeting until my loans for college came due.

Not only can you save money grocery shopping, but if you're careful you might even be able to eat healthier too. See, I'm doing you a favor. (Or giving you a tool... one of those.)

Honestly how much do you eat out? It might not be as much as it used to. It's getting more expensive nowadays. I wish I could figure out why...

The point is, budgeting. If you can cook at home maybe you should. So, you say you don't want to cook every day? Neither do I. Make something in the crockpot. If you make a double portion (I don't know how many members there are in your household, but double it.) then you make at least enough for two separate meals. Two days down and only one day of cooking. You can of course do this for more meals. I tend to cook on Sundays to get me through Wednesday.

When I do a little planning, I can make more food in the same amount of time as it would take to cook one meal. I think it helps to see it this way when comparing the ease of eating out to the chore of cooking all the time. The answer is don't cook all the time, cook more some of the time.

The reason I took time on this is, sometimes things that might seem easy don't occur to others. I myself found this out by searching online. I kinda wish someone would have pointed out how easy, cheaper and fun it could be to budget and cook! (I fear may be getting old.)

June 7

Rest on your laurels.

—

White Star Line

YOU just completed a huge task! Congratulations! You deserve a break. Maybe you actually do. How long would you say, exactly? The issue isn't with stopping and smelling the roses, or tiptoeing through the tulips, or some other fancy flower that you always hear lotus eaters spouting. (That's some mighty fine word play, might fine.)

No, I think that you should stand back and look at what you accomplished. Just don't stand back too long, or you might fall over on the couch. Ruts are hard to get out of. Once I was stuck in a rut, then a Land Rover came and pulled me out. Just saying.

Sometimes we need help. When is the last time you felt that you did something worthwhile? What about outside of your job, or providing for your family? Something for you, or for someone else perhaps? A new project. When was the last project? Do you remember what it was like to do something, perhaps with a group, or even alone and go from beginning to end?

Perhaps it's not important. If you're fine resting on your laurels, by all means, have at it. Much of the world does. Some even think their kind words are enough to rest on.

I'm all for rest. Love it, believe people need it. I also know there are those out there who are not resting because they can't, or they are lying in a hospital bed, or an alleyway. Perhaps outside, in a foreign country, or a war zone.

Resting helps us re-energize so that we can get back up and do more. Even if it's not helping and it's just going through our day. That takes rest.

All I know is, I'm tired of resting.

What about you?

June 8

Don't make a difference today.
—

I think I'm giving some good counter points to these pieces of advice we hear others say or simply thoughts floating around in our heads. The fact is, it's hard sometimes to make a difference. Do I make a difference, everyday? I suppose you could say the closer my writing gets to done the more potentially could be changed. Or each day I write gets closer to the finished product, that you're reading now. I guess that could be seen as a difference. Doesn't seem like that though. When we say to ourselves, "I'm going to make a difference, or I'm going to do something to support this cause!" we mean that we're going to take some sort of action that we probably don't normally take. Giving money to an organization, or helping out in a food pantry or handing out food at a salvation army. These are the things that make a difference. You might not do these things every day.

Me neither. I don't have time. Bills and work and rest required get in the way. I don't know how to help all the time either. It's too much work to always be 'on' you know? Certainly. But is that the only way to make a difference. If you're helping someone else? I say "Not at all!" Maybe it's a small difference. How do you feel about yourself? Do you feel good? I hope you do, you should. I already explained that you're special, even if you haven't done anything yet, you have the potential to do great things. How to grocery shop, how not to use your 'fit in' face. Maybe you need to make a difference for yourself today.

Maybe making a difference everyday doesn't have to be a huge event. Maybe great things aren't always huge. Maybe its picking up a book you never have time to read. Maybe playing catch with your kids after work. Stopping by the store on the way home to pick up flowers for your wife. Having a 'game night' instead of eating around the tv. Maybe having a family discussion about a summer vacation to somewhere, one that you'll really go on. Maybe just listening to your teenage daughter talk about her day. These little things make differences.

Sometimes the little things help us get ready for the big things. They build us up. Allow us to climb higher. So maybe the difference you make today is small, but what if that difference allows you to influence and create change through a smile and small conversation. What if that's really all it took?

Dare you to find out how much difference you make if you just try these little things. Worry about making a difference with the big things tomorrow.

June 9

Have 'awesome life changing' conversations under the influence, then forget what they were about.

—

WE'VE all done this. Or I suppose a few of you haven't. Good for you! Keep on keeping on. For the rest of us I'm sure that you've smoked some weed and you and your friend had this awesome, awe inspiring conversation and if you just could remember it, or in my case decipher the ranting scribbles, we would be so much better off. Some of us might even be millionaires!

So, I think we've established the fact, we can't have conversations that are world changing, and life altering when we're under the influence. However, we can talk more. That's saying something.

I know I'm not a talker. That's really not true. I say that a lot. I am even somewhat stoic and reserved at times. I'm serious about things. Quiet even, but I can talk. Sometimes I don't want to though, or I'm fine with silence more than others. If I can write a 360+ page book, I got some stuff to say. At least that's my thoughts on it. I used to think I wasn't a talker. People told me I wasn't. People still tell me that. I think they're wrong. I think it affected me, maybe in a negative way, maybe in a positive way.

I used to think I needed to be cool. The best way to be cool is to be quiet. As soon as you talk, people find out you're not that cool. Sometimes they find out you're stupid. I hate it when I'm stupid. Somewhere along the way (albeit, I still want to be smart.) I stopped caring so much about being cool and quiet. Now I don't go up to every person I meet and start an in-depth conversation about what I had for breakfast. (Now I'll totally do that on Facebook. It's almost etiquette after all, right? People gotta know what I eat and when I'm watching something.)

So, I don't think I need to be under the influence to be able to talk with people anymore, and I'm pretty sure I don't enjoy talking to people under the influence, when I'm not. I do think it gives us a feeling of ease. That's understandable, but once I figured out that I don't need to care so much about how others perceive me I have been able to start more conversations without it. Once you know people, for the most part, are friendly when you say "Hi" or even something odd like "How was your day today?" When you're in the elevator across from them, it gets easier to do it more and more. Hey, who knows, you might not even need drugs or alcohol.

June 10

Slide down the escalator.

—

Rain Man

RAIN man always did love sliding down the escalator. Remember that. That was a good scene. It showed us that he could be humorous even in a somewhat dreary scenario. It gave the audience a comedic break from the harder to watch scenes. It was a way to let loose.

Maybe sliding down an escalator isn't the thing to do. It's not safe nowadays with those circle knobs sticking out of the center lane after all. So, while this is some terrible advice that Hollywood gave us. (I mean, no one should take that risk.) It is perhaps something we've thought about. Maybe it's not an escalator, but maybe it's something else. Perhaps letting loose, or giving up when what we need to do is stay on course. Stand tall with your hands at your sides and wait until the escalator gets there. We shouldn't whoop and say look at this and slide down the center line like a surfer. Don't follow Dustin Hoffman's lead and throw danger to the wind. Stand still and ride it down. Slowly. Safely. Calmly. Sometimes that's how we need to approach things in life. If someone's built an escalator, there are really only two ways to ride it. Don't do it like Dustin. Follow the rules.

On second thought, I think that's wrong. I think I was confusing Rain man with Roger from Dawn of the Dead. My bad. Rain man. Sheesh. Yea, Rogers had zombies all around him. The world was over or ending. Never mind all that. If you have zombies chasing you, slide down the escalator.

That might be smart advice then. Depends on how close the zombies are.

June 11

Don't go to Paris.

—

No one. Ever.

TRAVELING is for young people and rich people, or retired people if you're lucky to save enough. It's too much to think about planning a trip like that. The cost is too high. We'll just visit the relatives in the next state. I hear you. I figured I'd take some time to break down some vacation costs. These will be relative to the current (2018) year, but you can extrapolate.

Say you have 4 people, two adults and two kids. I found airfare to Rome for about 800 big ones. That's per person, so 3,300. If you only really like one of your children, you could take them and it would drop the price, or leave the kids at home for two weeks with grandma and grandpa. It's not a bad idea, they need time with each other. It helps roundness or something. Either way grandparents, if they're good grandparents, and good kids they all will benefit from the time.

I found a place in Rome that has a condo for rent for 1,500 a week. That's another 3,000 there. If you get a condo chances are you can buy food and cook it yourself. This could afford you getting by on about $600 dollars for two weeks and 4 people, if you cooked yourself.

This gives you a total of about 7,000 for 4 people and two weeks in Rome. Course you also need some spending money. I'd say it looks like many of the sites and attractions are free for Rome, but I've seen guided half-day tours for the Colosseum for 4 people around 250 bucks, but it only costs 15 per person to go in and they have electronic guides for an extra 7. If you go with the electronics and free attractions such as the Vatican (the Sistine Chapel and museums costs about 17 dollars but are combine), there's also many other sites, that's a pretty good deal.

Let's assume you go to one thing every day. Trust me you could spend days at just one of these sites. That's 4 x 20 x 12 ~ 1000, I'd say add an extra 500 to be safe. (I consider two days travel and you wouldn't spend money on attractions.)

This means you're up to about 8,500 dollars. That's 4 people for 2 weeks. It's not a small chunk of change, but if you have kids, or don't, something in Europe, or another country might be worth saving some money to go check out. So, a Europe vacation isn't as cheap, it costs about 4,000 less to go on a vacation in the states according to AmEx. Maybe save up one year and go on a two-week super vacation with your family. Memories are priceless. But budget for it. Because paying off loans forever causes stress. It doesn't have to be Rome, but give it some thought. I'm sure there's somewhere you'd like to go. Plan it, save for it, then go.

June 12

"You're gonna go out, you're gonna start a fight with a total stranger, you're gonna start a fight, and lose."

—

Tyler Durden, Chuck Palahniuk

LOVED this movie. Fight Club. Parents took me to see it. I forget how old I was. Older than 8. What I came to dislike about the movie was it had a bent (I feel) towards the existential (I mentioned this already), which I feel is pointless. I'm not sure that's what the author was going for. See existentialism/nihilism is not really a destination. Some people stop there, because their tired of trying, I guess. I don't believe that Friedrich Heinrich Jacobi or Friedrich Nietzsche or Soren Kierkegaard were for Nihilism, even though people equate them with the idea. It means nothing, promotes nothing. If you fancy yourself a Nihilist, I'm not sure you can even defend your view point. What would be the point?

That being said I think the book Fight Club does have a point. We are not our things. I touched on this earlier. Going out and fighting to feel alive isn't a solution to how we fit into society today. You can go out and fight, but it won't make you feel alive, it'll just make you feel pain. I believe the book does touch on breaking down barriers, even in a 'terroristy' sort of way. (Given the fact that terrorist wasn't really a buzz word in 1996 when the book came out.)

It attempts, I believe to change the status quo. Did it do that? You still buy stuff you don't need, and try to be someone you're not? Then no, I don't think it did. I applaud it for effort though. I think he was trying to get guys to start acting like guys, not being pushed around or oh hum about. I don't agree with the idea he had of what men do, but the movie was 'fun' anyway.

There are some who have taken this cause to heart however. Perhaps in a more constructive way, depending on your viewpoint. Building a camaraderie of sorts and leaning on each other in hard times. They are more than a support group, they are a family and one that might be teaching men how to be. They call themselves Fight-Club414. Maybe it's something to look into. I linked it in the appendix.

June 13

That's just who you are take it or leave it.

WHAT does this advice mean? You've heard it on commercials and in magazines, from various people. It's true right? You are just who you are. People should accept you It's not really what the 'advice' says though, is it? This is a statement. What it really sounds like to others, if you were to be so bold and say it to someone is this. "That's just who I am, take it or leave it." It means deal with a present attitude or get lost. It's very friendly. I get it, we're independent. We don't need others. We don't actually care. That's what I hear when someone says this. I am who I am, and I don't care if you like it or not, deal with it.

Now, I agree with sections of this advice. I think we should know who we are. I think we should act, and speak about things we know about. I know we fall short of this, we get caught up in drama from time to time. I believe we should say what we mean and mean what we say. If you say you are doing this, or mean that. I want to take you at your word. Although, sometimes I find our words aren't good enough and they don't reflect our actions.

There should be respect. Let me say, I don't want to tolerate you, I don't want you to tolerate me. When I'm outside camping, I tolerate the mosquito that sucks my blood, I tolerate that my car needs fixed. I tolerate that my parents are older and won't live forever. I tolerate a lot. I don't want to have to tolerate you. I want to be able to respect you. I want you to be able to respect me. If you disrespect others, how can I respect you?

When I hear this phrase, it doesn't have a tone of respect. It's about you. It's not about us. You need this. It's your way, or the highway. If you're not with us. See a pattern, I do. It's subtle, like a slope into white water. It's not like that a bridge or cliff your mother warned you about.

Maybe it is your way or the highway. Then say that. Mean it, or don't say it at all. I'm not saying you can't take stuff back that you say in a moment of selfishness. If you said something you didn't mean, by all means take it back, but don't flippantly go around saying things you don't, or that you're not wholehearted about. It's confusing, and we don't need any more confusion in this world.

June 14

Life's a party. Live it up.

SORRY, (Not really sorry. I don't know why people say that in the condescending way. It's so rude.) Life isn't a party. Don't get me wrong, there are times for fun and excitement in life. There are so many things to do in this world. (I mean the good things, you have that list, right?) You won't even have time for all of them. But life isn't a party. I had parties, I went to parties. They were great.

Fun, drama. Okay so maybe life is kinda like a party. You can get your heart broken, or beat up, or die at a party. But I'm going to stick to the whitewash Hollywood teen party image for this write up.

People have fun at parties. Drink, fight, breakup, get together. Then at the end, everyone goes home and rests. Good times, good food. That's a party.

Life has parties, but once again it isn't a party. I feel like I could use a Venn-Diagram or the Socrates' method here. But I won't.

I love homeostasis. Status quo. Get up, work, come home, write, relax, eat, sleep, repeat. I have fun, not 'party' fun. Maybe party fun, I haven't been to a party in a long time. Been to a few clubs. They're loud. Anyway. I enjoy myself.

One thing that seems to weigh on my mind, is that I have it pretty good. I don't have a lot, but I got some. Others, they don't have some. They live under a bridge (different bridge then the trolls, most of them anyway). They don't have a bed, or know where their food is coming from. That thought always seems to come back to me. I don't do enough, I can't really. There's no possible way. So, I'm trying to do something here. Hopefully it will start with this book.

Life's not a party. At parties, nobody is starving, nobody is homeless, nobody is without friends. Life's not a party. If you want to live it up, find someone who isn't and find a way to help.

Besides, we know about real parties. (Full circle.) At real parties, there are cliques, real parties have bullies, drugs, overdoses. At real parties people give you roofies, or 'rapies' (if you've seen the movie 'the Hangover'). Real parties have people who don't care about you, or anyone else. So maybe life is like a real party, I just know I'd rather be helping drive someone home who was sick of the party, than waking up the next day with a hangover, possibly one I could never get rid of. (That's a metaphor for, like bad stuff in life. Just in case I needed to make that clearer.) Take time to have fun, but remember the people who aren't at the party, maybe invite them next time. By 'invite' I mean give a meal or help find a job or buy a Christmas gift. Maybe it does mean to invite them to a party though. I'll let you decide. :)

June 15

Be a 'yes' (wo)man.

Corporate Ladder

CLIMB that thing. That's what it's all about. Or just work hard enough not to be noticed and hope you don't get fired. Either way I think the above applies. Suck ass, it's how you get ahead. Not by trying hard. Not by showing your worth. This isn't entirely true. There are many, many of us out there that train, and work and learn new things. It's only some of us who don't, or hopefully less than the many. I can't be sure. I don't know where I put my statistics on that one.

Can't complain about this too much. I'm a writer. So, I sit in a room and write. Sometimes I interact with people. Co-workers, usually talk to them over the phone for an hour or so. Not too many board meetings in my gig, ya know. But it does sting when you see someone who doesn't really 'get it' and climbs the ladder over top of you. (I'm not talking about me. I'm still in line to get to the ladder.)

I'd say in these cases, the brown nosers. They have it made. They climb the ladder and get more than those who don't. It's easy to do. Just suck up, just make sure you find the right one to suck up to, or you might actually end up sucking something. I can't say it's easier than learning, just different.

It makes the corporate structure of a business weaker. In my opinion. I'm sure there are plenty of VP's out there that pull their weight in gold. Gold has some intrinsic value (unlike bit coins or dollars). But I'm sure there are more that just pull their gold simply because they're a 'yes ma'am' or 'yes sir' kinda person.

Maybe I'm wrong, it's not like I can know, right? Are you just a 'yes 'em' or are you providing value?

I hope so, if not, why not? Are you focusing your gifts somewhere else, or are you just after things?

No time like the present to make a difference.

June 16

Don't walk alone at night.

WHAT'S wrong with this? "You think I can't take care of myself?" Perhaps. It's more than that though. It's not terrible advice. You should watch out for creepers in the night, but you also have to watch out for 'em in the day and maybe at home. How could this be bad advice, it's a fear thing.

I don't think fear is very helpful. I'm not saying jump off the bridge to get over your fear. I'd say, don't jump off the bridge 'cause you might die. But I don't think that means I'm afraid of jumping off the bridge or dying. I just think it means I don't think it's smart. That's risk for what reason? Maybe you have a 'sensation seeking' personality trait. I wish I had that just a little bit. But I'm comfortable without it just as well.

I don't see points in taking risks, unless it's breaking the sound barrier or building something bigger, or somehow it might help more people if you succeed.

However, I don't see a point in living in fear either. In other countries they have to worry about being shot, or worse. Not knowing where your next meal might come from or if you 'eye' someone the wrong way. Those are reasonable things to be concerned for, but they shouldn't be feared. These are just true things in life, but their presence doesn't mean you fear them to the point of not living your life. (Yes, I understand in a war-torn country this statement might be offensive or wrong. Context is key after all. That's one of the take-aways.)

What's fear? An unpleasant emotion caused by the belief that someone or something is dangerous, likely to cause pain, or a threat.

It's an emotion. Remember when I mentioned leaning to stoicism. This is an emotion that might have been helpful, but it has created a psychosis for some. We should teach our children to take notice of things, not to fear them. Fear is a tool stupid people use, i.e. terrorist, dictators, aggressors really. If you can't teach, just use fear, then you don't have to explain. Explaining is hard. Explaining creates understanding. Understanding takes time.

Both results help us to not walk alone at night, but in understanding we become equipped to take action instead of simply cowering. In understanding we can walk alone, keep an eye out. Take defense courses. Maybe that won't help from being attacked, but you can't live in fear. You don't live that way. You die that way. If only there was a way not to live in fear of the things in the world, and people actually shared it? That would be something wouldn't it.

June 17

Bigger is better.

School Stopper, "Intern, BP" Paul

BIGGER is best. Just that little bit more. We see this in everything. A model of car has a different type, just a little bit more horsepower, or a few extra miles per gallon. A toy doesn't just have one thing any more, but a whole world to purchase for just that little bit more. For just a little more, you can have this and this!

I remember back in the day, transformers had a few toys you had to buy to make the Devastator, or the camera Reflector! (You had to mail in to get that one). I thought those were expensive and a lot of work. Nowadays it's even better! Everything is connected into little universes!

If you buy something, there's an app for that. You can keep track of all your items. They really needed to come out with an app for comics back in the day. I could have used that. Now, not so much, but back then. I had a lot of comics.

Anyway, bigger is where it's at. More. I know it's hard not to want the next best thing, but I'm kinda tired of the next best thing coming out as soon as I bought the last best thing. I don't think when they built this vehicle called consumerism, they installed brakes.

I love all the things. I just can't buy them all, and I feel like I should, like it's something inside of me that's urging me on. I think I've been conditioned a little to think this way. I'm not trying to get all conspiracy like, it's just how our society reacts to the marketing. I know businesses have to make money. It's the way of the world, but I don't think I should always feel an urge not to get the 'lite' version and get the 'extra special limited-edition bingo bango thingy majig', or one of the three levels in between.

Just sell two things. Then I'll know I can afford the 'lite' thing and others can afford the 'extra special'. Giving me different levels just helps me step up to spending all my cash when I didn't want to spend more than 20 dollars. I wonder what would happen if companies made less options. Why do we have so many options? I only need two. I'm only gonna buy one anyway, the cheap one. Rich people will buy the extra special one.

That's how America is though. Bigger is better, cars with bigger wheels (and I understand there are more variables than size, although 'size matters', right?), while they tend to not help with fuel economy, there are a lot of huge tired vehicles around. Why because they believe bigger is better. I don't know who told them this, but it's a lie.

There might be a few things that are better bigger. Like big macs, but I'm not talking about those. We don't need to buy the next level up. Course maybe it's just me who thinks this way.

June 18

Never compromise.
-
Me

SOME can see this is just stupid, others might say it's not. I don't think it is, entirely. But it's a relative world. If you know you're right, if what you are doing is correct and the best way to do something, why should you allow another obsolete idea into the mix. It would just weaken the project. That could be true.

There are times when no compromise and no quarter can or should be given. This really begs the question "How do you know you're right?" How do you know? Experience, did someone else with experience tell you, or write it in a book? You just know? Or is it deeper than that? Is it that you know you're right, or that you can't allow someone else to be? Or perhaps your pride is at stake?

What's the issue we're talking about? Well if it's never compromising it should be a big one, right? Not who the best sports team is, or never letting anyone else drive your car even when you're too tired to. It should be big. Really, not just big to you. It should be an issue of weight. What's that mean?

Well, if you compromise. Let's say in a marriage it's for the better. It's to nurture and create an environment of harmony or growth. In marriage, compromise would seem like something to do at times. Pride does not come before love. It shouldn't even be in the same room.

So, we still need to find something that we should never compromise on. So compromising means changing your opinion, or actions on a matter. Webster says 'lower than desirable'. That's right, isn't it? For both sides, regardless of the stance.

So, to compromise requires change. If there's no change, there is no compromise. If compromising means changing 'our' opinion or 'our' actions, how often do we truly compromise? I say not that much.

We as individuals balance our lives out, and if we accept a lower than desirable outcome somewhere, someone else we know will accept something that lowers their desirable outcome and our lives will remain 'balanced'. If the above is true, what about below?

Values. Can we compromise these? Remember we have to change our opinion, or action to compromise. To get someone else to compromise and change their action or opinion they have to be persuaded. Can you honestly say you've persuaded someone? How do you know? Do they talk about it differently now? Did it change their life? Did you do it on Facebook? What was the goal?

I think this advice is easy to take. I think it's easy never to compromise in this world. We just don't listen to each other. We talk a lot. If no one brings valid points to the discussion, or with research, those points are found wanting, how can we trust someone's position? Whose word do we take? Our parents word? Joe Facebook's word? Why should we take anyone's word at all? (Societal breakdown is why. We would cease to function.)

Point? I'm not sure that people have changed my opinion (but rarely) during an argument to change my opinion. That's usually when I'm head strong and donkey Kong. It's only in quiet moments that I find my opinions are truly formed, where my actions really take place. We feel this advice at a time when we are already on guard, but when our actions and opinions truly form this advice is a ghost.

So, if this feeling is nowhere in sight when we are building our foundations of what we stand for, how is it so prevalent during an argument against those values? Where does the standard in those values come from?

I'll tell ya. We care about those values. We might live based on them. How did we learn them though? Did we question these values as we went, or accept them willfully? If we excepted those values willfully without question, why would we see others as any different?

Final thought. Know what you stand for. If you believe in something, understand why. That means research, that means time and action in your life. Be willing to listen to others. Arguments with clever soundbites rarely change minds. Take your pride out of the room. Are the values you defend supported? Could you support them in an argument, properly? If not, then stop talking. I'd rather know what you ate for breakfast this morning. It would be more useful to me than your regurgitated words.

If you want to change people's minds know what you stand for, be able to defend it through research that you did. Actually, that will only allow you to come across as knowledgeable. If you want to create understanding don't only talk about what you believe, show it in your actions.

June 19

Be obsessed.

Ananke

IT'S good to have hobbies. But obsessed? I'm not obsessed with Star Wars simply because I can tell you that the Jedi first split into two factions on a world called Tython and the race of Sith were conquered by 'Dark Jedi' leading to their Empire, and before that were given gifts of the force by the Infinite Empire. But Disney changed all that. That's merely stuff of legend.

I'm not obsessed because I can tell you that the first world series was in 1903 won by the Boston Americans who became the Boston Red Sox later on.

Those things don't make me obsessed, but I think it's easy to do. I'm not as versed in Star Wars and baseball as an American should be, but I enjoy them both.

Now we create universes in games. We create Hollywood icons. Causes. YouTube channels and products. There are a lot of things we could obsess about. Cool things.

I bring it up because we know to be obsessed is a bad thing. We know that. We shouldn't obsess. I think we do and don't realize it.

I'm not trying to pick on our entertainment, but I'm gonna. Television. I'm obsessed with that, watch it every chance I get. Couch. I smash couch every chance I get. I think if I could be a sloth. I might consider it. My power animal could be a Koala (Because they sleep more.) I need to check my phone. Someone might have liked something that I like. It's easy to be obsessed. Is it technology's fault? I don't think so. I think we don't fully understand how to properly use it. We've been granted all of this tech and it keeps getting better, but no one has shown us how to integrate it into our lives so that we function. Now I function just fine, I'm sure you do to but as a society, I think we may have some points to work on.

We tend to waste free time in the process of using all this technology. Time that we could use for better and bigger purposes.

But to pretend that we aren't obsessed because we aren't like Ali Larter in 'Obsessed', Robert DeNiro in 'The Fan', or Michael Douglas in 'Falling Down' then maybe we should take another look.

If you're like me and want to bicker over the meaning of words lets go with these three characters instead. Robert Downy Jr. in 'Less than Zero', Michael Keaton in 'Clean and Sober' or Mr. Washington in 'Flight'. Obsess, addicted. Whatever.

It has become quite easy to be obsessed, over work (Family Man), Drugs (My Own Private Idaho), games (Wreck-it Ralph...or maybe Ready Player One). In this day and age, you need to be careful that you're not already obsessed. Maybe it's the 'good' kind though, maybe its health snacks and weights for you. Still obsession. Try rounding yourself out, every once in a while. I say this to you as I sit typing, looking into the techno void.

June 20

You can take it with you.

WE store, we build for retirement. We gather for the next day. We have to really. We have to plan for the future. We are humans, heck even squirrels gather nuts. I can't remember if they remember where all the nuts are though. That's how trees are made.

Those are true things. We need to plan for the future, but how much do we really need? If I buy a Maserati GranTurismo for 130k is this something I need? I keep going back to the needs of others. I'd love a fancy BMW i8 (remember), but the fact is I can't take it with me, and while driving it would put a smile on my face. If I bought a Hyundai Sonata, I'd have 100k to spend on children, or a child and that money might help their situation. I'm not saying it would make everything better, but I think we need to try something. (Not even try something different, there are people trying things all the time.) We, as individual people I mean. We need to stop looking at others to lead the way. They won't. They're waiting on you to lead the way. No one will step up first. I repeat, no one. But maybe you can.

We can't take it with us, but we can make a difference. That difference can continue on after us. Instead of leaving a sweet ride for some other rich guy to buy, what if we could leave, just one life changed for the better. Hey let's ramp it up, what if we could change just two.

What if it were possible to help just two people in your life. What if those people helped two people? And those? And those?

I wish it were true. Could it really be? I hope.

Is it too hard to help two people? To teach them, or support them, share what you have, make time for them, even when you have none to give.

I'll tell ya, we can't take it with us. We leave stuff behind, everything. What kind of stuff are you going to leave behind?

Fancy cars and diamond rings, or an opportunity for someone to leave an opportunity of their own?

That's a true gift right there. It's better than a 130k car, I tell you that much. Again, what is it that you will leave behind?

June 21

If it feels good, do it.

NO ONE can tell me what to do! I will do what I like, and apart from societal rules I'm required to abide by (that's a fun bunny trail, if ever there was one!), I'll do what I want, when I want.

Okay buddy, fair enough. I would say that if people don't speak into your life and your activities, maybe they just don't care about you. Maybe that's what you want. People not to truly care.

People don't like to be told what to do. It's not fun. It wasn't when I was told I had to clean my room and I decided that I was going to run away from home.

My mom helped me pack. I got a bookbag and some toys. I think she made me a sandwich as well. I started walking away. She let me walk away. I kept turning around. Think I got to the stream in the woods before I decided that I kinda wanted to play in my room again, but was still disappointed that a bigger fuss wasn't made.

I got what I wanted though. I ran away. But was that really what I wanted. It wasn't that I couldn't clean my room, I'd done it hundreds of times before. It was kinda nice having a cleaned room, it even made me feel good after. I didn't want to at the time. It was too much for me to handle. I wanted to do what felt good now. Turns out, running away didn't produce the 'feels' I thought it would. I didn't even have a room to clean down by the stream. I liked my room, it felt good. It was safe. The wind wasn't there. I just didn't want to clean it at that moment in time.

I'm not saying this is terrible advice at face value without context. I'm saying it's terrible advice through and through regardless of context. It's incomplete. If you think about it. If you can realize what good is to you, and for you it changes the advice entirely, I think it's much better advice than doing what 'feels' good at the time. It would be quite different if we understood what 'good' was. I'm sure both groups have lists for this though. Good luck. Just a note as you go off in the wild world. If harm is in the goal it's not the good group.

Trouble is, we use this advice at Woodstock and parties. What feels good doesn't harm someone. It doesn't harm you. If it does it's not good is it? And its masking something, hiding some hurt.

Just something to think about. Unless you look at the actual context, simply feeling good, it's not helpful. I feel it's good to say here, we've lost a lot of context in this day and age. Maybe if we examine and research what good actually means, we might find this lost concept once more.

Or take Hunter S. Thompson's advice on the matter and forget the whole thing.

"Sex, drugs, and insanity have always worked for me, but I wouldn't recommend them for everyone." - Hunter S. Thompson

June 22

Nice guys/girls finish last.

Me

I honestly don't know if this true or not. I haven't finished yet. I'll try and let you know if I come in last place. (I'll leave a note for my 'grave stone writer'. I don't know what their title is. Ghost writer? No, that's not right.).

Self-fulfilling, I think. What are you finishing last in? Mating? Have you taken a look around at some couples? I think I'll take last place if some of these guys are in first. If all the nice guys and nice girls are finishing last. Maybe it's time we get up and find a new race?

That's what I say. How important is it to finish whatever race you think you're in? I'm not trying to be dark here. To say that I would never want children, that would a little white lie. But the truth is I'm quiet, and reserved. I won't start talking to you, even if I'd like to, unless I can think of something to say in the moment. If you gave me an hour, I think I could write something up. I'm a nice guy. Does this mean I'm gonna finish last? Why's it gotta be hard? Why do girls like bad boys? Don't feel sorry for me though, there is also a flip side to this coin.

I have things I want to do. I want to finish this book. I want to travel. I'd like to write a novel. I have some things I'd like to study. I have movies I want to see and books I want to read. Causes I want to support, cancers I want to bring down. People I want to free. I don't think I'll finish last in these races.

So back to the race, I'm gun shy too, what can I say. I'm not saying I want to be alone, but I also remember what my relationships were like. I see people's relationships. I'm not sure that's much incentive for me to start looking for one. People fight a lot, needlessly too. Maybe it's something you really want though. I say go for it. Get out there. Join a group, a social group. Not like the ones on Facebook. I know Mark Z. would agree you should go out.

I'm not so much concerned about that. I think if it happens, it happens. I know I won't be meeting anyone in a bar anytime soon, but I don't think that's my race. Maybe I'll finish last there, but maybe it's a triathlon and I can finish first in a different section. Now all I have to do is learn to swim and ride a bike. Great.

What I'm talking about here is maybe you need a new race, you agree? What trophy are you trying to get anyway? I'll warn ya, the prize probably looks different up close.

Also, for the record, It's really a blatant lie. Nice girls/guys finish first all the time, but you gotta get out there, and take off your 'fit in' face and smile.

June 23

Let it slide.

HOT button issue! Should we, or shouldn't we? Maybe it depends on context. If only we had context. Since we don't, let's just throw some stuff at the wall and see if it sticks. That's how most of us debate anyway.

Little things. Your brother takes the last can of 'not so good for you, but marketed as the cool kid drink so you have to have it' soda. Or perhaps an off-color comment from a friend. I think the honest truth is some people would find that a bigger deal than others, so maybe it's a 'big thing'.

What's small to you? I think the truth of the matter is that a lot of things are 'small' to us. If they weren't small infractions, we wouldn't let them slide, right?

Sadly, I think this post will be darker than lighter. I'm not trying to bring you down though. Just make you think about it, for at least a few seconds. That's all we really get is a few seconds to influence or explain. Everyone has ADHD now. I'm not trying to be funny, I think our attention spans have decreased. Not to say everyone falls under this category.

Take me for example. I watch the news. I see people protesting this or that. I see good causes and bad ones. I see commercials for supporting animals and people. Sometimes it feels that it's all I have time for. I'm an observer. It's not to say I disagree or agree with different things, but if I don't take action, how much outrage or support do I actually have or give?

I would say many of us fall into this category. Sliders. Now there are more outspoken people that would condemn what I just said. If I truly believe in something, shouldn't that be made manifest in my life and actions? I agree. It should. I'm trying to get started with this book as a matter of fact. You could say I'm slow to pick things up. I've been busy working.

I hope this writing will help you examine your life. I'm not saying pick up every because you come across and say you care about. We don't have time for everything. It's nigh impossible with our daily lives, but maybe there is something. One or two things that you might determine are things to stand for, research, or know about for a greater good? Something you believe is important enough not to let slide, something that you would research from all sides because it's so important. You see examples on your phones and TVs causes to take up and support. Take a minute to see if you care enough about an issue to try and do something about it besides observe, either for or against it. Everyone has different things in their lives they are passionate about. Perhaps it's difficult to join a cause you hear about, take a waiver. I'm not trying to put you down with the choices you've made up to this point. Just trying to point us all in a better direction.

June 24

The only way to the top is to climb over others.
—

THE only way to the top is through others, but it's not always over others. Sure, you can work really hard to get that promotion before Bob does. Maybe throw some people into the fire, if you do that, I have to ask, are you actually good at your job? Or are you the guy who cheated off me in science class? (Maybe that was me doing the cheating, forget I said anything...second thought keep reading.)

It's lonely at the top, if all you do is use others to get there. Maybe you're the smartest. Maybe you know what's what, and others don't. I'll accept that. So, does that make others dead weight? Or give you an opportunity to share what you know? Perhaps you don't want to, because you're scared, they will take that promotion over you. Perhaps you need the money, maybe you haven't been able to manage your money so well. Reminds me WARNING Rabbit trail! Did you know that they make drugs now with side-effects that give you an addiction to gambling? (That's a rant unto itself. Maybe they need to spend a little more time on these drugs, but it's not about helping, not really, in the board room, it's about money so let's get serious. Never gonna happen. Unless someone were to do something... any takers?)

Back to this. Sure, you can climb over others. You can maybe even make it to the top. It'll be lonely, maybe you don't need others. I think you do though. Remember it's not about things. Take Mark Zuckerberg for example. He just made news as Facebook has made changes that decrease the time people spend on the site. I know, it's still about money, right? But I see in that effort an example (small as it may be) of a man trying to support connection over potential profit. That's what it's about, connection. Even allowing third parties to have access to our information :) We all signed the contract no one takes time to read. Just saying.

I think the road to ruin is paved with money. Money provides comfort. If the purpose in your life is to acquire money and things, you might get those things. I ask again, are things what's important? Clearly the answer is no. But that's not how we behave. Things are important. I think our definition of 'things' needs reevaluated. It's too relative. It has no meaning outside of what you think it means, or what I think it means. And both of those thoughts could be on opposite ends of the scale.

I understand that this world makes it hard not to desire comfort. I wish we were all comfortable, but I feel that comfort in the end, leads to death. I know, I'm being a little Spartan. We strive for comfort, but if it's at the demise of those around us, then how can we be comfortable? Are we monsters? Or are we simply conforming to the world around us? Which phrasing makes you feel better?

If we were to support each other, in business and life, couldn't that lead to more possibilities? Am I a dreamer? It might be lonely at the top, but I don't see why it has to remain that way. We just have to get this advice out of our heads and trust a little more. (Just...:)) Good luck with that, right?

June 25

Party while you're young.

—

POPPYCOCK I say! Who came up with that stupid notion? Granted when you're young your body is in shape and you have more energy. Some things are easier, right? So, its good advice. Live it up and go on adventures when you're young.

Okay, they got me there. I can tell you I don't really feel like partying now. Not the way I used to anyway. Ragers, I think they called them. People jumping off roofs and hot tubs. Yea, I remember. Those were times. Or perhaps it's just trying something new, traveling, Europe maybe. Better to do it when you're young, right? By all means if you have the means, do it.

I don't think we have to stop though. Sure, maybe some things we can't do anymore. Maybe because we partied a little too hard when we were young. That sucks. So maybe partying when we were young, helped us not be able to party when we're older. I mean I'm sure I turned it up to 11 at times.

Now the only thing I have left is retirement, then maybe I'll get to travel more. Seems a little bleak to me. So, you're telling me that I have about 10 to 12 years on the front of my life to really 'party' and maybe if I'm lucky 10 to 20 to 'take it easy and relax'. Bullshit. I call Bullshit.

There's work in the middle. I'm doing it right now. I'm sure you are too, but I think we don't have to stop having fun. Granted I don't want to throw a rager anytime soon. I enjoy different things now. Rock climbing and canoeing (which none of my friends seems to have time for.) I enjoy remembering the things I do now. Not waking up at 1 o'clock with a hangover that seems to get worse with age.

I say maybe we should continue to party, I'm not suggesting a Beerfest. I mean find things you enjoy doing. If you have a family find something to do together. Often, not just once a year at Disney World, the most magical place on earth! Little things, big things. Be smart about it, don't blow all your money, but have fun. Don't waste your time on this big ball of a planet thinking about how much fun you'll have when you retire. Have fun now, today. Isn't there something, even if it's a small thing that you've always wanted to try or place you've wanted to go? Have fun today. Make it a priority and never stop.

June 26

Buy an island.

GROWING up I spent time on an island just about every summer. (No, my parents didn't own it.) It was a small island with shops and islander things. I grew up in the 80's and 90's so while the need to be 'connected' was there, it wasn't to the internet. I would actually look at people and hang out and make real conversations and stuff. Play video games at the arcade or at the camp grounds.

I loved the island. Things were so laid back. It wasn't like home where there was work to be done. It was nice, relaxing. That's what it would be like buying an island, right? If you could have your own.

That's what I thought at least. I looked into it once, of course it was not because I could ever afford it, simply out of curiosity. I remember reading an article about a couple who bought a private island. Good read, bad island. Mosquitoes, and getting water. Not to mention electricity. Also, no television, that may not be an issue with streaming and satellites now, but still. It sounded like a lot of work. I'd be curious if they still own the island and live there.

In my search I found some other interesting articles too. I put them in the appendix. Islands aren't cheap. Not that I needed to say that. There are surveys to do, and resources you might have to bring in.

Not to mention the solitude. This isn't like going into your room for a month and being alone. I mean like, you're basically on an island by yourself. You have to boat or take a plane to get to civilization. That means you have to afford a plane or boat as well. The cost really does start to add up.

And if you pick an island that's farther away, it will be cheaper but if you get sick, you'll have to travel that much more.

Oh, sure there are upsides. You get to tell your volleyball friend Wilson that you own an island in the middle of the ocean. Or you could buy an island with people already on it. Maybe just 97% of the island. That's what one guy did.

I'm just saying, there is a lot of overhead, and it might not be as cool as you think. Maybe just vacation on one that's populated. It might not actually get better than that.

June 27

Better get used to it.

THAT'S just how it is. It's the way of the machine. There's no stopping it. Nothing we can do. It's gonna happen. Maybe those are true for some things. It feels true for bigger things too though, doesn't it? At least at times. This is how the game is played.

It seeps into your being. Nothing we can do. It's the way things are. Resistance is Futile. But I can tell you that just like the Federation fights the Borg (Old time reference), we can fight this advice.

First off, it's not true. Everything changes. Time will change things, better or worse. If we do nothing, if we sit back and watch our screens. Complain and argue about how things need to change, but we don't take it as a call to action then yea. We better get used to it. Go with the flow, because you don't know how to swim upstream to change it.

I don't think we have to get used to things though. If we can make things better, if we have a feeling that we even care, shouldn't there be an obligation to do so? (Right, strong word 'obligation'. My bad. I can't tell you what to do.) I'm not trying to tell you 'what' to do. I'm not sure I feel an obligation to write this book. I just know that there are children out there that need help and perhaps with sales from this book I might be able to provide some of that help instead of just sitting around waiting for the next work day. That makes me kinda feel good about doing this. So, I'm not trying to tell you 'what' to do, but maybe how you might feel about it when you think on something that is near and dear to your heart. Have you made time for that thing today?

I think the only thing we have to get used to are things that we decide that we don't care to do anything about. If you don't care about something, admit it. Don't waste your breath trying to save face on something that doesn't concern you. Or maybe we just don't know what to do about it, but someone out there has to have an idea. Seek them out. If you feel that a cause is worthy, is it worthy enough for your time, or just your breath, maybe it's just something for others to handle?

I struggle with this. I don't do many things that I say I believe in. Sometimes I don't know how to approach an issue. That doesn't mean I'm going to accept what I don't do, or feel that I can't. I don't have to get used to something that is jarring or wrong. Unless I don't stand up for it, unless I sit down on the bleachers. It's at that point I better get used to it and watch the game play out.

So, I say, don't get used to it. If there's a cause you feel deeply for, fight for it, get in the game. If there is an injustice, speak up. Even if your wrong at least you've chosen a side.

June 28

Ignore the classics, stick with the new stuff.

WHO has time to read Jack London's 'The Sea Wolf' or Homer's writing. Perhaps Oscar Wilde's work. There are others. Many, and better and worse. Who has time when we have so many YouTube videos to watch? Those don't take as long either. Now vines. That was a good idea. It was only a few seconds long. (I'm not sure how long I spent watching millions of those videos, but I might have been able to read a book in that time.)

Busy, busy. We don't have spare time. Only 15 minute blocks nowadays. 30 minutes if you're doing it lazy-like, right? It's about doing more, not about finishing anything. Now I know what you're going to say. "Alex, maybe you don't finish things, but I do. Speak for yourself." I am speaking for myself, and the millions of others who feel this way about time.

One thing is for sure we have the world at our fingertips, but our focus is off. Or all over the place. There is just so much to do. So little time. No time for Jack or Oscar though. We need to create and work and have fun. When we read something its 140 characters. Or 280 now!

If you have some time, make some more. Try a read. Course if your reading this, I'm probably preaching to the choir, but maybe not. I used to read all the time when I was younger. Then came cell phones, I still read. Then came iPhone, Bluetooth, Facebook, myspace. I don't blame technology, it's just something I've noticed.

I need to move about more. I multitask (even though that's not really a thing humans do.) I have many different projects, rarely books. Granted I read every day, but only a small amount of my time is resting and reading. Little sound bites, short blogs.

It might be less for you, but I'm going to encourage you. Take some time to read an old novel, or history on something. It just might be more interesting than what the Kardashians are up to next. (This might be a dated reference, I'm kinda hoping it is.)

June 29

Dance... on a chair.

YouTube

DOUBLE dog dare ya. Joking. Don't do this. It's interesting to find that there are people that do, do this. I'm not talking about professional chair dancers now (I'm sure that's a thing.). I mean amateurs. Check it out.

There are so many videos on this. I mean fail videos. It's like there was an unstated stupid internet challenge (Don't do those, they're stupid.). You can spend minutes watching them, hours even.

Don't do it though, it's almost as bad as dancing on a chair. Remember what I said, try reading a novel. Think of it as gaining achievement points in the real life.

June 30

Sex is love.
—

SEX isn't love. Sometimes we mistake it for love. If we're lonely or alone sometimes we want to be held. Sex involves holding, to some degree. It requires a lot from someone. But it isn't love. Sometimes we confuse the two. Let's stay on the 'lighter' side of this for now.

In dating, people sometimes get involved quickly. They go out a few times and then how many ever dates later, they have sex. It's your body, your choice. But it's not love. I'm not talking to the people that know sex isn't love, or those who simply like sex. I'm talking with those who believe that sex is equivalent to love.

Good sex doesn't mean good love. They can go together. "Well," you say "Sex is an expression of love." That's one of the things that makes it confusing. If someone has sex with me, then they're showing me love. That's not true... at all. It's Bullshit.

We get confused about this though. I don't want to feel sad, or lonely. Sex gives me instantly, a feeling of 'love'. That's a lie. Sex is similar to a drug. I'm not trying to demonize sex in a relationship built on love. I'm talking about sex outside of that.

It might give us a high. A euphoria that will help us not feel a certain way, but it doesn't equate to love. It doesn't build bonds of commitment. It can make bonds stronger, but it doesn't create them in itself.

I'm not telling you, you can't have sex don't put me on a soap box. If you want to have sex, you will. I want you to know what sex isn't though. It doesn't keep someone from leaving, it won't make them stay longer, that impression fades. It won't fill a hole for you, at least not very long. It has qualities of a drug, but there are good things to it also. However, it is not love.

I don't know why we confuse this so easily, it's not that we don't understand. Of course, sex is not love. We know that. But do we? As a teenager I didn't really see a distinction.

Is it so important for us to have sex, to get to that level in a relationship? Don't get me wrong, sex is great. But it's not love, and it doesn't produce love. In our society it seems like it's more and more about sex. If you don't, you're strange, odd. What's wrong with you? Don't like sex?

In truth it seems more and more, just another thing that we run after, but like any drug it has side effects. Some are life changing. I guess it just depends what you want to do with your life, right?

July 1

Learn Sanskrit. Teach it to your coworkers, even if they don't ask. Interject in conversations at the water-cooler. That's how friends are made.

—

ABOUT 14,000 people in the world spoke Sanskrit back in 2001. That's not a lot. I couldn't find any statistics today. There are some historically and communication...ally significant uses. We have old text that need read, but on an average person's day-to-day, unless you're an average person in the one of the four Indian districts its spoken in, it's not going to help you much.

Of course, I wouldn't do that. Waste my time learning about something not even a few people care about in this world and focus on it so intently.

It's hard to say that in this day and age and actually mean it. Even now that statement sounds disingenuous. Truth is I just don't want to learn Sanskrit, it doesn't hold a 'fun' factor. For some people it might. I'm thankful for those people. It allows me to watch Netflix and at the same time not risk losing a piece of history. But I will never learn it, and if something happens to those other people, I wouldn't even know how to start translating if push came to shove. This is a rabbit hole topic going into the importance of what we do... I'll see about coming back to this in another edition, if this makes enough that is. I'm sure listening to someone talk about Sanskrit myself would be absolutely boring. I would have a hard time feigning interest, but listening to why they found it interesting would peak my curiosity. (That might be a good conversational approach.)

We all have interests, unless we're nihilists (They're not really supposed to, if they aren't careful, it could disprove something) then water-cooler conservationist wouldn't mean anything. So, we all have interest, and they're different. Sometimes boring, sometimes, like if it's something with entertainment value, it might have very little point outside of capturing interest. That doesn't mean pointless. Entertainment is very important, it helps us wind down, relax a little.

So, learn Sanskrit (or anything), share it with someone. We all have our Sanskrit, some people won't get what we're talking about, others will. I'm not recommending actual Sanskrit here, unless you run in those circles, but find something and share it. Someone might find it worthwhile to talk about it for 5 minutes. That's one way to start a conversation.

July 2

Wait till the last minute.

Starbucks

THIS is my go-to advice. 'Till the last minute'. It's not that I've intentionally done this, it's simply that life gets going and sometimes you forget the time. It's then we realize that the next day we have something due. Bring on the cram session!

Things fall through the cracks and then appear instantly once they're due. Happens all the time. I'm thankful that we can catch some of these, even if it means staying up till 3 a.m. to get them done for work or school.

For this little write up I've taken a look at some of the things to do to avoid this from happening so much, and what to be ready for when it does.

Thomas Frank's YouTube videos and blog, I think are pretty straight forward and to the point. We don't have time to waste here after all. Learning tips galore!

Plan things out. When you first know about an assignment or project take 10 minutes and write down dates and times you are going to use to go toward that project. That's it, then put the calendar away, know where it is. Get used to writing in a calendar or scheduler. When that time comes devote some effort to the project.

The first 10 minutes of starting a project, or starting it back up again are the hardest. This is where focus is important. Make sure you have a 'work area' away from distractions. Find a place. Libraries work, even if you're no longer a student. Point A is sitting down and looking at the work, Point B is when you pick up a sort of rhythm, it will come, trust me.

Studying can be boring, or we might feel it's hard and call it 'stupid'. But like anything learning about the tools it requires can/will make it easier. You wouldn't try to put a nail in a board without using a hammer, would you? Take some time out to learn about the tools. If you understand the tools, you can build anything.

With these tools, learning, studying, even cramming become different. Maybe not easy, but more approachable. If you have children, I encourage you to check these out. Learning about these tools will help ease the pain when the last minute comes up, be it for school, or work. And it helps with work let me tell you! (Check out the appendix on this date for some links to Thomas Frank's YouTube channel, he knows more about the tools than I do.)

July 3

Don't take a road trip with friends.

Brought to you by that guy who bet you wouldn't drink a whole bottle of ketchup for five dollars.

ROAD trip. Who has time for that! I tell ya, I'm busy now. Work, work, work. But when I was younger, I had a few. Colorado, Canada, Florida, Maine, London, Paris, Italy, etc....etc. Never really thought about it much. I recommend it highly.

They don't have to be long, like you see in the movies. Going out for a whole summer, or a 'gap year' but it broadens your horizons as they say. It's fun too.

Friends are fun, even if they aren't 'true friends' like I talked about before. Remember true friends actually care enough to get you to not do things sometimes.

So, some of the things you do with your friends are crazy. Maybe even death defying. Some not so defying. We've all lost friends we care about along the way. Whether just moving away or leaving this world. That's hard. It doesn't change the road trip you had back in the summer of whenever. The laughs, the tears, the fun times. Memories. Treasure the memories. Barring something like Alzheimer's or dementia you keep these with you. You take them with you.

These small trips, day trips, weekend, whatever. These trips stick with us through our lives, they shape us. Road trips help us get to know each other. I mean you're forced into a vehicle for who knows how many hours. It's an experience.

It's good times, good food. Again, I recommend it highly. So, when you're sitting on the couch watching tv this summer, perhaps you might want to make some plans for next summer. I don't know what you want to do, but be safe doing it. Bring friends. Create memories. Don't miss the opportunity.

And later when you're off in the real world, making money and living life you'll have those times to look back on and I hope you continue making new memories with new and old friends. As long as we are here, we have that opportunity.

Don't miss out on that.

July 4

Dude(ss), whatever you do, don't celebrate your life.

DID you know you're special? Did I tell you that before? I think I did. You realize it's still true today right? Right now. We have talents and gifts. Maybe they seem small to us. Insignificant even. Let me tell you, hopefully I'm not the first. They aren't insignificant.

Life's not easy, they say it's not fair, but I'd say that its equally so. We all live here. We don't have the OASIS yet. (I shudder at the thought.) We don't always get along, because our ideas get in the way. Our thoughts, even experiences. It's sad, but it's as fair to someone else as it is to me. There will be people who disagree, and they're allowed. It's about context after all.

It's easy to get caught up in the world, work, chores, duties. We do what we have to, to survive. Sometimes we don't. Sometimes people forget to. Did you know that we influence people every day? When we throw our 'fit in' face around, because we didn't wake up after one of our REM cycles, but instead in the middle of it, or we have a work project on our minds that we waited till the last minute for. Or we aren't happy at home, or our parents are abusive so we take it out on other children at school. The one that's geeky and quiet and mostly goes unnoticed and perhaps feels alone at times.

So, we have power. That's what influence is. Our arguments are powerful, but we underutilize them! Or we allow our thoughts to darken our own day. These thoughts are lies, lies we hear and tell ourselves, sometimes it is hard, chemically there might not be a balance. It's not as easy as telling you that you're special. It's something you can't control. I say seek help, because even if you don't believe me, there is purpose, even if there feels like there is none. There are people out there that need more help. If you're one of them speak up and out. There are those who would listen. Remember they hand out water on the road side.

Did you smile at someone today, did you ask them how they're doing? That's the influence I'm taking about. Now that's only the tip of the topic, more needs done. Dedication needs to happen inside of that question. Work, I know you already have work to do. People to care for, you can't be bothered to care for others outside of that circle. I get it, sometimes life isn't fair. (See what I did there.) Whether you go out of your way to help or simply smile and say hi, you have influence. You are important, don't forget to celebrate that. For those of you who may have forgotten this, perhaps because of environmental reasons, or chemical ones, I've written some links for support in the appendix under this date, check them out. Don't forget you have significance, sometimes we just misplace it, but it's there. We touch others' lives and we (You) are important, celebrate today.

July 5

Get lost in sad songs.

The Rain King

I listen to slow songs. Counting Crows, Passenger, Cat Powers, Cold Play, The Frames, Lana Del Ray, James Blunt, David Gray. I like the piano and the ease of the tunes, the soft flow, if you will. However, I do find that if I'm in a low mood I start listening to the words. (You'd think I listen to the words normally, I don't.) Some of these guys have sad songs. I used to listen to sad songs, watch sad movies perhaps. I didn't really cry or show my emotion very much, not to say I don't have emotion. Just didn't show it a lot, so I remember one day I was watching a sad movie, 'That was Then, This is Now' with Emilio Estevez. My mom asked what I was watching (just cuz parents check when your teenager mopes about). I explained I was watching a sad movie cuz I liked it. She asked me why.

Hard question really, I guess I didn't feel sad normally and I was trying to create that. Over time though, maybe even then, I've found that I don't like that movie. It's sad. Don't see a reason to watch it again actually. Life has so much sadness in it already, I found I didn't need to artificially create that emotion.

Now I know that when I was actually sad, I'd listen to slow music not because I thought it was sad normally but I'd hear the words in that state of emotion. You know if I broke up with a girlfriend or my life wasn't going the way I thought it should because of my expectations, or thinking of someone that was gone. So, I stopped listening to music I liked when I was sad. For me that meant I just pretty much stopped listening to music (you've seen some of my play list).

Now, I still listen to the same music, and now I sometimes hear the words. If I do, and I feel like they are creating an emotion that I'm not actually feeling. I turn it off. It's just like that movie.

I've found it's not productive. It doesn't help as I thought it did. It dulls your senses. It creates a little white lie. It amplifies emotion, or creates it, that's what songs do. Don't get me wrong I like a certain style of music. I think there are things to be said. However, it's not good to get lost in sad songs. If you are sad, dwelling isn't the thing to do. Listen to some upbeat poppy music. I'd recommend something, but you've seen my play list. Maybe some Justin Bieber or M. Cyrus, I don't know what you kids listen to nowadays.

July 6

You are in fact the center of the universe. People should know that.

—

I think I'm funny. Clearly this is stupid, and if you think you are, clearly… well you might be I don't know you. More context is required for me to make that judgment call. Anyway, I have a somewhat dry sense of humor. In fact, someone once told me my humor was so dry and deadpan at times people have a hard time knowing when I'm joking and when I'm being serious. I explained that I was always joking, unless I was serious. That got a little laugh. Let me tell ya, on a personal level I find this not only extremely hilarious, but profoundly frustrating.

This lovely gem is also one of the things I say from time to time, which is normally completely out of left field. I'm pretty sure one of my friends believes that I actually think I'm the center of the universe, and some days let's face it. I am. ;)

Sometimes you need to show your worth, and ooze confidence like that TCRI canister back in 2014 or the TGRI canister from 1991. At work it's important to use affirming language, not things like "I'll try, or I'm not sure I can, or that's not in my job description." They want to know you're good at your job. It's important.

People don't care for arrogance, and if you pretend to know something whether at work or at home you're most likely compensating. (Read 'most likely' as 'are') That's because you're not confident. That's a difference we don't see between the good guys and bad guys. We mistake arrogance for confidence, and believe bad guys are just more confident, cooler, collected. WRONG.

While you should be confident and maybe you do know the square root of e and can figure out why that algorithm that no one else can works. If you can't be kind and helpful to your team, what's the point. Perhaps they can't get along without you. That might be true. You might be the smartest person in the room. Congratulations.

I hate to break it to you (what I mean is I really enjoy saying this next part. I wish people would speak what's on their mind instead of talking sideways.), but there's someone smarter. The person who shares that knowledge, the one who is able to teach others, to make the entire team better. It creates value, it gives you more value if you must look at it that way.

We are all special, but we are not the center of the universe. Another point here, when we think we are, and we all do at times. Remember there is someone out there who is in more need of help, then our small issues, no matter how big they are or seem. Unless you're the 'someone out there' in this sentence. Got to have context, otherwise these are only useless words.

July 7

Check your locks three times. All of them. Dwell on if you did it right.

—

HUMOROUS on the face of it. I don't do this... too much. I believe I dodged this in my life. Sometimes I check something a few times. Like the stove is off, or the door is locked. I told you about how my dad helped break me of the anxiety of being late to school. Not that I ever truly got there, but I'm not as concerned about it on a neurotic level any more. Another time when I was young, under 8 I'd say. I was thinking about something sad, not the movie, again my mom was there and asked what I was thinking about. So, I explained it to her. In another awesome mom moment, she helped me understand that I didn't have to dwell on that thought. I could though and let it consume my head. She explained I could do that with anything, but I had the ability to stop thinking about it too. For me, turns out this was true. I was young, mind you, maybe its truer when you're young. Parents, keep that in mind.

Sometimes as we get older it's harder. Especially now, it's hard to focus on anything for a length of time because of all the things we have going on. Sometimes we get trapped in a cycle of thought. Me talking about cycles again.

I can't convey how to correct OCD, if you have it, or if you think you might. I can tell you, trust yourself. If you checked it once, its good. I know Santa checks his list twice though, so I understand if you need to check it twice too. But that's it. It's good. Do it once. Check something twice and then leave it for tomorrow, see if that worked. I bet it will. Checking twice is as good as twenty. It's better even.

I've added to the appendix on this date some support for ADHD and OCD. I would say check it out if you feel you need it, also if you check things more than twice you might give it some real thought.

Not too much thought though. Just go ahead and call.

July 8

Find a Charity you care for. Plan to give with your whole heart. Put it off until tomorrow.

WE care. I'm not saying that we don't just because we don't give time or money. I know that sometimes we have life going on. We would if we could, we just don't have time. People should be able to relax, right? I agree, people should be able to relax. I'm not saying I'm going to be one of those people that say "I won't rest until this is done." I'm not sure I have it in me. I relax. I rest. I watch tv, and smash couch like the best of them. Heck, I could be a gold medalist.

Sometimes I relax more than I should though. I put things off when I have time now. Like writing, I've put it off to do nothing all day. Nothing, all day. I feel I'm lazy when I do that. That's my problem not yours. I'm sure you handle things better. But even when I do nothing my mind doesn't stop thinking. It's insane. No rest for the wicked, that's what they say. Maybe it should be no rest for people who watch YouTube all day while thinking about how they should be writing.

With that said, I'd say that it's okay to take time off, a whole day, or vacation week or two. Those are good things. You just have to find a way to rest your head.

What about when we do want to do something though. Give to that homeless person on the street, or help out locally by giving our time to build or repair houses. We see a commercial and plan to give something. We just have to wait for money or time off. I understand. I do this too, not enough time right?

What about when that day came that you did have time and money. What did you do then? Go to a movie, hang out with friends, watch tv instead? It's easy to do. Not judging here. Just giving some motivation. That homeless person is still cold outside, or that food pantry just doesn't have that one extra can to give out. They could have though.

Sure, these things take some planning, but how much planning does it take. Look up a number, visit a website. Find the local pantry or that person on the street and buy them a sandwich on your way out of the store. 5 minutes of your time, 10 if you want to say something besides 'Here ya go.".

Maybe it will be like studying, only the first 10 minutes are hard, after that you might find it easier. Hey you might like it! Ever give Christmas gifts to a family who can't afford them? Pass out food on the street? It's not about the feeling you get from this though, it's for them. Take one day, plan on something, big or small. Just try it. If you don't like it, never do it again. But try it at least once, I dare ya.

July 9

You have to binge watch this!

—

BINGE-drinking is bad, binge eating is bad, binge watching? Well that's not really bad. Great! Another piece of great terrible advice that we all do. I'm going to say, binging, which is 'an unrestrained and often excessive indulgence' according to Webster. It isn't by definition good, or fine. It seems to be that its bad even. So why is it that it's so okay?

I'll binge watch a show. Weekend. I got the time. It doesn't hurt no body. I disagree. I think it hurts me and others. Not in the short-term sense. But as a writer I think only watching tv takes something away from my imagination. It corrupts my ability to think for myself in a sense. I don't think there are new ideas, simply new arrangements of those ideas, but I believe it can narrow my focus and perception of possible delivery. So, I need to make time to read books too.

Now you say, 'Well, I don't watch that much tv." Okay, then maybe I'm not talking to you. Chill out, you're reading. I get it. I'll give you a break. I'm sure you're not on your phone or YouTube all that much either so you're probably scot-free here.

I read a study once, about electronics and sleeping. They actually can keep our mind active. I don't know where the study was, I linked a similar study about binge watching tv.

I think you can enjoy your favorite shows, but just like a drink or food, if you indulge too much there could be issues later on. Perhaps tv won't have any lasting side effects, but I know that when I first tried putting cigarettes down it didn't work, and it didn't work for a few more years after that. I would never say give television up! It's gold! But we have so many electronics now, we are immersed to such a higher degree than in the 80's and 90's or even 2000's and it's not going away.

You don't have to restrain from watching the entire run of Firefly, (They cut it off after one season anyway. Can you believe that!), but I think it's something to be aware of as we sink into the 'sea of technology'. (That's cute how that last bit rhymed just there!)

July 10

Read the phonebook, while driving.

FUNNY today. No need to think about helping or not binging. Now everyone is sinking in wave after wave of technology and instead of gaining knowledge and riding the wave, most of us are being pulled under by the rip tides. Becoming numb to the pains of the world, nothing more than a cog in the machine pumping out crap other people don't need. Sorry didn't mean to go all Black Mirror on ya. I'm giving you a non-sense piece of advice for today. It's just funny No one's ever said this and you've never thought it. Crazy, right? It might not be humor for you, but it made me laugh. Then I thought about it again. We do this. People have died doing this. You ever browse through your contact list? Text a friend that you're on your way?

They have devices you can use, so you don't have to restrain your urge to not pay attention to your digital drug dispenser. (to some degree making it better). You can't tell people what to do after all. Only provide a way to do it better, safer, faster, right? *Heavy breath*

So, don't text and drive today. Try not to do it anymore.

In the UK people get 6 points on their license if caught doing this. That's half the points you can have total! Caught texting and driving your insurance might go up, 'might' as in 'will'. Insurance companies love their money, I mean providing helpful ways to line their pockets, I mean provide a service you need.

There is also the fact that you could kill someone, and the secondary fact that you could kill yourself. I'm not sure which is more important here. I'm thinking others.

Don't text and drive. I feel like I'm making a PSA here. I have put a few links in the appendix on sites that work to help support not texting and driving as well as placing those links here as well. Don't worry, as soon as we fix driver-less automated cars, you can go back to not paying attention again.

It Can Wait -- http://itcanwait.usaa.com/

Maria's Message -- http://www.mariatiberifoundation.org/

July 11

Nobody is watching.

GOOD as any reason, right. I mean if you're going to do it, might as well do it in the dark. It's an interesting understanding. We're more comfortable doing bad things, or things we think are bad when no one's watching. Why? I'm not sure I'm okay with being a proponent of accepting bad behavior, but I'm going to feign naïveté on why it's done in the dark.

The truly monstrous out there. The dictators and tyrants. They shouldn't care on a personal level. They can do what they want, at least in their own mind or corner of the world, if they do seem to care, I garner it's probably only on a more global scale but not locally. Perhaps another country might work to dethrone them and if you're a leader in that position you most definitely want to hold on to your power. This applies to all the criminal's goings-on, rapist murderers, child mongers. They can't come forward or they could go to jail or lose their way of life.

What about the common woman/man though? What is it that you do in the dark? If you do it in the dark, why? Would it be detrimental to your life, or family? If so, you shouldn't do it in the dark. You should find some support, help? Do you fear that your family wouldn't understand? Find outside help then. I understand just like the criminals we fear what someone would do if they knew we lied, or didn't support a cause, watch porn, struggle with anger, or cutting yourself to feel.

So, we hide things because they could ruin us, right? Sure. Is that all we hide in the dark though? It's not. You hide good things too. The world is so judgmental that we hide who we are, bad, and good.

We hide our opinions when we hear others have a different view, perhaps more vocal. We hide our interests, maybe they aren't that interesting to others. We suppress our humor and perhaps our skills. We don't just hide bad things in the dark, we hide good things. Things that make us who we are. They make us interesting, not simply a cookie cutter design from your major shopping center.

We hear in the media and with causes we should be able to accept others for who they are, but we hide so much of who we are from each other. I feel that what we do accept in others are not always real. So, for the bad things in the dark, seek help, support. For the good things, open up. Share, if they're good you're depriving yourself of an opportunity to live a life with more flavor.

July 12

Take yourself seriously, always. People are watching.

TRUE, people are watching. Everyone is watching through their phones. It's only a ruse that they pretend their focus isn't on you. Look, I've already explained, I'm somewhat stoic at parties. The short silent type you know. I've found that in some situations being serious is called for. In others maybe a little faster and looser is how it should be played. It's not even a mask. It's just how I am, or is it?

I've considered myself responsible for most of my life, give or take a few moments as a teenager, or more than a few. I've always had plans and I'll say I might struggle with what others might consider 'fun'. I'm not sure if it's that I'm getting older, or that I have always been older. I may have mentioned this, don't take yourself too seriously. You might find it difficult to have fun. I'm not saying I'm like an ex-heroin addict. (Did you know that you can do enough heroin to take away your happy. Take away your happy! Like for good. That's your emotional feeling of happiness just gone! Riding off on a horse somewhere. I tell ya, I need all the happy I can get! That's terrible, just wanted to share. Not worth it!) I have fun, I'm not saying I have the same level of 'fun' as some people in their 30's, but I'm enjoying my time most days.

I'm not sure what that's supposed to be, 'fun'. I have to get ready for retirement. Nose to the grind stone and all that jazz. Then I can have fun. Sounds like crap to me. Have fun now. Remember how I was talking about hiding your good qualities just yesterday. Don't do that. Share them. Sure, maybe there will be some 'fit-in' faces you get. Who cares?

Don't fear what others will think about you. You shouldn't, perhaps there is a point to fear, but it isn't to have it for the society around you.

Have fun with your family, your friends, have fun at your place of work, but get work done. If you can't have fun now, when are you going to start? At the end of the race? What's wrong with a little pre-celebration?

Stop worrying about what people think. If people would just begin to say what they mean, and mean what they say, I wonder how different our world would be.

Maybe it can start with you, but remember as Ellen would tell you 'be kind to one another'.

July 13

Good things happen to good people. Or good things happen to bad people.

NOPE. First off, it's not that good things don't happen to good people, but you have a responsibility for some of that. Others hold some as well. Bad things happen to bad people, and good. Great things happen for bad people. They know how the system works. Life isn't fair, but it's not fair equally. Of course, where you're born helps. There are places with many opportunities, and places with none, but the context of our media only allows our eyes to be open so wide.

If we take this advice at face value, we simply wait. Wait for good things to come along. You can't. Not here. You have to grab opportunity. Otherwise someone else will. It's not enough to want it, you have to fight for it. It's not what we heard growing up. I could be whatever I wanted to be. Well I wanted to be a cowboy and an astronaut and pirate, a native American, and video game designer and live in a castle. I'm not every close to being any one of those. Although I may have 1/16th pirate in me on my dad's side.

It's not that fortune favors the bold, sometimes fortune favors anyone who would try. Check out YouTube. I mean check out Rhett and Link. If they can do it, maybe you could too. (Honestly, they've got a pretty awesome channel and have worked pretty hard to develop their fan base.) If you want you could just comment on video games in a funny way. I guess that pays well too. I'm sure there is some work involved in that. I don't think I could do it. I'm not that good at anything past Street Fighter II: Turbo, probably not too good at that anymore either. (Button Masher here.)

So, we should really change this advice. Good things happen to those who work for it. It's not that good things don't happen outside of that, but we need to take notice of these success stories. They pop up overnight. Instantly they show up in our little worlds, but they worked for it. It takes blood, sweat and tears. There is no get rich quick. That's a lie. Leave it at the door. If you want good things, you need to work for it. Otherwise, you'll only get what you've always got, because you only do what you've always done.

Encouragement. Make a plan.

July 14

Guys/Girls will talk to you if they want to know you.

THAT'S not true. It's not that someone has said this, you say it. "Well, if she likes me, she'll look over here." No, she won't. Maybe she doesn't like you. After all you're over here, not there. She doesn't know you. She's not going to talk to you. It's not going to happen. He won't come over either. Maybe he's shy, or just self-involved. (Come to think of it, if he's self-involved, he might come over. That's why nice guys finish last, right?) It's not gonna happen. If you want to meet someone, guy or girl. You have to make the first move. It won't happen any other way. And of course, I'm speaking from personal experience.

Let me tell ya. In order for him or her to like you, they need to know you, otherwise they're sure you like them, and as another rule you can't know if they don't care. You can help them in that process. Go on up, say hi. They won't say hi. They won't come to you. It's just not going to happen. Forget about it. Wipe that lie from your mind. Nice girls/guys finish last in this stupid race, for this reason.

So, in knowing that, that they will never come up to you. I don't care if guys are supposed to make the first move, I don't care if girls are supposed wait for a guy to approach. I get it, maybe it's the stereotype that's just ingrained into us, guys that don't approach, don't want to know you, or are too timid to be a good provider. I can tell ya, that's bullshit. I'd love to hit the dickweed that came up with that gem, or perhaps if a girl approaches you, she might be too aggressive. It's a waste of opportunity.

If you don't take the chance, you'll miss it. Then they will be gone, and you will be alone. So, how is that different than if you get shot down, at least you will have the knowledge that you two weren't compatible. You don't have to wonder about that. You get to rejoice in the fact that you tired. Just put yourself out there. It's just 5 minutes, if it's worse, it's even less. So many missed opportunities.

Try it, I'm begging you. Do it one time. The average life span of a human is 79 years. So that gives you about 50 years, (assuming you start at 20, and your last 9 years are set in stone, which they aren't) to approach someone. 50 years, 5 minutes is all it takes. Or don't. I'm sure rejection is worse than sitting alone, right?

Find people, and just talk. It doesn't even have to be at a club. If you don't try you can't complain. To your friends or in your head. And I know we all like a little complaining. I say earn it. (P.S. Second thought. Don't complain about it, come up with a viable solution, and fix it.)

July 15

The internet/tv is an excellent babysitter.

FIRST things first, before I start poking this hornet nest. Clearly, clearly the internet has pockets of good things laced overtop the rampant backdrop of porn that fills in the dark spaces between its potential. Sometimes children are a handful. You need some time. Clearly, clearly, I'm not addressing you. It's the people who don't engage their children. The sad fact is, it's easier, and we have too much going on. I wasn't alive before we had television and the internet came up pretty quick in my life. It must have been boring for all those kids just sitting around with nothing to do, right? How did they entertain themselves, I mean honestly? (I feel I could add more here...in a later edition perhaps.)

Now we have television in our cars. Everyone has a phone. What's wrong with looking at your phone. I'll say this as writer, I love the internet, I love tv too. Good things about it.

Here's an example of what I'm talking about and why I think this maybe, possibly a little bit important, especially in this day and age. I remember growing up with my brothers and sister. I would play hide and seek tag (in the country with acres and bases. It might not sound awesome, but it totally was.) with my brothers, I remember building a Sherwood forest fort out in the woods. Digging an underground tunnel that my grandfather drove his tractor into. Oops! Walking around the back roads with my friends. Checking out haunted houses. Playing in the pool. I remember those things.

So why do I say that you ask? To say this. I don't remember the last thing I watched on YouTube, in fact I don't recall many video games I played with my brothers (Save Golden Eye, and Halo), or music videos I watched. Now I can recall them by name, the video games, but I don't have full memories attached to those names.

I do have a full memory of playing paint ball with my brothers, granted it was most likely because I shot myself in the finger while running, or the time my brother shot me, not once, not twice, but five times in the back of my head! I mean, come on! Once was enough, don't ya think. He said he was scared, but five times?!

I wouldn't trade those memories for anything, especially spending my life hooked to a phone. I have a phone now. I'd give it back if I could.

Make memories, not chains. (BOOM! Legend in my own mind.)

July 16

Do what I say, not what I do.
-
Me

THIS command infuriates teenagers as well as adult teenagers everywhere. (Me being one of them.) Really, it leaves a bad taste in everyone's mouth when they hear it.

This is not how it works. We do what you do. We don't care what you say. We care what you do. Parents. If you smoke, your children will smoke. If you don't care, at least you can step up to that fact. Maybe you don't care, maybe you're too addicted. I feel sorry for you, hopefully you can get some help. Unless you die of cancer, your child will smoke. You've showed them that it's okay. It doesn't stop there. If you do crack, good possibility, if you don't go to jail for it, you kids will too. Crack is not cigarettes. I understand. I'd encourage you to stop doing crack, it's hard. I don't do crack so I can't say how hard it is. Your children have a better than likely chance of doing drugs. I haven't seen the numbers, but if you do it, they can and will too.

Now, I speak not from a parent's point of view. I don't have children. I was one. (Arguably, I am still.) If a parent curses, I'll curse. If a parent hits another parent, I'll think that's how it is in families.

Children will do what you say, but they will also do what you do. And if you don't want them too, chances are they'll do it behind your back. I'm sure it's hard to be a parent. I tell ya, it wasn't easy being a kid. I'm a little stone faced about this topic too. Children are special. They should be cared for and protected. They should be taught, they need to be taught. Electronics will not do it. The world will though. It's a hell of a teacher too. If you think I'd be the person I am without my parents, you'd be dead wrong. Sure, I have genes, but my parents taught me things. Some things they didn't teach me, and I learned them the hard way. Others they told me 'do what I say, not what I do' and I didn't listen. It happens, but don't stop trying to teach, but you have to be an example. Not just to your kids, but everyone.

Another finger I'll point is to groups for causes. If you stand for something, then shouldn't you follow it, support it, live it. If you don't, if your life would look the same if you stopped supporting the cause. Was it really being supported? If nothing changes, if you do or don't support something, you're probably not really supporting it. So, stop lying to yourself. You're damaging what others are trying to do. You pretend, this only gives a sense of support that's not there.

If you don't truly stand or believe in something, parent, group, expert internet arguer (Unless you're in debate club. At least you are probably learning to research the topic before speaking. Carry on.), don't talk about it as if you do. If you do and are seen doing the opposite, it will deafen people to you and to the cause. So, stop lying (to others and yourself) and say you care when you don't. (P.S. I hope you do believe and stand for things. Just thought I would send a little encouragement your way after that oh so awesome pep talk.)

July 17

Wear a cape to work. All week.
(Just have to say if you can and no one mentions it, and more people start doing it too.
Let me know where you work. I'd love to work there!)
-
Me

CAPES: why don't more people wear them? I don't get it. Okay, maybe a full-blown cape like superman is out of the question, but what about a medieval shoulder cape? Maybe a trench coat like Sherlock Holmes. Not the double hat, just the cape. Or a cloak! (I love that word.) People don't wear enough of them.

It's interesting, we read fiction books with people dressed in intricate clothes. Hoods. I know, we have cosplayers who bring those designs to life.

I don't know that I'd want everyone walking around with Starlord's fashion sense. (I mean, I'd want to be original…) but I think hooded cloaks have a pretty good functionality to them. They keep the wind and rain away. Now if they could just make them so they wouldn't mess up my hair.

I've seen a few that might work for walking around in. They aren't as loud as Altair's hood from Assassin's Creed. Don't think I can pull off the widow's peak myself.

I'm not saying we should cosplay every day, all day. There wouldn't be enough time to make things for everyone, but what if we punched up our fashion sense just a little. I mean, if they're talking about flying cars like the TF-X from TerraFugia, maybe we can afford to punch it up a notch on our blue jeans and suits. I'm all for the classic cool, but if Hollywood and video game land, and olden days can come up with these interesting fashions why am I stuck wearing cargo shorts and a tee shirt on the weekend, every weekend? Go ahead, bring some flavor today. Not too much though, you don't want to scare the faceless masses, they might not accept you.

July 18

Demand less from yourself and those around you.

EVER said this. Probably not. Ever felt it? We all can't be astronauts, we might as well take a step back and get a grip. While it's true in a sense. Sometimes we can't achieve our dreams. We have to walk on the ground at some point. I say don't let failure stop you though. What's that catchy thing that 'old what's his name' (I've heard either Edison and Franklin said this. Here's an excellent reminder to check sources.) said about building something. He didn't fail 1000 times, he succeeded in finding 1000 ways not to make that something. It's a good way to look at it. Course if he had 1000 opportunities to make something, chances are he might have been doing something on the side to support that effort and the finical aspects that go with it Don't quit your day job is what I'm saying.

We follow this advice though, demanding less of ourselves. In our culture we have stated that people should be able to do what they want to do. Although it's a pretty notion on its face if looking at it from one side everyone is happy and good, but on the other, you get chaos run amok. Everyone doing what they want. The monsters would come out of their cages in droves. But the point stands on both sides. People can't just do what they want, even if society was accepting, we put ourselves down because we don't always see how we can accomplish things. We tell ourselves we can't.

People need encouragement, they need help. Perhaps a vast amount of people do want to sit down and eat Cheetos and watch tv. Maybe they enjoy the day to day work and home life they have. We can't force someone to push themselves, especially if they don't want to, whether from their own will or perhaps believing what others have told them throughout their life. It's interesting though, because as a child I thank my parents for pushing, and encouraging me. Even today they do that. Granted maybe I find irritating at times, but I accept and listen. I take their feedback and hopefully go forward and grow as a person.

We should always push ourselves. Just a little every day, or heck every once in a while, if every day is too scary for ya. There has to be something you want to do. Today is that day. If you're reading this, perhaps you're 79, in which case maybe you only have a few days left to live, perhaps you're younger and you haven't hit the average life span. In either case you should make the most of your time here. It's not too late. Demand more of yourself. You can accomplish something, maybe something bigger than you thought possible. I know there are others who agree with me. (Shout out to read history books!)

If you, just you, could do something, perhaps give a kind word. Be there for a friend, paint, create something, no matter how long it took. The effort in that would be a success, it would be something. Demand more of yourself, in doing so maybe we change the world. Maybe others will follow suit if they see your actions and maybe, just maybe they'll change the world too.

July 19

Go ahead, live in a van down by the river.

CHRIS Farley—remember him? You might be too young. On SNL there was a comedy skit where he was a motivational speaker, Matt Foley. You can check it out online, or in the appendix. Funny guy.

He talks about how you shouldn't do drugs and gets in David Spades face about it. Tells David that he will end up in a van down by the river! It's good stuff. I mean people in vans, they must have it together right? Don't have a house. Don't want to have that life No sir!

Another thing that's interesting is while it's true, living in a van might be because you've had a hard row to hoe. There are people who do it, and not because they have to. It's because they can. I'll say it's not for everyone, gotta be pretty determined for this lifestyle, but perhaps a summer? I started following the YouTubeers who did exactly that. Apparently, they got it figured out. It honestly might be worth looking into with our rising debt issues in this country.

This economy is tough, its expensive. Just because someone might live in a van, doesn't mean they can't afford to live in a house. Actually, it might mean their smarter, more resourceful. Let me explain where I'm getting this.

Van Life. There are a few YouTube channels on it. Interesting stuff. I'm a little for the 'soft and cushy' myself, but I find the idea pretty cool. If you watch some of the channels they bring up great topics, how to budget for living in a van, places to see, and areas to stop in.

One of the draws to being an author is, you could write practically anywhere. Travel anywhere. You can do that with vans too. I mean you'd have to use a boat for some places, but you get the idea.

I'd say if you were thinking about taking a 'gap' year, or simply wanted to move around, check it out. If you're set on doing something, you might as well do it right. I tell ya, Van life isn't for just anyone, but these guys do it right. I've linked to a few videos on this date in the appendix.

Even if you don't want to live in a van down by the river, and I'd check it out. Some even have pretty good budgeting tips for travel.

July 20

Never make a shopping list.
—

WHEN I lived in Boston for a time, I never made a shopping list. I'd buy groceries, but I'd just wander in. The trouble with this is obvious. You over spend. Now if you don't have a budget maybe because you don't need one, you're filthy rich and buying groceries isn't an issue. Or the other, you're not sure how to budget. If it's the later then read on! If it's the former, I'd like to ask for a hand out. From one class level to another. (Never hurts to ask, the reply might, but the asking doesn't).

The great thing about the internet is you don't have to make a shopping list. Millions of people have already done that for you. In fact, there are tools and apps! (You knew that though, there's an app for everything now.)

Some stores even have apps that you can order online and the store will now shop for you. I tell ya for the time it saves me, it's worth it in some cases.

I'd check out to see if your local store has something like that. In the meantime, check out this date in the appendix for links to various articles and shopping list ideas. Please note, I only included healthy food. I'm not saying you have to eat it, you can have Oreo's. I love Oreo's. I'm not suggesting you buy those either, but they are good. (Even that stupid cinnamon kind.)

Do make a shopping list though, it will help you save money. If you're a college student this is a must. You're probably gonna have a massive loan to pay off. You gotta watch those loaners, they're cycle starters. I wonder if we could just start learning what we needed from establishments through the internet or somewhere that didn't cost us so much of our future. Anyway, student loans seem to start a cycle that we all seem to be in. That's what they say anyway. (Or maybe I say that. Maybe they'll start saying it now that I brought it up.)

July 21

Don't be there for your family today. Think about yourself.
—

SOMETIMES we need space. Relaxing, unwinding time. That should be something that is given in a relationship. It's healthy. Maybe you don't need as much alone time as another. Just something to keep in mind, but with our busy day to day, and electronic baby sitters and eye catchers sometimes the opportunities slip by. It's not even that you are trying to be neglectful. Perhaps you're even in the same room, just preoccupied with work, or emails or television. Maybe you always watch tv together. It's how you unwind and relax.

In our day to day, sometimes, maybe even more than that, we don't realize how often we don't make time for those around us. It's not intentional, its passive. We need to check our apps during conversations now. We need to be constantly connected, but sometimes the ones we are closest to, we forget how to connect with.

Take some time to talk. 15 minutes without your phone, maybe a game night if you're feeling froggy. I've linked to a site that has a few different ideas in the appendix, but wanted to mention a different one here.

Family nights allow for communication, we have a lot of devices that allow for this, but sitting down and having fun with each other helps build bonds. You get what can be a non-invasive (if you're careful) way to learn about your children's lives, their likes and dislikes. How school is, how they feel about boys and girls.

I think it's worth a shot. It seems like a pretty powerful tool. It doesn't have to be every week, maybe once a month. If you all enjoy it, maybe have a bi-weekly night.

See what happens. Oh, I don't think I have to mention it but maybe put the phones down for a few hours on that night. You might find that you enjoy each other's company. I hope you do!

July 22

Before giving a speech, write it down, memorize it. Stick to the script. Never deviate.

TERROR. A word I normally reserve for H.P Lovecraft or Stephen King, possibly Dean Koontz if I'm alone. But giving a speech or talking in front of a large group of people all staring at me. Gives me 'meat sweats' just thinking about it.

What's even better is reading cue cards. They do this on tv, but it's a little more advanced. Perhaps we should have a guy standing in the back of the room with a large board that has the things we're supposed to say so we don't look down every other word. Oh, how I loved college speech class!

I can write the cue cards no problem. I can make up little scenarios in my head, ones where I'm able to know everything I'm going to say and it just flows out of me like a famous poet. I'm so awesome I get a standing ovation. Women swoon and guys want to be me. I'm an awesome orator! Then I snap out of that lovely daydream and stare at the crowd. Meat sweats. What was my line? I'll look down. It's on my card. Eyes up, eyes down, eyes up, eyes down. I'm a real Frederick Douglass, or Winston Churchill. That's me. Up, down, up, down.

One thing I've learned. You know what you're going to talk about. All about it. Write down points, or put them in a PowerPoint, don't read the PowerPoint. Your audience can read the PowerPoint. Don't write enough on the points that they are reading the PowerPoint and not listening to you. These are your cue cards.

I know it's not easy. Even if you could give a speech, and I'm sure you've practiced in front of an empty room, right? It's different with people in it. They're judging you after all. If its college, you should try and do a good job, but other than the professor, why do you care so much about what the others in the room think? They don't grade you. You've practiced in front of your one friend and did okay, right? So just do it again. Make eye contact with the room, but only one person holds the key to your grade.

If you're at work, its different. They trust you know what you're talking about. You're talking about it. This is your baby. Breath, tomorrow will still come. Unless there's zombies, and they're fast. Then you might not have that long.

July 23

Listen to your heart.

-

Roxette

WHAT does your heart tell you? What lies in the heart of mankind? We tend to think our heart as a source of good. I think it's good. It keeps me alive. I say it's the 'source' of our emotions, our gut, our instinct. Our mind is more analytical. I'm going to talk about that source and point out its functions. Basically, I'm going to rant about why this advice is nice at face value, and terrible to its core.

We say this, so what does it mean? It means listen to your feelings, right? But there are many sites and doctors and sources that tell us our feelings can be misleading. They can cause us to commit heinous acts in single moments that can change our worlds. Our hearts can lead us across the world only to find out that what we were after isn't there.

People say our hearts are the source of love, passion. I won't disagree. As you know I've mentioned stoic a few times and that I relate to it in some ways. I'm showing my bias, so you know where I'm coming from.

We see movies and hear stories about people listening to their heart and getting everything, they want. It's a pretty picture. Maybe it's even happened like that for you. I haven't met you yet, so I have no point of reference outside of Hollywood.

It's hard not to listen to your heart, or feelings at times. Let me tell ya, they're fickle though. They make things hazy, maybe an investment isn't the right approach, but you 'feel' it is. Did you consult any historical evidence? Is it a chance of a life time, a get rich now or never kind of thing?

I'm not against listening to your heart, but I don't think our hearts care as much about the rest of ourselves as they should. It's rash and brazen. It throws words around like it means them forever, although it shouldn't be so bold and can't be sure about such things. It makes promises it can't keep, and takes trips it can't complete. It doesn't have an end game. It's out for itself, and only cares about how it feels today.

That's why we have a helper to rein, that's why we have a mind. If you listen to your heart maybe it will work out, but let me gently remind you, don't forget your head out there.

July 24

If you can make it here, you can make it anywhere.

New York, LA, Las Vegas

THAT's not true. If you can make it in New York city. I don't suggest you move to Montana. I'm betting that state might chew you up. If you can make something of yourself in Texas, maybe pause before heading to Cali.

It's similar to 'If I can do it, anyone can do it." That's a false statement. What if you're a doctor, what if you can pick things up by hearing them and I have to actually step through them?

So, if the statement is total crap, what's it good for? What's the purpose in saying it? Encouragement. Helps people work harder if they're on a certain track. If they apply themselves a little more, they might make it? It gives a confidence boost that isn't really even direct. It's not saying you can make it here, it's only saying if you make it here, everything else will be easy.

I'm not saying stop using it. It's 'cute' encouragement, but it's certainly not true. I've made it here, wherever that is. But I don't think I could move to another part of the world and make it. I'm not saying I couldn't, I'm saying it's not 'in the bag'.

What about the other advice, the self-deprecating kind that intends to pull others up, but rarely does. If I can do it, anyone can do it. Irks me when I hear someone say that.

If I can do it, I can do it. If you can do it, you can do it. Maybe you can't do what I do. So, it's not true in that sense, but also it 'harmlessly' puts yourself down. Just because something is easy for me, does not mean it's easy or obtainable for you. Stephen King writes, I hear James Patterson writes. Doesn't mean I can. Maybe I'll find that I can't. I'm going to try, but just because they can, doesn't mean a thing for me. I wish it did.

I'm not trying to make this into a downer, it's just an observation. It doesn't take away from what these pieces of advice attempt to do. They don't do all that much for me. You hear them and get a boost of confidence. I'm here to tell you, be confident. If you think you can, try it. But understand that these words, while they seem helpful, aren't all that weighty. It should go 'If you can make it in a place, you can probably make it somewhere else.' It just doesn't have the same ring to it, you know. It's all about marketing after all.

July 25

Whip your hair back and forth. Come on, whip it. Whip it good.

Neil Young

CATCHY. It reminds me of headbanging, but it might be a little safer. Wish I had more hair. I'm jealous is what it is. If you can whip your hair, good for you. Or if you can only whip it good, then maybe do that.

Not at work though, most of the hair whipping should be at the club or in a safe location away from the walls. It's not something to laugh at. Whipping your hair can bring in the big bucks. You can't use that for a get rich quick idea, it's already been taken, but maybe it will get your wheels turning.

July 26

You only live once. YOLO
—

I'VE heard this described as the poor man's 'Carpe Diem'. I would agree. The way I see this little gold nugget of drug circle philosophy is telling someone that they might as well do it, you might not get another chance. Well, that's true. You could die tomorrow. The End. Never get to go to Paris, or dine in Sydney with a new set of friends, no sunsets in Hawaii. But while that's true enough, things that we do require judgment., maybe not that much, but some decision needs to be made. That hit of acid your 'pal' just gave you as he says 'YOLO' is the hard truth of the matter, its where this tidbit's power shines.

Unlike Carpe Diem, which is Latin for 'Seize the day' (or 'Seize the Carp' if you watched "Out Cold"). This Latin phrase conveys that you should make the most, the best of the day. Take the bull by the horns and go after the goals you set. Unless those goals are doing as much acid as you possibly can.

YOLO tends to slide in a negative fashion. That's because words mean things. This catchy, nausea inducing phrase doesn't convey that you should go after goals, it says try it, do it. Screw it. It's not the same thing. It pulls from the older phrase to try and sound important, deep, meaningful. It adds unwarranted risk to the equation, for no purpose other than to harm. It takes away meaning, in taking away the context and creating something new it becomes watered down. We do this a lot. Technology has allowed anyone to share their thoughts with millions. Sometimes my thoughts aren't worth my time, let alone sending them out to waste millions more. While YOLO allows more bottles of 'YOLO' to be sold to younger people, after all, we all want to do, what we want. It takes away caution and planning.

If I wasn't so right, I'd be wrong. Words mean things. If we use them wrong, we get varying results. We are living in an age of watered-down information, some of which is time consumingly wasteful, just like this sentence.

July 27

Things get better the more money you have.

MONEY makes things easier. Maybe. That's what I hear. I'm still waiting to figure out how exactly that's the case. I'm not poor, but I wouldn't call myself rich either. I get by pretty well. I still have loans and bills. They don't seem to go away. They seem to grow as I get more money. It seems relative. The more money I have, the more bills, or bigger things I'd buy.

Take rich people. I was gonna point some out directly, but since I don't personally know any, I'm not sure I want to poke at them. Yet. They buy jets and islands, multiple houses, cars that drive underwater, gold filtered cigarettes, cure diseases even (That's pretty chic though). I don't know how much in land tax islands costs. I'm guessing a few bucks. Some are so rich they can't possibly figure out how to spend it all. I'm looking at you Bill Gates and Warren Buffet, Jeff Bezos. (If your reading could I borrow just 100,000,000. I figure it's kinda like asking for a loan of 5,000 or so. Heck I'd take half that.) But seriously I'm not sure these guys could figure out how to spend everything. For the average rich person though, I mean the paupers, you know, millionaires. Many have so much tied up in assets and going to bills their lives might seem awesome. I'm sure that's kind of the case, but they are still who they are. They only see a standard of living, and it's probably just a little higher than where they are now.

Money doesn't make things better. People do that. Communication does that. Caring and action do that. While money can alleviate worries it doesn't change character. It does by you a boat though. Wish I could buy a boat, a boat with friends on it!

I'm trying to let you know that money is not the answer. Working to be content with what you have goes a whole lot further. It's fun to dream, "If only I had a thousand bucks, I could buy that lawn mower. If I had a little more, I could pay off the house and take the kids on vacation." It's pleasant to think about how many people could be helped, but if you don't think about how you can manage without it, how you can mow the lawn or take a smaller vacation for family time, what you might be able to do to connect with your kids now, today. How is it that money will make those things better?

Don't wait to do what you can today, in hopes that you can do more with money tomorrow. It's good to have dreams for tomorrow, but remember to put effort behind them today.

July 28

Stay away from the groups.

YOU don't want to put yourself out there too much. Sometimes these groups can require a lot. It's like a relationship with a crowd of people. Maybe that sounds fun to some, but it's a lot of work.

It's definitely easier to stay home. You can join groups online after all. It's the same thing. Too much sunlight causes cancer. I know some people get anxiety in crowds. It's a thing. It's called Enochlophobia. I get that. I don't have as much of a concern with crowds, although I can get aggravated if there is no space, but I think that's more of a normal reaction than something I need to dive into, dissect and discuss.

And there's the idea that some groups could be 'bad', I say that's good to stay away from those groups, especially if they make you eat only certain things and stay in certain locations, that's kinda 'off', if you know what I mean. But don't cut yourself off from any groups. Explore, there has got to be something that you have always wanted to try. Maybe there is a group for that.

Don't let a fear of something stop you. (Now taken out of context you could use that line to say I mean YOLO, or jump off a bridge, but that would be nowhere near what I'm talking about, huh. It's interesting how context is important though.)

What's the worst that could happen? You join a cult, yep that's bad. I highly advise against that. Stay away from those groups. I don't know if they all carry signs that say directly, "Hey, we're a cult. Join us for cookies and cake!" though, two of the signs would be supplying your only food and requiring you live in a certain place, so keep an eye out.

Sometimes we aren't worried so much about cults or being in large crowds. There is just not enough time in the day and we get buried in work and family. Family is definitely a good group, so if you've got that 'game night' thing then you're on your way. If not, maybe step outside and find a group, small or big. Just something that interests you. Just for fun. How else are you going to meet people, Tinder? Grow up.

July 29

Penny stocks are the fastest way to get rich.

IF you find the right one. But I think its kind of a gamble. Did you know there is software you can use that will do the trading for you? Course that's kind of a gamble too. You know what I love? I love wasting my time watching those videos about how to get rich quick, or the vitamin videos that will change your life. "It's just after this next thing." The voice says before the next piece of paper is flipped a new drawing is made and the voice begins droning on about pointless point number 7. Crap. Words that mean nothing. I wonder if they make money on the time you waste. I think that's a thing. Grrrr…

I believe that the reason they 'got rich quick', is because they're selling the idea of how to get rich quick. It's snake oil, humbug, balderdash. Harrumph I say! Fills me with ire! Wasting people's time. Human leeches. (That's one of the nice words I have for them.)

Stop it, just stop it. No one, not a one, gets rich quick. Sure, there's the lottery. Let's talk about that, in the vein of GMM. (Linked in the appendix for that ref alone.) I don't think I want to win the lottery. It's seems just like a bad idea, read the other link in the appendix to understand that one. People don't know how to manage money. I mean our entire economic system seems to be based on that principle alone. I not an economist, but I don't think that's too far from the truth. If people started actually managing their money, everything might come crashing down.

Forget about rich quick. Live your life, work to be content, share your time with others. Don't get that next best thing. You can be rich in so many other ways besides money. Something to think about.

July 30

Eat all the candy you want.

Willy Wonka

TONS of gobstoppers out there. "Come with me, and you'll be, in a world of pure imagination."

There are too many to count, but just like anything I believe tastes should become more distinguished over time, or something like that. I've linked a few sites in the appendix but wanted to mention them here. You can probably find these online somewhere. Perhaps worth a try.

1. Reber Chocolate Marzipan Mozart Kugeln Hearts
2. Rom Bar Cel Mare
3. Peppermint Crisp
4. Kägi Fret
5. Denmark licorice – Warning, it don't taste like the whips! SODIUM! It's like a salt lick!!

Let me just say, I highly discourage eating excessive amounts of candy, but who cannot love the original Willy Wonka and the Chocolate Factory with Gene Wilder. Although, it's something to note, too much candy will make your stomach hurt, or turn you into a giant blueberry, so watch out for that!

July 31

Save sick days for when you're sick.

—

I'M all for responsibility. I'm diligent and always stay off the grass where the signs tell me too, I try never to be late, and always 15 minutes early. Do my best, and keep my head down😊. But I'm sick about once a year for maybe a week. That's it. I have more sick time, some people don't. I realize that. Sick leave is for just that, when you're sick. I get it. What happens if you get sick a lot. Well then you probably shouldn't listen to this, call it 'humor' and forget it. But for the rest of you, check it out.

How many sick days does one get in a year. I think I had about 24 hours or 3 days at one point in my life. As an author sick day don't really play into it as much. Some people get more, upwards of a week or two max. For those with that much, how often do you get sick? Maybe a few days.

Students have sick days too, now if you're in college. You're out of luck here. Go to class you're paying for it. More than you probably realize. Some is at least.

If it's high school. You should go to school, learn stuff. But I recall that there were times my parents allowed me to go on small vacations. We'd go to museums or week trips to historical sites. Some of these translated into sick days at school. They didn't have mental health days in my days at school.

That leads to another topic, mental health. Sometimes you're not sick, but you're spent. You're run down. It should be acceptable to charge your battery backup. I'm not saying take advantage of the system, but being allowed to take a day for yourself. Especially if you're a workaholic, it is important.

Manage for it, but take one. Be okay with it. Let your boss know and do it, if it's not something your company offers, look into how they could start.

Don't forget that we all need time away and even though we aren't sick with the flu, if we run on empty other things in our life can become mismanaged. That 'empty' or 'disconnectedness' can harm your relationships or your well-being. I'm not saying take a vacation, just think about allowing yourself a recharge.

August 1

Don't try, you'll never make it or a difference anyway.

WHY try? It's not going to happen after all. You feel this way? Sometimes that thought occurs to me. Not so much anymore, it seems to mask itself as watching television or reading a book. A distraction from what I truly would like to do, which is write my own book. It might be different for you. I recall the famous quote by Michael Scott via Wayne Gretzky, "You miss 100% of the shots you never take." Or the one from Henry Ford, "Whether you think you can, or you can't. You're right." I mentioned that before. This advice comes from our self-doubt. It's a mash up of these two quotes in the negative. It takes the possibility of success away and leaves us with only a defeatist attitude.

Do you feel you haven't done anything? In looking back at your life, have you not learned anything impressive, or found a friend, someone that listened? Sometimes we have feelings of depression, that what we do or could do doesn't matter. On a tangent, this is one of the reasons nihilism is not an end goal, or shouldn't be ever treated as such. The truth is, and I'm going to get a little Zen on ya here, when you throw a rock, or skip one across a pond, do you notice the ripples?

We all make ripples, these ripples, no matter how small have an effect on this world. You can deny it, but it will never make it untrue. Take how long we live, about 80 years. I'm in my 30's. I've been to different places, and held different jobs. My circumstances change. I've noticed this about life. Nothing stays how it is. I think that's awesome and terrifying at the same time. Somethings we don't want to end, good things, comfortable things, but life isn't fair, so it changes. Then we have bad things, terrible things. We would love these to change, they do as well. Sometimes they get better, sometimes they morph into something just as bad or worse. But they change.

People make ripples, stop listening to your feelings, your feelings can lie to you, your heart can hide truth. Stop listening to it and do something positive for yourself or someone around you. You have around 80 years to work with. This is truth. It might take work, hard work, blood sweat and tears work. The work it takes is one of the things the news casters never dive into enough but they keep trying new things, because everything changes. These events in your life too will change into something else, in some ways you control what that change will be.

August 2

Be superficial.
—

I am not superficial. Just because I like the fact that my tv responds to my voice and turns on, or I have to wipe the drool from my mouth when I see an expensive sports car, or I care about what's going to happen on my favorite television show more than I do about what the most current crisis is, or taking 5 minutes to buy that homeless man a sandwich. Wait, maybe all those things actually mean that I am. Crap, and here I thought I was on a high horse.

Regardless, let's dive into this. Is it really superficial to care about the finer things? Let's point out that the finer things include television, phones, public transportation, let's not think that it only applies to rich people. I don't know if it includes shelter and food at your fingertips, but if its more elaborate than most have, it might. Compared to many countries we live in excess.

It's sometimes hard not to be superficial, especially here. (Think earth.) There are so many cool things, better things. They're shiny. Shiny things distract people. On some level we need distractions from time to time, so we can recharge. Other times, distractions lead us to not reach our full potential. I tell ya it's easier for me to listen to music and read a book than it is to sit and write this up. Don't get me wrong, I'm not sure all of these 'gems' are worth the effort, but it might provide some support to children in need, as well as giving me more opportunity to continue doing what I love, writing and helping in a small way. Remember that small way, it makes ripples.

So, it's easy to fall into the shiny trap, "look at my cool watch", "my car can go up to 220 miles an hour and reaches 60 in 3 seconds!" (Even though the speed limit is set at 85 as a max in most of the world. Even the autobahn has a suggested limit around that, per accident rates.) I'm sure the speed limit problem will go away as we allow the machines to drive us, as time goes on, so don't worry about that. It will give us more time to stare at our phones on the way to work in the machine. (Sorry, I'm reading a dystopian novel at the moment. Bad in bad out, 'paranoid much' in, 'paranoid much' out.)

We care, (myself included) more about our comforts than thinking of what we can do for others. (I know, not all the time. We might carve out a day or two here and there, send checks in the mail, or post things on the internet, or write terrible advice books... 😉). It's hard to not be superficial in ways, but sometimes we can see it. In those times, ask yourself "Am I being superficial right now? How can I instead use this to help someone in need?" Not an easy thing, but as G.I. Joe says. Knowing is half the battle.

August 3

Knowledge is power

Me

THIS is a good one. Its sides up nicely to my last comment. G.I. Joe cartoons always ended with a PSA of some kind. Cartoons don't do that nowadays. Writing has gone down the tubes for some of them, IMO. Anyway, sure people who know things have power, but is knowledge power? Just because I saw a video, or read a book and possibly wrote something about it, what's that mean exactly?

I think like G.I. Joe says, its only half the battle. If you never do anything with that information. I'd argue its useless. If you watch a video on say, swimming and like some of the kids in the G.I. Joe PSAs fall into the water, if you don't use that knowledge to swim, (and perhaps tried practicing first) it's pointless. If you watch a news broadcast on some crisis in a part of the world and put it in the back of your mind never to bring it up or create a call to action, it's useless to you.

Perhaps posting information, or writing about something is a little more useful, but if it never reaches people who act on that information, what's the point? I'd argue for little. Knowledge is only power if one creates an action from that. That can be a small action, or something bigger.

Knowledge is not power, doing something with it can be powerful. If you only watch videos of cats on YouTube (which I love to do!) you might have a knowledge of what they do, but how is it helpful? If you hear a call to action and think it's a good idea, but then do nothing with it. How powerful is that call to action?

I'm not saying respond to every cause, that's equally pointless but find one and stand for it. Make it a good one. I trust we went over the good and bad ones enough for you to know the difference already. Remember the list you have?

I've also linked a video on some of the nuances in the G.I. Joe PSAs. I'll give the guy some points, he definitely broke up the short videos and explained why some of them failed to hit the mark. I think it goes well with the theme in this book about context and needing the proper context when giving advice or arguing a point.

August 4

Make something big, and structurally sound, now call it 'unsinkable' or 'unmissible'.

— *White Star Line*

I'M of the belief that if we put our minds together we could create wondrous things. Things that would astound and bring us into an age that few of us could imagine. But even though I believe it's possible, we need to get over ourselves first and stand up against the evils in this world. Call me a dreamer. It's hard when everyone thinks their way is the right way.

I'm also perhaps a little superstitious, if I could be labeled that. I believe that our pride gets in the way of things. I don't believe in counting your eggs before they're hatched. Or putting all of your eggs in one basket. (Let's just say things with eggs, I tend not to believe.)

It's not to say you shouldn't take 'pride' in your work. Which I feel is a terrible derivative for 'confidence' in our lexicon. I think you should have confidence in your work. I think you should have an enjoyment for your work, whether that is because it merely provides you food on your table, or provides food for someone with no table, I believe either is enough in many cases. Be thankful for your job. This outlook is important to have. If you don't have confidence, you should take time to learn your work to a greater degree, take my writing for example. I should work on honing my skills as a writer. Otherwise what can I hope to amount to?

Careful in tooting your own horn though. Comfort leads to death. (I know, so dramatic.) Just dot your I's and cross your tee's is all I'm saying. If you forget to buy the good rivets for building the project and think it doesn't matter, the idea might end up sinking on an unseen iceberg you didn't plan for, no matter how much you believe in it.

August 5

Never say Never.

The Pickwick Papers

IT could happen. Words are sweet. Good advice, but how often is it followed? I'd say not often, if not never. That's because this ruby of knowledge only gives a hint of hope. It's hardly ever followed up with a plan of action. We as individuals tend to give up. That's not to say it doesn't happen for the people on the movie screens. It's a platitude. It's meant to lift someone up, without giving a way to do it outside the moment.

If you're like me and consider yourself a Toy'R'Us kid (May Geoffrey rest in peace) you should probably be able to say 'Never Never Land' and smile, (which if we break that magical isle's name apart almost seems like it's 'Always Land' or 'Whatever you want Land'. That's vexing to me.), so my generation (your generation) if we know who Peter Pan is, must have Never in our vocabulary. All joking aside though, we tell ourselves, never a lot. Sure, things could happen, you might get a raise or travel the world. This tidbit of info gives us nothing but blind hope. Put us at a quiet ease with our current situations. It's something friends say to us to lighten our moods, but then after it does and we move forward, what then? Are we supposed to only admit that something could always happen? What about the work behind that? Rarely do things just fall in your lap in this world. I spoke about success stories you hear about and how it's not as easy as the media makes it seem. Sweat, tears, blood, jazz. It takes all of it.

So, while never saying never might be a good start, you need to push that a little further for it to be helpful. What good is it if you were to go up to someone on the street who needed help and told them that tomorrow could be different, if only they applied themselves and then walked on, disappearing into the faceless masses. I see this nugget of inspiration as the same thing. What's someone supposed to do with that? It's pointless, it's like arguing on Facebook. It might be seen by millions. But how many will remember and or be able to utilize that advice?

I mean this needs to be followed up. Never say never, sure, but what do they want to do? How can they get there? Do they have a plan? If not, are you going to help them with a plan? Would that take too much time? Then perhaps its best if you don't give them any time? Especially telling them this mindless drivel. If someone was lost and you knew the way, are you going to take the time to get them there, or just throw a finger in the air pointing to the left, or right? It's going to be one way or the other. Maybe we feel with the empty words you've that at least we've narrowed down their chance to 50/50. Now they can at least go south and not entirely in the wrong direction. You think that would help? Of course not.

We need to stop simply giving worthless advice our collective mind has cobbled together and create actually paths for people. If people don't know which way to go, and we merely have an inkling from something we've heard but never looked into the thing personally and can't say if it's true. Why say anything at all?

Don't ever say never, but give better directions than a compass app could.

August 6

Never be satisfied.

NEVER say never. That's what I always say. In this case it's about pushing forward, striving for the next goal. Keeping things moving. Not being comfortable standing around. These are good things. You should push yourself. Always have a new goal, and when you finish one, move on to the next. Don't rest on your laurels.

Good stuff, it's hard not to admit. But sometimes the opposite is true. What if never being satisfied means you're depressed or you've done heroin and it took your 'happy'? (PSA don't do heroin, ever.) Perhaps never being satisfied takes a toll.

If you're never satisfied you might not ever stop striving for betterment, or you might simply stop trying altogether. If you can never find satisfaction then why bother?

This gem feels like one of those pieces of advice that tries to correct a social/individual failing by overshooting the mark and expects us to figure out the puzzle. It's 'the secret'.

It's also untrue. You should be able to find satisfaction, find it in your job, or hobby, or side project or cause.

What you shouldn't do is never be satisfied. Perfectionist, if there is such a thing, I would argue there isn't, (I'm sure that will send a few people into a tizzy. Mostly perfectionist are those who lie to themselves.) think this way. There is always one more thing to do to make it 'perfect'. Stop. Relax, just for a second.

I'm not saying rest on your laurels. I don't want you to be lazy. I what you to have confidence in your work and look back at it, or glance back. Take 5 minutes, yep just 5, or 10 or a day. Then move forward. Recognize your achievement, don't gloat, see it for what it is. Be glad in it, then move forward. On to the next thing.

Successful people are satisfied in some regard. Don't let them fool you.

And successful people, please stop saying this. It's not true, you know that.

August 7

Follow the crowd.
—

I love a parade! I watch them from time to time, I think I've been in a few, or at least one. Parades know where they're going though. Sometimes crowds don't. Big crowds or small crowds, cliques. I know you've all heard of 'group think'. There have been different psychological experiments that show its dangers. If you haven't, I've added a few links in the appendix on this date. It's pretty interesting stuff. It's pretty dangerous stuff. I'm not saying in every case following the crowd is bad, but I wish the crowd was full of people who came to a decision on their own and the 'crowd' merely all came to the correct outcome without any outside pressure. I'm a dreamer, what did I tell ya?

As that's never going to happen, following the crowd is normally considered a negative term. It implies mob mentality and the aforementioned 'group think'. Some of these things are 'baked' in our societal structures and its even how stocks work. It's inevitable that we will follow the crowd. No way around it. Even not 'following the crowd' is following another crowd. There are too many crowds not to follow someone. Nobody has their own drum, they got it from someone at some point.

The things we hold dear, our passions, our families, our jobs. These are in different ways influenced and created by the crowd. I'd say Russia might know something about the bandwagon effect. It seems that it's hard to get away from.

Following the crowd is not something we see as a 'good' thing per say, unless it's a worthy cause, but we hardly use the term 'just following the crowd' unless you're trying to insult the person's ability to think and act on their own cognizance.

I say to this, never follow the crowd. (You will, it's inevitable, remember.) I would tell you, find your way, don't wait on someone to lead you. If you're passionate about knowing something, then research it. Don't read Wikipedia and spout off quotes, or defend something you don't understand. When you do that, you're following a crowd. And maybe that crowd is a bunch of lemmings.

Some of you might know lemmings as animals who when scared will run off cliffs to their deaths. There's a game Lemmings. They walk forward, your job is to lead the herd to a safe exit.

So, if that's what you think, let me open your eyes to the truth. Lemmings don't try to kill themselves, which is most likely came about due to an observed behavior, compounded by a misconception followed by reinforcement. Which seems rather curricular in terms of how it came to be, by other people simply following the crowd that came up with the notion.

August 8

Don't follow the crowd.
—

SO, we all want to be individuals. We tell ourselves we are independent. Our own captains. (I like boats, I really need to learn how to swim though.) Take for example this blog entry on Gizmodo.

I'm not trying to pick on them but something's off. (Personally, I love this site. I'm using it merely as reference for my point.) In the last write up I spoke of Lemmings. I referenced an article on Snopes that explains how Disney faked the lemmings mass suicide. The film apparently pushed them over a cliff. Now in the video I linked, the narrator explains in once scene that 'all seem to survive the ordeal'. Now perhaps that's because they returned them to the Inuit people, they bought them from after the fake scene. I don't know, the 1950's are so very long ago to do proper research.

In the Gizmodo article, however the actual narration is cut off by a music in the background so the reader doesn't hear him say this, which might lead to some questions. More to this point the article references that in the movie Ben-Hur in 1959, (I assume, the article says 1950's) a single scene was responsible for killing 100 horses! Outrageous, right? Totally. I was appalled. I went to another site, an article about 25 things I didn't know about Ben-Hur. Turns out this article says in 1925, one stunt man died and 5, count it, 5 horses, in 1925 died. In the 1959 movie with Charles Heston, there were no serious injuries to people or animals but one man died. A producer died of a heart attack. That's way different than killing 100 horses in a scene. Who do I believe? Let's check the sources… or… where are the sources?

I'll tell you, research it. Another site says that the 1925 film killed 100 horses! So, which is it? 1925 or 1959. 100 or 5? It tells me I can't trust these writers. And when I click on the link that mentions 100 horses, well it doesn't exist anymore (Which might be the case for my refs as well. That's the reliability of the internet for ya. Sorry about that). Nice huh?

This other article references 7 other animal cruelty incidents in films. 7, with no source references. None! They want me to simply take them at their word. I really wish I could, but that's impossible now, and rightly so. (I suddenly feel that I'm arguing for not following crowd, when I'm supposed to argue against it…That's the theme of the book right. Sorry, goofed there.) The point stands, I guess. How is it we find ourselves following causes/articles/people that can't reference their own points? We do, all the time. We even do it as individuals. Follow our own way, when we have no source material at all.

We read things and take them at face value. We don't look into, we simply follow. We believe ourselves to be individuals, independent. But we rely on so much from others, even to the point where we simply nod our heads and become outraged tweeting on Facebook how we should stand up for something that may have happened in a totally different way. Context isn't important, its who yells the loudest.

Counterpoint, I believe we need to follow one crowd, but it leans out from blind conformity, and hence the idea of community or crowds. You might mistake it for leaning to relativism but that's a crowd of its own. Where everyone does what they please, where people make their own truth. There are truths out there to be found, but if we don't care enough to dig for the truth ourselves, how can we expect others to do it for us?

If we don't care, that's one thing. I think we should be able to simply say we care enough to find it, or say we just want to be part of the crowd. If that's the case, I'll stop listening to you. I'll start listening to the head of the crowd, that's where the researchers or the wackos are, the ones who care. Or are their motivations as pure? Maybe they're only after fame and money, maybe they'll say anything to make a dollar?

Support things you believe in, but know what it means to believe in it. It's not something you just say, so stop just saying it. Live it, or leave it behind.

August 9

Buy things from late night television paid programming.

2 AM. Perfect time to buy that lawn equipment for the back yard. Buy the knife that cuts cans. The magic leaf blower/weed-eater. Get that little glass rabbit to go on your shelf. Go ahead and get the necklace with glass in it. No shame in it.

Just know that it's not the best quality. I think it's junk. ShamWow. I can get those much cheaper in bulk. Now Billy Mays, I honestly liked him. I still use Oxy-Clean. Knives that cut cans and the cordless yard trimmer. Junk.

This might stem from the fact that I grew up listening to Kevin Trudeau. What a character, this guy. Think I first saw him when he was talking about Mega Memory or some variation of it. I thought it was awesome. Through the years I saw him pitch diets and how to win in real estate (I think). I watched imitators sell similar products, he was pretty good. I hear he wasn't on the up and up. I read that he was a total fraudster. No doubt the first time I saw him doing it, I may have thought that. Too good to be true after all. I enjoyed watching his corny infomercials. They remind me of those videos that you have to keep watching because in just a few minutes they're going to tell you the secret of their success, or product. They just irritate me now.

I dislike knowing that people are being taken advantage of. It irks me. Not sure what can be done about it. It's not even on a small scale, the products are junk and come from manufacturers who make things cheaply. Cheaper than they can be made locally. Even on a global scale, (if you are reading this in another country) they create lower quality products that people buy and we can't compete or provide.

It's not nearly the same as the dark web, you should know better to buy things from there, but like my grandmother always said. Nothing good happens after 11 PM on a week day.

August 10

Keep up with the Joneses

NEIGHBORS or social equals, just those around us. We need to make sure we have the same lawn mower Ed has or that new car Mary just got. I'm sure that's just the spoiled. "We don't all feel that way Alex. I don't need a fancy car."

It's in our nature though. We want the next best thing, for the most part. The new phone, or app. A better house. Perhaps we're good, we're content with what we have. There's always tomorrow. Tomorrow something new comes out. At least here, but in other parts of the world tomorrow someone needs to find some food, or figure out how to provide a future for their children. Tomorrow someone might lose their child. Or someone might be gone to old age.

Many times, we focus on what we need, or what we can get from something. We even think about what we can do or must do for our children. Sometimes it's hard, we have to work hard to provide. Good stuff there.

It feels like a rat race sometimes. Our intentions might even be good toward others. Helping to balance the scale, when we have so much and others have so little. Keep it up.

It's a 'get up and go' world. We have to keep our eye on the prize.

These are good things. No doubt, children being supported and even helping others. But you got to keep up, right? Otherwise you fall behind.

After all we don't make the pace, its set for us. Question, who sets it exactly? I'd like to know. Differing opinions set it, people in high place set it. Our neighbors set it. Life sets it, our needs, and our wants. We can't control many things, but we can control some.

We provide for children, that's something that sets the pace. What else? Bills? We could have set them if we tried in the beginning. If we did some research at the start. If our parents took the time and taught us how to budget, and we listened.

It's true the life we build sets the pace that we run, but don't mistake that pace for something you don't have control in setting. As you grow older that control slips by, things need done after all. Even now you have the ability to take control of your pace. Perhaps you need to seek a financial adviser, or step back and see what the rush is even about. Maybe keeping pace with the Joneses is what you need to stop doing. Maybe you can set your own pace. But only if you're running your own race. (Nice! Rhyming.)

August 11

Failure is not an option.

Me

WE have this odd understanding that if we fail at something then it's over, or we're not good enough. That's inane. It's interesting that when we fail at something, we feel bad. Why do we do that? Possibly because we let someone down? True. If we aren't as good as our word that can make us feel bad. If we failed to finish a project on time, or pick up our kid for the weekend.

Perhaps though its learning something new, or making it all the way to the top of the skill set. It could be many things. We say failure is not an option and it breaks down confidence, in ourselves and others. Then if we fail, we feel worse, because we couldn't pull it off. So maybe just stop saying this.

I understand a boss might say this. It adds more weight to a project or deadline. Helps you understand the importance. And it truly might be, if you're a doctor a failure could mean a life. But we don't just use this in those dire situations, do we?

We use this coming right out of the gate, at least some of us do. We have to succeed the first time, why because we're smart enough. Because we all win. Everything we do is magic. At least that's what we've told ourselves. It's true, we're pretty good at most things we try, or learn about. We're like T'Challa or Tony Stark. Smart as hell. First time, every time! It's not sustainable. Successful people fail. They fail a lot! Not at everything, they get better. Learn from their mistakes.

Sometimes, every once in a while, there's a person who doesn't seem to fail, they simply learn from others. Let me tell you, they fail too. It's just that it might not be covered in detail by the wiki article or media when talking of their success.

Einstein didn't speak till he was 4, or 9 depending on what source you look at… that's a failure right there. Disinformation and misinformation abound. (Ire.)

People build from failure. Failure isn't fun, but I don't see why it has to be so bad. If we never failed, how much could we really hope to grow?

Try this, the next time you fail at something take note of it. Analyze it. Why did you fail? Did you do it too fast, or over schedule something? How could you improve? I say failure is an option and it leads us to success, if we stop beating ourselves over the head about it.

The next time you fail, smile, you're learning and that's okay. Do it again. Better.

August 12

Try and try again.
—

SO with failure being an option, outside of surgery or clinical trials or blanket irritating prescription ads explaining death as a side effect(I consider death to be an 'effect', not a 'side effect'), followed the next year by class action suits. (Seriously can't they just stop with that already... it's a broken cash grab cycle and its killing people or ruining their lives simply in pursuit or the almighty dollar)

Let me start over...if failure is an option then trying and trying again is the reaction to that. How can trying over and over be terrible advice then?

Some of us, when we were young have been told we can be anything we want to be. I agree, if we have the drive and determination, we can push toward that. They never told me about how stubborn I could be, or our futile some endeavors can be. Take the book "The Lost city of Z" it's about an 'explorer' Percy Fawcett. Spoiler Alert!

Percy Fawcett whether you believe him to be who he was portrayed as in the movie or something else, it seems to me he spent a considerable amount of effort to find this city of Zed. The movie explains, at least in my head, he wasn't really present for his family or wife. He insisted on making numerous trips for years at a time. Each time he failed to find much of anything. He brought his son and friend along on his last expedition, on that trip he disappeared. That was 1925. (The same year as Ben-Hur and the 500/5 horse death scene...)

Now maybe on the backbone of some of Percy's writings and I say maybe, Michael Heckenberger found some structures they now call Kuhikugu around the area Percy and his son disappeared. By 'around' I assume that could up to 500 miles. So, Percy's lack of findings may have led others to look in the area, but it may have been the stories Percy himself studied, or another source entirely. You could argue Percy wasted his time, and his life as well as his son's life trying and trying again. On the other side of the coin, perhaps he found his life full of adventure and no regret.

So, try and try again, no question. Failure is an option, but sometimes we need to understand that we can't do things. We have limits. Percy spoke of the Lost city of Z, but he never found it. Maybe at some point it's okay to stop trying, perhaps you want to be like Percy and search for the thing you know exists out there. Trying and trying again until you disappear in the jungle. Or perhaps there is a time to quit, perhaps failure is an option. Not failure exactly, but moving on to the next great adventure.

August 13

Sign up for every credit card you can. It's more money for you!
—

FREE money. Do you know what a 'debt-slave' is? Well it's a pretty simple term. It refers to people who work mostly to pay off debt, Wikipedia says "Debt-bondage...is a person's pledge of labor or services as security for the repayment for a debt or other obligation, where there is no hope of actually repaying the debt". Now in third world countries or in colonial America we see this in its classical definition. In America people would 'bond' themselves voluntarily to someone who would pay for their trip across the sea. This was not the same thing as slavery, bonded servants had more rights without a doubt, and benefits. Not really going into that.

We don't perhaps think in those terms anymore. We don't 'bond' ourselves to a credit company and perform work as they tell us to. We're somewhat free to make money our own way. That's pretty much the difference as I see it. I'm not saying its slavery, I mean we volunteered for it. Although, I'm sure we read the fine print, and even if you did. You still signed it, it's not really a choice. If I want to listen to my music, I have to accept the iTunes agreement, right? It's an interesting concept, all the paperwork we sign and no one but lawyers read. Anyway, it seems a rather frivolous action in the face of something that could matter, or useless waste of trees if it actually means nothing.

Now that I've vilified all the credit lenders and pointed out all the contracts, we pay no mind to. (I'm sure that will work out to my advantage just fine...) I want to bring us to the point. Stop not reading the contracts. You're allowed to make them wait. Sit there for an hour, and ask questions. I urge everyone to do this. Maybe they'll start making the contracts smaller. (I doubt it.) It's your job to know what you're being bonded to.

Maybe we're being taken advantage of. Being preyed upon. I think a lot of it could be because we're not taking the time to research the context of the situation. That's what this book is somewhat for. Research your points, know what your signing. Don't talk about things you don't know, it truly is a disservice.

I know there are situations we can't control, and we need cash now. But it's not every situation, there are plenty of times we could think a little longer, but choose not to. It's time to stop signing things we don't read. Take the time, no one will give it to you. Take it.

August 14

Model yourself after your favorite Disney character.

—

I know I wrote about not imitating famous people to get away from yourself. Don't do that. Sometimes it's fun to pretend though. Have fun today. Believe in yourself. I'm sure you have a plan now that you've listened to all this bad advice. Take it and have fun today. Your future is ahead of you, even if you only have today.

August 15

Take Time out of your life to watch Godfather III.

I know Godfather was a great movie. It's one of those top 100 AFI movies of all time. Godfather II, long, but I enjoyed it. Poor Fredo. I don't think God Father III was the worst movie of all time, but it lacked some of the 'mafia' I could feel in the first two. I would recommend the first two, although they are not for the faint at heart. There is plenty of violence in them, so be warned. SPOILERS AHEAD!

On the other hand, it does complete the trilogy of the Corleone family. The pacing is different, even compared to the second. The second was tragic, to me it showed what happens when you come into that life. Your family becomes broken. The changing seasons at the end after Fredo's last scene spoke to my heart.

The third however worked to accomplish the same feeling. Bad things catch up to you. For me, that was clear at the end of two. Even if Michael got away with it. It was by no means the end, but I felt the darkness of it. The third worked to accomplish the same, but also reestablish the Godfather. I have to say I enjoyed Andy Garcia's character, but felt that Al Pacino's Michael lacked the fire he once had. I suppose age will do that, and it's not for lack of his performance, but something felt as if it was missing. I just can't put my finger on it, perhaps it was too grandiose with its reach.

All that being said I feel it's a movie that must be watched, but only if you've seen the first two, then you have to see the final. Since we're talking about movies, I'm going to list some others that I have seen. Perhaps I wouldn't say you will like them as much as they should be watched.

In no particular order:

North by Northwest Raiders of the Lost Ark Goodfellas The Gladiator
    Casablanca Cool Hand Luke Star Wars (OT) The Princess Bride
    It's a Wonderful Life Manos: The Hands of Fate Blade Runner
    The Goonies The Deer Hunter The Hustler The Color of Money
    Close Encounters of the Third Kind Schindler's List
    The Sandlot

There are more, I'm sure we could all make lists. Maybe make one of the top 100 today. If you don't watch movies, bully for you.

August 16

No time to Relax.

—

IN this day and age, we don't have time. Things need to be done. We need to keep writing, we need to make that project deadline. That term paper is due Friday. On top of that we are constantly being barraged with marketing, via our electronic ball and chains. Gotta love technology, you can't live without it, and you can't live without it.

I've begun to notice my quiet time. Now, I'm not really a mediator. I don't consider myself a talker or think I require a huge amount of space, but I've noticed there are always sounds. Either from an outside source, like music that I'm playing, or television that is on. I'll admit I even speak these words out loud as I type them. There's always sound.

Even when I sleep, I'll put on white noise. It drowns out other sounds with sound. Do we remember what it feels like to be truly in a quiet place? Have you ever found a spot, in a park or woods that is quiet? Perhaps there are a few animal's or wind.

It's really hard to find such a place. Can you say if you've sat in a space for more than 3 minutes without thinking about what is going on or hearing the hum of electronics around you.

If you can great. I'm not sure I can. Find a quiet place. Don't think too hard. Do that 'clear your mind' thing you always hear people mention in movies or from that yoga class down the street. Just breath and relax. Don't think too hard.

I'm not saying it will work, but try it for 15 minutes. It's going to take at least 7 to 'wind down'. Find a quiet place, maybe that's your car in the morning.

Most of the time we never stop moving. In our sleep we still move about and are working to recharge.

Take some time in a quiet place today. Or try to find one, I bet it's harder than you might think.

August 17

Don't take risks.
—

I mentioned this before. Remember. It's a hard concept to get out of our heads. Risk means danger. Some people gravitate to danger. They're wired differently. Sometimes that pays off, other times it can end in tragedy. YOLO. Stupid.

But the risk takers have points. If you fail to try, if you don't get out there, what are you going to do? Just work, play it safe, then retire and hopefully live to old age. That's a pretty good dream. A lot of people would love for the opportunity. Not everyone has it. If that's you, good on ya.

Sometimes though we don't take risks because we might be taken advantage of, or lose something dear to us. What we might consider risky might not even be on someone else's radar.

Not taking risks, whatever the level of that risk might be, is similar to not trying. Or not ever failing. At the end of your life you can say 'I never failed.' That's something to say. I don't know what type of metal that trophy is, but it's not the point to never fail. I think needing to never fail is a failure in itself. So be warned if it is, you've probably failed at realizing it.

It's a catch 22 in a way, isn't it? In convincing yourself not to take risks, at some point you risk never doing anything. I'd say it's impossible to not risk somethings.

It's the act of taking calculated risks, not simply doing crazy life thrilling things that's important. Put yourself out there, go talk to that girl or guy. Instead of meeting only online with a group of friends in a game, maybe meet up at BlizzCon. Clearly, I'm talking with my somewhat introverted cohorts. Maybe save for a trip and go. I don't know what it could be, it could be anything, a beach trip with a few friends, or a road trip, it doesn't have to be a huge risk.

Try and make something, maybe you risk failure in not finishing, but at least you try. Maybe reach out for help on something. Try it, not just once, multiple times. When we fail to take risks, sometimes we box ourselves into corners that we feel are real.

Take a chance. Take a risk. Calculated. Don't get too comfortable.

August 18

Shame your pet today.

I don't have a lot to say about this. It's a rather cheap plug, but I ran across it in my internet travels. I got lost there. Be warned. And if you get lost, at least come back here for tomorrow's advice.

Of course, we don't think about doing this to another person, but animals don't mind so much. They know we love them. They can't read after all. Or at least they can't tell us they can...

http://shameyourpet.com/

August 19

Put someone down to make yourself feel better.

WHILE pet shaming might bring "Awes" and giggles to our lips, people shaming is something we'd never do. But people do it all the time. I don't know if it's getting better, and in fact, I'm pretty sure it's getting worse. What can we do though? The simple answer is, more. I'm sure there are people that would say it's more complex than that. While I don't disagree, talking about doing something and doing something, to me seem like two different things. It's time to stand up. More of us need to.

Bullying. I remember when I didn't want to go to school because I might get picked on. I wasn't a fighter, but I'd been in a few fights. I don't believe I was ever fearful for my life. I didn't want a black eye, but I wasn't worried about being shot at, or stabbed. I'm sure in many areas this might have been the norm in the 80's and 90's but my school was small.

Today we have cyber bullying. Kids don't even get to go home and be safe. The internet is everywhere. Children kill themselves because they feel they can't get away from these bullies. Not just in the US, but all over the world. They kill themselves, or each other. How does it come to this?

Some of you might say, well there isn't much I can do. If you're one of those people, I'd say you're probably right. You can't do much at all, not with that attitude. We are all consumed with the things we have to do, until something reaches out and touches us, maybe that's this book (forgive it for being so frisky and assuming.) maybe it's the death of a loved one, think child or cancer, or one of the multitudes of other events that could happen that flip our worlds upside down. I hope it never comes to a tragedy for you or another to take up a cause, but it is sometimes an initializing action. I've put a link to a few bullying sites in the appendix, from the US, UK, India, and Australia. If you're being bullied, reach out. It's not okay. Also, I included a site called Iamawittness. They have an emoji. It's been out since 2015. It's a giant eye. I haven't seen this around the internet enough. It should have a hash tag #iamawitness attached to it.

Maybe you'll use it, you know about it now.

Think about your kids. Let them know about it. Word of mouth.

Perhaps we could make one for trolls too. #Ihatetrolls.

August 2

Don't read to your children.

AGAIN it's the time thing. Electronics. Heck, it might be our kids are smart enough to read on their own. I'm happy for you that your child can pick it up just fine. Maybe they'll be one of those "I'm fine" kinda people. They're 'nice polite quiet' people after all.

If that's what comes to mind, you don't see the whole point. I'll give it to you, our children nowadays are pretty fancy with the tech. But it's more than just reading. It's reading together. It's helping them learn, and not simply what you're reading to them, no doubt. Here is an example, my mother read to me when I was little. I'd say, and others agree, it creates a bond. (Not like the financial debt bond, mind you.) It's an opportunity to help them love to read, and love and interact with you.

Okay, so I'm a writer. Hence, I read. I don't think we do all the time. I stopped really for about 10 years back in the day. Not to say I stopped reading, I read articles and cereal boxes, milk cartons and road signs. It's different reading actual books and not just news feeds. It's only now started to come back to me. My attention span that is.

Of course, reading makes you smarter too. You ingest more information. Not like how its shoved in our faces with our electronics. When we read, we wish to consume the information, although I want to point out, and maybe it's just me but I can recall a novel I read 5 years ago sometimes a lot quicker than I can the article I read 5 minutes ago. Maybe that's just a fault of my own. It's information, it's just not always worthy of being stored.

Reading with your children helps them to create a desire for it, an acceptance outside of playing Candy Crush and Angry Birds, or Clash of Clans. (Which reminds me I need to upgrade my Town Hall.)

Make some time, I'm gonna say 30 minutes. I know it's a lot. So, a half hour before bed, your kids could listen to you read. This will do two things, it will bore them to tears if you read like Ben Stein but it will also wind things down to help them sleep, and draw you closer to them. FYI, it's been said that electronic devices can help stimulate your brain and cause you to remain awake longer than desired.

As a bonus, as a child I remember being read to by my mother, and as an adult I get to appreciate those moments all the more.

30 minutes. If you can't do it every day, try it at least once a week. And do a game night. It could be worth it in the long haul. Just saying. Make some memories and teach not only through action not words. (Or in this case, words, but time spent reading them to/with your kids.)

August 21

McDonald's regular coffee isn't hot. That lady wanted the big bucks.

— *The Internet*

YOU might understand the reference. In fact, in the US around the 1990's it might have been considered a jab or joke about people suing for things that were stupid, or as they say "frivolous lawsuit". I admit I'd be one of those people (to joke about it, not to make up a frivolous lawsuit). The event was that a woman ordered a coffee and subsequently spilled that coffee on herself. So, she sues McDonald's for that event. Not McDonald's fault. The lady's fault. Case closed. It's like if a robber were to impale himself on a knife in your house, and sued you for it. Crazy.

Let's look a little closer though. Some context if you will. I'll give you this, she spilled it on herself. No question there. Her name was Stella Liebeck and she was 79 years old. Still she shouldn't have held the cup between her legs, like everyone does. Still her fault.

Did you know that the coffee hot? Sure, that was in the initial story. But really, hot. Like scalding, right. It's supposed to be though. It's coffee, not like the iced sugar syrup you order today. It was hot coffee. It's hot. Well hot in this case was between 180 and 190 degrees. That's really, really hot, some might too hot.

Okay, well we knew it was hot. Coffee only came hot back in that day. That does seem a little much though. Maybe 140 to kill things in the water like Legionellae, but 180 is pretty high. I understand McDonald's might have some other funky stuff they need to kill off, but that's somewhat excessive.

Ms. Liebeck received third degree burns around her inner thighs. In fact, she offered to settle for around 20,000, after all she required skin-grafts for her burns. I can't imagine that's very cheap. McDonald's, well they offered her 800 dollars. So, in order to probably pay for her medical bills, she went forward with the case.

In the end they settled for an unknown sum. And I only looked up the first source I found, some 'facts' may vary. But if I heard this story back in the 90's maybe I wouldn't say I know the coffee is hot every time they hand it to me at the McDonald's drive through. Maybe it was hotter than it seemed. Question of morality perhaps. If as a company with a small profit margin comes across an individual that was caused harm by an operation or process. Is it worth helping? I'm going to say no, it's not worth it. If you help one person then anyone could come crawling out of the woodwork. It would kill your profit to do the acceptable thing. Not because you as a company don't want to, but because there are people who would walk all over you. So perhaps it's not the company that's big and bad, but our circumstances. What might the solution be, perhaps we need to start being more helpful on an individual personal level. Maybe we caused this in our world from our 'fit in' faces? (Maybe I'm on to something here.)

Now, back to context. It's terrible we can't trust the knowledge given to us, isn't it? I think it requires us to stop and check the sources. We can't simply trust anymore. Sad really, but how often do you simply accept the things people tell you. I do it all the time. I guess I need to stop. Maybe you should to. Maybe we all should really start to question these things. Maybe stop showing our 'fit in' faces. Maybe we wouldn't need as many lawyers. Ha-ha, that's funny.

August 22

Start a show about nothing, without prior approval from Jerry Seinfeld or Larry David.

I grew up watching Seinfeld in varying degrees. It's a show about nothing. It's almost one of kind. Sure, there are other sitcoms, but there was something different about this one. I don't rightly know what it was. Larry David, he also made another show, Curb Your Enthusiasm. It's kinda about nothing too. I mean there are a lot of shows that follow characters' lives. You could say they're about nothing in particular, but I feel that Seinfeld and Curb Your Enthusiasm embrace this concept. Not in a way that makes it pointless to watch or a waste of time, but oddly captivating. It's a show about meaningless day to day, with purpose. To make you laugh.

Fourth wall stuff in a way, but not. I don't know how to describe it, magic might be a good word. Not everyone liked it. I won't say every episode was a hoot. I can't say I've seen them all. It went out on top though. That's saying something.

I've linked the wiki pages on these two series in the appendix below. Jerry Seinfeld didn't stop there. He's got a new series, Comedians in Cars getting Coffee. Let's hope they don't burn themselves.

Also, of note, I guess someone is now suing Jerry over the idea. Interesting it took about 6 whole years before it was important enough to do so. It's all about the money though.

Maybe you might start a show about nothing, just make sure the nothing is worth something before you do. Take an example from Larry and Jerry.

August 3

Beat that dead horse, go ahead, beat it. (Not a real dead horse sicko. Although that would be terrible advice.)

—

YOU ever find yourself in an argument or conversation that's already been concluded, but the other person doesn't know it. That's happened. Even on an amusing level. I'll pick on my parents here. (I'm sure you could do the same. Don't judge me! 😊) I know I might not always remember how to do things, especially in my teen years. Instruction helped me understand. However, it doesn't stop once you're 18. Your parents at times forget you're not perpetually young, one of the lost boys of Pan. Granted I've started to ask them to write things down, but that's mostly because I tune out. They will go over things they think I should do, then go over them again with some lost detail. Then again since the third time is the charm, and how charming it is! I just require them to write what they want to tell me down. I had it the first time, but then more and more information is piled on. It was clear, but now not only do I know what to do, but the exact steps to do it in too. (I love you family.)

Or how about the person at work who explains the marketing plan, over, and over again. "You get it, ice cream. People will do anything for ice cream." Got it. Please stop Bob. (I'm sure that's where my parents got it from, dealing with business people. Tell 'em what you're going to tell them, tell them, then tell them what you told them.)

What if it's you? Do you have to run a point into the ground before your teenagers listen? That might be, I wasn't always the brightest crayon in the box. Or perhaps you see that argument on Facebook, that just keeps going on and on, but neither see that the other side has disproven the other's point and they keep throwing words around as if they are going to save the world in their PJ's and gaming chair.

If you're like me and find the humor the advice offensive, good. It is offensive. If you find yourself beating a dead horse, stop. Now, it might be that you are talking to an idiot. It could be that, but it could be that you're just calling them an idiot. In which case that is offensive too. Or the third you could be an idiot for thinking that it matters what you say on an obscure Facebook posting. If you want to change, you must show that change. Not on Facebook, too much noise.

Now, in my parent's defense I can't rightly say in every instance they shouldn't drag out the horse and flog it from time to time, but for the rest of you I urge you to think about it before you do.

August 24

There are no absolutes in this world.

———

THAT would be kinda fun. I mean we wouldn't have to be so concerned about all these things we show concern for. I mean, that's right, right? Maybe you don't use this statement, maybe it comes in a different form. Perhaps we've moved past that argument in the world, and know only some things are relative, but things like "Live your truth", "Do what you will" still fill our minds and influence society. So, what's wrong with that?

It's not hard to point to any one thing. If we all simply did what we wanted, (and trust me we tend to do that anyway,) there would be chaos as they say, but as we have laws in place and a greater 'moral' society so perhaps this chaos only happens on a smaller scale just quiet like. So, what's it matter, what a person believes or how they act? Why? If we're good and relatively we are working toward the same goals, then it (the overall effect) should lean toward peace. I agree, if we're actually good, it would lean toward peace. It seems though we as a public body lean toward indifference and others lean toward what they will. Else wouldn't things being to look better around here? If we were of a mind to do actual good?

So, we can't simply do what we want, that's absurd, right? And clearly not working, as we do what we want regardless of someone's moral high horse or religiousness or logical reasoning of working toward a future and preserving it for human kind. I think wherever you stand you can see that doesn't work as a model for society. So where does that leave this post? I think relativism has a place, many places. In the study of other cultures, in relations to Einstein's theories. In relation to opinions and experiences, but in math there are absolutes. In fact, we have something called Absolute values in math.

So, it's not that absolutes don't exist. They do, math has proven that. Math people. Math did that. I'm not sure what kind of math kids now a days are learning but they should know that much. Some relativist may have forgotten though. I'm sure we don't use the statement above much. Unless we're not using logic. I think an argument on such is pretty much like beating a dead horse myself. But if there are absolutes, what are they? Can we start to create a list of those things?

I think this is where we get into the discussion about 'who' is qualified to make such a list? You? Me? Them? Us? Should we have two lists? One for one group and one for another? I like the idea of two lists, just two. Do you think we could do that?

I say let's give it a go. We can create a website for the two lists and allow people to weigh in on what's on the lists. We'll have a committee for the two lists. But who would we get to be on the two committees? Which list do they get? List 1, or List 2. How do you know which list you should be looking at? I suppose it's relative to you at that point which list to follow, but I might argue that the list itself wouldn't be. Otherwise why would you follow it at all.

August 25

Don't drink water today.

ONE day won't hurt. I mean you get water from the cans of soda you drink and the coffee you consume anyway. It's no matter. I'd agree. Sometimes I go weeks without drinking water. At least in bland water form. I have coffee and hence water every day.

So, the healthy people would tell us we should drink at least some amount of water, but now instead of 8 glasses of 8ozs each, we can get it from coffee. I could have told them that back in the 90's when I only drank coffee and beer and mountain dew. Gotta do the Dew.

Chances are you've already had the intake of water required, we do need water to survive. That's never really been in question.

Maybe start a new trend today, try some straight water. From the tap if it's not contaminated with chlorine and fluoride or whatever else they tell us is bad for us in water these days. Drink a bottle. Heck go ahead and put that flavored drink mix in it. See how it goes.

All in all, terrible advice not to drink water. Terrible. Some people don't have water. Isn't that amazing? There are organizations that help.

I have added 'Clean water for Everyone' in the appendix on this date. They focus on providing water to schools in the hope that this will give children more time to focus on learning. That's an amazing thought, give kids enough water so they can focus on learning. Interesting. Honestly, I would have never even thought of it. I suppose because I've always had enough water. We don't give a lot of thought to things we don't know about. Make sure to read, and not just your news feeds. Deep huh?

August 26

Live to work.

ANYONE seen the movie *Office Space*? Well it's about a guy who decides he no longer wants to work all the time. He ends up doing something illegal, but in the end gets out of it. It's not a movie you should watch to get your relative moral values, but its humorous.

Sometimes it feels like we simply work all the time, if we're not at work, we're working on something that needs done. Work, work, work (No commas, commas imply pausing).

Some companies have come up with work-life balance efforts. These are helpful. They are coming to terms with the wellbeing of their employees. It's important. I think globally so. I don't think that globally its being addressed. I think we should start.

There are people who also choose to live to work. I myself like work, keeps me busy. It's not busy work, it's just busy. It helps me feel productive. That's really what I want to do, is be productive, not saying I want to work all the time but I relish the feeling.

Sometimes we can be dragged down by our jobs though. Another day at the grindstone. We can't quit, we need our jobs to provide for our lives. No way around it. It's one thing to talk about how we can 'one up' ourselves in this world, it's another to do it. Sounds bleak, but in those cases I think we're looking at the forest and we can't see the trees. We aren't breaking up our days, but we seek them as one long week.

I have a schedule. I even mark down the hours I work. It turns out if I work 8 hours a day, and I sleep 8 hours a day I'm left with 8 extra hours. So, we mark off 2 hours for driving to work and back, that leaves me 6. Mark off another 2 for television, that's 4. Mark off 1 for cooking and one for shower. (I don't take an hour-long shower, I do brush my teeth for an abnormally long amount of time though. Still can't get them as white as the tv people. I'll keep trying!) That leaves 2 hours for something else, every day. That's 10 hours during the week and even more on Saturday and Sunday. It might not seem like a lot, but I think it's enough to take notice of and maybe fill with more than my favorite past time, which is 'smashing couch'. What do you think? Have a project you want to start?

August 27

Superfruit. Shumooper fruit.

IT'S a bird. No, it's a plane. No, it's Superfruit! (I couldn't resist. It was futile.) Not a lot to say here. Superfruits came about in 2004. As a marketing concept. In fact, according to the source of all knowledge and understanding Wikipedia explains that it's really not backed up by science, but merely the manufacturer prerogative. Interesting. So, it's kind of a white lie? Seems like there are a lot of those around. Or maybe that's misinformation. Wish I could find context.

I was on a superfruit kick a few years ago. Star Fruit. Awesome looking stuff. It looks like a star. It tastes like water, I mean really, it's just water. But apparently it also contains, just the smallest amount of something called 'caramboxin'. In summary it can be bad for people with kidney and liver issues. Perhaps like grapefruit shouldn't be taken with medication. I'm not making that up. Don't eat grapefruit with medication, it might be worse than drinking, might. Don't do that either. (I've linked the wiki articles on it if you want to look into that more.)

So, it looks like super fruit might have in some cases higher antioxidants. These help against free radicals, free radicals in my limited understanding of medical things can damage cells which leads to possible cancers. I assume. I've never studied it. No time after all. I have to take their word for it. I do by the way, but on second thought, I don't have to take their word, I can look up the research myself. Actual research, not from Bob's blog. We should all research things that are important to us. I think that's part of the point of this book and wouldn't want to misinform you there.

We all want to be healthy. It just makes things easier. Eat apples and bananas. Eat grapes. They're good for you. We don't need them to be called super for you to do that, do we?

Learning about this, (in the whole 10 minutes I looked into it) I feel that me buying into the 'superfruit' idea and picking out the more expensive items is similar to being treated like an emperor and someone trying to sell me 'new clothes'.

August 28

Google your ex. Facestalk them. Like their posts. All of them.

—

I really have nothing to say about this. Don't dwell on the past. Move forward. Don't listen to sad songs. Nothing good comes from such things. You're better than that. Turn a new leaf and go forward. There is more to life than finding someone to love, or being loved.

Of course, we want to be loved and accepted, but I believe there are others that we must think about. Maybe we haven't found someone. Maybe we are alone. Many people are. It's the way of things, maybe they don't really know how to approach someone and stick their necks out there. Rejection is hard, it actually probably takes up to about two whole minutes. Crushing. After that two minutes we insist on dwelling on it.

"Maybe I smell.", "Why don't they like me?". We dwell on it. We do that to ourselves. So, they don't like you, currently there are about 8 billion people in the world. 8 billion. (Okay, maybe it's still 7.6 or was it 7.5?) So, one doesn't have the time of day. I know, maybe they mean something to you. Rejection, even if it's only 2 minutes it can affect us deeply.

All I can say is move forward. Forgive and forget. Not doing so, doesn't hurt them. It damages you.

August 29

Look down or away from a person who has disabilities. It shows you care. Or stare hard like a creeper would.

—

SO I get it. Honestly, we probably don't address too many people directly in this day and age anyway. We nod or say "How are you doing today?" where we actually mean, "I'm acknowledging you, but I'm going to keep walking because I didn't really want to start a conversation.". Personally, I like the head nod, "Sup?" combo. It's shows you're cool, while also conveying a mastery of condensed language so as not to waste any extra time.

We would give more credence if they popped up on our phones with a text. We might actually start a conversation via our key pads. Face to face is becoming awkward in itself.

Personally, there's a chance that someone doesn't want to talk to you. I get it all the time. I'll ask how someone is doing and they give me their "Fit-in" face followed by the standard "Fine, you?" They don't mean for me to tell them how I'm doing. I get that.

Sometimes though I'll ask someone and they'll actually stop and talk. I tell you this can be awesome. (I'm not saying every person should stop and have a 5 minute conversation with me when I ask. I'll never get into the store.) When it does happen though I think it's pretty cool. I find that its mostly older people, or people in handicap spots that give better answers.

Sometimes I'll answer, maybe they seem like strange answers, because they are strange right? People don't answer "How's it going?" with an actual response. That's not normal. Someone says "How's it going?" and I'll tell them. "Well I'm going in to this store to pick up a drill. I'm going to try and build a table today." Some people will just look at me and keep walking, some stop and share some advice or ask what type of wood or details about whatever I say I'm doing. It's nice.

What's also interesting is that you never know who might be dealing with something they want to talk about. Some are more direct. Some aren't. I wonder if we could actually start asking in earnest. "How are you?"

August 30

Don't be spontaneous.

-

Me

I'M not spontaneous. Unless someone asks me how I'm doing. I just don't have that get up and go. I can't go across country on a road trip, or just decide to take swimming lessons. These things need planned out. It's crazy just to decide that you're going to travel the country side or go for a hike after work.

Maybe. What is spontaneous mean? 'Performed or occurring as a result of a sudden impulse or inclination without premeditation.' So, we know a general definition, right? It's true I plan things out. In fact, as you read earlier, I plan most of my days. I have little time for anything but perhaps an hour here or there. I can't do anything impulsive in one hour's time! I'll just play on my phone.

I think we do have a lot going on. In fact, we fill our time with either work or couch smashing. That's not true of all of us. Perhaps you're at the gym 4 or 5 days out of the week. I wouldn't call that spontaneous, simply active.

One thing that stops me from being spontaneous is all the stuff I still have to do. If I've finished one project, I start another. Does spontaneous really mean you have to do something huge and go somewhere exotic though? My younger self would tell you that's true. I don't know anymore.

I think I can 'plan spontaneity'. Now I'm sure you're thinking to yourself. That's literally impossible. You can't plan to be spontaneous. You're right, but I think you can plan for it.

Finish your tasks. Schedule your time. Create blocks, big blocks, little blocks. Of nothing. Not relax time, just spur of the moment time. Maybe you don't do anything in that time, just keep it open. Next time it comes around, maybe an idea will pop in your head. If it happens to be within that time frame, hey what do you know, you've given yourself time to be spontaneous! If you of course fill it with something you thought of outside of that block of time, its most likely not spontaneous. It might be a start though. Schedule your time so we can be spontaneous! You know, it might just work.

August 31

Don't make a bucket list today.

—

SPONTANEOUSLY make a bucket list. Okay that might not work. But do you have a bucket list? I know you might have thought about what you want to do, and even when you might do them, but do you have one? Do you keep it on your refrigerator? Does it change? Mine changes. Swimming, sailing, skiing, canoeing. I'll even add locations. Sometimes it's not places, but projects. Causes I'd like to give to, but can't at the moment. Books to read, books to write.

I've included a few links in the appendix to help with this project. If you have a family maybe make it a family project to come up with a bucket list. Combine your ideas.

I think it's worth the short amount of effort it takes to come up with a list. It doesn't even have to be world travels. Maybe it's something else. But take the time to figure that out.

There is so much that we can do in this world, but we have to put our minds to it. If we simply live in our phones and internets, we might miss the life around us.

September 1

Swim in waters with large alligators.

I saw a YouTube video once, I'm pretty sure it's gone now. It was I believe, this man in Texas (Not trying to pick on people in Texas. Just this guy.) and he was going to prove that he could swim with the gators. I suppose he proved that, but it cost him his life. The sobering point I took from this is, don't try to prove how much of a man you are by doing dangerous things. It might work out a time or two. This brings to mind some of the internet challenges as well. Just stop, trolls laugh at your misfortune. I understand doing something for the thrill of it, but when you jump in a body of water with an ancient creature that lives off meat… because you have a desire to, or internally you want to impress or show off somehow, I have this to say, Come on man. Think it through. The best case, nothing. The worst case, you're dragged under the water by an ancient creature that lives off meat. Whereas if you stay on shore, the best case nothing happens, the worst case, nothing happens. See what I'm leaning toward?

It's purely statistics people, not fear. Although I'm man enough to admit I would not like the sensation it brings of being dragged under the water by an ancient creature that lives off meat. Not like it at all. To put it another way, if you jump in, you probably can't do math. If you don't jump though, the sky's the limit. Unless you're that guy who was trying to prove the earth was flat by building his own rocket. Surprisingly, that guy is still alive after the rocket didn't get high enough and he had to bail.

September 2

Accept what people say about you.
—

TAKE me for example. People say I'm quiet. Maybe I am, but I didn't used to be. I would talk to anyone about anything. Go up to total strangers and ask about their day. I'd tell 'em about mine. I don't do that so much anymore.

I wouldn't always talk though, and in those times (the good ol' days), I'd hear. "Oh, you're such a quiet boy." Or, "You're kinda shy aren't ya." No. Not really.

But after hearing a million times "You're kinda quiet.", I began to think I was kinda quiet. Let me tell ya. I'm slow to speak. Others don't seem to be. So, when someone says, "You're kinda quiet." And you respond, "No, I just think about what I want to say sometimes." They probably would be offended by that. Perhaps those people think faster. I'll give that to them, or some of them. So, you just don't answer. That's how you become quiet when you're not.

Or 'you should be more outgoing' or 'put yourself out there', those sound strange. I guess none of these people saw me as a teenager. Then you focus on how you're not outgoing or don't put yourself out there. Awesome thanks for the direction.

Maybe you are shy, and quiet. I've met people that I would say fit that discription.

You ever hear someone call you something your entire life and deep down you know it's not who you are, but you believe it because it just seems to fit?

Stop doing that.

I linked to a few books in the appendix. I haven't read these. You can if you think they might be good reads. I mentioned them as they are books on ways to change things in your life, how to look at things differently. The point of these (hopefully they're not dreadful) is to make you aware that change is a possibility. There is time. I know that they say life is short, but it's the longest thing you will ever do.

You can accept what people say about you, and accept your lot in life as the saying goes. Maybe it's a good lot, maybe it's a big lot. Good for you, hopefully you're sharing it.

There is time to change. You need to believe and come up with a plan. Maybe it won't work, but you will change.

Either life will change you, or you will change your life. (If someone makes a bumper sticker, I want royalties.)

September 3

Brush up on conspiracies, ignore anything that discredits them. Get angry at other people's inabilities to see the truth.

—

LET me be the first to say. I enjoy a good conspiracy. I suppose they happen. I see people get charged for conspiracy to commit murder on various tv shows. JFK, the moon landing, actually that's it. That's all I can recall on such short notice, besides the mysterious groups that rich and powerful people are a part of, or the really secret groups that the rich and powerful are a part of. My question about those super-secret groups is, if no one knows you're a part or them, is it really a group? Or is it like the Anonymous cracking/hacktivist group where you just need to say you're part of the group to be a part of the group. Who knows?

I enjoy conspiracy theories. I enjoy reading about dragons and rings that rule them all as well. I'm not saying all the conspiracies are matters of fiction. There are a couple that were right, although I'm not sure I would call the ones I found conspiracies as much as groups of people secretly planning something evil together in the past... :) I'm not sure anyone had a clue they were happening, or had a theory about it.

I've linked a few in the appendix on this date. I do find the theories fascinating, of course I'm a budding fiction writer by name so I'm not sure you should jump on the wagon I'm sitting in. I'll say this though. I'm a fan of Occam's razor. If your theory has too many moving parts, I'm not going to buy into it very easily.

I find that the motivations that individuals have can usually be scaled up. Granted with more people involved in a thing it can take on complexities within itself, but the overall outcome or root purpose is usually easy to discern.

Some of these newer conspiracies I've heard about perplex me.
http://www.thebeatlesneverexisted.com/
https://theflatearthsociety.org/home/index.php
KIS out there.

September 4

You have to see this!
—

TRUTH is, you don't have to see it. Don't buy into the lie. Somethings are better left to the imagination. Of course, we can go directly to porn and how it dulls you to intimacy and creates a chemical reaction similar to the level that many addictive drugs do, as well as distorts your ability to interact or just think. But even though I think that should be understood, that's not what this section is about.

I'm talking about that YouTube video that your friend just tells you that you can't miss. The one with the cat that falls off the back of the fish tank and scrambles out. Or the one where the skater racks himself in slow mo. Or the one that you wish you could just get out of your head. (Which ever that one might be. You know the one I'm talking about.)

The unending rabbit hole of videos we think we have to watch. I myself get lost on YouTube for hours watching amazing people. I used to watch fail videos, but I find that the People are Awesome videos are more uplifting. We shouldn't want to watch people fail so much. (I understand we do. I just wish it weren't so, is all.)

Most things I see though, I could do without seeing. Not because they're bad or there is some moral stance on it, simply for the fact that its time you can never get back. It's almost impossible to not fall into the rabbit holes, they're everywhere. A new app, a new phone and features. A talking car! (The 80's made everything.)

Just keep in mind, it's okay not to see everything. In fact, sometimes not seeing something at least back in the day was part of the fun. One of our friends would do something, you know, like in RL, and then tell us about it, in person. It did two things if not more. It allowed someone to use words to describe something, that helped my friends and myself at least increase our brain power. It also gave us things to share, and not just posting a video or pushing a phone is someone's face. But we actually shared a moment, discussing or talking about something. Some of my best memories were made when I couldn't see something, but my friends shared it somehow without a video.

Maybe I'm just an old fuddy duddy. (That's a Duck Tales Reference. Another timeless masterpiece from the 80s).

September 5

If you're not married you better start looking. Don't want to be alone, do you?
—

AHHH. The dreaded single life. I'm a bachelor. I could be for life. Women on the other hand get labeled as 'spinster', or 'old maid'. Or the new term of endearment 'the cat lady'. Okay so maybe the first two are dated, but sometimes you still get the feeling like the world around you sees being single in your 30's as a sad thing. I think it's better than being divorced in your 30's. Ahh, you say it would be nicer to be in love and have someone around. Would it though? Granted I like doing what I want, but I can also see upsides to relationships. What is it you expect from a relationship?

So, let's say, it's us, as singles that are longing for a relationship. (I kinda feel like the only reason we think that we need to find someone is that it's been told to us in our sleep and places we look. After all, "Sixty-two thousand four hundred repetitions make one truth.") What do you expect will happen? Happiness? Support? You expect someone else will provide that for you? How often should they meet those requirements? 50% of the time okay, or should it be more?

I for one, don't think I'm alone. I mean I'm currently single, but I don't think about it. If anything, I think about all the time I would have to spend on the other person. (Not, that I'm against that per say. It just helps to know.)

Being single isn't that bad, even for your life. There are articles about how it's actually not that bad. I've linked two. There are more. The fact is. It shouldn't be a thing.

It's thinker. You should ask yourself. Do you want to be single? I know why I'm single. I don't make time to meet people. I'm writing this book for you all. I'm busy doing what I want. It happens not to be joining a club or group or church or going to social outings. Maybe I'll meet someone if I do one of those things. If I'm not busy doing the things I want to do.

Maybe you've tried, and keep falling short. Take a class. Find a group that enjoys doing something you enjoy doing. Go to that group. Pick more than one. Talk to people. That's all I got. Work on talking. All this coming from the writer who doesn't. 😊

If you like being single, but every so often get a thought, like maybe I shouldn't be single. Ask yourself if it's really your thought, or from someone else before you worry yourself too much.

September 6

Germs are everywhere, wash your hands! Then make sure to use a disinfectant after you touch the door.

—

GERMS are everywhere. This is true! You should wash your hands. Your kids should wash their hands. But there is a limit, what is that limit? Well I think if you have to ask if you passed the limit of reasonable, then you've passed it. If you check on WebMD for your symptoms, you might be passed the limit. If when you see a commercial and it says this drug might be right for you, and you should go and talk to your doctor about it, and you do, you might be passed the limit.

I mention all that because if I have to bring up to my doctor the medicine that I need then they need to be paying me. I pay my doctor to know what medicine is right for me! I pay his student loan, or for her Maserati. (That's another expensive car I'm not sure I could own, but wouldn't mind trying.)

Sorry I'm back, I had to go build a Maserati on their website. Can't afford it, but it looks so nice! Germs, that's what we were talking about. You know there's a limit to worry. If you think about germs more often than when you're in a restroom, or if you have kids whenever your kids interact with other kids or come in from outside (if children actually play outside anymore) or if one of you is sick then you might have passed the limit.

A great show with Tony Shalhoub is called Monk. Here is a show about a guy who has taken the word Mysophobia just a wee bit too far. I recommend it if you're bored. I linked to it in the appendix. I believe it might be on Amazon if you have Prime.

If you believe that you may have a serious issue with this however, I've also linked some sites for that as well. I believe it can be a serious issue and don't want to down play it. Check those out.

If you don't have a problem with germs then more power to ya! Be thankful and have a good day knowing that you don't care that much. No reason to start now I say!

September 7

Vape, it's better than smoking.

OKAY, does anyone believe this? Perhaps. Is it true? Well, let's break down the process. How it was first explained to me. So, you burn oil, that creates a cloud of vapor, then you breath that into your body. It's water vapor.

Well it's not really water vapor. It's oil smoke, it's hot oil smoke. So, stay with me here. I cook with olive oil. It gets hot, oil burns and has a smoke point. At the smoke point you can create burnt flavors for your food. But if you go too far beyond that it could break down the oils in more hazardous ways. Free radicals, remember those back in the day they were all the rage. That oil smoke can get in your food, if it's above the smoke point too much its bad. We've known this as cooks and chefs for a long, long time. (I might not be able to include myself with the likes of Gordon Ramsay, Rachel Ray, Jamie Oliver or even that evil Chef who tried to kill Sebastian in A Little Mermaid, but I cook and it's not all bad.)

So, if we burn oil, oil that has things in it like Propylene Glycol, Vegetable Glycerin, Distilled Water, added flavoring, and Nicotine. Well those things aren't that bad. Water, vegetable sugar(?), flavoring, nicotine. Those sound-like good things to me! Okay, okay. And even if the Propylene does prove to cause sores and inhibit your ability to heal wounds, so what! It's got to be better than cancer. I guess… But if heating things up to a certain temperature could create carcinogens it's still cool right? Still better than smoke after all, that is so gross. And you get to look like a dragon, breathing out all that smoky smoke. Awesome. (This is me being sarcastic, or is it witty? I forget.)

Smoking cigarettes was cool back in the day and they didn't even smell good! Vaping smells good!

So maybe I can't reach all of you. You're going to ingest hot oil vapor into your lungs and call it water vapor regardless. I mean if soma is good, soma is good, right, no matter what its form? (Brave New World Reference, if you're curious.)

If you're going to vape, maybe just smoke. It's the same thing. I don't want to breath it either. But it's all about the devil you know, right?

September 8

Don't bother loving those that are hard to love.

PEOPLE are hard to love. Listen to me, it's probably REALLY hard to love me. Sitting here writing a book with terrible advice and giving questionable advice back. I mean who am I? Besides Alexander Loch. True I am hoping to make some money (for myself to continue this line of work but more importantly donate half of it to children who might be able get some medical care or support from the cash). I mean, you might say, 'that's a good cause, and I respect that writer for trying to make a difference.' But I'm not sure I put off that 'lovable' vibe in person. Ya know? I'm not a grump mind, you, it just means you have to engage me and talk about something I like. You know, like 75 to 80% of the world. Maybe that's a generous estimate.

Sometimes we have that one uncle or aunt who is just hard to love. I mean it takes effort. Who has time for that? The next show is coming on soon, or the next sale, or you have to work on yourself first. Or that project can't wait, because you know, you have to save for retirement. Then you can really love others and take the time.

I say hooey with that! You can work on yourself till the pigs go to market, or the cows come home, or the chickens come home to roost, but until you get off that high horse, you'll realize that the best laid plans of mice and men are just that, small in the cosmic sense of it all.

It's hard to take time, or make time for people, even your own kids. It's even hard for them to make time for you now. They have to do something on their devices. I'm not saying you don't love your kids or they don't love you. It's just we don't really have time for that, do we? We have to do the next thing, sporting events, or business trips or vacations, or bills or doctors and dentist or college or retirement. If we stop, not only are we going to fall behind, we're going to be left behind. Us and our economic community. The world will not wait.

If you're too much trouble then you're going to left behind. If you want people to give you time, you have to plan for it and if someone is a time soaker or too difficult then that's a point in the negative column my friend.

I'm not dark about this, I'm just being honest. We only have so much time and we can't be expected to help those who can't help themselves, can we?

P.S. This is what I call reverse psychology. (I just made up the term...believe me?) Just trying to make you think and take action. Is it working? I hope so, only you can make a difference in the world around you. You can't wait for someone else to at least.

September 9

Answer everything with a question, or a correction to the original question, just like they do online! It makes you look smart, and it's helpful!

Internet Troll 404

I think this is just humorous. Do you think you can do this? Some people have, sometimes it's actually needed to verify what is being asked. Perhaps you feel cornered, I get it. This day is not about a special lesson turned on its head. It's simply a stupid challenge. I think it would definitely start some confusion on the internets. I love those brainy sites where someone will ask a question that they think should be simple enough to answer then someone comes along and rakes it though the coals. The answer could be obvious, but some genius wanted to flex his mental muscles, or some keyboard jockey thought it might be snarky for the zillionth time to tell them to Google it. Now that said, if you don't Google it first, probably shouldn't be allowed on the internet, I think that's a good rule of thumb.

If you already fall into this category, maybe ask yourself, why? Perhaps it's a layman who doesn't actually understand the depth of what they're trying to ask. Is it not a simple answer? Don't berate them, that's troll help. We're not trolls. Ask them about it, in a nicer way then telling them how to search on Google, or explaining why their question makes no sense.

I for one don't ask questions online, I feel it's rather scary. Being online is brutal. It's like the wild west.

So, to that end, have fun with it. Challenge! Do it in real life though, not on some internet site. See if you can for a day. Not in a I'm going to be pompous today, but I'm going to see if people notice. You might have to get pretty witty about it, if you don't want to have your boss talk to you in their office later.

September 10

Do the latest internet challenge.

I come from a time where the internet didn't have challenges, it was actually a challenge to get on the internet. I'm talking dial-up of course, did you know that the internet made a sound. If you didn't, they might have an old modem in a section of the natural history museum. I know they should capture that sound. There used to be a sound you would hear when 'logging on' to the internet. You had to log on, to the internet. Strange right? Probably wouldn't know how to log on anymore, huh? I don't know if it's possible, it's just there, right?

My fear is that while we have all this technology, we no longer understand the underlying foundation of that technology on a similar scale. Actually, I take that back, I don't 'fear' it. I think I can bang out my next novel in the dark ages to come on a type writer, (I might have to learn how to spell words right the first time though…) but there are a lot of things that I have come to rely on and I don't know how they work at all.

(So…I'm sorry about the rabbit hole, jumping into the aftermath of WWIII is a little bleak for me too, I'm sure we'll be just fine.) Back to the advice though, some of these internet challenges are just bad and I think rather old, the Cinnamon challenge (even though it's a fact you will choke and vomit with too much…) or the hot pepper challenge. There are more. Almost all of them are equally idiotic. I suppose it's similar to the 'challenges' that me and my friends would give to each other at the 'ragers' we used to have. I don't have a defense except that the 'atmosphere' at the time effected my ability to think logically.

It's never a good idea to jump off a house. I repeat, it's never, a good idea, to jump off, a house. I do think we should think of some challenges to put on the internet though. Perhaps teaching us something or learning, or networking. Something to think about.

September 11

Create a holiday, don't tell your boss until they ask why you're not at work. Become indignant about their insensitivity to the day.
—
C. Columbus

SOMETIMES being silly is terrible advice. Take this for example. Utterly stupid. We are so serious about life a majority of the time. When I'm out and about. I'm serious. I don't goof around. Even when I'm with friends nowadays, I'm pretty calm. Stoic to a fault. Boring. At work, I'm the same way. If I want to take myself lightly, I have to work at it now. Everything is judged. Everyone is serious. That's why I love stand-up comics, not all of them mind you, but many are philosophers of our time… (Well, Louis C.K. might not be) at least they understand how to have fun.

It's hard to set things down and take things easy. Comedians know how to do that. They've found the 'secret', I'm not talking about that movie that's I giant infomercial. They've found gold. Why don't we grant ourselves this? So, you can't just make up a holiday, why not? We do it all the time, Valentine's day? You think that was a holiday. I'm pretty sure Valentine, either one of them, didn't enjoy that day.

Let's just take September for example. Labor Day, Skyscaper Day, Read a Book Day, International Literacy Day, Pardon Day, Grandparents Day, Video Game Day, Peanut Day, Positive Thinking Day, Uncle Sam Day, Play-Doh Day, Citizenship Day, Wife Appreciation Day, Talk like a Pirate Day, Oktoberfest… Comic Book Day, Stupid Question Day, Confucius Day, of course todays remembrance of the towers. It's not a new concept.

Try it out, maybe it's not the greatest advice in the world, but check out the holiday calendar and pick one. Maybe it's important to you…or at least warrants a Mental Health day.

Don't forget to be silly. Being silly brings flavor to life. It helps create a salve for some of the hard things we go through. Too much seriousness, I find, just dries things out.

September 12

Watch 'Manos, the Hands of Fate'

M.S.T. 3000

I did it. You should too…or not. Manos, is of, I might say, a 'lesser quality' than Ed Wood's films of the same era. If you consider yourself a movie buff though, you might consider sitting though some of it. It's truly dreadful, and I don't just mean the plot. They should give out an achievement award for sitting through the sucker, like they hand out achievements in all video games of the new Millenia. It's not one of those movies you regret not watching. And might I say if you fancy yourself a movie writer or someone who knows movies and story elements, it might be agonizing. Like eating a ghost pepper for no reason but to see if you can.

There are some movies I would recommend, but this is more a test of endurance than recommendation for enjoyment.

September 13

Drink a bottle of ketchup because a friend bet you 5 dollars you couldn't.

J.K.R.

REMEBER I said go on a road trip. I recommend it. I don't know if you can fully appreciate some things unless you go and do them. Not to say that's true of everything. I can appreciate that Desomorphine destroys your skin without needing to partake in the drug. Don't do drugs, (Who knew McGruff the crime dog was right?) But taking a road trip with your friends is definitely one to try. I went to Colorado, and once to Florida, Maine and Maryland. Crazy times, fun times.

I do recall some incidents. I'll share just one. I think driving out to Colorado took about 24 hours. I drank coffee and smoked at the time. I drove I believe up to Kansas. I trusted my friend, see. I still do and I thought sleeping in a car was something I could handle while he drove. It was really, that is, until I woke up. You see, I didn't wake up as one normally would to a road in front of you, my friend just driving along. I woke… differently.

So, you know when the world is spinning, it jostles you. You wake up, I raised my head in this case, and there was spinning. I think I was in about degree 114 out of the total 675 we spun for. It was about this time, after raising my head, that I came under the impression that we had, or more correctly, my friend, my good buddy, my pal, well he had lost some control over the motorized vehicle we were in. I took that time of reflection to grab the dash board and turn to look at my friend. He was to say the least, somewhat concerned. His face displayed that quite well. More so I would say than myself, having been spun around in a previous vehicle incident of my own.

I didn't feel that we were going to flip, so that brought me some comfort. What didn't bring me comfort was, after we stopped. We kind of slide to a stop off the side of the road. My friend looked at me and told me, "I can't, I can't drive any more man!" I wanted to call bullshit, I really did, seeing as how I was pretty sure I only got about an hour or two of sleep max. But I didn't feel I could argue as I could see his point.

Anyway, I get in the driver's seat. I'm thinking we never completed the whole 720, because I recall needing to turn around on the highway to head in the proper direction. Thankfully being in Kansas, there wasn't a soul around from horizon to horizon, as you can see such in the corn fields of Kansas, when you're out of the season.

So, I turn around and start driving, still tired mind you, and with a thought that maybe my friend spun around on purpose so he wouldn't have to drive. I don't believe that, but when you're tired you don't think too straight and your heart tells you little white lies, just like Stevie Nicks would.

We stopped for more coffee, else I might have fallen asleep again, and my friend was definitely pleased as punch to not be in the car for a minute. Funny thing happened. We ordered coffee, but it seemed as if no one in the diner in the middle of nowhere actually engaged us. So, my friend and I were wondering if perhaps we had died in the spin out. I thought it was an interesting concept, but as we still had about 300 freaking miles left that I had to drive I figured I'd worry about it once we got there. If St. Peter met us at outset of the city of Denver, I'd ask him what we do there now we're dead. (That's a movie reference for you theater/movie geeks out there.)

So, you see, road trips give you stories. Interesting stories. Amusing stories. Flavor. If you can, I highly recommend trying one.

September 14

Ask a total stranger to play you some 80's music.

-

The Man out of time

"ALEXA, play me music." I've gotten quite used to saying that. In fact, it's become almost common place. Alexa, play me this, Alexa order me that. Add this to my shopping list. Convenient. The issue is when she's not with me, I sometimes forget. I can't say I forget, but I misjudge distance or range. So, when I'm at the gym and I'm running I'll listen to music as well. Alexa doesn't work on my phone. I have to wait for an upgrade or something. "Alexa play Mr. Sandman by the Cordettes", (What? It reminds me of 'Back to the Future' and 'Riverdale' on Netflix.)" Everyone at the gym hears me, but 'she' doesn't. And now I can't get anyone to talk to me. They think I'm a little off.

I recall when Bluetooth devices in people's ears were a new thing. I once saw a man in Rome walking down the street talking to himself and I thought, "Hey. Well, he's crazy." I mean he was crazy, he had a little tin foil hat on. Literally, tin foil. Shaped into two antennas like you might see on a television. That was before Bluetooth, though. Now if I saw that guy, I might think he's just trying to get better reception. Stupid 4G bars. Am I right?

September 15

Forget math. It's not like it's really everywhere.

Me

MY algebra teacher explained to me that I would need algebra in the world. That's what he said. He said it's everywhere. Did you know that petals on a flower have math in them? Yep, someone told me that. Helpful. Especially to a high school kid. The number e, pi, Fibonacci, factorials. Mathematicians love these numbers and operations of all kinds. (Factorial would fall under an operation I believe but for the sake of brevity.) Fibonacci is more of a set or sequence of numbers.

The point is, math does seem to be everywhere. All I need to do is balance my check book, actually I don't have a check book anymore, because I'm transitioning to bit coin, or perhaps putting a NFC device in my hand, but the point is still valid. What does one need with all this math? It's easy enough without it. That's what my phone's for after all.

Maybe you don't, but it is everywhere. Understanding math can give you a leg up on how things work, you can see how stocks are influenced by different equations. That's fun stuff right there, am I right?

Math can be hard too, but it really is everywhere. The problem I had is that I need to understand how it's used, and what it's for before I can learn something. Sometimes my math teachers just showed me how to do the problem. I can memorize formulas, until I am out of the class. I can get 100's on tests, but if I don't understand the purpose, if I can't see the functionality in practice, I'm going to forget it.

The craziest job in the world to me would be a theoretical mathematician. They come up with formulas for things that might be true! Crazy. I had to have someone explain math to me before I could do it, how could anyone just know enough to make it up?!

I need to understand the function. I've linked to a site on math that I found explains things a little bit better than I've ever had them explained.

I would encourage anyone young or old to take a second look at things in math, not getting into the field, but just checking things out and how different things work. It's pretty interesting! (I know I'm old.) It might even help you budget your credit card bills a little better, and who doesn't need help with that!

September 16

Don't bother with warning labels.
—
Doug "Wrong End" Burton

I don't read warning labels. Unless it's a power tool. Chances are I'm not going to stick my tongue in the light socket, or splash water around the device I'm using. I'm not going leave it on all the time, and I'm not going to put it near an open flame. I'm not going to taste test my cleaning products and I'm going to keep my fingers out of the device. I'm not going to try and stick anything inside of me, unless its food, and I'm not sure who that customer is, but I'm pretty sure I don't want to meet them. They probably have a tin foil hat.

I don't read instructions either. I try and put it together the first time, by myself. I used to have transformers as a child. I got this. If I don't it's probably a major project, and it will never get done anyway.

Sometimes warning labels can be helpful. I mean, maybe there are people who don't understand that they need to keep things out of the reach of children. I would ask why they are allowed around children, but maybe that's just me.

Sometimes we can't be bothered with warning labels, they are more for the lawyers anyway. That way the company can't be sued because someone stuck a curling iron somewhere it shouldn't have been. They can at least say, I told you so.

Ranting now, but maybe it's time we separate shopping items by IQ points. When you enter a shopping mart or mall store, they should greet you with a small survey "If you can't pass this quiz, you're not allowed to buy things on this side of the store. You can go to this 'beginner' area of the shopping mart, but you're not allowed past the velvet ropes." Is that too much?

So, I hate to say don't read the warning labels, as I don't, but it seems that they are for a different audience, either lawyers or the people that are going to need them. They aren't for us, not really. Are they?

September 17

Only your parents play board games.

Cthulhu Wars

I recall game nights. That's why I recommend them. My cousins, parents and relatives would meet down at my grandparents' house. We wouldn't do it often, but we'd set up card tables and play different games. I'd always want to be on my grandfather's team because I knew he could count cards. Actually, I think my cousins could too. They had a system. So, I can't say anyone ever cheated, but we'd poke fun when one team lost and my grandpa won a lot. Or at least I thought he did. Regardless of if someone did or didn't, it wasn't about winning or losing. It was about being together, and we were. We would play until the wee hours (That's the late hours for those who aren't sure what 'wee' means in this context, small. Side bar: What's 'small time' mean?). I'm grateful for that time.

Its true though, older people played more board games. You know on Star Trek, there was this kid. Wesley Crusher. The Wil Wheaton of Big Bang. Awesome character, I wanted to be smart like him... anyway. There is a YouTube channel, GeekandSundry and it has a show called "Table Top". I don't play games anymore, my grandparents have passed and we don't get together as much, except on the holidays. I watch this show though, it brings back happy memories. I mean we only played cards but games create a camaraderie that is hard to duplicate.

I'm not trying to drive home a family game night again, but just reminiscing about the fun times. Not a lot of those to go around. I don't mean in the sense that life is dark, but you should make a point to take a snapshot of those times when they happen. They are a wonderful thing to look back on, and an even greater thing to look forward to in the future!

Ah, heck, have a game night. Invite the relatives, just the ones you like. Hopefully it's a lot of them though! Maybe even invite the one that's hard to love. Might make it easier to love them if you do!

SEPTEMBER 18

Don't work out if you're pregnant.

—

I'M not a woman, and I've never been pregnant. I know it's hard to believe after 'Junior', but it's still not happened for me... So that being said. I don't have a whole lot to say about this. Although I have run across some interesting ideas that women shouldn't workout, and also the quite interesting and amusing responses from the women who disagree.

As I don't want to put a target on my back, or front. (Not to mention I have no opinion for or against.) I have linked to some work outs that seem to be good for pregnant women to do. Now if you are or aren't interested that's totally up to you personally.

I know that as a man, I work out to stay in shape. I do it because it makes me feel good about myself, and I'll never find a woman if I allow myself to become a fat slob. I hear, and I want to say this as sensitively as possible, but I hear that women can feel concerned about their image when they become pregnant. I mean I'm not saying that's you. You're probably fine with how you look, I think that's good. Great, don't kill me. I'm not talking to you then. I'm sure... you're glowing.

I'm just pointing out that it's an option, and being active helps to combat stress and depression. At least it does in me, and any articles I've read, ever.

Anyway, they're in the appendix, take it or leave it. Some of the links have more articles than just exercises that might be worth reading. So, look at it as they're available. Maybe it's something you haven't considered, or care about, but I'm sure not a whole lot of people cared that I pointed out that there is math everywhere either.

September 19

Don't watch Homestar Runner. It's so Old Skool.
—

IT'S one of those treasures of the internet. It's old. It's flash. Flash is bad. The link might not even work anymore. Hours, I've lost hours of time to this site. I just listen to the voices. They're funny. Then there are the simple games you could play, now people play games on their phones. College days consisted or Halo, drinking, HomeStar Runner, Ramen, Red vs. Blue, some D&Dish stuff, oh and class can't forget class. Most days anyway. Tuition is too high.

I wouldn't call myself a 'nerd' as I consider that to be reserved for the smart people, but I was more of a nerd than popular. I suppose I'm somewhere in the middle of that still.

Good times back in school, but I don't think I was on the internets as much as I am today. I'm just waiting for my google glass to make a comeback in AR so I never have to leave.

If you have some time, and you probably do, if you're ever on YouTube, check out the list of websites from the 2000's, some are still around. They're like Ramen, they never really go out of style, or expire. Or maybe that's disco, bellbottoms and twinkies. Oh, maybe that's just me.

September 20

Put all your eggs in one basket. They'll be easier to carry.

Chicken "Free Range" Big, Little's younger brother

INVEST in one set of stocks, only save enough for one rainy day. Put all your money down on that one dream, the idea that's going to make you a star. Sell everything and go out to California. You're good enough to make it. You have one purpose in life, find it and shoot for the moon.

I'm all for following a dream. I mean I'm writing a book and there are billions you could read, but I'm hedging my bets that this will work. Hopefully it will make some, (A lot) of money for the children St. Jude's helps. Again, it's my intent and purpose of this book to take the profits (50% first two years, thank you lawyers.) I get from this book and give half of it to St. Jude. The other half I would use to support myself, but hopefully get into a position where I can do more to help causes like St. Jude or others in the future. I have personal dreams beyond that, but for this book project and anything (for the first 2 years) that comes out of it the goal is to support children in need in various ways. If you're interested take a look at the back section. Moving on.

Like I said, I'm all for the dream. You only have this one life to live… (as far as we really know, faith being another thing). You might as well take a chance. But that doesn't mean YOLO. It means come up with a plan. Work it out and attempt to grab the stars. Don't shoot for the moon. Don't do a hail Mary, take it to heart and work for it. Maybe tomorrow won't come, maybe you only have today, but don't rush it. Enjoy it, step through the moments and look at them.

Remember them. Sometimes you work hard, sometimes you take a breath, always look where you're going and always, always look for ways to enjoy the moment you are in. If it's only about the destination, you'll end up missing the trip. Maybe you won't spin out in Kansas, but I wouldn't have missed that story for the world.

SEPTEMBER 21

One word: Gravitron.

—

I loved this carny ride. I would get in it every homecoming. The streets closed down, and the rides went up. It was wonderful. I'd ride it as many times as I could, probably another reason I was calm about the Kansas incident. I'd spin myself around using my own energy when I was younger. Circles were great.

This is great advice, if you can stand being whipped around in a circle at 24 miles per hour. I couldn't get enough.

Terrible advice if you don't like going around in circles. Just terrible. I'm not sure what exactly happens but I had vertigo one time in my life and that's not fun at all. If you experience something attune to that. Terrible.

Another thing, going upside down in circles. That's fun or terrible too. If you can manage, I highly recommend it.

You can test out if you would be okay with it or not. Stay with me here, we are talking about spinning in circles. So, what I need you to do is pretend you're a dog. (Dog or a cat. Both have tails. I think dogs are more likely to be behind this experiment, or kittens. Or cats on acid(catnip)).

So now that you're an animal with a tail, just turn your head, slightly to the right, or left and then spin around like you're trying to catch your tail, (or whatever they think it might be at the time, am I right? They can't be thinking "OMG, that's my tail, I gotta get it, I gotta get it. It's gonna fly off. I mean it's their tail, how do they not know that?)

If you don't fall down and bust your head on the coffee table, (Careful, that can happen. Gotta research these things, you know.) and you don't mind the wait when you stop, as you have to wait for the world to catch back up to you, then you should be golden on the carney ride.

I think everyone should be able to handle this, I mean we are already spinning in a circle going about 733 to 1000 mph (or 1100 to 1600 km/h). If you want to stop you better head to the poles, I hear they travel slower. Guess they don't like the gravitron up there.

September 22

Trust no one.
—

X-Files. That's the first time I heard this saying. 1993 was the year. I believe I was on the internet at that time as well. I think my parents bought me a 486 for either my birthday or Christmas. It was a good time to be alive. Jurassic Park, The Sandlot (I still let people know whatever their real name is, if something goes wrong then they instantly are branded the name of 'Smalls' and they're as it was, 'were killing me'.) Pauly Shore was at the top of his game. It was fantastic. But X-Files, a show I adore, would teach us about aliens and government conspiracies.

It followed the tone of old Rod Serling openings, like the Twilight Zone. One of my favorite characters was the Pusher. He could make people do things he wanted, similar to the Kilgrave character in Netflix's Jessica Jones. I don't respect these characters, but they were awesome bad guys. How can you beat someone that can make you do things?

It's interesting, because sometimes I do things that I don't want to do. Not like Dexter, or Mr. Brooks, but to lesser degrees. I think everyone can agree with that. We are able to convince ourselves we don't want to do something, rather easily, just by saying we don't have time. That something isn't worth the squeeze. Instead of writing these next few pages, I should probably go check YouTube for episodes of the 'X-files' or watch the newest season of JJ. It won't take too long.

So, while X-Files taught not to trust anyone but yourself, it failed to mention the fact that sometimes you can't trust yourself to varying degrees. We hold ourselves back just as much, by not trusting that sometimes we don't have our best interests at heart. We have at the center of ourselves, an idea of what is the most comfortable at the time. That idea we give ourselves, keeps us from reaching our potential.

We should keep that in mind the next time we think twice about a project. Can we really trust that our heart has our best interest…at heart as it were?

September 23

Don't go white water rafting.
—
Bob Newby

THIS should read, don't go white water rafting with Kevin Bacon. Sticking with the theme of reminiscing of my childhood. Another movie pops up, you see we didn't have fancy phones, we had to rent movies back in the day. I don't mean rent them through Amazon or a Streaming service mind you. I mean my grandmother would have to physically put us (my cousin and I) in the car and drive us into town. We would pick a VHS tape from a shelf and take it home to watch. It was quite an adventure in itself!

"White Water Summer" It had the goonies kid in it, you know him as "Samwise Gamgee" from Lord of the Rings or "Bob Newby" from Stranger Things. It taught that you needed to be responsible and whatever you do, don't go whitewater rafting with a crazy guy. In Kevin's defense, Sean was kind of a 'lay-about' in the film.

I've never been white water rafting, but I tell you. I think I could handle a class 1 or 2. If we always give into fear, how can we hope to really live. I know in this day we have to worry about school shootings, and terrorist movements, along with tons of other dark things going on in the world. We can't let them hinder us from trying things. If we allow outside forces, or inside voices to take the wind from our sails, what can we truly hope to accomplish?

So, on that wave of thought, I say do go rafting with Kevin Bacon, maybe not him personally, but your own Kevin Bacon. You friends or a group. Maybe it's not white-water rafting, maybe it's just hanging out at a mall, or going to a concert or an event to help pass out something someone needs.

So, go, don't let the fear of something get in the way.

September 24

Spend all day on the internet.

Kip

I'M on my computer or phone checking tweets and posts. I'd say at least 50 or 60 percent of my day is spent staring at a screen. Going back to 1993 it was less. I had to get up and go outside. The parents made me. They wouldn't say I had to get off the computer, while the internet was fun, there was only so much text-based gaming one could handle.

I had to go play hide and seek, I had to spend time convincing my parents that I needed to be driven into town to get some toy. I mean I had to spend time on that. They wouldn't simply give into my desires. Madness, I tell you. Parents nowadays have it right. Just let the kids do what they want, everyone gets a trophy is the way to go. (Maybe that's dated, maybe that horse is dead.) Everyone gets a phone now.

We spend 5 to 10 hours on the internet. Adults spend about 33 hours a week watching television. I don't know if these figures are accurate, but they feel pretty close to the mark. Even if we halve those figures. Say 2.5 hours a day on the internet, and 16.5 hours of tv a week. That's a lot of time. Right?

I could build a...well I probably couldn't build anything in that time, (my brothers would be able to though) but I could write a lot of pages in that amount of time. Are we actually utilizing our time to the best of our abilities?

I love the fact that I can spout off movie quotes to get a laugh in a conversation, but if that's all I can do, is it worth it?

I don't have a solution to fix any of this, all I know is, it seems like that's a lot of time to be spending on something that provides little in return. Do we really need upwards of 40 hours to zombie out? That's on top of our sleep time. So, for about 50 hours (assume 7 a day) a week we sleep, Let's say conservatively we watch 16 hours of something (tv, internet tubes, Netflix, Amazon) a week.

That's 66, we also work 40 hours so that's 106 out of 168. We'll add another 20 for chores, and another 12 for kids. That gets us to 138. So, we have 30 hours left.

So, we have 2.5 a day for 7 days which is 17.5 round that up to 18 for that cat dancing video that caught your eye. That leaves 12. We could fill that with more rest or tv, or special events, traveling. So, there is the break down again, questions are, could we spend our time more wisely? And do we really want or care to?

September 25

Don't get involved.

—

Kitty Genovese

IT'S easy not to get involved. There are so many other things to get involved in. Why should I be bothered to help a guy out on the street when I'm heading to a movie? Or how can I give money to a cause when I have so many bills of my own to pay? Barely getting by, how can I be expected to help someone else get by?

Maybe you're not this person, maybe you're not like me. I feel for those who need help, but I don't have time to help them. What does that mean? I think it means, I don't care. Not to say I don't care about them. I haven't really given any thought to it, the thing that tugs on my heart string. I have to move to the next thing. I have kids and a future to worry about, I can't be stopped by everyone in need. I'd be torn apart. It's an outlandish idea to think that I could. Yep, I agree.

Question? Besides your family, and I use that with a huge assumption that you actually spend time cultivating those relationships, who do you help?

Maybe no one, and why should you, right? Just because someone else can't hack it in this world, doesn't mean that it's your problem. Am I right? (I feel a rant coming on.)

Honestly, I don't agree with this mind set, but I believe that many of us have it. Secretly, in ourselves, hidden from ourselves, behind our things and responsibilities. My question is why? Why should it be a secret? I would rather someone tell me that they don't care about starving kids in who knows where, or animals choking on plastic soda pop wrappers than someone who would stand there and say, "That's atrocious! Something needs to be done about that!" Then walk away and bury themselves in the things that are their life.

I think I'm tired of feigned interest. I would rather someone speak their mind, then attempt to placate a conversation with a white lie. I understand that people should be kind and attempt to build bridges and not burn them down. I also understand some people don't care, or don't care that much. That, being enough to do something besides talk about it.

I guess what I'm saying is, if you don't care. Let me know. If you think you care, keep it to yourself. If you do care, let me know. But don't waste my time. I'll respect your opinion just a wee bit more, if it's truly yours. If I wanted to hear my own opinions shot back at me, I'd record myself and put it on a loop.

September 26

Join a gym, never go. Never cancel the monthly dues.

WHY is it that we do this to ourselves? Why do we lie so much? Do we feel better in knowing that it's an option for us to go to a gym anytime we want? Do we have a voice that says, "I know we don't want to go to the gym today, but we should keep paying, because next month! I'm pretty sure we want to go next month."

Stop listening! The voice is lying to you. Get a Netflix subscription like everyone else! Perhaps you do want to start going to a gym, what's your workout routine look like? You need one of those. What about diet, did you know that dieting helps weight loss more than exercising alone?

It's tough. I've tried numerous diets and exercise routines over the years. Sometimes I will go all out and get into them for the length of the routine, and sometimes I fizzle out.

The newest I'm trying is the Atkins diet. I actually think it's working a little. One thing I've come to expect in my routines is, well, not much. I'm not saying you should lower your expectations, but I've found that when I start any project with a preconceived notion of how it's supposed to turn out. If it's anything else I'm a little, or a lot, disappointed. I've tried to take that out of my diet and exercise routines. I understand that this isn't a get thin or ripped quick routine. I don't have that discipline. I need something longer term, gradual incline.

I have a goal to lose weight or see muscle tone, but nothing concrete or connected to a time line. I'm not making movies after all. No one is watching me, they aren't expecting anything. I am.

I've also found that through my years on this earth that if I put my mind to something, I can do it. It just takes time to do something right. Takes work, sweat and tears. Possibly a little blood, not too much though, I'm kinda squeamish.

So, if you pay for a gym, go. Or come up with a new routine, do a little workout when you're spending 33 hours a week in front of the television. I think if we all did that, we'd all be ripped!

SEPTEMBER 27

Don't chew on the iPhone.

Your dog

DIRECTIONS are for lawyers and those who aren't allowed in the higher IQ areas of superstores. Warning labels are for children and people who don't want to think.

I've never thought about chewing on an iPhone. I bet some babies have, babies can't read. If you can read, you shouldn't need to be told that you shouldn't chew on an iPhone. You should be done teething when you can read.

I've already mentioned warning labels about ten days ago, but I really want to make sure I drive the point home. Don't chew on your iPhone, even if you're getting a tattoo that really hurts and you need something to bite down on. Ask for Gary the artists stash of rawhide for just such an occasion.

Don't put hot coffee between your legs, I feel terrible for the lady this happened to. Thankfully I'm now warned every time I get coffee about its temperature. I also never use a curling iron internally. I don't know who I have to thank for that special gem.

I don't ever plan on letting my dog operate heavy machinery or drink when I give him worm pills. I'll try and remember from the warning label never to wash a baby, in a washing machine.

I'll try and refrain the voice in my head that tells me, "Eating that toner, might pay off."

If I'm in California, I'm to understand that most things can cause cancer there.

I should also stop using my hair dryer in the shower.

I need to remember that not all balconies are on ground levels.

The list goes on…

September 28

Buy rocks with little plastic eyes pasted on them for your kids. Or anyone.

—

I'M impressed. I wish I came up with the idea. In fact, this is still a copyrighted idea. You can't sell Pet Rocks on the open market. You might be sued, I believe RoseBud Entertainment owns the right currently.

Gary Dahl was the guy who came up with this idea. It was simple. You really paid for the entertainment value of it. The box of rocks came with instructions on how to care for your pets. He was already in marketing, for years. He knew the game, and he knew the players, it wasn't as simple as having an idea and selling googly eyed rocks in a bag. He put work into it. He found a winner because of everything he had done before that. Sometimes we forget about the work when we hear these stories. He sold the rocks for 4 dollars and sold 1.5 million I'm guessing the packaging material was the most expensive part of the 'toy'.

Maybe you don't want to buy pet rocks, but if someone can make a million on this simple idea, maybe you've got one in you too. Just need a little time and elbow grease and it might be the next million-dollar idea, but don't forget there is work involved. Unless you start a twitch account that is.

September 29

Take what you can, give nothing back.

—

September 19th

PIRATE code! Did you know that ten days ago was International Talk like a Pirate day? Again, you could make up your own holiday. It's an option that's out there.

Terrible advice, unless you're a pirate. Those still exist too, by the way. I linked to a site that explains where they operate and what they do now. Pretty interesting stuff. You need to be careful out there.

September 30

Let your kids do whatever they want. They'll love you more for it.

—

YES this is probably a dicey topic. "Yea, this guy is going to tell me how to raise my children. Whatever. Next. Stick to the jokes."

You're absolutely right. I can't tell you how to raise your kids. I don't even have kids. I don't know your circumstances, or environment. I can't possibly know the struggles, so I should shut my mouth. But that would make for a very short page wouldn't it. Now I'd be okay with it. It's less words I have to type after all, but you do know a few things about me. One, I used to be one, that is, a kid. Maybe I still am a little bit on the inside. And two, I want to find a way to help sick kids. That's the whole point of this book, nothing else really. If you found some nugget of insight that wasn't totally stupid, great. But this hard topic is important to me. I don't have kids, but I care about them. I know you care for your kids, but the world doesn't. It will be hard on them like it was to you, maybe harder. You have an awesome opportunity. You're a parent. You can make a difference in a person's life! And they might even listen to you, but you have to make a connection.

Today it's even harder to keep someone's attention. I heard somewhere our attention span is decreasing, and I'm hoping that it was a joke, but don't think that it was. It wasn't published on April 1st and no one seems to be laughing at Time magazine.

I'm sure it's hard to be a parent, but again you have an opportunity to provide a future for someone, to help them accomplish their goals. I know, some people just don't care and it makes it hard for everyone. But you can't give up, even if your life was hard, you have a chance to help someone else have an easier time going forward. I'm not saying, give them everything they want. I think sometimes love means doing what's right for a person, over what makes them comfortable in the moment.

I can't know how hard it is, but hopefully you do and hopefully you want to help your children, and others develop skills that help them survive in this world. Allowing someone to do what they want doesn't mean you love the it might just mean you don't care. Children watch us, and imitate what we do. They will try and do whatever it is they want to. It's up to us to show them the way. Maybe in doing so we might make the world better and easier for everyone. Did I tell ya I'm a dreamer?

October 1

Take up miming at school.

STARTING off, whimsical like. There are schools for mimes. That would be good advice. Miming at a mime school would be expected. I'm talking about what a lot of us do, but don't see it. Do you realize you mime? The fact is you might. You ever nod your head to something you didn't actually understand? Even pass someone in the park or hall way without a kind word? Maybe even at work. You're a mime. Of course, mimes aren't idiots, they just can't talk to express questions or feelings. I try to mime things. I use body language to do it. Let me tell you. I'm actually terrible at it. I understand they say we have expressions that mean certain things, I don't think it matters. If someone can't 'read' your body language they aren't going to get it. If I move in a certain way or have some reaction to something in class, if the teacher doesn't notice they aren't going to clarify what they just said. You have to ask questions. If you don't you might as well go to mime school. They can at least teach you how to express yourself in a manner that will make things clearer.

We are all mimes at different times. Sometimes those moments don't truly matter if we're silent, but more and more often as we connect on our devices to the world all the more, we act like mimes to the world directly around us. Try not to be a mime today. Hopefully people won't give you their 'fit in' face, be gracious anyway.

October 2

Go shopping to fill the hole in your life

I buy movies, games, books, gadgets, books. I buy things when I'm bored. When I don't want to do something I should be doing, like writing. Sometimes I think I buy things to take my mind off being single, sometimes. Or distract me from some awful chore I'm supposed to be doing. Sometimes I buy things when I shouldn't simply because I think it's really cool. It normally is pretty sweet.

I feel on the fence about this advice. I can see that in some cases I would buy things to take my mind off where I was in life, but not everything I bought had that center of motivation. I'd say in truth I may have 'over-analyzed' my intentions. Sometimes we just want to buy things. That's not bad, but how do you know if you're buying something because it's cool or if you're using it to escape something in your life?

Should you break it apart and look at the details, perhaps what happened that day or week? Look for the root cause so you can correct it? Maybe. If you're spending too much definitely. We seem to analyze a lot these days. Everything has a deeper meaning, and we need to understand it to better ourselves. We don't just do this with ourselves though, we'll break apart other people's intentions, even when we really don't have a clue. It's about context, walking in other people's shoes and it's something we are lacking in our busy 'connected' lives.

What did they mean when they said this, or posted that? Were they trying to tell me something? Perhaps, maybe they just meant they were going out. Maybe there was a slight inflection in their voice. What could that mean? Are they mad? We could analyze things to death.

So, you shop a lot, and people say they think you're trying to fill a hole. It's getting to the end of our session. Are you trying to fill a hole? Answer now, yes or no. If yes, why? Answer now. What can you do about that? There should be something. If the answer is no. That's the answer. Don't dwell on it any more.

I'm not trying to mitigate issues for people who might be worse off finically. If that's you then seek help for it. I find though, in my own life that the first answer I give myself is usually the right one. Why am I buying this book? Is it because I am trying to escape the reality, I'm in. No, the cover is awesome looking and the description of the story pulled me in. It's the autonomous marketing machine of the world. I'm not sure that makes my purchases worth it, but I don't have to break it down any further than that.

What can I do about the autonomous consumer creation machine? That's a harder question to answer.

October 3

Hold the door for someone and when they say thanks, respond "You are welcome milady." No matter who they are. Do it for large groups.

—

WE take everything seriously. I do at least. I lean toward a stoic demeanor, and over-analyze just about anything I want. You should know, we've been walking through my mind, a little in these pages, but not everything I say I agree with or think you should. Context is so important, but let's get back to my personality. Let me tell you, I am an awesome party guest. If I were on a game show, I think I might be the most boring person to watch. "You just won a million dollars! How do you feel?" I think my first response would be, "Well, relatively the same. I need to talk with a financial advisor. How much did I actually win? Is that before or after taxes?" I analysis everything first. Makes for ho-hum television.

(Rabbit Hole Warning!) That brings up an irksome point. Why don't they just give you want you actually win? Just tell me how much money the winners get, after big brother takes his money. People win cars on game shows, they have to pay taxes on that. Did you know that? Some can't and have to forfeit the prizes. I call bullshit. The prize should include the taxes. If it's for a cool million, then the taxes should come from an amount more than that. Maybe that means we don't hear that we win one million, but only 625,00 or whatever it is after taxes. I've never won anything to put actual number in my head.

I think I went off track a little, but the point of this advice is doesn't take yourself seriously all the time. Make sure you have fun with your friends, sometimes doing stupid (but safe things) gives life flavor. We work all the time. We worry and analyze the future all the time, or we tune out until we go back to the grindstone.

Make time for silly, and fun. Make time for helping others, it might be the most important you do in life.

This is terrible advice. People will look at you with their 'fit in' faces if you open the door like this. They'll get annoyed with you. Why are you acting silly? Grow up. Fit in. Get to the grind stone.

What's the purpose in life? I suppose its whatever you want it to be. I believe that's what Douglas Adams meant when he said 42. That's what that means. Look it up if you don't believe me. Fact check me. I encourage it. Is the purpose to wear a suit and jacket and get a 401k? Or is it to do more? Could it be for us to stand with our true friends and begin to change the world, here and everywhere?

Do you think that starts by going to the grindstone, or changing the grindstone?

October 4

Wash your car at a car wash. Make sure to get the inside with the soap and water. Use the sprayer.

—

I watch YouTube videos like a lot of us do. I've found a special little gem out there. People washing the inside of their cars. I'm not sure if it's an intelligence thing, or something that actually works, or perhaps a revenge type thing. I feel it goes against common perception, and I'm not going to try this in my car. There are many videos. Most comments make fun of the person, I wonder if they watched the lady I've linked to in the appendix and believed her? I'm not sure exactly what happened that day to provoke these individuals to do such a thing. Perhaps someone told her that she had to clean the car, and so she did. Maybe they heard this was a good idea. Maybe it wasn't stupidity at all, but spite. Or maybe it works? I don't think that makes as much sense honestly, but why are so many people doing it? Either way, its humorous to watch. Google: 'People wash inside of Cars YouTube'.

OCTOBER 5

Go on a date to a dance club. Bring the Robot back. They're coming anyway.

School Stopper Intern, "Button Pusher" Paul

DATING. Best face forward. I find it interesting when I talk with singles about dating. A lot of the time, I hear "I hope I'm likeable and they see my 'fun side'." Why, I ask? Shouldn't it be the other way around? I know, I know. We want to be liked, but what about the other person? Why are they the one's we feel that we have to impress. Shouldn't they have to impress us? We're both looking after all.

I understand that we want to show our good side, but why do some people feel that the other person has more value. Did you ever think that perhaps they should have to win you over? It kinda feels like instantly settling to me. I'm sure it happens on both sides, "I hope that person likes me". Why, because you know they're worth it? They had an excellent gym selfie. Their travel record was exciting? You don't know them at all, you haven't been on one date yet. Perhaps they're as boring as watching paint dry. Maybe they aren't worth what you have to offer.

So that feeling of uneasiness goes away within the first 10 minutes of a date, either because you both enjoy each other to some degree, or you're too busy thinking of an escape plan to listen to their awesome stamp collection stories. Hopefully you can ease up and begin to enjoy yourself. It goes into that whole 'terrible' advice of being silly, or having fun. Of course, I'm talking to introverts but even extroverts have concerns about how they come off. Maybe to a greater degree even.

About 50% of the US and 50% of the UK are single, I don't even know the statistics for the rest of the world, a lot of people are looking for someone to spend their time with. It's an interview. But maybe you're not the one who should be worried about getting the job.

Just have fun. It's only a few hours of your life. Be yourself, you don't want to sell yourself as someone you're not. How long can you pretend to do that?

October 6

Always listen to your friends.

FRIENDS. I mentioned true friends and friends before and what the differences were. Peer pressure. It goes beyond school. It happens throughout life. We don't want to look like outsiders. In fact, sometimes if you're of a different opinion you risk being shunned. Groups have the amazing power to mold ideals, and sometimes those ideals are truly for the good of others, while much of the time they can contort individual thought.

Most of us want to be liked and accepted. We will allow ourselves to do things, even terrible things simply because our 'friends' require it. Sometimes even at the threat of being ostracized from the group, or killed. Groups have this power, it's almost fascinating to look at it. For the bad groups out there, they realize this and feed on that principal like it's a weakness to be exploited. The good groups use it to garner support for causes.

Both groups utilize this to their benefit. Of course, groups and causes are needed, but we shouldn't derive self-worth from these causes, good and bad. We should realize that we are worth more. People do not give enough worth to themselves, and place their worth in being part of a group. The sad part is sometimes those groups don't give enough worth to the individuals within them.

It almost seems to synergize with what was said yesterday. We need to understand that we are worth something. Sometimes our 'friends' are not about protecting our best interest. That's not a true friend, no matter what they might say. A friend would see you prosper, they would lift you up in time of need. They would see that you don't waste away on drugs or worthless pursuits. A friend wouldn't put you in danger. There are many true characteristics of what a friend is. However even 'Greeks come bearing gifts', in other words, people may lie about their intentions.

Find your self-worth. You are special, there is a purpose for you. You may have to search for it, but if you are bringing hope, kindness, and working to uplift and not put others down you might be on the right track.

October 7

Roll your doobies with writing paper.

—

Matt Foley

FIRST off, I want to say. I don't roll doobies. And if I did it wouldn't be with writing paper. That's what rolling paper is for, am I right? I could use this section to point out the downsides of doing drugs and wasting your life. Instead I want to point you to a motivational speaker who can do a better job of it. Awesome talent. Take it from ol' Matt Foley. You don't want to end up in a van down by the river, unless you planned ahead and binge watched some Van life on YouTube.

R.I.P. - Matt Foley

October 8

Streak.

ALWAYS something you hear that some sports fan did, or teenagers did on a dare. It's interesting to me. Is it an act of rebellion, or freedom? Is it to show the masses you aren't going to play by their rules? To stir the pot, make the crowd laugh? Is it an expression of our inner selves to be noticed in a world that has an attention span equivalent of a 1980's stock broker coked out in the bathroom at the 'Berlin' in NYC?

Love, respect, notoriety. It's interesting how people do some strange or even terrible things to get these from others. I still wonder why we can't just get along.

So, if you want to streak, go for it. It's thrilling right? Gets your heart pumping, but nowadays the people at the game might just be too busy looking at their phones to actually notice.

OCTOBER 9

Don't think about helping the homeless guy you pass every day.

HERE'S something else we pay little mind to. In 2005 the UN attempted a global survey. Around 100 million people were found to be homeless, and around 1.6 billion had less than proper housing. Now, we can probably figure some of those chose that lifestyle for one reason or the other. Some are drug addicts, others might not be able to function due to mental handicaps and no places for them to go. Still some merely had a run of bad luck, not to say the aforementioned couldn't fall into the 'bad luck' category as well.

There are about, at the time of this writing roughly 320 million people live in the US. We might not have 100 million homeless, but I'm sure we have some of the 1.6. It's interesting to think as I sit at my computer in my place, that outside somewhere someone is homeless. Truth is, I don't think about it often. I have my things I have to worry about. I have to maintain my life so I don't have a run of bad luck and get eaten by the machine.

It makes me sad that I can say I don't do more. I'm still under the impression that if I really cared I would do more, but does that mean I'm not concerned about their plight? I'll still stick to my guns here as they say. I don't mean to say I'm not for helping them, but if I'm not helping then why would I say anything? If all we do is talk about what we should do, how is anything going to get done?

I think that's an interesting dynamic. I'm trying to tug on your heartstrings to help the homeless, but I just admitted I don't help them. Why should you, right?

Since I don't help, maybe I really feel it's up to them? Why would I try and lie to myself and say that I care, when my actions show different? Do I need to feel better by saying sweet words, just so I can sleep at night in my comfy bed?

I think we do this a lot in our global culture. We profess action, and fixing issues, but we provide no solutions, or intention on addressing the problems ourselves. We just don't have time. We are merely cogs in the machine, if we stop turning, our lives will fall apart and there will be no one around to help us, but to simply say that we should be helped. I'm of course not talking about groups or individuals who do hear a call to action in their lives. They are out there. This is about us, the regular crowd.

Thankfully I don't entirely buy into that concept. Everyone has to start somewhere. This little book is a start for me and my group. In the appendix I've referenced many organizations that have started actions above words in addressing the multitude of issues in our world. We don't see these in our media every day. We focus on the negative, and can't see the positive. There is positive change, but if we don't turn our focus there, we won't see it. Perhaps the media, the main stream news could focus on more positive stories. I'm not saying ignore the negative, but if the only thing we see is the negative, how does that effect our outlook as a society?

I encourage you to start somewhere, homeless, elderly, children. Find a cause that means something to you. Start small. Just one thing, do it every day. When it becomes easy, add another. Maybe things can change. Maybe I'm dreaming but why don't you try dreaming with me?

October 10

Be sullen, dark and stoic. It makes people think you're deep and complex. They'll approach you to get to know you better.

―

YOU know how many people approach me in the coffee shop every day? None. Unless it's the wait staff to ask about filling my coffee. Tall (Averagely so based on your location in the world), dark and handsome only works for characters in stories. You have to present yourself. Best face forward. Smile, get rid of that 'fit in' face.

People don't tend to approach you if you have your arms crossed, and a resting bitch face. It's not something to have. It's not cool. It doesn't make you intense or interesting. It isolates you. Obviously, right?

So, why do you still have your 'fit in' face on? If you know that to be inviting you need to show a smile, that you should express your interests, you can't expect people to stick around if you're just going to play it 'cool' and aloof.

People like to read mystery novels, but they don't particularly care for mysteriousness. It's annoying. What's that children's nursey rhyme? "Secrets, secrets are no fun. Secrets, secrets hurt someone.". (I know I still say it whenever someone whispers to another person around me. Maybe I should stop that.)

Sometimes you have to give up the goods. Show people what makes you tick. What are you interested in? Where have you been? What do you do for fun? Do you sit and drink coffee and think about how to solve the world's problems and then upon realizing they are too big for you, sink into a solemn melancholy and finish your coffee in silence? (Just a wild guess I mean I may or may not do that at times.) No, you need to focus on what you enjoy, doing the things that bring you joy bring others joy, or are they too dark, or intense for others to understand? Perhaps it's just that there isn't that much to talk about?

If so, find something to talk about, you have interesting things. I know you do. If I can watch 'Manos the Hands of Fate' and find it interesting, I know there are people that will find certain things you don't see as entertaining, interesting. Make a mental note of a trip you took, or something fun. Put on a smile and drop the 'fit in' face.

If you do, you might find someone does approach you. Just a thought. Don't just try it once, try it a bunch, with no expectations.

October 11

Eat fast food every day for...at least a month.

The Name of Convenience

WHEN it's written above across the page I can feel that it's just bad. It's not the best advice, you could call it terrible, but again, no one says it. This is promoted in commercials we watch, in the restaurants we pass going home or to work. Honestly, I don't think I've seen a McDonalds or Burger King or Chick-Fil-a(or Chic-fil-a, or Chiq-Fil-a depending on what Mandela universe you hail from originally) commercial in years. Maybe they don't have to any more. It's been burned into our psyche. It's burned into mine I tell you.

I don't eat out because it's just too expensive when you start to look at your budget. It's cheaper to make your own meals. I mean if you can afford to eat out like the upper class does, go for it. I have to manage my spending. It also seems to help me eat a little better. I say a little, because I still eat Swedish Fish by the handfuls.

It's interesting that when I was younger it seemed eating out was a money saver. Healthy food was harder to manage. Eating quick was cheap, or at least I thought so, but to be fair I was a teenager at the time so in the 2000's I might not have been paying that much attention.

Is your time worth the money? I don't think it is anymore, but perhaps technology has a fix. Soon we'll probably have robots working in the fast food joints. That will drive down costs, some. We won't have to worry about minimum wage there anymore. Robots don't need money, just enough for maintenance which will be lower I imagine. That's a nice hot topic I'm going to side step right now.

So, think about it the next time you go out to a restaurant. It might save you time at the drive thru, but is it more than you make an hour? Might be time to think about planning a cooking schedule and making some meals over the weekend for part or the entire week if it is. If time is money, isn't money your time?

October 12

Buy a plane, not a regular prop, a Luxury jet, the more expensive the better.

MORE, better, bigger. That's what it is. It doesn't go away. If you make more money, there are bigger things to buy. Money issues don't go away if you can't manage money in the first place. There is a car, it goes underwater. It's 2 million dollars. The car that gives me 'feels', (Although I'm not sure about the low-profile body on most roads.) Is the Lamborghini Veneno, its 4.5 million. I'm sure it's totally worth it.

Private jets, the Golf Stream G500 is about 44 million. A Chinese company owns a Boeing 787-8 BBJ, price is 334 million dollars. On a jet for people. 334 million dollars, seats about 40. That's impressive. Let me be clear, its impressive to see how much we don't care.

I admit. I'd love to be able to walk around and fly from England to China in one hop and in luxury. I'd love it.

Let's compare this purchase though. I'm going to pick on Bill Gates for a second. I'm sure he's got his bad habits. I don't know. He owns a plane. I mean, I think he is currently worth 81 billion dollars. So how much did he spend on this plane of his? About 44 million dollars, seats about 20. It's a luxury jet. Apparently, its bottom of the line too.

I'm sure this 787-8 company is worth more than Mr. Gates, and perhaps their purchase was justifiable. I mean they might be in the travel business, however it's a plane that holds 40 people. I can make travel arrangements that widdle that cost down considerably.

So, let's look at this, for a middle-class person to live a life with perhaps more than reasonable comforts compared to most. I'm not going to do the math for you, but let's assume in 2018 a person would need about 5 million dollars for their life. They could make some good and bad money decisions with that estimate. So, let's assume the big company bought a 44 million dollar jet like the conservative Mr. Gates. That leaves 290. Let's round that down to 250 for 'fees'. So, if that company spent 5 million to care for someone, not saying giving 5 million but putting 5 million toward the potential for someone. They could sponsor 58 people for their entire life. It's not much, relative to the 8 billion people, but its more than 40 for a single plane ride. Is there anything that you buy that might go to a better cause?

October 13

Follow your passion.

—

The Heart

OKAY so I was picking on corporations for wasteful spending. The fact remains, it's their money, they get to spend it how they want. And would changing the lives of 53 people really make a difference? I mean how much can one person do?

It's hard to gauge. We have different people on the scale. Some don't have passion. Or desire to help or do better. There are terrible in people in this world. Maybe it's not even that, maybe they don't seek to harm others, maybe they just truly don't care. They have no passion. They live in this world, but they are simply plugged in. Work, home, sleep, work, home, sleep. Some might even have families. Perhaps the world has just pulled the passion out of them. That's sad too.

We say 'follow your passion', but the world doesn't care about your passion. Most of the people, even those you love won't fully be committed. If you have a passion, you have to work for it. You can't just follow it, you have to lead your passion. It doesn't know where to go. It's wild. It will stop and graze and get happy and fat and sit down and die when it runs out of energy, that is if you so let it.

You also have to manage 'normal life', the machine, if you will. It seems to eat some people up and spits out indifference.

I'm writing, not to take the wind out of your sails, but to give you a motor for your boat. Sometimes there is no wind, and the waves will capsize you.

You don't have to limit yourself to the 'one' passion either. Sometimes passions go away. Did I tell you I wanted to be a cowboy? I mean I could still do that, but I have other things I want to work towards. Helping children who are sick with the proceeds of this small book is one of those things. Hopefully it propels this passion forward. If it doesn't, I tried it. I still get to help those in need, I'll just have to find another way about it.

Follow your passion isn't bad advice, but without context, without direction, its terrible advice. We hear about passion everywhere, but somethings we don't hear. I don't know if it's to the level of 'conspiracy' but it's strange that we don't ground ourselves a little when thinking about 'following our passion'. Did you ever think your passion could/would change, and that it is okay? That it will be hard, blood sweat tears hard, no one will care as much as you do, but if you see it through, it will bring flavor to your life. And hopefully positive change to the lives of those around you.

October 14

Hold grudges. They mean you're right.

———

PEOPLE do you wrong. Some do it on purpose. I could tell you, you need to forgive them. It's to your benefit, it has little to do with them. Holding it in eats you up inside. It becomes a rage, and hatred. It consumes you. It can, I mean, it probably will. And they wronged you. Terrible people. They might actually be horrible examples of humans. Perhaps they caused real damage, and not just superficial drama.

You can't let it go. They're scum. Maybe they've already ruined your life. You have nothing left. I mean I can't know how bad it is for you. Perhaps you've been locked in a basement and molested for years and kept in a cage. I can't possibly relate to that, I'd not try. But the truth is still the truth, no matter what angle you look at it.

If you don't forgive them, for yourself, they win. And they win again, and again, and again. Let me say. I'm tired of them winning. I'm tired of watching the news and hearing about how someone was hurt or taken advantage of. I'm tired of just being sad about it, I'm tired of being mad about it. I think its time we do something with it.

Someone hurt you? Okay, people are out there today who have gone through something. Something terrible. Unforgivable. It's tearing them up. Did you go through the fire and come out the other side? You know what it's like. You want to truly get back at the people who wronged you. It's time you stand up. Forgive them. You have to. You can't really beat them if you don't. If you are to enable the future generations to withstand the evils of the past, you have to equip those who are in the fire now.

If it's less than terrible, if it's simply they spoke over you at the meeting, or stole a rake and said they gave it back, but you know and they know they didn't. You need to let it go. Forgive them and move on. It doesn't matter how small or large the wound is, if you keep picking at it. It will never heal.

It's our job as we move forward to enable the next generation to achieve greater things. How else are we going to create the Federation in San Francisco in 2161? (Props if you don't have to google that.)

October 15

Wrestle a bear with a set of 'finger knives' (you know like Freddy Kruger, or Edward Scissor Hands). It's fair, and manly.

Me

THIS is simply something I say, or did when I was younger. People look at me strange when I say it. I suppose that's because I say it deadpan. I can see they're trying to evaluate my level of sanity. There was that one guy from Alaska who went to live with the bears. He ended up wrestling with one. He didn't want to but that's what happened. It's not a fun story. So, I wanted to include it, not the tragedy of the bear guy dying but the funny little quote on this special day. I'm probably touched in the head a little. I mean, crazy. No one should want to wrestle a bear. Even if it had its claws and teeth filed. It's not a good piece of advice.

Metaphorically speaking we all have bears we have to wrestle. Hopefully we have our finger knives handy for such an occasion.

Speaking hypothetically, don't wrestle a bear (finger knives or not) you will die. I will not have your death on my conscience. You'll be like that guy who decided he could swim with the alligators. If you didn't read that one yet, the answer is. You cannot swim with the alligators. They kill you.

It's like that other bear saying I love. "What doesn't kill you makes you stronger, unless it's a bear. A bear will just kill you."

Again, a bear will kill you. Literally, kill you. I can't drive that home enough. Be thankful you're not wrestling a bear today.

October 16

Take your imaginary friend to work. Introduce your co-workers to them.

—

I had a few of these. I don't recall them in any detail. All I remember is my mother mentioned I had a few. I believe I asked her about it when I was a teenager after I had seen the movie "Drop Dead Fred". I recall she said I had a few, but one was named 'Tiger'. I think imaginary friends are interesting. "Little Monsters" with Fred Savage and Howie Mandel was another one. I'm afraid to watch them again as it might ruin some of the nostalgia of the memory. I made that mistake re-watching 'Flight of the Navigator' after I was older. I don't want to ruin it too.

So, I find this topic interesting. Invisible friends. I linked an article in the appendix. As a budding writer, I can relate to this idea. I don't consider that I have 'friends' that are invisible anymore but I believe that it has helped that I once did. I can't say it helps me 'get' the characters I create a little better, but I'd like to think it does.

I do advise against taking them to work however. This might rattle your boss, unless you want to rattle your boss. Although the joke might cost you your 401k.

If your kids have imaginary friends though, that might not be such a bad thing.

October 17

Make animal noises in the elevator and halls at school and work. When someone asks why you're doing that, ask them why their doing it. It will make you popular.

—

JOKES this month! You got to add flavor every whip stitch, otherwise you dry out the content. That's what my editor always says. That's what I keep telling the other School Stopper writers anyway. People can't just hear about actual terrible advice, talk about funny things. Funny sells books. Maybe that's wrong, but you can't say that this isn't up there.

To be fair, when I was younger (like high school) I started writing some. I actually think I wrote about 6 or 7 editions of the School Stoppers Newsletter. Technically it wasn't an 'authorized' newsletter. I would put stacks of the print outs in the boy's bathrooms when I excused myself from class. I can't say what happened to all of them, but I hope a few of them found some high schooler's hands. I believe I included some jokes and puzzles, as well as stupid things to do in school. Nothing bad (I don't think, at least I don't remember), just obnoxious teenager stuff.

So, this is something reminiscent of those editions of the 'paper'. In fact, this advice might actually make you part of the 'popular' crowd. Although if the popular crowd at your school thinks it's fun to make animal noises in the halls, then perhaps you should find a different crowd anyway.

Don't give in to the peer pressure.

October 18

Make up a language and teach it at a college.

THIS is a thing! No, it's not just a thing, it's a way someone can make money. It's not that I don't think the Dothraki, Klingon, or Elven languages are cool. In fact, if you do know how to speak one of those languages, more power to you. I personally would like to go the other direction with this. Maybe we won't ever all speak the same language. I mean the world is huge, and the dialects would still end up being quite varied. I think it might go a long way to overcoming international issues though. But I'm just a writer. L. L. Zamenhof thought it wasn't a bad way to go either so he created a language to try and bridge that gap.

And while Esperanto gathered momentum for a while, and while it is still spoken by a few today it never really grabbed hold, it's not a natural language after all. I think we should take a hard look again though. I can't say I have any votes for which language we go with. I believe it would be a generational change over anyway, but maybe we should really give it some thought.

I referenced an article to a naysayer. He uses the word 'Never' in the title of the article. I'm not trying to pick on him. He's probably close to right. Esperanto, I thought it was considered a secondary language according to my other source, not one to rule them all. You have to love the missteps in information, in the information age. So, we have like 8,000 different languages in the world. That's a lot to change.

That's not what a 'universal language' is for really. It's not to say we should only speak one language. I'm not sure I agree with the scientist/researchers who see language as something important to culture. I mean I'm just a person in the culture so what do I know, I just feel that even though I speak English, if that changed as a nation, I'm not sure how it would offend or strip away my 'culture'. But perhaps it's just that I don't care enough. I'm too busy looking at a future, and not so concerned with keeping a past alive.

For those of you who feel that your language defines you, I didn't mean to offend or insist your language isn't important, but I think if we ended up with only a few hundred languages instead of 8,000. Maybe we might be able to understand each other better. What do you think? Is it worth the effort for a secondary universal language? Should we even attempt such a pointless endeavor? I mean I know we need to Dothraki, but maybe a universal language is just too 'whimsical', Am I right?

October 19

Trust that the internet will set you up on a date.

I suppose my profile was never really up to par with everyone else's. Everybody loves to go hiking and camping, or museums. Travel a lot. People love to travel. I mean really. Almost all the profiles I see talk about how much they travel, and there are pictures of them traveling. They have groups of people around them. It's really amazing to me. Maybe I just work too much.

Here's a story about me. When I was younger. I traveled around Europe for 6 weeks in the fall time. I took pictures. When I got home, I still lived with my parents in this story. So, I got home and told them a little about my trip, you know the sites, how it was 'cool' and 'fine'. I showed them pictures. I believe of the hundred I took, I think there were two that had me in it. Just two. I think my friend even took those, because she came up with the idea.

My mother asked me why I hadn't taken any more photos with me in them. "Well" I said. "I was there. I took that picture. I know I was there." I still have the same sort of mentality about the places I go. Barring dementia or Alzheimer's, I'll remember till I die. Granted I don't have pretty Facebook pictures to be the envy of all my digital friends, but I know where I go. I just don't have the dating profile presence that gets the 'right swipes'

Traveling, it's amazing how many successful people travel and date. Especially on this 'Tinder' app. Everyone is successful and parties and is active and doesn't like tv. Except the ones who aren't. I guess I'm not one of those successful world traveler party types. I don't think I am. I don't have time. I have to work. They should have a peoplewhoworkdatingapp.com. I'd be too busy to sign up, but just saying.

I guess I should try to find a dating site that has 'regular' people on it. I would hate to have to just walk around and hope that I bumped into someone that I said hi to on the street, or hallway or park and asked out. I mean RL is totally scary. I get the 'meat sweats' just thinking about it.

October 2

You deserve a raise, two even. Ask for one. When your boss agrees (and he will because, you know, skillz.), ask for a second one.

—

FUN stuff this one. It's always good to get a raise. Sometimes it happens when we aren't expecting it, but most of the time we have to work for it. Do you ask for raises? Do you have the chutzpah for one? Do you need chutzpah? Do you have the skillz so someone like Napoleon Dynamite? If you have the skillz ask for it. How long has it been? Now perhaps you don't want to ask because you'll lose the job you have. That's something to think about, in which case maybe it's time to think about how you can get the skillz you need to advance. Maybe even outside the company you work for.

I understand the older you are the more uncomfortable it is to try new things. But jobs aren't getting easier to get. They will only get harder. Minimum wage is high, robots are coming to take blue-collar jobs, and with machine learning, some white-collar jobs as well. No one is safe from the robotical revolution.

I jest, a little. We have to continually improve ourselves, if we don't look to the next step we could be left behind. If you deserve a raise, make note of your accomplishments, what you want. Then ask. And if they disagree or can't give you what you want you at least know where you stand. We should know where we stand and why we are standing there. In my opinion. (Reminder, some of these things I say aren't my opinion. Always research and look for context in things.)

Keep in mind, if you stop learning, if you only do just enough. At some point someone will pass you in this race. So, grab some water and pick up the pace.

October 21

Burn books.

THERE are a few books I've read that were bad. I mean badly written, or simply stupid. Books that would help propagate their idiocy through the human culture. Books that would just give people bad advice, or completely missed the mark. Intellectually or otherwise. It's terrible, and the fact they even exist poses a risk to more wasted time, or wrong impressions. But even though these books are atrocious, I could not bring myself to burn them. Wipe them from existence as it were. I'd like them to be filed in the library under 'completely wrong concepts and or terrible prose from our collective human history', but burning them seems so, so, Nazi-ish, but it is not limited to that group. Book burnings go on today. Although I hope with the advent of the internet the actual effect of such an event is limited to purely that. A truly useless symbolic gesture.

I find history interesting. A German named Heinrich Heine in 1820 wrote something in German. The translation is "Where they burn books, they will also ultimately burn people." He said that in 1820. Clearly a student of history as book burnings didn't start in Germany. They started in antiquity. People burned the ideas in books for ages before.

It's interesting that we can be so opposed to one thing, but completely miss the point when the same idea changes form. Burning books represents, at least to me, the statement that someone's idea is not necessarily wrong, but opposed to the core of a ruling class or regime. It's not the book, it's an action to snuff out an idea, that someone or a group finds abhorrent.

People around the word burn books and we turn away in repulsion as it's so direct, but if the idea is destroyed in a different way, we might even cheer and applaud at its demise. I'll leave it to you to think about what those different ways are.

So, I think it's something to ask yourself, what's the difference between the ways we snuff out opposing ideas? Why is one appalling and another other praise worthy?

October 22

Play a guessing game with a stranger. When they answer wrong, giggle.

IF someone came up to me and did this, I'd probably give them my 'fit in' face, no question. It's crazy, people don't engage others playfully at all. It's too scary. If it's not scary for you, it's scary for the other person. We don't connect on that level anymore. Only children do that on the playground. If we can't just give you a 'like' then we don't know how to react. Maybe I'm bias, right? I mean I am an introverted writer. So maybe I'm simply not approachable, or give off the wrong body language. That might be, but I think as a people we keep our heads down, looking at our phones perhaps, and actually avoid interaction, even though we are 'connected' online.

I remember going out as a teenager and I would have the intention of meeting people. Nowadays I have the intention of buying what I need and going home with as little human interaction as possible, I get enough of that online.

It's subtle, isn't it. You're never asked to jump, just slide a little. I don't think it will change society that fast. You and me will probably be the way of the Dodo before its noticeable, but with the rise of technology I see changes in our cultures that while on the surface seem inventive and helpful you have to wonder where it leads. Throughout history, if you read history, you'll see men/women working to horde power over others.

Now, I'm not saying anyone is trying to be a masterful puppeteer. At least not yet, but tools are being created now, that make for some interesting situations down the road. The way we interact reminds me of the old maxim 'Divide and Rule'. Maybe with all this 'communication' we're just dividing ourselves, and later it will make it easier for someone to come along and 'rule'. While technology has been expressed as a way to connect us with the world, it also seems to divide us into little cubicles.

We seem to be less apt to approach each other in RL (real life) as they say and more comfortable, as well as feeling connected, when we're linked to our phones.

No solution, I'm not being helpful. Just paranoid. It's like one of those post from some random you always see online, stating a possible problem with no solution. Simply an observation. I'm sure everything will turn out right, the world is built on that. Right?

Maybe if you have time today, looking up from your phone connect to someone in the RL for more than 10 minutes without looking down at your window to the world. I'll give it a shot if you will. That's a lie, I'm going to do it anyway.

October 23

One won't hurt.
—

YOU ever have a friend tell you this? I'm pretty sure I've heard it from my friends, as well as my own head. One won't hurt. Did you know that some people are allergic to alcohol? So, like if they drink it, they could just die. From the interaction. Reminds me of the stories where teens had done just that. I, myself was and am not allergic to alcohol, unless you count the morning after with that massive axe-splitting headache as a symptom.

For some reason this is taken as a truth in our younger brains. Let's put alcohol down. Let's talk about drug use. In the world, there are about 29.5 million people who have a drug problem according to the internets I looked at. So, that's not a lot. If we have about 7.6 billion. That's less than the total cost of a private jet at 44 million, right. Someone else can work on that.

That's how I see statistics. Numbers. (That's quite original you say. Statistics as numbers! Brilliant!) It's 29.5 million people, but I just see the number. So, do you think if I saw some of their faces, I'd be more compelled to help? I don't know. It's possible. If you're trying to start somewhere, as you can't start everywhere or you'll run out of determination maybe this is one place to think about.

However, you have to think about starting somewhere. No one really told me about drugs. Drugs were bad. They would mess up your life. I got that, I stayed away, mostly. I wasn't rolling doobies at the riverside, but I had one or two.

Some kids hear that drugs are bad, and that's great. They hear sex is bad too, but from what I recall it doesn't feel bad. How can something that feels good be bad for you? "It just is." Is not an answer.

Well, Heroine can take away your ability to be happy. I need 'happy', that's scary to me. Acid, you might get a 'bad trip'. I don't need that shit, walls bleeding, squirrels jumping out of mushrooms. No thanks. I'm trying to make my 'trip' (of life) as good as possible. I don't need the detour. Coke, destroys your nose and you stay up for days, and you fidget like a coke head. Great. Sounds awesome. New drugs, they give you alligator skin. What? Excuse me? Bath salts, you kill your mom, try to eat people, and you generally just might try to kill someone. Thanks, but I'll pass. Meth, teeth. Wash the inside of your car with a power washer. Super. Don't show your kids a video of eggs cooking in a skillet. Put the phone down, yours and theirs and talk to them. That cat video can wait.

October 24

Play the lottery every day, and put all your financial hope into it. Make no other plans for the future.

―

NOT to burst your 'win big' bubble, but it's not worth it. Unless you win, of course. I myself like the idea. I spend a dollar, and I get to daydream about spending millions. Then I check my ticket and the dream crashes down. I pick the dream up again with another dollar! Yah!

We might not put all our hopes into the lottery. I mean most of us are reasonable people, but I can tell you I spent a lot more time buying tickets than I did in buying bonds or investigating how to properly budget my money. It's like everything else. It's easier. Easier is better right?

Get rich quick. That's the dream.

When did that become the dream, exactly? I thought the dream involved hard work? I think that it used to. If we read about some of the players in history. It really doesn't anymore. That's not the dream, the dream is to live on a beach. Although that's impractical. No one, including Jimmy Buffett wants to live on a beach forever. You might for a while, but if you retire at 65, you might have 15 years, on a beach. I'm not knocking beaches, but that's a lot of time in the sun doing nothing. Maybe I'm a different breed.

For some reason it seems that we have come to the conclusion in our media and marketing that we want things to be easy. We want convenience. I get that. Sure, I want things the way I want things, but do I really expect them to be handed to me without any work? My mind thoughts are screaming right now, "Of course, idiot! I've worked hard enough!"

Life isn't easy, and it's not fair. If you truly want success, you're going to fail. And you're going to do it more than once. Then you'll build on that, and find success. Maybe it won't be in the form of an Audi R8 or a Lamborghini Veneno, or BMW i8, but you can find it. It will require work, time, boring amounts of waiting and more work. If you can manage that, you can be successful, but life will never just hand it to you. You think its time that we get to work.

October 25

Download Clash of Clans, Angry birds, Farmville, etc. Time…well…spent.

—

LET me be the first to say. I have all of these wonderful games. But as we have all this ease at our finger tips, we forget other things in our lives. I recommend the games themselves, but there are some who might need assistance in breaking free from their tech. (Links in the appendix.)

This is something to gauge. You probably don't have a problem, but how much time do you spend on electronic devices outside of work?

I can tell you. I spend about 16 hours at my computer. Probably another 2 on and off using my phone. Maybe another 15 watching television. Plus 40 at my day job. I spend a lot of time. In fact, I gave up electronics for a weekend. Let me tell you, I thought about taking up smoking again.

What am I supposed to do with my hands? I also found that it wasn't silent time. My mind would bounce around to different things. Things I needed to do. World problems I could solve. I couldn't google anything! Do you know what that's like? Realizing that you can't finish an entire thought without wondering if google has something to add to my jerky ADHD knowledge base.

I bet you can't do it. Just for a weekend. I tried it. It's hard. Plan it if you have to. Your leg will vibrate, or your ear will twitch. Oh, but you won't have a call, just the feeling that you're missing something.

And you have to log in or else you won't get your gems or coins. Is that only concerning to me? These are symptoms of an addict.

October 26

Live in the moment.

Seize the Carp

FAVORITE saying. Great advice. I encourage you. Do this. This is possibly the only 'good advice' in the book. But do people tell you this? What good are words if they don't explain it. How do you live in the moment? What if these moments suck? I don't want to live in these moments, I want to live in the other ones!

We have too much to worry about to 'live in the moment'. We have bills to think about, and kids and work tomorrow. There is this big project coming up, my girlfriend is mad at me. There is no way I can live in this moment, I have others to think about. Come on, Alex!

Okay, breathe, exhale. Count to ten backwards, then open your eyes. Cross them. Real yoga stuff. Feel better? Me neither.

It's hard to live in the moment when we're linked to all these other moments, or linked to all these apps and ease of use devices.

I love technology. It's not ever going away. It's awesome, and scary. When I gave up tech for a weekend there was still no silence. My thoughts kept racing. They would flip from one topic to the next, never ending. That's not living in the moment.

My mind was still and is still preoccupied with noise, useless stuff. I can't find my center, because I don't have a center, everything moves and changes. Its fidgety, my mind, like an 1980's coke head and I don't even do coke. I like my nose, and septum.

I could tell you we need to break away from technology and 'find our centers' but I don't want to do that. I want to think about all the things coming out tomorrow and how tech will change our world and think about how I can save money for retirement and help my family and give to worthy causes. There is just so much, too much, to think about.

We can't turn this off. We don't even want to. Sometimes though we should slow down, breathe, exhale. Count to ten, backwards, and do yoga stuff. Enjoy the moment, breath, slow, because before you know it, everything will change, again.

October 27

Be offended. It shows you care.

I'm not sure how offended I'm supposed to get. Don't get me wrong I have my understandings of things. I have core values and standards. Sometimes I see things or hear things I don't agree with. I don't see why other people should kill one another. Clearly there was an offense. Someone was offended by something. And now that we are connected to the world, we have that much more to be offended about. Yah, connectedness!

Let me just clear the air. I'm right and if you agree, you're right too. If you don't agree, your wrong. You shouldn't be offended, it's just true. You should just tolerate me. Like a bug or a cold breeze. This is true if we live in a relative world. In a relative world, anyone can be right and 'live their truth'. Why should you be offended by anything? In their eyes, they're right.

I think it's obvious this is impossible. People are offended often, very, way too often. At everything. It's crazy, right?

We are offended by oppression. Oppression is offensive. I believe that. I don't want to be oppressed. I don't think that others should be oppressed. I think trolls should be oppressed, but then who should squelch them? Who should be in charge of that?

I don't want that responsibility. I'm running over the same old ground. Perhaps the same old fears.

So, if we agree that oppression is bad, why do we see it so much? Is some oppression good and other oppression bad? I think that stands to reason. We shouldn't tolerate, intolerance, right? It actually makes my head spin. Just like Beetlejuice.

But the problem is an actual paradox. I looked it up. The gist of the paradox is, we tolerate others that we don't agree with. But if we come across a group that is intolerant then we don't have to tolerate them. The guy (Karl Popper) explained the 'tolerant' group if faced with an 'intolerant' group who is unwilling to see reason, then the tolerant group can use force, because the intolerant group would be pushed in the direction of using force because of their intolerance to what is tolerated. I don't claim to be a deep thinker, but what does 'reason' mean in that statement to you?

How can I know as an individual, who is pummeled daily by various sources of information and disinformation, know with reason, which would be based on my experiences, and conclusions, which group in that scenario comes out on top as reasonable? Perhaps it's up to the larger group? It's getting historically scary up in here ('here' being the world, just to clarify.).

October 28

You can make it.

—

YOUR friends give you this advice? You have time to dodge the train. It will work out.

It's always close. But you pull it off. Weaving in and out of traffic, because you don't care about human life. I mean let's be honest here, if you give it much thought, you really don't. You have to get to work, killer 😊. Did you know on trips up to an hour, speeding by 10 mph only saves you about 12 minutes? That's great if you might be late for a meeting, but is it really worth it? Is your life worth 12 minutes?

Are you going to stop a nuclear bomb? Is your name Jack Bauer?

Don't get me wrong, you can probably make it. If you have a trip over 500 miles you can save almost an hour. That's where the math helps your teacher always told you about. Open roads and long distances. Don't speed. It's against the law.

That math though is only for clear sailing. If you are in the city, forget about it. Potential lights knock down those savings at even the longer distances of 50 miles down to about 6 minutes.

If you're late, you're late. Let it slide. Breath, exhale, do yoga shit. You're not the center of the universe, but if you kill someone speeding to work, I guarantee that will consume your mind for a very long time.

October 29

Jealousy is just a 'different' love language.

NOPE, it's not. It's created by various things. One is insecurity in who you are or if your partner is the jealous one, who they are. I suppose there can be little instances of jealousy, perhaps you aren't spending any time together because you both work and you're jealous that you don't get that time, but it's really not the same thing. We just use the same word in the media from time to time and that's conflated the term. You simply need to figure out that time dynamic.

Jealousness however is dangerous. Your partner could insist on you spending more time with them, or stop seeing others. Now on one level this could be healthy, if you're spending all your time in a relationship with your friends, and I do mean a significant amount going out, while your partner either does the same or stays at home there might be an imbalance in that relationship. I might be old fashioned, but I assume that if you are in a relationship your time would be divided into portions and just as a job is, a somewhat big portion would involve time with that other person and not friends.

Jealousy I think for most of us is a pretty obvious and marked emotional state. You can reach a pretty clear conclusion if someone's motives are inspired by jealously or simply caring about the relationship. Although there are some tricky bastards out there. And I use that term for either sex.

The quick of it is, jealous behavior is not cute. It's Marky Mark in Fear. You remember that movie. It was scary. I like him better as a dad.

If you deal with jealousy, there are some links in the appendix on this date. Check them out, for your own well-being as well as any relationships you hope to have.

October 30

Work to be original. Otherwise nobody wants it.
—
The Marketing Department of the World

EVERYONE wants to see something new. Although I have to day, Hollywood doesn't seem to care about it all that much. I don't have any links for this, but there are a multitude of movies in Asia that have simply been repurposed for Hollywood. Most have been recreated badly.

Pet Rocks. That's what original means.

You know any new stories? I know stories that have elements of other stories. At work we are told to use or reuse something someone else created and change it to meet our needs.

I think we should be honest with ourselves. There aren't new ideas, simply new ways to view those ideas. Of course, it seems like we have new things being created every day, but when you break them down, they are simply proven ideas that have been reorganized into the latest tech or with a different skin.

I'm not saying innovation isn't great and we aren't making new things, but they aren't what Webster defines as original, in the original sense of the word at least. (Yeah, the definition has changed just like everything else.)

What people mean by original is to take something and make it your own. And don't think that there aren't people out there who wouldn't still buy Rocks with eyes. Why do you think one company still holds the patent on 'Pet Rocks'? They know it will come back around. Cycles. Everything has cycles. Just gotta see them.

Don't worry so much about being original, or with the in crowd, or independent. Just follow your passion (Also see October 13th to thoroughly grab for context... 😊).

October 31

Test the gods today.

WHAT is it that you have always wanted to do? What's held you back? Why? What can you do to make it happen? (I assume this is a positive thing in your life and the lives of those around you and its not to be a space cowboy on the new Mars colony.) We have so much time in this place, surely there is more that we can do as a people together, as a global force. How can we work together? Do you think it's possible to come together, to work toward a common good? To bring light to this world? Do you think it's something that we could do, forget our pride and create a future that would make the machine stop, if not just for a second? Let's dream big.

November 1

Dress up in your favorite Halloween costume, go to work in it for a week. When they mention to you it's not Halloween, say "I know." And smile, run back to your desk, make appropriate noises for the theme of the costume.

—

LIFE is so serious. I keep bringing this up, maybe it's a dead horse or a broken record. It's always about what bills are due next. How much you need to save for 'retirement'. 'Not enough ever' is the answer by the way. I'm not saying don't try, I'm saying try to remember to have fun today. You can't know what tomorrow brings. Money doesn't buy happiness, only facsimiles. Just remember the things you worry about today, will not be remembered in 5 years. If that is true of something you are worried about then maybe you can let it go and go out and do something about it. In the meantime, remember to have fun.

I guarantee you'll remember the story where you walked into work on November 1st in a Viking custom because a terrible advice book mentioned it might be fun. (while at the same time giving little gems of wisdom for your life☺... maybe...). You might not remember the time you got a flat tire and had to call a tow truck. Remember to always look on the bright side of life! (Monty Python Shout out!)

WARNING: Only really flavorful people can pull this off with class. Don't be creepy, be fun. Maybe the back story will help keep this light instead of strange. Maybe you'll mention where to buy this book. Some of it goes to me, but the other half is going to a good cause, and who couldn't get behind that!

Have fun today, don't use your 'fit in' face. Smile. Spend time with your family, do a game night. Read to your kids at bedtime, buy a homeless guy that sandwich on your way home from work. Wear a cloak to work, go on a date and be yourself. Have fun and bring some flavor into this world.

November 2

Drive across country to the ocean. Never get in.

YOU ever get up to the very edge of something really life changing and then back away out of fear. It's just about the same as taking this advice. Maybe taking a trip every day is not worth the gas, or electricity you'd have to pay, but every once in a while, something comes along and it just screams for you to try it or make an attempt at the very least. It you throw 100 darts at a board, chances are one of them will stick. It's possible that one will even hit the target.

You say, "But Alex, I don't want to drive across the country. It's too far." Okay, don't. What are you going to do with your life? Any plans? Any aspirations at all? What's your bucket list look like? I say "Attempt some of them. Maybe you fail, maybe you drive right up to the ocean, and then say. 'I can't swim.'. Well, then don't drive across country and get in the ocean I say. Start at a pool and get an instructor. Learn to swim. Then maybe you'll want to take the trip that's further."

My life is perhaps rather boring. I write and don't go out much, but I have attempted many unsure things in my life that have brought me great joy. I will continue to do so. Even if they amount to "Jack Squat!" as the late great Matt Foley might say.

Maybe you are scared to take that leap. Perhaps you shouldn't, maybe you don't have what it takes. I know people out there that don't. But if you aren't one of those people, you would have known it before you started agreeing with me back when I said jack squat.

So, my advice is, maybe you should take that drive, but make sure you know what you're going to do when you get there. Sink or swim. Sink or swim.

November 3

Money makes the (wo)man.

School Stopper Linda

MAKES them what? Rich. Sophisticated? Smart? Loyal? Happy? Perhaps fills their days with joy? Nope, money comes and goes, or makes money or buys things. Still with the things, and wanting them.

I can't say I don't get it. Fancy cars and diamond rings, or mocking birds, or Shetland ponies, goats, or looking glasses. I mean who doesn't appreciate a good looking-glass, am I right?

Things seem to be what it's about though. If you have money then you can buy all these things that we 'need'. I tell you, we seem to 'need' a lot more than other people. It's amazing actually. Did you see the statistic on the FAO site about how 1.3 billion tons of food are just wasted? About 680 million from industrial countries, and 310 million in developing ones. That's sad. It's food that might go bad or simply be thrown out due to policies. If the store can't sell it, they can't give it to the homeless, if one of them gets sick the company could get sued. I'm not sure how that works for canned goods but I'm sure there is a lawyer somewhere around to explain why they would need be thrown away too.

If we waste so much food that might be able to feed some people, I mean I'm conservative here. Let's say only 2% of all that waste is probably useable and/or able to be used by people. That's about 13.6 million tons of food for industrial countries and 6.2 million in developing ones.

We waste a lot of stuff, we waste a lot of time on gaining stuff. Apparently stuff we don't even need. If we can waste food, something we should be able to agree on that is needed. How much easier would it be to waste money?

Money comes and goes and money makes money. The only thing it seems to do to people is make them want more money.

Money holds no character value. What I mean to say is, money does not and will never make someone something. You decide what your character is, not your money or the people next to you. You are ultimately responsible for your character, and if you're looking at someone else's wallet, you're missing who they really are.

November 3

Start a pirate radio station in your basement.

HHH

PIRATES! ARRR! On top of wanting to be a cowboy I also thought it would be fun to be a pirate. Not a bad one that plunders, and kidnaps and kills. Everyone I would get treasure from would be okay with it. I was 8 after all, I didn't fully understand the concept of plundering.

Another thing that happened was (probably not at the same time.) I saw a movie called "Pump up the Volume". Let me tell ya, I was ready to build a radio station in my basement. Only problem was, I didn't have a basement. Nor did I understand all the equipment I would need. I walked up to the edge of that idea though. I looked for parts at Radio Shack. (Yea it was an electronics store that used to sell components and what not.) I mean I had the right idea; the store was called Radio Shack after all.

Turns out radio equipment wasn't within my budget, and I couldn't very well tell my parents I needed an increase in allowance to start an underground pirate radio station and blab about who knows what.

So, I put that idea off, later I found out that its indefinitely. I mean as a child sometimes playing tag with your friends is over all more important than becoming a vigilante radio rebel by night. There is only so much time you know. Pick and choose. Pick and choose.

Today there are still pirate radio stations that operate across borders and spout ideals and anti-whatever. They talk around the world. Interesting stuff to look into. What's also interesting is anyone can actually do this nowadays. I'm not promoting going out and starting one, but with YouTube and podcasting at our fingertips its actually within arm's reach of the average 'weekend warrior' type.

Don't get me wrong, there is a lot of work to it. It's not simply plug and play. You need content, and platform. The tech is there, and easy to buy, but if you don't have motivation, if you don't have a drive and determination, it will simply not last. You'll decide you want to play tag with your friends instead. That's okay too. Follow your dreams, and put a plan into action.

By the way, I don't recommend starting a pirate radio station. They are illegal, hence the moniker, 'pirate'.

November 5

Don't worry about the issues; the politicians can handle it.

WHO has time to read about these issues? I mean we don't, not really. That's what the politicians are for, to represent our interests. We trust them to do this. They've let us down in various ways. We've found out they're just people, which is amazing and shocking, right? (This shouldn't actually be ironic, but it feels that way when the votes come through.) We turn on the news and find out that most of them are not above reproach. I don't know if we are truly shocked, but sometimes the media makes it seem like its news, when it's really not. I mean they are politicians and, in that culture, or 'sphere of influence' there comes a need to play ball. Sometimes playing ball requires scratching backs. Sad, but true.

I'm sure there are a lot of them who are trying to make a change, but with so many outside influences, as well as red tape that has to be cut, I'm sure it's hard not to have your direction altered in different ways.

My point is, how many letters have you written to your politician about something that needs addressed? If you have, you're one of the few. Most of us simply rest on the belief that they can do their job without our help. I'd love to say there are so many politicians out there that are able to withstand the negative influence of what life throws at you, that we don't have to worry about supporting them, but I can't.

Wherever you find yourself in the world, our leaders need support. They require input into how things are going. Think of it this way. We're a team. A business has the workers (that's us) and a team leader who reports to the ownership or higher ups. If the team leaders are only talking with themselves, they can't fully understand the details of a project. I don't care how good a leader you are, if you don't hear from your team you don't have the full picture. Your team is not going to perform well, and it might be impossible for a project or game to function properly.

It's like any fine print we sign off on these days. No one really reads what the small font is asking of us. We simply trust. What's stranger is why we trust? To save time? I think that's a poor excuse for damaging our future, but don't take it from me, just read a history book.

November 6

"You can't handle the truth."
—
Jack 'the man' Nicholson

TRUTH will set you free. Which truth is that? You're truth or mine. I don't mean to steal Dennis Miller's classic tone when he was an icon of sorts, but it seems we've lost sight of the truth. Not only lost sight of it, but we don't even remember the direction it was in. We're all turned around. We watch the news about all these tragedies happening all over the world and locally. Not really all over the world, we only get a sliver from outside. Nonetheless we hear of people killing each other, while others starve, drugs are rampant in our society yet we can't seem to do enough to stop it. We have jobs after all, we need the next best thing. Our jobs are to make money so that we can pay bills and scrape by, so that we can go to work to make money to pay bills and possibly see hope of retiring at 70.

Let's face it, most of this generation will never get to retire. We don't make enough money, or have the infrastructure for that anymore. It's a pipe dream going through Baker, Montana, although unlike the other 2.3 million miles of pipe already strewn about the US that dream will happen. Hope of a classical retirement is gone. The average life span in the industrialized world is around 78 to 80 years. If you retire at 62 that means you have to have saved around 700,000 dollars. This assumes you will be able to live off of 36,000 dollars a year. The average income in 2016 was around 32,000. That means all I need to do to retire is save about 26K a year until I'm 62. Sure, I'll just take out a loan for that, put it on credit.

Hopefully you reading this have been a little better with your money than me and managed it well. I've linked an article that made me laugh. It talks about pensions and how you can withdraw around 12,000 a year if you've saved 300,000. That's legit, that's 1,000 bucks a month. That could work if I'm old and don't want to do anything outside of gardening. Maybe start a 'Pet Rock' collection, if they're not too expensive with inflation. Where I'm from that's within the low-income range. Not that I plan on retiring though, horticulture was never part of my skill set.

I mean, I'm a writer and as Billy Crystal once said to Danny DeVito. "A writer, writes, always!" So, until my fingers and voice don't work, I think I'll be doing something. Hopefully this has actually given some hope. I mean if you start saving money when you're 18 (recall the importance of budgeting) you might have saved a nice chunk for yourself and be able to hire your own gardener in retirement.

November 7

Reach out, pour into someone, if it doesn't work, give up. Don't try helping anyone else.

—

LET'S say for a minute that you aren't one of these busy people. Let's say you have tried to help others out. Sometimes people just don't want help, sometimes they don't change for us fast enough. I mean, we see some change, but then they just go back to their old ways. Perhaps our time line requires effort quicker than their time line.

I mean, if we poured all this work into helping out these other people. We should be able to see a change, there should be some sort of reward or yield, right?

I agree, sometimes it is hard to watch others not change, or even worse change and then revert. It takes something out of you. Giving the way you do, it's exhausting. I mean, life is hard, but you don't let it get to you and you've tried to help others. You've given money and time, shown how to grow and displayed that growth to those around you. You work hard to practice whatever you preach.

It takes a lot from us when we dedicate so much of ourselves to helping others and they seem to disappear once more into the rift. It's disheartening. This is where we sometimes break down and think that we can't do this anymore. It's too much. Maybe it is too much, maybe you can't do it anymore.

I've found that there have been points in my life where things were tough. Where I didn't know if I was going to be able to handle something. Let me tell you, I was wrong every single time. I might not have succeeded, I might have failed to live up to a standard I set. No question, I'm sure I've let people down, and even been responsible for putting people down at one time. Some situations just don't work out.

But as bleak as that last paragraph is, there are people out there that need you. They need that glimpse of hope, and strength. Those things that you have provided in the past. You might not feel you can be that person anymore, it's too hard, but we have jobs to do. We have a future to build, and while the future might not know your name, if you endure, if you continue to show support and love, even though the times when we see people slip back into their old ways. If you do that, if you give hope out like candy, the future will be better off and what better reward could there be to give people hope, not false hope mind you but one for a bright future, one built on a foundation and not simply empty sweetness.

November 8

Open the box that holds all the worlds woes.
—

HAVOC. We all probably know the story of Pandora's box, or Pandora's jar. (It's funny to me this is now a jewelry store as well, since the original name was so ghastly.) So, the story goes, Zeus, (a pretty angry fellow if you ask me) was mad because we managed to get fire for the cave men from another tale. Anyway, he decided to get Pandora, who I guess might as well have been a cat (You know, cuz curiosity and all that.) around a box that wasn't to be opened. Guess what, Pandora opened it and we can thank her for all the troubles in the world, or maybe the dudes who might have explained better that she shouldn't open the box. I don't know, seems like a toss up to placing the blame solely on one sex though. Regardless, it's a pretty epic story. If you have some time look it up.

We don't do that do we? I mean, we can't. There isn't a box, or a jar. But we do have words. As a writer I find that words are important. Even stupid words like Supercalifragilisticexpialidocious, or jujube or Wabe. They can have meaning. These are just fun words, there are more and you can arrange them in such a way that it can tear someone's world apart. Let me repeat that, as I think you might have missed it. Words can tear someone's world apart. And so easily. So quick are the organs of our mouths at times that we don't even fathom rightly what we've done.

Maybe you'd say, "Ah, Alex. Your being dramatic." I wish I was, I truly, truly do. Let me give you a statistic that shouldn't be. Some range from 4,000 up to 6,000. Let's be conservative and say 1. If one person takes their life from being bullied or being put down. It's too much. This happens because of loose words. People giving no regard to the power they hold.

As I've mentioned before, you are worth something. You have purpose if you choose to find it. Your words, whether you're a troll on the internet, never seeing the damage you cause and not caring, to an actual human being who slips up once in a while. Know that your words have power. I hope you don't forget that.

You have the power to uplift or put down. Create or destroy. This is not simply a trivial thing. When you open your mouth, either hope or woes could come out of it. It's up to you to decide what your jar is filled with.

November 9

Only pretty people really count.

RICH and pretty, that's what the media shouts. Or scandal, and tragedy. Maybe I'm being too hard on the media. Sometimes out of the sea of consumerism and woes, sometimes there is a story, that is only slightly bent. Pardon my pessimism, or don't.

Perhaps it's not as bad as I think it is. I exaggerate for effect and passion, after all I'm a writer. I have to get you to think about these things somehow. Why do I, have an internal 'something' that pushes me from time to time to compare myself. Not to epic people of importance, not the true heroes of this age, but to the latest six pack action star I see on screen or magazine. Where does that come from? Well I think it comes directly from the media I watch, from the marketing I see.

Who doesn't want to be pretty. I'm not saying that it's the fault of pretty people. I love pretty people, but why. Throughout time, different cultures had different ideas of what pretty was. I won't go into all that, but it seems to be, that if I were to work on exercising and dieting to get into the shape, I felt was actually attractive now, I'd have to work out as much as I work. I don't even think that I'm bad looking, but I can't compete with all the models out there. And I'm poor, relative to the successful people I compare myself to, so that effects my ego as well.

Why though? I've been writing about how these things shouldn't matter, right? (I think that's what I've been trying to convey…) When I look in the mirror in the morning, I should be able to say, "I look good. I enjoy who I am. I have worth and importance. I have goals and they are worthy goals."

So why is it that I don't do that every day. (Some days I'm pretty satisfied with myself, let me be honest.) I don't do that every day because I forget, as you might have from time to time. I then begin comparing myself to others. NEVER, NEVER compare yourself to others. Compare yourself, to who you were yesterday. Are you better than you were yesterday? No, then what do you need to do to be better than yesterday? One thing, name it. Do that that thing. After you do that one thing. Ask yourself how do you feel about yourself compared to yesterday? Better is the word you should be looking for. Remember that feeling. Now, lather, rinse and repeat. Every day, compare yourself, only to yesterday not to anyone else. If you're better, great. If not, you have that one thing to do. Go to it. You are worth it.

November 10

Take up prancercising.

Joanna Rohrback created a revolution. Honestly, I'd never heard of her. Course I just spoke about bullying and how it's not something cool to do. So, don't do that, but some things you see, you just have to look twice. It's like a car wreck really, that's the only parallel I can think of.

It's just one of those things that make you go hmmm? It just goes to show, there is an audience for just about anything. If you haven't seen the YouTube videos on prancercising, you should check them out. I can't recommend the prancercising book. I'd prefer to give thousands for the Big-foot adventure in Canada myself, but to each their own. I've linked to this little gem of the internet in the appendix on this date.

November 11

Text your friends. Don't call them, you don't have that much time for a 10 minute call, but only 600 10 second keypad punches. Now that's social interaction at its best.

School Stopper Intern, "Button Pusher" Paul

DO you talk to a lot of people throughout the day? I mean like, talk. With your voice muscles, not your finger muscles. I prefer texting. I used to not be on board with it. I believe my brother still doesn't like it. He prefers to talk. It makes sense. It's faster in some situations, but I find myself texting even in those situations. I tell myself it's easier. Easier than talking? Who am I Stephen Hawking? (R.I.P.)

When did I decide that typing everything was easier than a conversation that would last half as long? It seems counter-intuitive when I break it down like that. Is my time so important that I don't have time to make a call? I don't think I'm alone on this one, or maybe I am, and I'm just the worst person in the world.

The thing is, what do I do with all that extra time not talking and only typing? Nothing, I'm still typing. Multi-tasking is a funny, funny concept. Let me share, computers multi-task. They have different, what's the word? 'Streams' or 'strings', maybe it's 'threads'. Whatever it is. They can do different things at the same time. We can't, sorry to burst your bubble there, Bob. It's impossible. You can only handle one brain intensive process at a time. That's not to say you can't do more than one thing at a time, but you can only perform one process that requires actual thinking at one time. You could try to dispute me, but it would be a waste of your time. (Check out the smart brain people's link in the appendix if you don't quite believe me.) It's one of the reasons why machines might be able to take over. They can multitask. We only wish we could.

With that in mind, one thing to remember is maybe we should make time to actually talk to one another instead of always glancing at our phones, how else are we going to make sure we aren't simply talking to a machine sent from the future to divide and conquer.

Words to live by…

November 12

Hammer pants.

—

STOP, hammer time. I used to sing this, I mean "You can't touch this!" and "Stop! Hammer Time" were like the only words I knew, but when you're a kid that's really all you need to remember in order to annoy the Dicken's out of your parents. Broken Record, 100 times. "Stop, hammer time! doo, doo doo, dute."

If I thought they sold Hammer pants, I would have bought them. Course I was also planning to build a pirate radio station in my club house/garage so you have to pick and choose at that financial level. You understand, you were there once.

November 13

Build a labyrinth and find a minotaur to put inside it.

Minos

MYTHOLOGY! I'm a fan. So, Daedalus built this maze for a King, not the one who turns things into gold or makes tires and oil changes, but Minos a son of who else, Zeus. I'm telling you, that dude got around. Daedalus had a son named Icarus. You might know him for flying too close to the sun, whereas Prometheus was the dude who stole fire from the gods. Mythology! I love it. I could start to ruminate over all this but I'll try and focus on only the quote.

This is just a silly thing, I'm sure we could try and make it deeper than I intended, so many facets. I think a lot of people tend to do this. You could say we each build our own labyrinths to hold our monsters inside. That's deep right. It's deep because you have to really carve that apart to get there. We analyze things, sometimes past the point of any meaning the creator meant in the source material. We do it anyway. It brings new life to things, or corrupts their true intention.

So, this quote, it isn't really advice, I mean it's silly, right? I suppose if someone took the time to build an actual labyrinth that might be a terrible idea. However, we seem prone to break things apart and construct new things from bits and pieces we find laying around. It's not totally our fault, all the information and misinformation, missing sources and 'fake news' in the world. It makes it hard not to form cancerous opinions of things we have little actual context for. We can focus on something to such an extent that we lose the meaning it once held. In fact, marketing people are known to be able to 'sell' artists, sometimes that means taking liberties. I mean you can't sell a boring guy writing a book unless there is some 'appeal' right. Sometimes though its useful to step back, find the source and accept the information as intended and not look at subconscious context that never existed in the first place.

But just in case I'm over analyzing, I've also linked to an article that lists some places you can go walk through a real labyrinth. They are actually pretty sweet looking. I'm not saying I'd dedicate my time to building one, my outstanding masonry skills aside, but I might take a trip to run through a few of them with friends.

November 14

Don't go scuba diving.

I'M sure there is something out there that you think would be cool to try or do, or work towards but you just don't think you can. Well, I'm going to go with the opposite here. I'm of the mindset that you can do just about anything you put your mind to. I think if we could all get along for a single day and be kind to one another we'd see a vast improvement in the world. I also don't believe that we could simply pick one day to all agree on. That being said, I do think that we can accomplish very miraculous things in this life time if we could only believe in ourselves, what we are worth and that we have a purpose. Again, we do, have a purpose that is. In case you forgot, since the last time I told you.

I don't mean 'believe' without having something to back it up. That's stupid. If you believe in something and can't back it up, you need to understand what you think you believe in more. So, let me explain 'belief'. Say I've decided to go across country to Columbus, Ohio. Never been there. I've heard about it from that movie Ready Player One. I recommend the book, great read. Seems like a place I want to check out. So, I start my trip across the country. Don't see any signs but I have a GPS that seems to give a route. It's a long route. Soon, I start to see signs, about half way, so I'm probably in Kansas. I just see the road signs. I haven't seen the city yet. But I believe it's there, because I've seen other signs that lead to other cities that were there. I've spoken with people who have made a trip, but I believe based on the logic from signs pointing other places and previous experiences that Columbus is a real city. Say I've never been there, but I believe and that belief is based on seeing other signs leading to other places I've been. So, when the sign says 50 miles to Columbus, I believe that, because the last sign for Columbus I saw said 100 miles or 75.

That's the belief I'm talking about, something based on an understanding of the past and future. So, I'll say it again if you believe, based on past experiences that you can do something. If you've seen the things that have been done and you believe it's possible, if you strive for it. I mean really run at it, then you can do more than you think.

Don't let fear stop you from what you believe. Believe in yourself and what you've accomplished up to this point.

November 15

Never be satisfied.
—

I'VE already talked about this on August 6th. Running out of material, I guess. However, this little gem runs through our societal veins like blood. It's not even that we are aware of it. We seem to forget the moment. So, let's stop this race for just a second. We hear this in our lives, in advertisements. The next best thing. We need this, we need that. Don't rest on your laurels, there are more things out there to do. Comfort leads to conformity, which leads to death.

Yea I hear them say it, and I hear myself saying it when I'm in one of my "Go get 'em!" moods. It's good to not fall into the trap of being comfortable. Comfort does break down your ability to change and want to change in certain ways. But in some context comfort does stop you from reaching further, in others it can give you some breathing room. There is hardly enough room nowadays.

We don't want to stop looking forward toward the light of the goal, but we should stop and get a drink of water from that guy who is always handing them out every now and then and look back at the road traveled. It was a hard one, you've gotten this far, but there is still a little further to go.

Take this moment. Think back on the places you've been. The experiences you've had, good and bad. In this moment are you thankful for your life, the things you've accomplished, where you're at? I hope so. If not, you know what you need to work on.

So, I wanted to bring this point up again, in case you forgot in your day-to-day, take just a small amount of time out of your busy, busy schedule to recognize your accomplishments. If you feel you have none, then recognize that you can, it will just take some more time. (I know right? I hate that line too. I want it now. But you have to work hard for it. No trophies to hand out today.) So, if that's you and you feel you haven't discovered your 'passion life project' yet, know that there is time. You just need to attempt something, but plan it out. Maybe it won't work out entirely as planned, but that's why 'they' always say, life isn't fair.

Be satisfied in this moment. Life is long, then move forward from it satisfied, then forward to the next thing. Always forward.

November 16

If you believe you can, you can.

———

RIGHT. It's almost like I threw these together on purpose. Remember this is all terrible advice. And I just said, believe in yourself, right? Got me, I did. But I know I'll never be an astronaut. Granted, I don't care to be, but even if I did. The chances of me being successful and even picked for the job is slim. Sometimes no matter how hard we try at something, we will fail.

But this isn't the end of the world. Did you know that there are around 7.8 or 8 billion people in the world right now? (Or did I say 7.5 or 7.6. Guess you'll have to check my sources.) Did you know that the earth has about 15.77 billion acres of useable land? That's a lot of land. I don't think that I've see all that land. I think I'd like to see more of it.

I guess I told you how big the world is to help you to infer, or conclude there are more opportunities out there for you. More tracts of land the buffalo roam on than you've been able to see or can hope to see. I'm of the belief that if you want to change something, that change can happen. Or 'a change' can happen. It might not be what we want or expect, but there is enough out there to find something.

The statement 'if you believe, then you can' is dangerous. It's terrible. What do you think believe means? If you believe that you can leap tall buildings in a single bound, well let me tell you. Lay off the PCP, it's not helping. Remember life isn't fair. If you believe you will win the lottery, it doesn't change the probability that you will more likely be struck by lightning 7 times. You should base your reasons off of logical deduction from statistical experience and those outcomes. This strengthens your beliefs, that and actually looking into things yourself.

So, people say this all the time, if you believe you can, then you can. It's makes you feel empowered. If I only believe! It's true, you can do wonderful things you believe you can, but you have to actually know what you believe before you can do anything.

November 17

Go ahead eat the whole bag.

NO one will stop you. I can't say it's because they don't care, maybe you're too hard to argue with. You know what I don't appreciate. Serving sizes. Nothing in the general market comes in serving sizes shown on the label. A can of soup, that's not a serving size, that's about two and a half. I eat a can of soup, A whole can at a time. Maybe it's a can of fruit. All the servings and portions at one time.

I eat the bag, I take two hot pockets. Although, one is a serving. They give us these labels, but do we look at them? I'd say we don't. If I have a bag of Doritos and a case of Mountain Dew in front of my game console you better believe that's what I'm eating until its gone. You need fuel. That's on me. I get that.

I mention it, because we, of the industrialized nations consume more. Waste more. It's our right after all, right? (Wrong, I'm being sneaky, I disagree that it's our right to be as wasteful and indifferent as we are.) But who am I to tell you how to eat? Well, I'll say it. I'm someone, and we should think about the things we do.

I'm not saying don't eat the whole bag, I'm saying don't eat the whole bag as often as you do. Don't simply sit on the couch as much as you do. This is your life and its ending one day at a time. Let's be cliché. If this was your last day. What have you done for others?

That's the question we should be asking, it's not how much did I get? How comfortable was my lifestyle? On your last day, none, not one of those stupid little things matters. I don't care how powerful or full of yourself you might be.

If the only thing you've done in this world is think about yourself and eaten the whole bag, you really need to re-evaluate things. Now, you say "Who are you to tell me what I can or should do." I repeat I am someone, and I care. I care for your being. I speak out, not to stop you from making the most out of your life or YOLOing or having fun. I speak out in the hope that you might find a true purpose. A purpose I know you have.

Perhaps I am a dreamer, but rest assured I am not the only one.

November 18

The Sopranos should have had an actual ending!

Half the viewing audience

STORIES, television shows, movies all end in multiple ways. Some have hard endings and others keep going. Many we have grown accustom to, at least in television, that they give some sort of closure to the topics or issues we've come to deal with over the series. And it ended like this... (I've tried to keep it spoiler free. So, forgive the generality and overall blandness in the words. It's a pretty good show.)

Tony was the head of the family. He managed to beat many of the odds and pulled off some major things. Some of his crew weren't so lucky. He had some tricky operations at the end but he had to protect his family! He wasn't a very great guy in the least, and the doors to the restaurant never swung open. You're a gangster for life, as they say.

Or like this, Tony was the head of the family. He managed to beat many of the odds and pulled off some major things. Some of his crew weren't so lucky. He had some tricky operations at the end but he had to protect his family! He wasn't a very great guy in the least, and the doors to the restaurant swung open proving it. You're a gangster for life, as they say.

I believe I changed two things. I took out never, as you should never use that word and I added two words to it. It changes the entire story from the success of a mobster/monster, to the tragedy of criminal life.

Both play in my mind even today. They exist as one, just like Sheldon's cat Schrodinger. I actually think that was a pretty fantastic way to end the series. Some people think they half-assed it and there should have been a proper ending.

We like resolutions. We like to know how things will go. Do the bad guys win, or do the good guys win? We like stories with endings.

Of course, we don't live like this. There are many things that we don't see resolutions to, half-ass projects we lost passion for. That's fine, maybe they weren't worth it. The news is like this, sometimes we never hear the actual end of a story. It just gets dropped. Sometimes we give money to a charity and then never think on it again, but wonder why there is so much pain in the world. We desire so many resolutions, but time and time again, our own resolve fails to perform.

I'm talking to myself just as much as I'm telling you. If you're going to do something great, try not to half-ass it. Make a plan for positive change and see it through.

November 19

Don't talk about your feelings. Ever.

WHO do you have that you can talk about your feelings with? Some of you might say, "No one. I don't talk about my feelings." Others might say a loved one or a family member. It's hard to talk about feelings. It's hard to know if someone cares, or if they're just placating to you. Perhaps they're only tolerating you sharing. How can you know given how fake people seem to be? If people can argue points without context, how can we trust them to be sincere on a personal level. I don't think it should be like this, we shouldn't think this way.

I think we should stop faining compassion. It seems like it's everywhere. I'm sure I'm wrong. Someone would love to tell me that. Good on ya. I have found that there are people who listen, and I've found people that simply wait for their turn to speak. It's not an extroverted/introverted thing. I know introverts that will do the same. These people make me not want to share. If they want to talk, let them talk. I'll listen, but they don't really want to listen to my day. I mean not really. They simply want to talk.

Another thing that helps my attitude on this topic is 'men don't share feelings'. Archaic, right? I agree. In various places its being addressed by some men, and I applaud them for working toward that goal, but the thought still lingers in my mind. I believe we should share more, not information. I don't need to supply any more of my information to the great marketing machine in the cloud. I don't need to know what my friend had for breakfast, or care about the trip they took to Spain. I care about connection and being with those we love. I mean actually sharing life with each other, not just pictures of it. Not posts of breakfast, or cats. Feelings. I'm not talking about 'deep sharing'. I'm talking about regular feelings. Not just "Hi, how are you?" "I'm feeling well. Thank you." Those aren't feelings, those are words. Not experiences, they're shallow soundbites.

Let me try to explain, I'm sure I lost half of you. That disappoints me. We seem to give off, I guess a 'vibe', not just with body language but something in our core being. It's a conformity to perform. We are expected in polite society to carry ourselves in certain ways. All the time.

It's interesting how many thoughts and feelings we share, but for some reason I feel like we still hold things back, not actually making connections anymore, just followers. There are rules not to be crossed. Lines not to break after all. If we are shown displaying these non-conformities, we are pushed to the outsiders, the ones beyond the walls. Shunned until we conform to only sharing plastic pictures once again. (Sometimes I like waxing, I'm a writer. It's what we do.)

November 2

Resistance is Futile

"I have nothing to say to you, and I will resist you with my last ounce of strength." Alexa tells me this when I tell her that resistance is futile. It's rather quaint.

The thing is, people don't really think like this, do they? I say this a lot, but only in a quasi-witty way. Afterall, I'm under the impression we could and would resist the borg, unless we really are the borg and not the federation that is. Who's to know?

Resisting something that is wrong, or against positive progress is something many of us do. We can resist a warmonger or a direct threat to our well-being. That's easy. We can prepare with suits of technological armor and tanks at the ready. Direct threats are something we resist easily.

We don't stand for certain treatment. We are all against child labor, and finding treatments for cancer, even fighting against evil ideas. We're prepared, mostly, for those things. We will resist with our last ounce of strength. Our dying breath.

Feel good? I do, knowing that I would stand up to oppression and harm and fight against it. I know you would if it were in front of us... directly.

I think I mentioned 29.5 million people in the world suffer from drug use. I'm sure many of them feel, or felt the same way. That they could face threats head on. That might even be well and true for them even now. Head on, we can face our enemies.

The problem with that is, not all of our enemies are of the warrior, death knight class. Some are rouges and scoundrels, others are hunters with traps. (I'm digging this WOW reference by the way.)

Many times, undesirable changes are made slowly, small increments. Barely noticeable fluctuations. Over time these subtle changes create large differences, at that point they're almost irrefutable.

It's nice to say that we will resist with our last ounce of strength, but if our enemy comes at us with tokens of 'improvement', can we hope to see the bigger picture and resist the future that is inevitable? I think we can, but only if we read the papers we sign, research the points we speak of and argue against. Don't agree to something you don't understand simply to save yourself time.

November 21

Idea: Every smelling scent candle. First scent, once through baked beans.

Me

I 'm not really a candle guy. I can take some scents, but if they are over whelming, I don't find it cute, or nice. I find it nauseating. I've linked to a few sites that would probably give me some grief, but I've also linked to one that might provide a more 'manly' scent. Hopefully they meant manly in a sort of 'applewood', 'oak' sorta way and not a 'gym locker room', 'lumberjack at the end of the day' way.

I did run across a bacon scented candle and while I appreciate the attempt, I'm not sure I want my house to smell like bacon. I mean when I cook bacon it smells like bacon, so I'm not sure I even need a candle for that.

They don't have an 'every smell' candle yet, but if they did, I'd submit an internet challenge to light the sucker in a room without windows and sit and eat those every flavor jelly beans until you couldn't stand it. I could maybe last about 3 to 5 minutes. Hopefully they would start with an Odin scent and a bacon bean, if they start with a Sunset Tide candle and some cotton candy jelly beans I'm sure it would be even less.

November 22

You're Batman. Tell everyone, use the voice. You know the one.

MAYBE you don't want to be batman. I'm not sure I understand that. I'm not sure we can be friends, but let's pretend I'm joking. Bruce Wayne is a millionaire, maybe a billionaire nowadays. He also has a Batcave, which is the most awesome mancave money can buy. I think when you logically break it down, it's hard not to want to be batman. It's just common sense.

However, maybe it's not so much. There is a guy who has a YouTube channel. You might have heard of him. Batdad. I can't say all of the videos are funny, some of them I look at and go hmmm like the C+C music factory would. Ridiculous humor. Still, it's been around long enough for me to mention it.

People, Batman is cool, I mean why wouldn't he be. Just don't break it down like John from vlog brothers and you might be able to stay in that mind set. Also reading the comments section shows that many, MANY people disagree and they think Batman is cool. I mean, he is Batman after all. Although John does bring up a good point about cleaning up the city, and his clearly fractured personality disorder. I'm not going to speak to the validity of either side of those points. I have to make coffee and I like to think I have priorities.

Have fun out there today. And if you're the guy who owns any one of the bat-mobiles, I'm interested in driving any of them. Just throwing it out there. That's a pretty good dinner conversation…explaining how you got to drive a bat-mobile, but maybe I'm projecting that I'm eating with geeks like me.

November 23

Do what you love.

Your heart

"TERRIBLE advice? I think you've got that flipped, Mr. Loch. This sounds like good advice." I totally agree. It sounds like good advice. What if I love smashing couch? What if I love binge watching television shows on the weekend? What if I love explaining things to people when they're wrong? What if I love not doing anything but helping myself and my status in this world, but pretend to care? What if I love taking advantage of people and getting ahead more than helping? What if I love something, say video games so much that I cut myself off from the real world to envelope myself entirely within the electronic? What if I love dancing naked under the light of a full moon in spring time?

Well, all except for that last one, I think if you think those are fine things to do then you should probably reevaluate your perspective. Sometimes the things we love are simply bad for us. Let me break it down in simple terms. If you saw someone banging their head against a wall, wouldn't you try to get them to stop? I mean it's true-ish, they are only hurting themselves...although I would say their sphere of influence is about 95% of the time probably a little bit bigger than just themselves. The things we do, good or bad, effect those around us. That's just how it is. You can take that and stick it in your pocket. It's a truth.

So am I saying you should stop smoking, yea. It's bad for you. I'm not going to make you stop smoking. I can only care so much, before it becomes like creepy totalitarian/helicopter parenting type stuff.

Go for it, do what you love. But keep in mind some things are not good for you, or perhaps others.

I'm gonna pick on Felica Day.

Felica Day is considered, what's the word I'm looking for, somewhat 'epic', perhaps 'legendary', but is she really? Let's take a quick look. Felica grew up in Huntsville, Alabama. She went to college at 16. She could have gone to Julliard but decided to go to University of Texas in Austin. (Points for full ride there. No loans. Good on her. Money minded.) After that she wanted to try acting. She got some roles and got a spot on Joss Whedon's Buffy the Vampire Slayer. Good stuff here, but what's this have to do with anything. Why am I picking on her? I'll tell you.

She has also noted how she loves video games, I mean really. She has a focus you might say. An addictive personality to say the least. It's been an issue for her. That's pretty relatable. Addictions take time, it took time from her. Massive hours spent in pursuit of something she loves. But it wasn't productive, entertaining, fun, enjoyable, but not productive at all points intended.

It's easy to get lost in things we enjoy. We should be able to do what we love, right? I believe it could be argued that if Felica Day simply did what she loved, and pushed off to the side the effort and hard work and determination she has shown that we would never have the internet we have now.

So, consider that. These passions and loves we have, they can be good. Fun, but sometimes in order to make something, to actually be a part of something bigger, you have to put the thing you enjoy, the thing you love down, so that you can give other people things to enjoy.

'Mythic', that's the word I think I was looking for, 'Mythic', or at least on her way to it. No pressure Felica.

November 24

The end justifies the means.

—

Machiavelli, right? Wrong. Another piece of advice taken out of context. And it's so wide spread that its laced in the fabric of our minds. Truly an example of the Mandela Effect. I've linked to an article you can read about in the appendix on this date, but it goes to show. If you don't research things for yourself this might be a shock.

I mean, if Machiavelli said this, then it could show something about his character. But if he didn't, what did he say? A lot actually. In the book 'the Prince' which I believe we don't equate to satire, may truly be just that. But without reading it, how can we give a real opinion. It's easy. I haven't read it. But I've formed an opinion of what I have read about it. (Don't worry, it's on my to-do list. It's just that I find 16th century Italian theorist, humanist, diplomatic, political, historians, that write possible satire, fiction, or 'how-to-rule' books rather dry at points. I'll get to it.)

So, I think we can agree this is terrible advice. I mean terrible people have run with this simple saying to produce travesties. When you bring this statement up in a conversation, you are either trying to 'shock' people or make a point against it.

So, if it's generally excepted as terrible advice, why do we follow it so much? Maybe you say, "I don't do that. I work toward the common good." Okay, so maybe I'm talking to everyone else but you. Relax in your chair.

This nice little piece of simplistic crap wrapped in fake depth has a name. Consequentialism. Basically the 'rightness' or 'wrongness' of an action determines its correctness, as well as the overall 'greater good'. Or as I like to put it. 'It's right because it worked.'

We do this all the time though. We cut corners, or avoid people who could use help. It just so happens; our ends are focused on retirements and our families. Important things, sometimes we don't look at the cost though. What I'm saying is our focus is too inward, it's on what we want. Of course, our families are also considered, but rarely outside of that circle to the same extent. What if instead of working for ourselves we truly dedicated our ends to helping others, instead of just saying it. Here I go, dreaming again. What if everyone did that? Why can't we do this? I ask, who's stopping us? So how do we stop them? Are we even allowed, or does the end not justify the means in your mind? If you can reconcile that it does, for just one thing in your world, then you've proven my point and you follow this advice to a certain degree. Maybe that's okay. Maybe the point of this was simply to get you to think and research before drawing conclusions. We don't research enough, but we lie and pretend like we do.

November 25

Pay off your credit cards with other cards.

—

HEY, sometimes we have to make ends meet. Pushing that bill off with a credit card, it happens. But it's not the best solution. In fact, some places might not let you even do it. And if you could, while pushing off your debt might be helpful in the short term it's probably a bad way to go in the long run.

Black Friday. It's here or coming up or just passed. Did you buy all the Christmas gifts you needed? Did you get that new tv? Did you save for it, or just put it on credit? You'll worry about it next month, right? You will. You'll have to. This day's advice is simple. Think about what you buy, and make a budget for it. Budgeting can take a short amount of time, or up to an hour. What do you spend money on? Write that down. Just take some time to sit down and look at what you're spending each month. If you have a loan out, are you just making the minimum payment? Think about how to pay a little more. If you only make the minimum you might not be able to pay it off, it might not even be touching the principal amount. Look into that. The more you know the better off you'll be, right?

November 26

Plans, you don't need a plan. Wing it!

BUDGETING and now planning. "Why are you trying to bore us to death?!" I'm really not. In fact, I think that these two things can greatly improve your life and allow more time for fun. They aren't miraculous by any stretch of the imagination, but they work. Remember how I mentioned success takes hard work. Here is a platform for that work to start. If you're younger and just starting out, that's even better. Take these things seriously. They can be of great benefit to you over your life time.

Are you in a terrible place or position in your life. Planning might help, action might help too. I don't know your situation, but I know these things have helped me. You're reading this book right now, aren't you? If I can do it, well I can do it. But maybe you can too. You are worth the time, there are things that you could do in this world that would help many people, but you have to know that. You have to believe it, truly.

So, you good? You know that. You believe me. Good I'm 100% right 80% of the time. So, we're good, excellent. Planning. Take out a calendar and start blocking off work time on the weekend. This time you will use to work on a project that needs done. You have an area in your life you want to work on? Take an hour on Monday, Wednesday and Friday. That time is going to be used to focus on that task. There is no such thing as multi-tasking.

If it's a big project, say creating a YouTube channel. Use that time to research the things you need to set it up. Podcast, create talking points. Content generation, that's a killer. Start stock piling it. Create a back log, don't just make a YouTube video and send it out, make videos for three months and come up with a release schedule. You want to do something else, read up on it. Dig into it.

Set goals, and realize you're not going to meet all of those goals. Some days won't go your way, but remember you don't compare yourself to someone else in the world, you compare yourself to who you were yesterday. One thing at a time. There is no such thing as multi-tasking, don't lie to yourself. Elon Musk switches from task to task just like everyone. Maybe he does it more efficiently or less at times but he still switches back and forth like the rest of us.

Make plans, it's a big world, lots of land, lots of time. Get to it.

November 27

Strive to be different.

INDIVIDUALS. We all want to be them. We want to have our own style, just a little. We want to stand out from the crowd. Or at least that's what we seem to say, but then if it's something that we inherently want, then why do we care so much about being included?

I mean we are a society that believes individuals should be able to do what they really want, why then is there such a need for conformity that must be obeyed? So, it's really advice to be individuals that is given from sources that sit on a structure that says you should strive to be the same. People don't like different really. At least outwardly. We want to be individuals, different from others. Although, for some reason we tend to group together because of like-mindedness. We appreciate that our thoughts are in line with others.

To me, that sounds strange. Why do we look for differences, in ourselves and others, while at the same time also work to belong to something greater?

Maybe I'm being dense. It seems like it might be a paradox to me. That's a safe word.

How different is too different? What do we gain by difference? Lots of things, new skills, experiences, new ideas, collaboration. We don't all want to be the same. Take goths for example. Different, but honestly, not too different. They have a group, a mindset.

So, is our desire to be different actually a drive to be accepted? That doesn't make sense. If we wanted to be accepted, we would conform our thoughts, looks and behaviors to those around us. We'd work to 'blend in'. Oh, I guess we do form groups as such.

The media and our way of life seems to point in two directions. One, that we should be our own person. The other that we need to stand together. While at the same time desiring/concerning ourselves with 'fitting in' to a group. How does a touted individualistic nation have so many people/children taking their own lives?

It's because we don't want to be different, that's not our drive. It's simply a feature that provides depth or interest.

What we want is to be loved, respected. We want to be part of a community of likeminded people. Let me say this, we can stop striving to be different than everyone else. We already are. Let's work on creating something greater than our differences.

November 28

Introduce yourself as Duke/Duchess Muffin Pants the third. All. Day. Long. Go up to people, engage them in conversation, with an accent. Make one up, hone it.

—

Duchess Muffin Pants II

DO it. Internet Challenge. Consider it flavorful for others. If this is too much for you, do something else that's silly non-harmful fun. (I feel I needed to add the 'non-harmful' I'm not sure why exactly.)

November 29

Don't believe in what you're doing.
—
'The Man'

STUPID terrible advice you've never heard. People don't say this, but they seem to live it rather well. Do we as a people believe that we should have to build up wealth in order to survive and retire? Do we believe in our 9 to 5 jobs, or are they simply what has to be done?

There are many things we don't believe in, but we seem to do them anyway. Why? Conformity? Necessity? It's the way things have always been. This is how it has to be done. It doesn't really matter that I don't believe in it.

That's true, things aren't relative to what you think, and will continue on how things go even if you disagree. They still need done, people have to go to their jobs to make money and make things so others have things to buy and spend hard earned money on.

It's a nice little wheel. Circles, cycles. It's a big machine, we're gonna have to change one cog at a time, but I think we should believe in the things we're doing. We aren't simply going through life as zombies off to a factory. Okay, maybe we do work at factories. I did and maybe you don't really believe in the product. Maybe its stupid junk you're making. There is more to life than work after all. Tell me, what do you believe in? Something I hope, unless you're that nihilist I met that told me that "Nothing matters". Of course, I punched him in the face. And he asked me "Why I did that?" And I said, "Why not?"

Sometimes we get caught up in a loop of doing things because that's how they're done, or that's what we've seen or been taught. It can become monotonous and seems rather, what's the word? Blah, bland, boring. That's when you need to look at your purpose. Your job isn't your purpose, unless you believe it is.

Find something you're passionate about, something you believe in. Do that thing.

November 30

Show an arachnophobe a spider, or just say you see one.

I talked with people who say they are scared of this or that. "I'm terrified of heights.", or "I'm claustrophobic." They say as they step into an elevator. Sometimes we get confused about the meaning of words. My sister for example lives in the tropics. She mentioned that it had been a cold winter. So, I asked her what she thought cold meant. Turns out its slightly different in the topics.

Terrified. Intense word. It means 'cause to feel an extreme fear'. Petrified is a similar word meaning that you're so frightened that you are unable to move or think. I don't recall a time in my life that I have been either of those things then. I've been afraid and frightened. Terrified is pushing it. The 'Ring' girl never came out of my television screen though, at least not yet.

I have a friend who's phobic with spiders. We were driving somewhere, and okay, so my car is a little old. Sometimes bugs get into my car without permission. So, there was this little spider. It was about the circumference of a pencil eraser and not as big. One of those light airy ones that you can barely see their legs. Floats on air. It was on the roof, the inside roof of the car. It decided to drop down in between the driver side and passenger side and it wanted to land on the center console. My dear friend was going to have none of that.

Another little tidbit to the story. I'm on the highway and going the speed limit. (You always go the speed limit.) And this little guy decided to make its way down. Not with my friend there, nope. But they aren't going to risk squashing or touching the spider. Nope, they decide that the correct course of action would be to open the door. That's right. Better to be road burger than be close to a spider.

That's terrified. That my dear reader is petrified. (although they did move to open the door so scratch that.)

Oh, you want to know if my friend died. Right, makes sense. That's a cliff hanger, right? Shouldn't have stopped there. So anyway, I was able to grab the spider and dispose of it out my window while maintaining total and proper control over the vehicle at all times. My friend was also able to stay in the car and not suffer from a case of road rash, after convincing them I got rid of it.

What was the point there? Oh, yea, know words kids. There are more descriptors than awesome. Take time to learn some of them, if not just for your own understanding.

December 1

Dress up in your favorite Halloween costume, go to work in it for a week. When they mention to you it's not Halloween, say "I know." And smile, run back to your desk, make appropriate noises for the theme of the costume. — Wait, I used that already.
Here's one, write a song, then have someone else sing it, then have attractive people lip sing it.

—

GIRL you know it's true. Don't try to pull one over on the audience, unless you're a magician. Magicians are supposed to do that, they're liars and we like them for it. If you're going to make something, take the time to think it through, I'm not saying do it yourself, but just think it through. I think this came down to trying to make more money, but I can't be sure. Way too many people doing coke back in those days to be sure about the train of thought on anything. Kinda like today if you think about it. Without the coke, we just have the electronics to keep us up at night now.

December 2

Believe in yourself, just not in front of others.

—

LET'S pick on me for a minute. (Mostly because I know you don't want me to pick on you.) I'm a quite person. Through my years I've been able to do some pretty interesting things. I started going to college at 16, I believe I actually took a college course when I was 13 because I was interested in the subject and was able to audit the class. It was just one, but I had to play tag some time during the week, you know. I got to travel in Europe and drive across the US with some friends. I've had a classic movie college party phase, perhaps reminiscent something out of 'Animal House' or 'Dazed and Confused'. I can't say I ever reached "The Hangover" or "Risky Business" level of rebellion but I'm okay with keeping my hand out of that fire. I think there is such a thing as too much fun. I don't need to wake up with a Mike Tyson face tattoo, if you follow me. I've done many other things that were pretty cool, or took a lot of effort. School included, but this isn't about me, but about self-image.

So, if I look back, I can see that I've done some pretty interesting things, but I don't often think of myself that way. If you recall, I'm rather stoic. I also sometimes have an internal voice that says "Well, if you can do it. Anybody can." It's similar to the cute saying "If I can do it, so can you." Which if you also recall is a big pile of steaming bullshit. Not to say it doesn't encourage, it's just a lie is all.

John Glen and Neil Armstrong went to the moon. Albert Einstein gave us smart guy things. Newton relaxed under a tree and found gravity there. Steve Jobs created Apple, and Bill Gates made Microsoft. (I'm not trying to dis-clude all the others that helped to make these things, but not everyone knows their names.) I will never do or be able to do any of those things. So, if Bill Gates told me "If I can do it, you can it." I'd laugh, I mean like a real hard belly laugh that makes Santa's stomach turn into a bowl full of jelly, kinda chuckle.

But I have done some really impressive things. I don't tend to give myself credit for those things, either when I'm by myself, or in front of others. It's truly a disservice. It's not humbleness, to not take some credit for the successes in your life. You have the skills. They have been found in you, or do you not remember that time you did that awesome thing? (Come on you remember, it was awesome!) Look back at the road signs you've passed in your life. The cities you've been through. Did you not come out the other side of those?

December 3

The highway is a great place to get rid of your trash.

—

IT would seem that some people follow the rule 'if no one is watching then it's okay'. I mean clearly, it's a time saver. You don't have to hold on to the trash until you get to the next stop. Putting it on the floor would be way to inconvenient. Then you'd have to pick it up again and we all know that's not going to happen. Then you'll have a car full of trash that you have to clean up yourself. That will take at least 30 minutes, because let's face it, your car is already full of trash.

Now there are some who don't litter, but have things blow out the window or the bed of the truck. I can't say much to that, except maybe take 30 minutes to clean out your car or secure the things in the back of your truck.

I'd love to think that everyone would read this and no one would litter on the highway again, but that's stupid. I know that people just don't care. They don't care about a lot of things. Some might even admit to it in a conversation. I think I respect those people more than the ones who agree with me and do it anyway.

It's just something to think about. I believe my 'passion' if you would call it that stems from the commercial, I saw when I was little with the duck being caught in the plastic drink carrier thing. However, this isn't about protecting ducks, or even the planet. It's simply about courtesy. Think about it. Do you want to pick up trash after someone else? I don't. I would, but it doesn't mean I like to. You don't either.

Now that we've fix the issue for the truly courteous, we only have to deal with the other 70% of the population.

Take an extra 5 minutes and don't litter today. Try it again tomorrow.

December 4

Go ahead and switch to the Mayan calendar for scheduling purposes, but also in case the end of the world comes back around.

—

I'm not sure I have the energy for this. I'm more of a see it first kinda guy in many ways. I'll hear about the end of the world. Halebop and how the Mayan's knew the end of the world. It couldn't be because the stone was only so big or the dude working on it got tired. (Occam's Razor really works, I'm telling ya.)

If they would include something other than 'the world will end in so many days'. If they could give some event, or cause that I could at least be aware of. Some sort of context that made sense in the least. Perhaps I would listen.

After all I'm a big proponent of the sun burning up, and by proponent, I mean I can spell it and say it. That's really all you need, big words. No research necessary. I especially like it because it gives me the freedom to not gave a crap about it. I'll most likely (unless breakthroughs in reverse aging, or mind/machine transference come by within my lifetime) be dead. That means I can focus on helping people today. I can do that, instead of going to the group meeting to talk about hypotheticals. (Not doing as much as I would like, but we are busy people and I am getting better each new day.)

I'm all for finding entertainment and relaxing. I'm all for researching obscure ideas and working on going to the stars, but I think we also need to refocus on things that matter. People matter, their lives and health and living conditions.

I wish I was amazed that these things are still issues, but I'm not. There are people who care of course, but apparently not enough, people that is. More is needed. You are needed by those far from you and those close to you.

You have purpose, you are worth something. More than simply being consumed by ideas that functionally amount to nothing.

So, go have fun, be entertained, relax from time to time, but find something worthwhile, something that provides hope. Something that doesn't work to tear it down, or suffocate potential. Something for you and those around you.

December 5

Sarcasm is the humor of the wise. People will flock to your razor-sharp wit.

FOR this day. Let's say I'm full of myself. (I'm sure it happens on more than one though.) I'm smart and awesome and people want to hear from me. I mean if I fancy myself a writer somewhere, I must believe I have something important to say that can't be done without, right?

However, I've run across a few people in this mixed can of nuts we call life and see different kinds of humor. There are the 'shockers' those are ones that might not really be all that funny, but can twist it so that people laugh. Or the ones who stay up to date on current events and poke fun at how they were handled.

I myself am a sarcastic son of a wonderful, wonderful lady. That being aside I find my sweet spot to be dry and sarcastic in nature. In fact, I'd be hard pressed to be anything but.

But I don't particularly care for its definition. Webster don't know. He says its 'a sharp and often satirical or ironic utterance designed to cut or give pain'. I don't think I want to give anyone 'pain'. I think I'm rather against it. I prefer to be amusing, while intelligent. Maybe I'm just witty. Let's go with that then.

Although the 'witty' examples I've read on the internet, are far from 'witty'. I guess wit isn't a high form of intelligence. There are so many quotes out there. It's hard to keep things in context.

I think I'd like to be 'witty', it's not as abrasive. Or sharp apparently. So, does that mean I could be funny and teach people life lessons with less harsh comments? Is that what I'm trying to do with my sarcasm. I'd like to think it's more than just cutting people with razor blade remarks.

I don't mean to 'push' people away with my humor. Is it my fault people do interesting things that require commenting? I also don't really think I'm a 'jokester' in the classical sense. I find it easier to play off people's comments than recall lines.

This is really only an internal observation of mine, I don't know if it helps you or not. Although I want to lovingly point out the fact that in the appendix on this date there is a Smithsonian article that points to the 'fact' that people that can't understand Sarcasm could have a brain disease. How do you say 'Classic!'? It also points out sarcasm is everywhere. Yet you shouldn't use it? Great, thanks for the help.

December 6

Forget about Life Hacks and DIY books or free budgeting courses. You've got this.

YOU can do it. You don't need help. You've grown up and figured it out all by yourself. Maybe you have. Doesn't change what's true. You need help from others. Do you think that you've learned everything you know by yourself? So, you've never read a book that's taught you anything? Interesting view point. Did you write the book and then read it to yourself? I'm just being silly, and if you think you don't need help, you're silly too.

Someone else will need to help you in some indirect or direct way for things to happen in your life. Outside of no one knowing anything about you or what you've done, being raised by wolves and then learning the local language while hiding in a bush and eating a rabbit you killed yourself. Then you managed to come into the city and found a copy of this book and taught yourself how to read using it. All that aside, I think we can all agree we need the help of others. Let me just point out a few links that I've mentioned before for your use in becoming a more independent, while at the same time group conforming capable human being.

1. https://lifehacker.com/tag/life-hacks
2. https://www.instructables.com/
3. https://www.youtube.com/user/DIYNetwork
4. https://www.youtube.com/watch?v=VCr-54OH7IY- FunCheapOrFree – (Single Episode – Channel Link in Appendix)
5. https://www.howstuffworks.com/
6. https://www.cnet.com/how-to/amazon-echo-the-complete-list-of-alexa-commands/ -Bonus! – Alexa Skills

Take a look at these, there is some pretty cool stuff around the net. But come back and finish the book! I've got some good stuff left.

December 7

You can fight this. You can beat this! Everything will be okay.

YOU'VE heard this before, you've probably said it before. Sometimes for some personalities it is okay. If they had a bad day, or got bad news. Even terrible news, these people can take that advice and run with it. They see through things. Even the darkest things.

It's not always true though. Many times, in this day and age particularly its more acceptable, and probably healthier that we are more in touch with our feelings. Now, let me say. I'm not a real 'feeling' kinda guy. I don't believe it makes me manly or cooler. Honestly sometimes I wish I was more verbose with my emotions, but I'm a stoic in the head so they don't manifest as much as I think about them internally. That being said, I appreciate and enjoy emotions and having fun, I'm not a robot. (Although, I have to say I can burn up the dance floor, doing the 'robot'. 😊)

It's not just the highly emotional I'm talking about either, it's this advice. "You can too." Or "If I can do it, you can do it." Maybe not. Maybe they can't do it. Maybe its freaking hard. Maybe they're fed up with doing it, and don't want to fight anymore. Fighting sucks, some things can't be beat.

It's not that we really want to hear that bleak forecast of our future either, but maybe like this article I linked to in the appendix says, sometimes we just want someone to be there for us. Maybe we can do without the white lie that tells them that it will be okay. It might not be okay.

Another thing about this saying. I know I'm sure I've done this too. You give kindness and words of support, and then go back to your life. In war, soldiers fight side by side. They stay with each other, night after night, week after week. Until the battle is over. Sometimes it's not won, but it is fought together.

We can't always stay with those who have or are struggling with something. Sometimes we say these things, "Let me know if you need anything." They won't, they're too busy dealing with all the shit. They won't call, or ask. If you truly want to help, just do something for them. Remember, being present is sometimes better than giving useless, unhelpful advice on "how everything is going to be okay".

Sometimes what we need, is just someone to hold on to. Even if it's not okay. Use your actions, not your words.

December 8

The person over there said it was okay.
—

NOW maybe you've never directly heard this. I guarantee you've listened to it. We all listen to it, all the time. We are independent individuals who listen to what everyone else says and then applies it to our lives. It's almost, if not entirely, impossible not to fall into this. After all, everything we know comes from either other people, or our experiences, that more than not, probably involve other people.

Maybe we fancy ourselves 'modern thinkers' or someone who 'understands' the ways of the world. Great, that means you've got other people believing it to. Where did you get your information from? That guy over there with a Ph.D., or the one that died a thousand years ago. That's fine. There is really no way around this. None, forget trying. It's a waste of time. I've looked in to it.

Did you believe me? That I looked into it. I didn't. I lied. This book took me 12 weeks to write. I didn't dive into a whole lot. I'm trying to raise money for sick children, I'm not trying to prove a point that will save the world. Just perhaps, make you think a little longer when you read things. Maybe change things in a small way.

My grandfather, who of course was the greatest man in the world, (I'm sure you have the same.) used to say this, "Believe nothing you hear, and only half of what you see, and only some of what you read." It was something like that. Looking it up, I found that Edgar Allen Poe may have been the originator of the saying, which is pretty cool, because I like him as well.

Regardless of my fondness of my Pap-pal, I want to reiterate what another purpose this book might have. Context. We need to know context. If we don't have it, we might as well be shooting people. Dramatic, well, I'm a writer. You've read the section on words and how I view them as somewhat of a weapon. People don't seem to get it. What we say helps to create and destroy worlds. If you agree with that, and you go out in this world and explain something that you don't have a clear understanding of, how is that going to help? Especially if you're using it to argue with.

I don't mind what you're arguing, but if you don't have a foundation stop, go to the beach, sit in the sand, relax because you're wasting my time and yours. And potentially endangering people's lives by giving them stupid reasoning. That goes for what you hear others say to. I say try to know what you're talking about, but don't just take my word for it. For the love of God, please don't just take my word for it, look into it yourself. If you don't, then just admit you don't care and don't talk about it like you do.

December 9

I got an awesome idea for a character! I'm going to call him JarJar Binks! Like it?

TOYS! I liked Star Wars. I didn't mind the prequels... I don't actually think about those to be honest. I'm afraid if I do, I might have to mind a little more. JarJar. I don't know about that guy. I was also a little uncomfortable with Luke drinking blue milk from an utter, but maybe that's just me. I mean, me and Rey.

It's difficult to make sequels. The first one, you can make and its normally good. It's usually a complete story. Maybe it's got some unfinished subplot that the creator wasn't sure was important enough to finish, it might have taken away from the main story line. The sequel, they realize, they have something to prove. Gotta be better, and bigger and the sequel seems to come with 'extra'. This extra is character development or some more plot lines to continue the story forward. I mean if you made the second, you will probably make a third. Got to set that up, it will make it easier to come up with a story, right?

Sequels are hard for that reason. There are some notable good ones, Star Wars: The Empire Strikes Back, Blade II, National Lampoon's Christmas Vacation, Scream II, The Color of Money, Batman Returns, Evil Dead II, The Dark Knight. There are more, but on average we don't think of sequels as easy to make.

And when money seems to be the prime objective, plots goes downhill even more. CGI, action and explosions are king. I won't even start talking about video game movies. The audience is a tougher crowd because they've actually lived in the world that is getting ready to be on the screen. They've poured their personality, to some degree, into the characters on the screen. It's like viewing a movie with writers, and they've all written parts in their minds that never made it into the showing. It's a very tough crowd.

Don't make it about money. If you make it about money it will never be as good as it could be. Unless its Marvel, they seem to be doing a pretty good job at the moment. Good on 'em. See it turns out nerds and geeks were cool, it's just no one knew it until Hollywood told us...

December 10

Tolerate others.

I mentioned this. I tolerate bugs, and rain. Snow. I tolerate the things I find annoying. I don't want to have to tolerate you. That sounds like a terrible existence. People walking around 'tolerating' others.

And maybe I'm a little behind the newest terms, but I think tolerance is still in circulation even if I'm not on the pulse of the nation, as it were.

Now if I look at the word, (I look at words, cuz I write them a lot) tolerance means: "the ability or willingness to tolerate something, in particular the existence of opinions or behavior that one does not necessarily agree with." Or "an allowable amount of variation of a specified quantity, especially in the dimensions of a machine or part."

Clearly the first definition is what we want. We don't want to live in a machine. I mean doing the same thing over and over to feed the other cogs. That's not what' we're after. So, tolerate, what's that mean again. Here we go, "allow the existence, occurrence, or practice of (something that one does not necessarily like or agree with) without interference." Okay, sounds good. I do tolerate the rain then, I don't use an umbrella, even though I have one. I don't tolerate bugs. I normally shew then away or try and smash them. No tolerance for bugs.

I still don't think that I want to 'tolerate' my fellow man. I don't do this now. Neither do you. I don't care if you think you do or not. You don't. If Steve Urkel stops me in the hall and starts talking to me about how his suspenders are the best, and made by the best manufacturer. You know what I normally do. I nod and smile, then I leave. It might even be that I avoid Steve, because I don't want to talk about suspenders any longer. There's only so much thread-based conversation a person can take, you know?

What groups do you shew away? None, right? Do you go visit them? Do you hang out with those you tolerate so much? I suppose if you did then, maybe you wouldn't truly be 'tolerating' them, as the definition implies, but accepting. Maybe you would sit with them, share your life with theirs. Stop tolerating, start accepting.

December 11

Don't think too much of this VR stuff, they tried it already.

—

IT'S been around for a while you know? Looking into it real hard for context on Wikipedia I found that references to VR were made as early as 1933, in a fiction story, believe it or not. That's where our scientist normally get all their greatest ideas from, dead writers.

So, when you get a chance to talk with one of the great minds of our time, make sure to ask them what book they read when they were young that gave them the idea. (Of course, if you believe in a theory of forms or hylomorphism you could disagree.)

To be honest I think VR might come around and actually turn into something with this current iteration. I think a lot of things are like that though, good ideas and bad one's cycle through and eventually someone is able to figure out how to make them stick. People will try anything once, right? That's what they say.

On a personal note, (not too many in here) I think I'm more excited about what AR can do for us. While VR might bring us home travel options (feel free to take that one, just give me one of the prototypes, or better yet a version without the bugs) and entertainment and better presentation value, I think AR will give us the ability to see and evaluate more of the world around us. It's still a ways off, and I might be gone before it gets too cool, but I have to wonder, will the next generation that is immersed in all this great and world supporting technology, will they know how cool and good they have it? Will they be able to stop for the moment and appreciate how they got there and all they have done? Or will they be after the next best thing?

Maybe it's up to us, you reading this, to set the foundation for that next generation. A foundation that will give them hope and a future.

December 12

Buy all your Christmas toys from Dan Aykroyd.

CHRISTMAS is coming. It's time to go shopping, or make gifts. I find that the best way to prepare for buying gifts is to make a list of people I'm buying for (I used to be able to do this in my head, but it seems we have some rabbit genes in my heritage and it is getting more difficult as time goes by.) So, make a list on December 25th or 26th when you're at the Christmas party you always go it. It's not hard, you're probably going to be looking down at your phone most of the time anyway, just open up a notepad app.

Now throughout the year look at it. Once a month. See if there are somethings you can buy early. Did you know that things are cheaper after Christmas? (I didn't I just made that up. I think it's true though, fact check me.) Especially if you have something big, you're trying to get someone special. Saving a little a month might make that a smoother time then spending a dump load come winter wonderland time next year, or if you're in Australia more money on Boxing day. That's a good time to shop for next year!

All in all, it just takes a little planning, but make sure you don't just buy any old gift. The gift should mean something, I don't know what, but you should. I'm not saying it needs to be of the highest quality, just make sure it isn't the lowest, like Irwin Mainway might try to sell ya.

DECEMBER 13

Dolphins and squirrels come from the reptile/avian duck family of mammals.

EVER hear something so outlandish you just shake your head. There are ideas out there that have been proven, actually proven not to be true. There are people that simply refuse to accept them. I'm not talking about beliefs in God, dinosaurs, creation, the ice age, evolution, the big bang or the age of things. I'm talking about simple things. Everyday things.

Really though, it's not surprising. I mean this book is about terrible advice that people simply believe or give out, or repeat, or argue about without any real context or thinking about the effects the lack of information brings. I hope no one believes that dolphins are reptiles and squirrels didn't come from ducks, but there are around 8 billion people in the world. (Right? 8 billion, cuz I said, right. Not 7.6?)

Did you know your tongue doesn't pick up on different flavors based on where the taste buds are located? Your whole tongue simply tastes stuff. All the buds work pretty much the same. Did you know the earth isn't flat? Did you know that Nelson Mandela died on December 6th 2013, and not back in the 1980's.

Much of this can be attributed to the simple fact that we don't really care. We don't care to verify, really anything. We don't have time. We have too much information to share, it doesn't matter if it's true. We don't have time to look into it, you should do that. We just want to believe things, share things and connect.

It's sad that we can't just believe things anymore. We're too grown up for that. Remember when we learned things from our parents, and they were just true? Now we know there are things out there called 'lies'. In fact, there are a lot of them. Sometimes people don't even mean to spread them, they simply think they're sharing facts or truth. But when you probe just a little bit deeper sometimes these things fall apart. That doesn't matter much though because the misinformation is already out there. You can't take it back, and maybe you don't care.

When I say people don't care, and I kinda mean that. We don't always have time to care, we share things we think are interesting, but we hardly spend time verifying them. While you and I might be able to brush this off as if it doesn't matter all that much, I think the impact is greater than we acknowledge. Until we start caring about what we think we know, I'm not sure things will get much better.

December 14

Old black and white movies are hokey.

THIS is like history. Sure, I know that watching a movie without color can be a drudgery. I mean with all the eye color candy we have with the new movies coming out now. It just seems bland. I mean how can they expect to keep our attention. Plot! That would do it. Actual story line. Now there are plenty of movies that fail this, and plenty that are black and white too. Although I'm guessing by now the color movies without a plot actually outnumber the black and white ones. This is merely due to the fact that more are now in color though and not something to do with the fact that our minds are rotting out of our heads due to information overload and CGI action scenes that replace story.

I would be hard pressed to go see or watch a black and white movie. Unless its Laurel and Hardy or Paul Newman I'm probably gonna wanna pass. But I've sat through some, and they were cool. I consider it an achievement, and we all know how we like to collect those in this day and age! (I'm pretty sure I actually came up with the life achievement point system before Mark Zuckerberg was even in college. I was most likely 16 or 17, but try proving that, am I right?)

So, I thought I'd list some black and white movies for this section. They might be worth your time. I haven't seen them all, but I've seen the majority.

1. Metropolis
2. The Hustler
3. Whatever Happened to Baby Jane?
4. Psycho
5. Casablanca
6. It's a Wonderful Life
7. Scarface (1932)
8. The Flying Dunces

Now, if you're bored you can check these out. You can even consider it an achievement to be able to say you've sat through a black and white film if needed. But you have to put your phone down to get the points!

December 15

Dance like there's no tomorrow.

———

LET me first say. I'm not really what you would consider a dancer. It's not that I'm against it, I just know I don't have 'the moves'. No one really enjoys doing things they're bad at, unless you're Elaine Benes from Seinfeld. (What she does is really not dancing. It's more in tune with a seizure, but I digress.) So, since I'm not really a dancer, perhaps I'm a little jaded about this advice, so bear that in mind.

This little saying seems well intended, unless you're not a dancer and couldn't care for the sport less. Sometimes you don't feel like dancing, other times you just don't have time to dance. It's something of an oddity, it is saying you should have fun today. Perhaps as much fun as possible because you might not get tomorrow. It's not quite as unnerving as YOLO, and it is not as intensely determined as Carpe Diem.

Perhaps it's a pretty good piece of advice after all. Just right in the middle of the two, but what does it do, when you tell someone to dance like there's no tomorrow? What's the proper context for this advice? What does it truly mean to dance?

Dancing isn't always letting loose. If you know how to dance, you probably have a few dance steps that you know. It's got some structure to it. In fact, it might improve the way you age. (I've linked to that in the appendix.)

I'm just confused by the advice. When someone says this, and they have never told me to do this. They being anyone in the world. What does the advice truly mean? Should I learn to follow some structure, and if there's no tomorrow should I really be dancing? I should just have fun? Is it telling me to live in the moment?

Maybe I'm analyzing this too much, I just know that when I used to break dance at the age of 8, I felt really good about it and relaxed.

Perhaps its intention, albeit vague, is to advise someone to enjoy the feeling of living. So, it is not the same as YOLO or Seize the day. It's not saying do what you want, or make the most out of the day. It's simply telling someone to enjoy the moment.

Enjoy the moment. With or without a dance partner.

December 16

Watch a horror movie alone.

—

I'm a little too scared to watch horror movies, and I'm mostly always alone. I could watch things that aren't really scary, like Nightmare on Elm Street, Friday the 13th, Halloween, Saw, The Thing. You know the classics, but today the horror movies are intense. The Strangers, Funny Games, The Hills have Eyes, The Last House on the Left, Hostel, DTJ. I can't watch these. They can actually happen.

Whatever happened to good old monsters. If I want to watch something that can really happen, I'll just turn on the news. There is enough of that already. I'm just not really up for the shock to my system.

Sure, it's thrilling. I get that, but I still have to go to bed and get up in the morning and go to work. I don't understand why I would want to watch something that is going to keep me up at night. I have enough of that already. Now, if I was on a date. Sure, I'd watch a scary movie. I don't know if I'd like it. I'd rather watch The Witches or Gremlins 2: The New Batch (Not Gremlins, that's scary.), Little Shop of Horrors or Arachnophobia.

I know, I know. I'm a wimp. I suppose it has benefits, as the random links in the Appendix show, but why do I need to watch a horror movie when there are so many real things out in the world to be scared of?

December 17

Money makes the world go 'round.

MORE money. I'm rather interested in what money is. It's really evolved from a bartering system. In the olden times with knights and shining armor and dinosaurs' people would trade items. They would determine if one item was of equal value to another. One of the problems with this was sometimes we didn't need an item someone had. So that person became ousted from the community. They didn't create anything productive or useful and so they couldn't barter. We then came up with a sort of credit type system based on commodities, which eventually evolved into our modern system. Right? Sounds good.

Well, maybe. Although we see bartering systems in the world, some smarty people who look back at history and other cultures we've been introduced to, have found that that idea is rather weak. Bartering exists, no doubt, but some say it wasn't really a precursor to our modern system, or at least not to any degree past the first guy not being able to trade any of his junk for food. It stopped with that guy, or the dude right after him.

I mean, I know we aren't the brightest, but if you think about it, how many people stood by and starved to death on that system? Probably not many, because they most likely decided on an I.O.U. strategy just like Wimpy from Popeye, on that second day. "I'll gladly pay you Tuesday for a hamburger today." This would have quickly been stretched out into a longer form of payment and repayments.

That might be true. It's honestly the first time I've looked into it, I assumed the teachers in school knew what they were talking about when they taught me bartering came first. I guess I've fallen into the believing something and not having any context outside of I heard someone else say it.

That's not shocking to me however, we all want to believe that others tell the truth. Not because we think people are 'good' intrinsically but we don't want to take the time to do our own research. In fact, a lot of the time, we can't afford to take that time.

We just have to know, money makes the world go 'round, or does love make the world go round, or is it the conservation of angular momentum? I always forget.

DECEMBER 18

Drink a bunch of eggnog, then ride a roller coaster.

—

TODAY is a cheat day. Here's some advice you shouldn't take. Make sure to remember it and giggle to yourself when you're out and about. For me this cheat day means I get to write less, and play more. I am going to have some nog, I might not ride a rollercoaster though.

December 19

When in doubt, Reboot!
—
Holl'ow'ywood

WE are so lucky to have so many new movies! I wish they were actually new though. It's not entirely true. I know that there are only so many story concepts, and they simply take on new forms depending on how the writer envisions the concept. We get our ideas from everywhere. I accept and even appreciate the diversity in storytelling.

I've also seen a lack of depth at times, or perhaps effort. For a while we've gone through some reboots, and of movies that just aren't that old. The 90's wasn't that long ago was it? Am I that freaking old that we need a "The Craft" reboot? Oh, man. I just might be.

I think the point still stands. Do we really need a new Grudge, or Highlander or the Matrix? I mean what ever happened to "There can be only One!". I guess Marvel blew that idea out of the water.

I digress.

I don't mind the reboots, but at least do them justice. I'm looking at Ninja Turtles, Power Rangers (Although I don't know that this can be a true reboot since it was never a movie to begin with) and Superman Returns. I don't really care for pointing out bad movies. These aren't particularly bad, but the originals were better. Sometimes when you try to reinvent the wheel, you break the car. I'm talking to you Goodyear and your hokey-pokey spherical tires! Not that I'm totally against AI needing to drive.

So, the next time you go to a 'new' movie you might want to check around. It turns out it might not be that new at all.

December 20

Go Skydiving in 0degree weather.

Mr. "Polar Bear" Loch

CRAZY right? You'd freeze. While I would say you should probably work to mitigate risk in your life, (as I believe my power animal, if not a Koala, has got to be Reuben Feffer from 'Along came Polly') some might want to take that chance.

It's interesting as I just made this tidbit up in my head as I thought it would be on par with the Polar Bear club or something else crazy people do in the winter time, although to be honest I think skydiving in winter might be a little tame compared to the Polar Bears out there. They have different clubs all over, in New York on January 1st a bunch of people will go for a dip in the Atlantic. I'll wait till June thank you.

But if you fancy yourself a bit of an adventurer, I'd say this piece of advice isn't as terrible as some of the others in this book. Bundle up!

December 21

You are a Ghostbuster. Your Boss, the Ghost. Bust that ghost. Vlog about it.

———

JUST another one of those silly days. You have to find time to make yourself laugh and enjoy life you know? Did I mention before? Gotta drill it in before you move on to the next best thing. We get caught up in what we have to do. Helping and bills and what we have and haven't done. Sometimes we need to take a moment to be child-like again. Remember the fun you had as a kid, or perhaps the fun you allowed your kids to have, if you didn't come from a happy home? The next generation should have it better than the one before, right? It's not about us, it's about them, right?

It's okay to not be 'all-business' all the time. I know as adults we have things to worry about, context is so important and we don't give it enough thought, need to think harder about what we're saying and how we're acting. I mean we have worlds to save but if we forget the reasons, we're trying to save it though, what are we going to be left with?

Think silly thoughts today. Share them with friends.

DECEMBER 22

Buy a koala, keep it awake

DON'T do this. I repeat do not do this. You will go to jail. Or get hurt. Koala's are, I wouldn't say 'not aggressive'. I might lean toward aggressive. Not that they would hunt you down type of aggressive, more like get the hell out of my face aggressive.

I mean, they're tired from eating cough drops all day, and they have to worry about STD's. If I took a 16 hour nap every day, I might be a little "Hey, where's my coffee?!", you know?

Regardless, don't bother the koala, but if you'd like to support one, or two that's something to do. Nobody likes STD's after all. Did I mention that koalas have STD's, maybe I should have said that first? I can't say Ranger Rick taught me about that little predicament the animal kingdom faces, but I've put some links to that and others in the appendix under this date. Check them out if you have some time.

December 23

On a StarTrek forum ask why the Federation never attempted to stop the rise of the Empire, and why the Cylons don't assimilate with the Borg and become even more powerful. And what's up with the Empire not sending stormtroopers to the Outer Rim to get rid of the huge Reaver problem?

Brought to you by the guy who never got attention from his parents and now seeks it through aggressive comments online

WHAT'S more fun than trolling the internet right? (LOUD BUZZER SOUND!) Did I mention I have an Ire for trolls? I don't mean like real under-bridge dwelling, "I'll eat your bones and then brush my long lovely colorful troll hair!" trolls. I mean the internet ones. The ones that are the bane of humanity, you know, those ones.

Everyone is entitled to their opinion, but I don't think so. I don't think we really are entitled to it. Entitled implies inherently deserving. I don't think we are actually entitled to much in this world. I think we want a lot, but I don't think we are always entitled to it. Especially if what I think I'm 'entitled' to hurts someone. My opinion on things, if it's truly merely my opinion doesn't matter. Facts, I think matter. Truth. The way things are, matter. My opinion, your opinion, not so much.

I don't mean 'hurt', as in my feelings were hurt. I mean real hurt. Life hurts, it's not fair. We shouldn't lash out at others simply because life isn't fair. It separates us more. The more anger we spread, the less connected we truly are.

The above is simply out of fun, it might get someone's engine going, but it's not meant to harm or hurt. Trolls harm and hurt. They're just mean, awful people.

I suppose that has something to do with the way we feel we're still invisible on the internet. Some of us feel that we can lash out and because we're in a room alone no one will see us. It's an interesting concept, its wrong but interesting. As our technology increases and we become more connected, we might see less and less of an ability to hide behind 1's and 0's.

Who wants to go troll huntn' with me?

December 24

Cologne and Colon are interchangeable in sentences.

SO I'm still a child sometimes. This cracks me up. I found it online. I couldn't not mention it. It falls in with the theme of the book. Know what you're talking about. Apparently, there are quite a few people on the internet who didn't use Grammarly, or spell check of any kind. It's important to note that when you compliment someone's cologne, that you use the correct word. I've linked to one such example in the appendix on this date, I'll leave it to you to look up others.

Hilarity ensues. I don't know why, but it makes me lol. Even Roflcopter.

December 25

Christmas is all about the gifts anyway.
—

IT seems that this becomes more and more true through the years. While Christmas can be traced to its root meaning in 'Christ's mass', and there have been links shown to be obvious to Yule and Winter Solstice. Regardless of your stance on the day or range of days. I think we can agree that people come together around this time of year. The purpose, to spend time with family, reflect on the good things in their life ('things' here don't mean objects in the material sense of the word.). They might even look forward to what's ahead for each other and themselves. It's a time for thanks.

I think we can agree on that. The advice at the top of this section shows us a different mentality though. It's not about getting. It's supposed be about giving. And we do, we buy more gifts around this time than probably any other. We might even be gracious enough to give thanks to the people who gave. This time of year, is a joyful time. We get to celebrate what we've been through, and how we got through it. There's lights and snow(maybe), a sense of warmth perhaps.

I think we can agree on that too. With all this joy and celebration and thankfulness you'd think we'd be able to remember it in the new year. We've come to celebrate things. Not life, not truth. We want the new game console, or grill, maybe a book. Things.

Our focus still falls on things. The economy has built itself up around it. They feed on our desire for things. I'm not saying don't buy things and give things, but it's not about these things. Everyone can give things.

We say we desire connection. We build up technology to connect us to the world. So, we don't feel so alone. We're not alone. This holiday, however you feel about it, is an opportunity to connect. It's chance to know your cousin, or nephew, aunt or brother. It's a time to reach into someone's life, to get to know someone. It's not about material gifts. It's a season where we can come together.

This year, and next and the one after that till the sun sets over time, give a gift that means something. Don't simply give platitudes, or words. Create connections, build relationships, learn about each other, foster that, in the days and years to come. Whatever your understanding, I wish you well on this day and future days.

December 26

Don't give to St. Jude's Hospital.

Word of Mouth

WE'RE coming to the end of this ride and I wanted to take a moment out of the great advice I'm giving you, or at least a few smiles and thinkers and talk again about the real purpose of this book. I got the idea to write this because of something I was talking about to friend at work. I went home and started thinking about terrible advice I've heard. First, I was just going to list the different stupid things I ran across. Then I thought I should explain why I thought they were less than optimal. It sounded great, but I didn't care so much about the idea itself.

You see I feel that while my life is good, I need to do more. What do I leave behind if I don't do anything? I don't do enough, I'm not sure I have a personality where that's even possible. I've always cared for children. I don't have any myself, but I know that many are in rough places, and others are sick. St. Jude is one of the places that helps children. There are many other causes I feel strongly about, but you need to start somewhere, right?

So, I decided to start here, with this idea. The plan of course is to give 50% of the profit from this book to St. Jude (For the first two years of publication. I hope to reup it with a new edition of the book, but the lawyers say that I should place a limit of some kind for accounting purposes.) The other 50% I'll keep and I hope it will provide me a way to do more for others in the future. The book idea grew a little in scope. I believe context is very important as well. We don't have enough, we have information coming out of our ears, but if we lack context, I feel we more often than not forget the point and can't convey it properly. I see this so much in arguments, online and off. So, the book became more than just terrible advice, but hopefully a look at all the context that we don't have. Yet we walk around sharing information about life and times that we know very little about, and all this sharing while it might have good intentions, without context I have to wonder, how much is it helping? When I turn on the news at night, I never see how an argument on Facebook gave someone a meal, or provided shelter to a person. (Maybe it's out there. Perhaps we should refocus our media attention if it is.)

Find something that you are passionate about, come up with a plan, and implement it. We can only provide a way for the world if we try.

Also, since I'm plugging the purpose of this book right now. If you enjoyed any of it, perhaps recommend it. I'll thank you, and hopefully with enough sales St. Jude's children will have something to be thankful for from this little idea too.

December 27

Sūrat l-nisāa 4:34
—

CONTEXT is important. Sometimes it's all we have. If we get context wrong, we can get it all wrong. I want to let you know, I've never read the Koran. So, my context is not from a place of complete understanding. However, I've run across an article that speaks about it. Like so many others, we read something and we have an excitement or passion about it. We want to share what little we know.

This is one such case. I have little context, little insight, very little knowledge of the inner workings. However, there are a few things that have tugged on my heart strings within the article. Some are bad, others terrible, atrocious, ire and rage inducing, some are warming. So, the article (I included a link) speaks of things I know nothing about, except context. I believe it is important. On any side, on every issue, context is key.

If we don't have context, we can't hope to understand one another and in not understanding, to put it into simple words, shit happens. Actual deep, shit.

We can't all hope to understand every viewpoint out there. Some are just wrong, clearly. If harm is done in the name of whatever cause, it's one of the bad things. That's not debatable, right?

This advice up above, it's a chapter in a book. The Koran. I'm sure you've heard of it. Your belief for it or against it does not make it any more or less important for someone else. What's important here is understanding context.

This article explains that this verse along with other parts of the book are interpreted in a multitude of ways, mostly to fix the desired outcome. This isn't true solely in the Koran, the Holy Bible, the Vedas, and the Buddhavacana all suffer from this. The less context, the greater the skew.

The article also mentions philosophy and it having a negative effect on the religion in this instance. I admit I haven't read all of philosophy so it might be true that Aristotle may have had a negative viewpoint on women that crept into the Islamic culture, but I am equally unsure of any interpretations garnered from those writings to blame philosophy outright. I feel there are too many variables to conclude ill intent. Context, I don't have it. Maybe you do. Good, because that's the point. Here is a link to the article. Context is important, no matter what your belief.

The Telegraph - http://s.telegraph.co.uk/graphics/projects/koran-carla-power/index.html

December 28

Don't think for yourself.

I'VE written about various different things, and shared a viewpoint on them. Whether or not it's my actual viewpoint is up for some debate. I've done some research, but not a lot. Nothing that stands out where I would say "This makes me an expert." In fact, I'm sure some of the posts contradict each other. I did that intentionally for the most part. We are bombarded with news, real or fake. I've found that in digging in, just a little deeper opens up an entirely different side of things.

We all have different experiences and understandings. We come from different places. I've found that as we go about our day, we have more information thrown at us, than we can properly process. Much of this information is written by people like you. Take me for example. I'm not an expert, by any stretch of the imagination, but I've written a book. So, you might mention something you've read in here to another. "This writer Alex says that blah." And that might be passed along to another then another, before we know it, it's ingrained as 'fact'. (I'm sure I'm being grandiose in my belief I might 'reach' a huge crowd, but we'll assume it could happen.) Really most of this book is purely opinion, it might not even be mine.

The point is context is key. We have tons of blurbs and tidbits and gems out in the world, and lurking on the internets, but we more often than not lack true context. The media doesn't have time to give all of it, they might not even know it. It's really about marketing money anyway. Of course, there are those who feel they do want to bring people the real news stories, but how can you tell in this age what's true and what's not. Which people are on the 'good' list?

We don't provide much context in our small blogs and arguments mainly because we're playing a big game of 'telephone' and don't recall where things started, or the exact details. We just know we feel strongly about it. 500 horses, or 5 is a big deal, but if the facts are wrong and someone discovers that, your entire argument could be flawed. If its flawed, it doesn't help win people to your side for long. Now, we might not be able to fix this. There appear to be forces beyond our control as individuals.

What we could (I say could, because you might forget this when you put the book down. I hope not, as this might be the only true gem in this little book.) do is realize we don't see the whole story, and people won't and can't provide it to us. We must learn to think for ourselves. If you're offended by my implication that you don't think for yourself, sorry but statistically it takes too much time to really research something. We, myself include reiterate what we've heard and more often than not we blindly accept it as truth and run with it. Not only is this a disservice to creating a standing argument, it also allows us to be easily swayed and used for other people's goals. So, my suggestion would be, don't talk about what you don't know, really look into the things you care about, no one else will, and begin working on how you can truly help those around you. (Without real context it's probably not proving your side of the argument anyway.)

December 29

Speed safely.

School Stopper 'M'

THAT'S like saying hold on to this roman candle, safely. Did you know there is a warning on the side of these products that says, not to hold these? It's there, because someone blew their fingers off. Do you like your fingers?

Speeding might save you a half hour on a long trip, but on short ones it's only a few minutes. That goes down with traffic lights. I've talked about that. But you'll probably speed anyway.

It might not be that big of a deal, I mean you have somewhere to be and it's probably worth more than someone's life. I mean right? We don't really think like that, but that's pretty much the core of the issue if I'm going to be dramatic about it. Why should you care, your job is more important than someone's life, right? Getting to your kid's game is more important than their life, right? I mean if they don't get there on time they might as well be dead. Sports are life. I'm not picking on sports. I'm picking on speeders.

It's not that big a deal, right? I'm blowing it out of proportion. I'm sure I am, but if it's not that big of a deal, why are you speeding in the first place. Just admit that you don't care if someone dies. Don't think I'm not talking about your life either.

What could be so important that you have to shave off 5 minutes at the risk of your life, your children's lives, or the lives of someone else simply to be somewhere? I know, people drive so slow! I mean come on, move!

You can handle it. You're in control. It's the other people that don't understand how to drive. I agree. The other people don't know how to drive, so you should watch out for them. It's amazing how much trust we put into other drivers when we whizz past them. Someone we don't know at all and we assume they will stay in their lane, or an animal won't just jump out of the bushes.

Recently we had the first driverless car accident. A woman came out of the darkness and the car, I suppose I can say that, killed her. Of course, the driver was looking at their phone, I'm not sure who is to blame there. On the other side though, in 2017 there have been about 40,000 deaths by drivers. Clearly driverless cares need more attention before we hand over control, but at least we'd all be going the speed limit, or only 10 miles over it.

If you're stressed about getting there, leaver earlier. Please don't kill someone.

December 30

It's dog-eat-dog out there.

THIS piece of advice is true, it just makes me sad. It is dog eat dog. It rough out there, people won't help you. It's not that all of them don't care, it's just most of them are busy trying to make a way and survive. They don't have time, we don't seem to have time.

I wish I could say that most people care. Some people care to a degree, even fewer care to do more. I mean its dog eat dog out there, and people don't have time to coddle you. I wish people would coddle me, but maybe I overshare. Perhaps I expect too much from others in my day to day.

I wish everyone would just be nice to each other, support each other, help each other make good decisions, and get ahead. If we would just help provide for one another, but we still have those people who don't care.

Life is hard and it has beaten a lot of people up, and they don't have, or care to make time. They will take advantage of you, if you let them.

However, just because someone treats you or me badly, doesn't mean we have a right to do the same back to them. Speaking our mind, freedom of speech is a right, but doing harm to another is not, words or otherwise. It's just an option.

It's an option, we don't have to take. Although it's easy sometimes.

It's just my encouragement to be different than everyone else. Show kindness when you don't feel kind. Provide help, when you need it yourself. Give a kind word to that woman or man on the elevator, it doesn't cost anything. Buy a sandwich on your way home from work and give it to that homeless guy you pass every day. Find something greater than yourself to be a part of.

Don't treat others as they treat you, treat them better. I'd love to say this will change the world, right? Be the change you want to see in the world. I don't know if I buy into that, but I do believe we should help those around us, regardless of how it could benefit the world or ourselves. Maybe it will catch on and the few who aren't too busy with their own problems will see what you're doing. It might not create a wave of peace around that world, but we can't sit by watching our phones and programs and do nothing. If you don't do something, I can guarantee no one else will. You can count on that. Don't be like everyone else.

December 31

This New Years, make 2 or 3 or 5 resolutions, do them all for about a week then give up. Try next year.

—

Hopefully this book has given some sort of 'insight'. Perhaps a desire to do more, for yourself and maybe even those around you. I don't know. I do know that we make plans for change, and goals for a better future. Hopefully we are on our way. No one else will help you understand all the information you get each day. They won't share context that might disprove their point. You have to find the truth, you have to make a way through all the junk for yourself. In doing this, you can hope to find a more fulfilling life.

Goals, plans! They will help you. One last thing that I've found to be true. Life is short, but it's the longest thing you will do. You have plans and goals and dreams. Many times, in this life those will change and be broken. Things won't work out. You won't go to the gym three days a week for more than the first two.

That book won't be written, because you know, tv. Other people's plans will get in your way. People will need help, and you should help them, but it will ruin your plans.

That happens. It's okay.

In planning things, we tend to see an outcome we expect. This is the thing we strive toward, this is the end goal. Many times, more than I can count that goal was never reached for me. The outcome looked different. It's upsetting, breaks you down, makes you want to give up. My expectations of what the results should be are flawed. It breaks you down. Many, many people see things this way. It's too hard. The outcome is too impossible, only the people on tv, or someone really smart can do it. If you believe that, it's true.

That's the issue, we expect a certain outcome in those goals we set. If we would simply accept that the outcome is going toward something, and that something if we see it to an end will lead to another goal. That goal will be built on the rubble of the last, and these goals will give you experience, give you knowledge and that knowledge will lead to success in other goals.

With these goals and failed plans, you can find success, but it will take work. You will bleed, but if you endure through it to the end you will find success. And it's my hope that that success will spread to the lives of those around you.

Thank you for reading and buying this little book. I wish you the best in life and that you share it with others more and less fortunate than yourself.

AFTERWORD

Reader, I wanted to thank you for getting through this entire set of societal ramblings. This book has been a collection of terrible advice we give ourselves. Maybe we've mentioned somethings that stick out to you to be true. Maybe this is all rubbish. If I've sold any of these, then I believe I've done my job. As you may recall, this book was put together so that I might give some money to sick children out there. If you bought it, I thank you. I admit that in some of the days I may have tried to put some helpful information. But this wasn't to impress you with my actual thoughts and mental fortitude. That's all these were, is thoughts. Some of them might be wrong, some are probably wrong. Without context it's hard to apply something to a situation. If you found something inspiring or helpful, then I'm glad. If you found parts to be arrogant and wrong that's okay too. It might be the point, I should remind you, I wrote this book very quickly with the original sole purpose to be amusing in nature while helping sick children. It evolved over the time of writing to include opinions on things that I thought might be helpful, or some might not even be my opinions and were written to make you think about how people take things out of context. Someone out there understands issues differently, and that's all because of the context they were given. You've probably noticed that I would use sayings and 'advice' in one writing that I mention were terrible in another. This was done on purpose too. We do this in our everyday lives. You could think of it, like a satire on how things are perceived through someone's eyes. I can't offer an apology for that. That's another point of this book. We throw our ideas out into the world like they're gold, or hope they have meaning for others and simply walk away. I won't I know you as a person, I can't hope to speak into each of your lives. I do hope that it makes you think about your beliefs and stances, your thoughts and your actions in this world. I don't know if we can change things. I do know that I can change small things if I would try though. Watching the news, it seems we take one step forward and two back in different parts of the world. Sometimes it looks like people don't care, but people that care are out there. Sometimes you don't see them, but they're working and trying to help. Hopefully this book of terrible advice will motivate you to pick up a truly important cause, join a group (one of the good ones remember) and run it to ground. In this information age we can't take what we are given at face value.

Again, I thank you for purchasing this book. Its sale, will hopefully provide a meaningful funding source to St. Jude that might give some of these children more time to make a difference in their worlds. (A few legal and accounting notes: As mentioned, this School Stoppers book will give 50% of the profit we receive from this book, as we get a percentage from the various marketing sources i.e. Amazon, GoodReads, other outlets this book may show up in, to St. Jude for the first two years starting from publication time. This two year limit is to lessen any accounting burden as not saying it, implies 'forever' and that is a very long time. It is our hope that new editions of this book will continue this profit-sharing model while allowing our lawyers to sleep at night as well. Also, another note for our lawyer is while this publication is looking to support (in a small way) St. Jude, the writings and opinions in this book are in no way associated the opinions or ideals of St. Jude's Hospital.)

If you would like to become involved i.e. an author looking to write a book under the School Stoppers name please contact the group at theschoolstoppers@gmail.com. We hope that we might be able to produce more books that will help various causes going forward. It really depends on two things, people like you buying this book and us being able to find the time to write more!

—**Alexander Loch**
The School Stoppers Writing Group

If we always do what we've always done,
We will always get what we've always got.

BIBLIOGRAPHY

Structure of References FYI:
Last, F. M. (Year, Month Date Published) - Article title.
URL.
Website – Title
URL

January 1st
Wiki – Sticks and Stones
https://en.wikipedia.org/wiki/Sticks_and_Stones

January 2nd
Wiki – Hippocrates
https://en.wikipedia.org/wiki/Hippocrates

January 4th
Emotastictoaster (?????) - Jonathan Coulton - Re: Your Brains Lyrics
http://songmeanings.com/songs/view/3530822107858607660/

January 9th
FeedingAmerica.org
http://www.feedingamerica.org/
Wiki – NBA Jam
https://en.wikipedia.org/wiki/NBA_Jam

January 11th
The Kinks - Topic (2014, November 8) - Youtube Destroyer
https://youtu.be/A5yuCwmf2fk
IMDB – DuckTales – "Nothing to Fear" Quotes
http://www.imdb.com/title/tt0566947/quotes

January 14th
Thomas Frank – YouTube Channel
https://www.youtube.com/channel/UCG-KntY7aVnIGXYEBQvmBAQ
CollegeInfoGeek.com
https://collegeinfogeek.com/

January 15th
Good Mythical MORE (2015, February 6) - Youtube Do You Have a Stupid Name?
https://youtu.be/m8Q0I3bwzcw
Broadbent, E. (?????) Why Is Everyone Naming Their Kids Weird Sh*t Now?
http://www.scarymommy.com/dont-name-your-kid-something-stupid/

January 17th
lifePrint – ASL Introduction
http://www.lifeprint.com/

January 19th
Wiki - Burke and Hare
https://en.wikipedia.org/wiki/Burke_and_Hare_murders
Amazon - Burke & Hare
My Book
Wiki - Little Bunny Foo Foo
https://en.wikipedia.org/wiki/Little_Bunny_Foo_Foo

January 20th
Fox Foundation – Parkinson's
https://www.michaeljfox.org/
Amazon - Back to the Future
My Book

January 21st
Amazon – Ralph Waldo Emerson
My Book
Wiki – Gap Year
https://en.wikipedia.org/wiki/Gap_year

January 22nd
Hess, A.E.M. (2013, June 8th) 0 USA Today - On holiday: Countries with the most vacation days
https://www.usatoday.com/story/money/business/2013/06/08/countries-most-vacation-days/2400193/
January 23rd
Amazon - Short Circut
My Book
Amazon - Blade Runner
My Book
Amazon - Terminator 2
My Book
January 24th
Amazon – Ready Player One
My Book
January 25th
Amazon - Ferris Bueller's Day Off
My Book
Wiki - Aquarius
https://en.wikipedia.org/wiki/Aquarius_(astrology)
January 26th
Amazon - Brave New World
My Book
National Human Trafficking Hotline
https://humantraffickinghotline.org/
January 30th
Wiki - Clark Stanley
https://en.wikipedia.org/wiki/Clark_Stanley
February 1st
Reid, C. (?????) 7 Things That Happen When You Give Up Technology
http://healthandthecity.com.au/7-things-happen-give-technology/
February 2nd
Wiki - Chronos
https://en.wikipedia.org/wiki/Chronos
February 5th
Wiki – Fred J. Dukes (Blob)
https://en.wikipedia.org/wiki/Blob_(comics)
Miltimore, J. (2017, February 25) - FEE - How long does it take to Form Good Habits?
https://fee.org/articles/how-long-does-it-take-to-form-good-habits/
Kollmeyer, B. (2017, May 29) The U.S. is the most obese nation in the world, just ahead of Mexico
https://www.marketwatch.com/story/the-us-is-the-most-obese-nation-in-the-world-just-ahead-of-mexico-2017-05-19
February 6th
Hunt, K. (2015, January 19) Man dies in Taiwan after 3-day online gaming binge
https://www.cnn.com/2015/01/19/world/taiwan-gamer-death/index.html
Jensen, K. T. (2015, March 13) - The Greatest Gaming Tournaments in the World
https://www.pcmag.com/feature/332886/the-greatest-gaming-tournaments-in-the-world
Smith A. (2016, September 14) - Video Gamers Head To The Gym To Enhance Competitive Edge
https://www.npr.org/sections/alltechconsidered/2016/09/14/493881325/video-gamers-head-to-the-gym-to-enhance-competitive-edge
February 7th
Cut (2015, July 7) Be a Man | Men | One Word | Cut
https://youtu.be/KYvWhzSKoc4
February 8th
People are Awesome (2018, March 30) Youtube - People Are Awesome - Best of the Month (March 2018)
https://youtu.be/V3zl2qXVu-k
FailArmy (2018, Marach 30) Youtube - Best Fails of the Month: Is This Regulation Size? (March 2018) | FailArmy
https://youtu.be/RsPv94ljeC8

February 10th
JohnnyThunderzzz (2007, April 9) Sheb Wooley - Purple People Eater (1958)
https://youtu.be/X9H_cI_WCnE
Wiki - Purple People Eaters
https://en.wikipedia.org/wiki/Purple_People_Eaters
February 11th
Amazon – Matchstick Men
My Book
February 12th
Wiki – Milky Way Collision
https://en.wikipedia.org/wiki/Andromeda%E2%80%93Milky_Way_collision
Eicher D.J. - (2014, August 21) 14 Things You Didn't Know About How the Sun Will Die
https://www.huffingtonpost.com/david-j-eicher/14-things-you-didnt-know-_b_5692426.html
February 20th
Simmons, A. (?????) 15 Little Lies Everyone Is Guilty of Telling Every Day
https://www.rd.com/advice/relationships/common-lies/
McDonald, A. (2016, March 14) New Study Has People Rank The Severity Of The Little White Lies We Tell
https://www.huffingtonpost.com/entry/people-rank-severity-of-little-white-lies_us_56e711e5e4b065e2e3d6db2e
February 21st
Wiki - Lyssa
https://en.wikipedia.org/wiki/Lyssa
February 23rd
Youtube - The Game Theorist Channel
https://www.youtube.com/channel/UCo_IB5145EVNcf8hw1Kku7w
February 24th
Wiki - Running with the Bulls
https://en.wikipedia.org/wiki/Running_of_the_Bulls
February 25th
Delistraty, C. (2013, September 12th) 11 Ways To Create A Life You Don't Need To Escape
https://thoughtcatalog.com/cody-delistraty/2013/09/11-ways-to-create-a-life-you-dont-need-to-escape/
Wiki - Escapism
https://en.wikiquote.org/wiki/Escapism
Wiki - Dolos
https://en.wikipedia.org/wiki/Dolos_(mythology)
March 3rd
Wiki - Ate
https://en.wikipedia.org/wiki/At%C3%AB
March 4th
Wiki - Aergia
https://en.wikipedia.org/wiki/Aergia
Wikia - Sword of Damocles
http://snakeplissken.wikia.com/wiki/Sword_of_Damocles
March 5th
Wiki - Savitar
https://en.wikipedia.org/wiki/Savitar_(comics)
Amazon - Dodge Ball
My Book
Wiki - Sentinelese
https://en.wikipedia.org/wiki/Sentinelese
March 6th
Wiki - Ambrosia
https://en.wikipedia.org/wiki/Ambrosia
Culinary Schools.org - (?????) The 10 Most Disgusting Delicacies to Try Before You Die - Would You Eat These?
https://www.culinaryschools.org/cuisine/10-disgusting-delicacies/
HOSTELWORLD - (2014, August 21) The 50 Weirdest Foods From Around the World

https://www.hostelworld.com/blog/the-50-weirdest-foods-from-around-the-world/
GMM S13 E60.3 (2018, March 30) – Youtube 4 Grossest Foods Taste Test
https://youtu.be/wGSHDpX2_sA
March 10th
Amazon - Along Came Polly
My Book
March 11th
Wiki - Nova Corps
https://en.wikipedia.org/wiki/Nova_Corps
March 12th
Amazon - Jerry Maguire
My Book
The Uncool.com - Jerry's Mission Statement
http://www.theuncool.com/films/jerry-maguire/jerrys-mission-statement/
March 13th
David Byrne (2018, February 2) Talking Heads - Once in a Lifetime
https://youtu.be/5IsSpAOD6K8
March 14th
LifeHack.org
https://www.lifehack.org/
March 16th
Wiki - Alexander the Great
https://en.wikipedia.org/wiki/Alexander_the_Great
Wiki - Olaudah Equiano
https://en.wikipedia.org/wiki/Olaudah_Equiano
Amazon - Long Walk to Freedom: The Autobiography of Nelson Mandela
My Book
Amazon - The Gathering Storm
My Book
Wiki - Hannibal
https://en.wikipedia.org/wiki/Hannibal
Wiki - Rome
https://en.wikipedia.org/wiki/Rome
Amazon - Theodore Roosevelt
My Book
March 17th
Wiki - Peter Pan
https://en.wikipedia.org/wiki/Peter_Pan
Amazon - Peter Pan
My Book
March 18th
Nunez, C. & Pfeffer, L. (2016, July 21) 13 Amazing Coming of Age Traditions From Around the World
https://www.globalcitizen.org/en/content/13-amazing-coming-of-age-traditions-from-around-th/
March 19th
The National Domestic Violence Hotline
http://www.thehotline.org/ Numbers: 1-800-799-7233 or TTY 1-800-787-3224.
March 20th
Wiki - Jumpman
https://en.wikipedia.org/wiki/Jumpman_(video_game)
Wiki - Donkey Kong
https://en.wikipedia.org/wiki/Donkey_Kong_(video_game)
Wiki - Manos the Hands of Fate
https://en.wikipedia.org/wiki/Manos:_The_Hands_of_Fate
Wiki - Adventure(Atari 2600)
https://en.wikipedia.org/wiki/Adventure_(Atari_2600)
Wiki - Pac_man
https://en.wikipedia.org/wiki/Pac-Man
Wiki - Super Mario
https://en.wikipedia.org/wiki/Super_Mario

Wiki - Sonic
https://en.wikipedia.org/wiki/Sonic_the_Hedgehog
Wiki - Mortal Kombat
https://en.wikipedia.org/wiki/Mortal_Kombat
Wiki - Chrono Trigger
https://en.wikipedia.org/wiki/Chrono_Trigger
Wiki - Super Metroid
https://en.wikipedia.org/wiki/Super_Metroid
Wiki - Manic Mansion
https://en.wikipedia.org/wiki/Maniac_Mansion
Wiki - Time Lord
https://en.wikipedia.org/wiki/Time_Lord_(video_game)
Wiki - Life Force
https://en.wikipedia.org/wiki/Salamander_(video_game)
Wiki - Blaster Master
https://en.wikipedia.org/wiki/Blaster_Master
Wiki - Al-Qadim
https://en.wikipedia.org/wiki/Al-Qadim:_The_Genie%27s_Curse
Wiki - Wolfenstein
https://en.wikipedia.org/wiki/Wolfenstein
Wiki - Heritic
https://en.wikipedia.org/wiki/Heretic_(video_game)
Wiki - Zelda A link to the Past
https://en.wikipedia.org/wiki/The_Legend_of_Zelda:_A_Link_to_the_Past
Wiki - FF7
https://en.wikipedia.org/wiki/Final_Fantasy_VII
Wiki - WarCraft RTS
https://en.wikipedia.org/wiki/Warcraft:_Orcs_%26_Humans
Cannot be Tamed - Youtube Channel - Retro Game Review
https://www.youtube.com/channel/UCzwyF_IcyMP86ilsmKD1Pcw
Gaming Historian - Youtube Channel
https://www.youtube.com/user/mcfrosticles
Wiki - E.T. (Video Game)
https://en.wikipedia.org/wiki/E.T._the_Extra-Terrestrial_(video_game)
LGR - Lazy Gamer Review Youtube Channel
https://www.youtube.com/channel/UCLx053rWZxCiYWsBETgdKrQ
WatchMojo - Top 10 Retro Gaming Youtubers
https://www.youtube.com/watch?v=eV-4Hn33exA

March 21st
Wiki – Daylight Saving Time
https://en.wikipedia.org/wiki/Daylight_saving_time
Wiki - Bering Strait
https://en.wikipedia.org/wiki/Bering_Strait
Amazon - Revolutionary Iran
My Book
Amazon – Back to the Future
My Book

March 23rd
Davis, B. Ph.D. (2013, May 23) There Are 50,000 Thoughts Standing Between You and Your Partner Every Day!
https://www.huffingtonpost.com/bruce-davis-phd/healthy-relationships_b_3307916.html

March 24th
Wiki - Narcissus
https://en.wikipedia.org/wiki/Narcissus_(mythology)

March 25th
Spicy Pancakes
Cairns, M. C. (2016, Feb 11). Chick and Corn Bread Pancakes with Spicy Syrup
http://www.countryliving.com/food-drinks/recipes/a37593/chicken-corn-bread-pancakes-spicy-syrup/
Hot Coffee, Hot Jalapeno

Phronk, (2010, Dec 14) Comment by Mattukaisan at 7:31 am, on Main page.
https://puttingweirdthingsincoffee.com/about/
RedHot Fudge Sauce
The French's Food Company, (2014), RedHot Fudge Sauce
http://www.franksredhot.com/recipes/redhot-fudge-sauce-RE0019-1
Ice Cream Sriracha
Leland, J. (2010, July, 12) Hot sauce ice cream: Cold sweat
https://www.salon.com/2010/07/13/sriracha_icecream/
Hot Sauce Cookie
Recipe by @IAM_MALI (????) Spicy Chocolate Cookies
https://www.cholula.com/recipes/original-spicy-chocolate-cookies.html
Listing of Hot Sauce Recipes
McDermott, N. (2015, April 8) 50 Healthy Meals Made Even Better with Sriracha Hot Sauce
https://greatist.com/health/healthy-sriracha-recipes

March 27th
World of Meters : World Population
http://www.worldometers.info/world-population/
April 4th
Cohen, J. (2017, Jan 25) Top 21 Superfoods to Jumpstart Your 2017 Weight Loss
https://www.entrepreneur.com/article/288100
April 6th
https://www.childhelp.org/hotline/ **1-800-4-A-CHILD (1-800-422-4453)**.
April 9th & 12th
Bjarki (2013, Sept 5) 7 time consuming things an average Joe spends on in a lifetime
http://blog.tempo.io/2013/7-time-consuming-things-an-average-joe-spends-in-a-lifetime/
April 10th
Dedhia, D. V. (2017, Dec 6) Here's Why It's Not Weird for Indian Men to Live at Home With Mom and Dad
https://www.huffingtonpost.com/dipti-vaid-dedhia/why-its-not-weird-for-indian-men-to-live-at-home-with-mom-and-dad_b_6118022.html
April 12th
Kelly, D. (????) 9 Medical Reasons You're Tired All the Time
https://www.rd.com/health/wellness/tired-all-the-time/
April 13th
Rotten Tomatos
https://www.rottentomatoes.com/
April 17th
Kristof, E. & Chandler A. (2011, Feb 8) 8 Jules Verne Inventions That Came True (Pictures)
https://news.nationalgeographic.com/news/2011/02/pictures/110208-jules-verne-google-doodle-183rd-birthday-anniversary/
April 20th
A&E – Horders Treatment Resources
https://www.aetv.com/shows/hoarders/exclusives/treatment-resources
April 22nd
Evans, M (2017, Feb 2) Conservation Efforts: Why Should We Save Water?
https://www.thebalance.com/conservation-efforts-why-should-we-save-water-3157877
April 23rd
Messing with the Sasquatch
https://www.youtube.com/watch?v=1X0Hi4eml0Q
Sylvanic Bigfoot
https://www.youtube.com/watch?v=w4PNYMfbmVk
April 28th
Wiki – Existentialism
https://en.wikipedia.org/wiki/Existentialism
Amazon - Things to do in Denver when You're Dead
My Book
Wiki - A Million Ways to Die in the West

https://en.wikipedia.org/wiki/A_Million_Ways_to_Die_in_the_West

April 29th

Wiki - Dystopia
https://en.wikipedia.org/wiki/Dystopia
Vogue, A. (2018, April 1) CNN- Supreme Court hears same-sex marriage cake case
https://www.cnn.com/2017/12/05/politics/supreme-court-masterpiece-cakeshop/index.html
Wiki - Group Think
https://en.wikipedia.org/wiki/Groupthink
Wiki - Mob Mentaility
https://en.wikipedia.org/wiki/Herd_mentality
Rotten Tomatoes - Star Wars III - Revenge of the Sith
https://www.rottentomatoes.com/m/star_wars_episode_iii_revenge_of_the_sith/quotes/

April 30th

Amazon – Butterfly Effect
My Book
Fernandez, C. (2016, Dec 21) You may think you're grown up at 18, but our brains don't fully mature until after we hit 30
http://www.dailymail.co.uk/sciencetech/article-4055490/You-think-grown-18-brains-don-t-fully-mature-hit-30.html

May 2nd

Abraham Lincoln (Will Ferrell) and Fredrick Douglass (Don Cheadle) Drunken History Vol. 5 – Funny or Die
https://www.youtube.com/watch?v=ipV2u-MxlFc
Billy the Kid – Drunken History Comedy Central
https://www.youtube.com/watch?v=sF_0om--2Tw
[Clean]Terminator vs Robocop. Epic Rap Battles of History Season 4
https://www.youtube.com/watch?v=dfjIE1jv8BI

May 6th

Scientist –(?????) 10 Most Famous Scientific Theories That Were Later Debunked
https://www.famousscientists.org/10-most-famous-scientific-theories-that-were-later-debunked/
Wiki – Flat Earth
https://en.wikipedia.org/wiki/Flat_Earth

May 7th

Link By Link - A Christmas Carol: The Musical - Jason Alexander https://www.youtube.com/watch?v=Bumro1kOOTI

May 8th

Adult Obesity in the US – By State
https://stateofobesity.org/adult-obesity/
Nerd Fittness – By Steve (????) - A Beginner's Guide to Healthy Eating
https://www.nerdfitness.com/blog/healthy-eating/
Jillian Michaels - Website
https://www.jillianmichaels.com/
Goodrum, T. (2014, Dec 16) 35 Realistic Ways to Squeeze Healthier Habits Into Super Busy Schedules
https://greatist.com/grow/easy-health-tips-busy-lifestyles

May 10th

Alexander (2008, March 10) Top 5 reasons why "The customer is Always Right" is wrong
https://positivesharing.com/2008/03/top-5-reasons-why-the-customer-is-always-right-is-wrong/

May 11th

Sillesen, L. B. (2014, SEPT 8) - What America looks like in the media abroad
https://archives.cjr.org/behind_the_news/american_news_foreign_press.php
Engel, P. (2014, Oct 21) Here's How Liberal Or Conservative Major News Sources Really Are
http://www.businessinsider.com/what-your-preferred-news-outlet-says-about-your-political-ideology-2014-10
MoovieQuotes (2013, January 22) – Youtube - Life Finds a Way
https://youtu.be/dMjQ3hA9mEA

May 14th

Stewart, A. (2017, July 6) High Carbs And No Cardio? Transform Your Body In Just 12 Weeks!
https://www.bodybuilding.com/fun/high-carb-no-cardio-dieting-part-1.htm

Stewart, A. (2017, Dec 14) High Carbs And No Cardio? Transform Your Body In Just 12 Weeks! Phase 2.
https://www.bodybuilding.com/fun/high-carb-no-cardio-dieting-part-2.htm
Caffeine Informer Staff (????) Documented Deaths By Caffeine
https://www.caffeineinformer.com/a-real-life-death-by-caffeine

May 15th
BMW i8
https://www.bmwusa.com/vehicles/bmwi/bmw-i8.html
Lamborghini Veneno
https://www.lamborghini.com/en-en/models/one-off/veneno-roadster

May 22st
AzzyLand (2017, Sept 28) Weirdest Japanese Inventions EVER!
https://www.youtube.com/watch?v=G6wEX6E2meA

May 24th
Vans
https://www.vans.com
Foot Binding
https://en.wikipedia.org/wiki/Foot_binding

May 25th
Karabell, Z. (2017, Aug 9) Yes, Bitcoin Has No Intrinsic Value. Neither Does a $1 Bill
https://www.wired.com/story/bitcoin-has-no-intrinsic-value-neither-does-a-dollar1-bill/
JP Sears (2017, Dec 19) Bitcoin - Ultra Spiritual Life episode 86
https://www.youtube.com/watch?v=g-zIbVEjVpQ

May 26th
Mystery Science Theater 3000
http://www.mst3k.com/
Elvira – Mistress of the Dark
https://www.elvira.com/
Svengoolie
http://svengoolie.com/

May 29th
Breslaw, A (2015, March 20) Cosmopolitan - 18 Things You Should Know Before Dating a Cat Lady
http://www.cosmopolitan.com/sex-love/news/a38020/things-to-know-before-you-date-a-cat-lady/
Cat Lady Box
https://catladybox.com/
Xavier, E. (2017, Sept 18) Leading Cause Creating Cat Ladies Everywhere: Cats Are Awesome
https://kittyclysm.com/creating-cat-ladies/

May 30th
Frank, T. (2016, Aug 11) - The Most Powerful Way to Remember What You Study
https://www.youtube.com/watch?v=eVajQPuRmk8

May 31st
Amazon – What about Bob?
My Book

June 4th
Love is Respect - "I've Been Abusive. How Can I Change?"
http://www.loveisrespect.org/for-yourself/can-i-stop-being-abusive/
The National Domestic Violence HOTLINE - Help For Abusive Partners
http://www.thehotline.org/help/for-abusive-partners/

June 5th
Silver, M. National Geographic - After Utah Video Scandal, a Primer on Hoodoos
https://news.nationalgeographic.com/news/2013/10/131022-hoodoo-goblin-valley-state-park-utah-toppled-boy-scout/
Crimesider Staff CBS News - Warrants issued for men who walked on Yellowstone hot springs
https://www.cbsnews.com/news/warrants-issued-for-men-who-walked-on-yellowstone-hot-springs/

June 6th
Tuttle, B. TIME Money (2016, March 3) Why You Should Feel Even More Guilty About Eating Out at Restaurants All the Time
http://time.com/money/4245285/costs-restaurants-cooking-at-home/

Yancey-Bragg, USA TODAY (2017, Nov 27) Take a bite out of your food bill: How to save money on groceries and dining out
https://www.usatoday.com/story/money/personalfinance/budget-and-spending/2017/11/27/food-bill-how-save-money-groceries-dining-out/536108001/

June 11th
Erb, K. P. FORBES (2014, JUL 7) The Real Cost Of Summer Vacation: Don't Get Buried In Taxes
https://www.forbes.com/sites/kellyphillipserb/2014/07/07/the-real-cost-of-summer-vacation-dont-get-buried-in-taxes/#2acd2256597a
Rogers B. R. PLANET WARE (????) 4 Top-Rated Tourist Attractions in Rome
http://www.planetware.com/tourist-attractions-/rome-i-la-r.htm
Drummond, C. THE WALLET DIET (2015,Oct 7) How Much It Cost Us to Travel Europe for 2 Weeks
http://www.thewalletdiet.com/how-much-it-cost-us-to-travel-europe-for-2-weeks/

June 12th
Fight Club 414
http://www.fightclub414.com/

June 16th
WE Movement
https://www.we.org/we-movement/

June 19th
IMDB – Obsessed
http://www.imdb.com/title/tt1198138/
IMDB - The Fan
http://www.imdb.com/title/tt0116277/
IMDB - Falling Down
http://www.imdb.com/title/tt0106856/
IMDB - Less than Zero
http://www.imdb.com/title/tt0093407/
IMDB - Clean and Sober
http://www.imdb.com/title/tt0094884/
IMDB - Flight
http://www.imdb.com/title/tt1907668/
IMDB - Family Man
http://www.imdb.com/title/tt0218967/
IMDB - My Own Private Idaho
http://www.imdb.com/title/tt0102494/
IMDB - Wreak it Ralph
http://www.imdb.com/title/tt1772341/
IMDB - RP1
http://www.imdb.com/title/tt1677720/

June 21st
Nowell, Ph.D, D.D. (2011, Feb 6) – If it Feels Good Do it?
https://www.psychologytoday.com/blog/intrinsic-motivation-and-magical-unicorns/201102/if-it-feels-good-do-it-0

June 22nd
Keyser H. – Mental Floss (2015 April 15) Where did the phrase "Nice Guys Finish Last" Come from?
http://mentalfloss.com/article/62774/where-does-phrase-nice-guys-finish-last-come
Sama, J. M. (?????)7 Reasons Good Guys Win In The End
https://jamesmsama.com/2014/09/08/7-reasons-good-guys-win-in-the-end/

June 26th
Mooallem, J. (2014, Sept 23) Larry Ellison Bought an Island in Hawaii. Now What?
https://www.nytimes.com/2014/09/28/magazine/larry-ellison-island-hawaii.html?_r=3
Stone, M. (2015, April 29) 16 islands you can buy right now
http://www.businessinsider.com/16-islands-you-can-buy-right-now-2015-4
Neuman, S. (2012, June 22) The Downside to Owning Your Own Island
https://www.npr.org/2012/06/22/155591470/the-downside-to-owning-your-own-island
Amazon – Cast Away
My Book

June 28th

Amazon – Jack London's The Sea Wolf
My Book
Amazon – Homer's The Iliad
My Book
Amazon – Homer's The Odyssey
My Book
Amazon – Oscar Wilde – The Picture of Dorian Gray
My Book

June 29th
Some Dude dancing – Not on a chair - Sorry for the confusion
Hoyt J.L. (2016, Feb 8) Alicia Keys - No One OFFICIAL DANCE VIDEO
https://youtu.be/nCm_oD7lwrg

June 30th
Coleman, K. (????) 7 Big Differences between sex and Love
http://love.allwomenstalk.com/big-differences-between-sex-and-love
Hendel, H. J. (2016, July 19) The Difference Between Sex and Love for Men
https://www.huffingtonpost.com/entry/the-difference-between-sex-and-love-for-men_us_578e26fee4b07cc1115ad9f8

July 2nd
Frank, T. (2015, Nov 7) How to Study and Do Homework in a Time Crunch - College Info Geek
https://youtu.be/ib98J80AUNs
Frank, T. (2016, Aug 11) The Most Powerful Way to Remember What You Study
https://youtu.be/eVajQPuRmk8

July 4th
Amazon – Ready Player One
My Book
Depression and Bipolar Support Alliance - Hotline numbers
http://www.dbsalliance.org/site/PageServer?pagename=urgent_crisis_hotline
National Suicide Prevention Lifeline
https://suicidepreventionlifeline.org/
Boy's (and Girls) Town
https://www.boystown.org/hotline/Pages/default.aspx

July 7th
NAMI
https://www.nami.org/Learn-More/Mental-Health-Conditions/Obsessive-compulsive-Disorder/Support
OCD ACTION (UK)
http://www.ocdaction.org.uk/getting-support/help-and-information-line
SANE (AUSTRALIA)
https://www.sane.org/mental-health-and-illness/facts-and-guides/obsessive-compulsive-disorder
CHADD
http://www.chadd.org/

July 9th
Dodgeson, L. (2017, Sep 8th) Problems caused by binge-watching could go even deeper than previously thought
http://www.businessinsider.com/tv-binge-watching-can-damage-your-health-2017-9
Sleep.org (?????) Three ways gadgets are keeping you awake
https://sleep.org/articles/ways-technology-affects-sleep/
Yapbeelee (2015, Nov 6) Positive and Negative Impacts of Electronic Devices on Children
https://wehavekids.com/parenting/dlectronic-devices-and-gadgets-to-Children

July 10th
It Can Wait
http://itcanwait.usaa.com/
Maria's Message
http://www.mariatiberifoundation.org/
Wiki – Black Mirror
https://en.wikipedia.org/wiki/Black_Mirror

July 11th
Imafidon, C. (?????) 10 Things You Shouldn't Hide Anymore, No Matter How Others View You
http://www.lifehack.org/306039/10-things-you-shouldnt-hide-anymore-matter-how-others-view-you

July 13th
Street Fighter II Turbo: Hyper Fighting
https://en.wikipedia.org/wiki/Street_Fighter_II_Turbo:_Hyper_Fighting
July 17th
TerraFugia TF-X
https://www.terrafugia.com/tf-x/
July 19th
SNL (2013, Sep 25) Matt Foley: Van Down By The River
https://youtu.be/Xv2VIEY9-A8
Exploring Alternatives - (2017, Jul 2) Van Life - Woman Living in a Van for 3 Years to Save Money & Travel the World
https://youtu.be/0EupRH9K5y8
Minimal Millennials - (2017, Nov 8) 1 MONTH VAN LIFE EXPENSES | how much living in a van actually costs
https://youtu.be/EKJ2yboU-R4
Living Big in a Tiny House -(2017, June 15) School Bus Converted To Incredible Off-Grid Home
https://youtu.be/o7X2nOtwdUM
Wandxr Bus - (2017, Apr 29)Vlog #1 Q&A - How We Afford Van Life
https://youtu.be/Z1PF_eUFqZU
July 20th
Risher, B. (?????) The Ultimate Healthy Grocery List When You're Cooking for One
https://greatist.com/eat/healthy-grocery-list-for-one
Kirkpatrick, K. R.D. (2011, Sep 8) Healthy Eating on a Budget Pantry List
http://www.youbeauty.com/nutrition/healthy-eating-on-a-budget-grocery-list/
Lee, J. (2014, February 19) - The Only Grocery Shopping List You'll Ever Need
http://theeverygirl.com/the-only-grocery-shopping-list-youll-ever-need/
Bible, A. This grocery shopping list you need to get ripped
https://www.mensfitness.com/nutrition/what-to-eat/grocery-shopping-list-you-need-get-ripped
Out of Milk - (?????) Healthy College Grocery List & Recipe Ideas
https://www.outofmilk.com/ideas/healthy-college-grocery-list/
Oreo
http://www.oreo.com/
July 21st
Beyer, M. (2017, Dec 29) Fun Family Night Activities That Take Bonding to a Whole New Level
http://www.sheknows.com/parenting/articles/842477/50-family-fun-night-ideas-for-families
July 22nd
Ranker - Vote on Everything - List of Famous Orators
https://www.ranker.com/list/list-of-famous-orators/reference
July 23rd
Roxette (2009, March 4) Youtube - Roxetter - Listen to You Heart
https://youtu.be/yCC_b5WHLX0
July 25th
Youtube (2010, Oct 18) Willow Smith - Whip My Hair
https://youtu.be/ymKLymvwD2U
Youtube (2010, Feb 9) Devo - Whip It (Video)
https://youtu.be/j_QLzthSkfM
Youtube (2012, Jul 26) Bruce Springsteen And Neil Young Sing "Whip My Hair" (Late Night with Jimmy Fallon)
https://www.youtube.com/watch?v=9adAljIaKYc
July 27th
Das R. (2015, August 26) - SCOOP WHOOP 20 Things Super-Rich People Spend Money On That Poor People Like Me Can't Understand
https://www.scoopwhoop.com/world/rich-people-things-poor-people-dont-understand
July 28th
Dooley, P. (2008, Dec 6th) - Anxiety Guru - How to Deal with Crowds
http://www.anxietyguru.net/how-to-deal-with-crowds/
July 29th

Popper, B. (2014, December 3) Don't try this: meet the high schooler who made $300K trading penny stocks under his desk
https://www.theverge.com/2014/12/3/7319277/whiz-kid-penny-stocks-smartphone-mobile-trader
Mitchell, C. (2017, June 23) The Balance - Should You Use Automated Day Trading Software (EAs)?
https://www.thebalance.com/automated-day-trading-software-eas-4142824
Chan M. (2016, Jan 12) Here's How Winning the Lottery Makes You Miserable
http://time.com/4176128/powerball-jackpot-lottery-winners/
GMM S7 E83 (2015, May 5) The Unluckiest Man on Earth
https://www.youtube.com/watch?v=EU3d4PMBxkk

July 30th
Glavan, A. (2017, May 10) - BuzzFeed -36 Ridiculously Delicious Candies From All Over The World
https://www.buzzfeed.com/anamariaglavan/the-best-candies-from-around-the-world
Gallagher B. (2012, October 29) COMPLEX - The 50 Best Candies From Around the World
http://www.complex.com/pop-culture/2012/10/best-candies-around-the-world/
Youtube - LiveStream (2010, December 3) Willy Wonka (HD) "Pure Imagination"
https://youtu.be/r2pt2-F2j2g
World Market
https://www.worldmarket.com/

July 31st
Morin, A. (2017, July 12) Psychology Today - How to Know When to Take a Mental Health Day
https://www.psychologytoday.com/blog/what-mentally-strong-people-dont-do/201707/how-know-when-take-mental-health-day

August 2nd
Cummins E. (2017, September 19) Hunger and Obesity Can Be Two Sides of the Same Coin
http://www.slate.com/articles/health_and_science/science/2017/09/the_latest_u_n_report_shows_that_global_hunger_and_obesity_are_both_on_the.html

August 3rd
ChannelFrederator (2016, April 30) Terrible Advice From Cartoon PSAs - (Tooned Up S2 E30)
https://youtu.be/_v4j2FipbzU

August 4th
Waxman, O. B. (2017, January 3) - Did a Fire Sink the Titanic? These 7 Other Factors Could Have Also Played a Role
http://time.com/4620608/titanic-fire-iceberg-theories/

August 7th
Markmcdermott (2007, September 15) The smoke filled room study
https://youtu.be/KE5YwN4NW5o
Group Think
https://en.wikipedia.org/wiki/Groupthink
Mob Mentality
https://en.wikipedia.org/wiki/Herd_mentality
Band Wagon Effect
https://en.wikipedia.org/wiki/Bandwagon_effect
Mikkelson, D. (1996, February 27) Snopes - Did Disney Fake Lemming Deaths for the Nature Documentary 'White Wilderness'?
https://www.snopes.com/disney/films/lemmings.asp
Lemming
https://en.wikipedia.org/wiki/Lemming#Misconceptions

August 8th
Tarantola A. (2014, August 8) Lemmings don't commit mass suicide, Disney pushed them off a cliff
https://gizmodo.com/lemmings-dont-commit-mass-suicide-disney-pushed-them-o-1614038696
Susman, G. (2016, August 18) 25 Things You Never Knew About the Original 'Ben-Hur'
https://www.moviefone.com/2016/08/18/ben-hur-charlton-heston-facts/
The Week Staff (2012, Novemeber 19) 8 troubling tales of animal abuse on film shoots
http://theweek.com/articles/470272/8-troubling-tales-animal-abuse-film-shoots

August 9th
Tarm, M. (2014, March 18) Best-Selling Author Kevin Trudeau Gets 10 Years In Prison For Massive Deception
http://www.businessinsider.com/best-selling-author-kevin-trudeau-gets-10-years-in-prison-for-massive-deception-2014-3

Hill, M. (2015, August 22) 6 Insane 'As Seen On TV' Products That Are Worse In Person
http://www.cracked.com/blog/6-ridiculous-as-seen-tv-products-tested/

August 12th
Percey Fawcett -
https://en.wikipedia.org/wiki/Percy_Fawcett

August 13th
Roos, D. (?????) How Stuff Works - How Debt Works
https://money.howstuffworks.com/personal-finance/debt-management/debt.htm
Zimmermann, J. (2018, February 8) How to Get Out of Credit Card Debt
https://www.nerdwallet.com/blog/credit-card-debt/
Irby, L. (2017, November 22) The Balance - How to Manage Debt of Any Size
https://www.thebalance.com/how-to-manage-your-debt-960856
Debt Slavery
https://rationalwiki.org/wiki/Debt_slavery
Debt-Bondage
https://en.wikipedia.org/wiki/Debt_bondage

August 14th
SparklinDiamond, (????) List Challenges - The Ultimate List of Disney Characters
https://www.listchallenges.com/the-ultimate-list-of-disney-characters

August 15th
AFI - AFI's 100 Greatest American Movies of All time
http://www.afi.com/100Years/movies.aspx
GIOIA, T. (2015, December 20) Why is 'Godfather III' So Disrespected?
https://www.thedailybeast.com/why-is-godfather-iii-so-disrespected

August 16th
Isip, R. (?????) Life Hack - 15 Reasons Why You Have No Time to Relax and Have Fun
http://www.lifehack.org/articles/lifestyle/15-reasons-why-you-have-time-relax-and-have-fun.html

August 18th
Shame Your Pet
http://shameyourpet.com/

August 19th
Bullying UK
https://www.bullying.co.uk/cyberbullying/
Stop Bullying.gov
https://www.stopbullying.gov/kids/what-you-can-do/index.html
NoBullying.com (2017, March 26) Bullying in India Reaches Epic Proportions
https://nobullying.com/bullying-in-india-2/
IamaWitness - EMJOI
http://iwitnessbullying.org/
Gonzalez, R. (2015, October 22) The Story Behind that Mysterious Eye Emoji in IOS
https://www.wired.com/2015/10/i-am-a-witness-emoji-ios-9/
Steward, S. (2015, Nov 30) #IAmAWitness Stopping bullies one emoji at a time.
https://www.theodysseyonline.com/witness-campaign

August 20th
Ph.D, Mann V. (2012, March 6) Why you should read with your child
https://www.scilearn.com/blog/why-you-should-read-with-your-child
Joyce, A. (2017, February, 16) Why it's important to read aloud with your kids, and how to make it count
https://www.washingtonpost.com/news/parenting/wp/2017/02/16/why-its-important-to-read-aloud-with-your-kids-and-how-to-make-it-count

August 21st
Consumer Attorneys of California - The McDonald's Hot Coffee Case
https://www.caoc.org/?pg=facts

August 22nd
Cadwalader, Z. (2018 Februay 16) Jerry Seinfeld Is Being Sued Over Comedians In Cars Getting Coffee
http://sprudge.com/jerry-seinfeld-is-being-sued-over-comedians-in-cars-getting-coffee-130624.html
Seinfeld
https://en.wikipedia.org/wiki/Seinfeld
Curb Your Enthusiasm

https://en.wikipedia.org/wiki/Curb_Your_Enthusiasm
August 25th
Margolis R. E. (?????) SFGATE - Why Do We Need to Drink Water?
http://healthyeating.sfgate.com/need-drink-water-4301.html
Clean Water for Everyone
http://cwfe.org/
August 26th
Rizzo, C. (2017, December 28) Travel + Leisure 4 Simple Ways to Finally Find Work-life Balance in 2018
http://www.travelandleisure.com/trip-ideas/yoga-wellness/how-to-improve-work-life-balance
Bothwell E. (2018, February 8) Work-life balance survey 2018: long hours take their toll on academics
https://www.timeshighereducation.com/features/work-life-balance-survey-2018-long-hours-take-their-toll-academics#survey-answer
Moore, E. (2018, January 15) 8 Cool Companies to Apply to in 2018 With Awesome Benefits
https://www.glassdoor.com/blog/companies-awesome-benefits-2018/
August 27th
Ravn, K. (2012, March 31) LA Times - Superfruit, or just a plain old Clark Kent fruit?
http://articles.latimes.com/2012/mar/31/health/la-he-superfruits-20120331
Plackett, B. (2012, August 1) - 23 Healthiest Superfruits You Need Now
http://www.health.com/health/gallery/0,,20606331,00.html
Star Fruit - Wikipedia
https://en.wikipedia.org/wiki/Carambola
Super Foods – Wikipedia
https://en.wikipedia.org/wiki/Superfood
GrapeFruit - Wikipedia
https://en.wikipedia.org/wiki/Grapefruit
The Emperor's New Clothes – Wikipedia
https://en.wikipedia.org/wiki/The_Emperor%27s_New_Clothes
August 30th
Nelson, B. (2017, April 5) ODyssey - 11 (Practical) Ways To Be More Spontaneous
https://www.theodysseyonline.com/sit-here-and-look
August 31st
The Bucket List Family
http://www.thebucketlistfamily.com/
BucketList Journey
https://bucketlistjourney.net/category/bucketlists/
September 1st
Animal Planet (2014, Aug 29) An Unwelcome, 10 Foot Long Pool Guest | Gator Boys
https://youtu.be/X47yLp_eeBc
Blidner, R. (2015, July 4) NYDaily News - Texas alligator attack victim mocked animal before jumping in bayou
http://www.nydailynews.com/news/national/man-mocked-alligator-fatal-attack-texas-bayou-article-1.2281325
Sept 2nd
McCann, G. - (2012, August 27) Who Do You Think You Are?: Aligning Your Character & Reputation
My Book
Scott S.J. & Davenport B. (2016, August 23) Declutter Your Mind: How to Stop Worrying, Relieve Anxiety, and Eliminate Negative Thinking
My Book
Scott S.J. (2017) Habit Stacking: 127 Small Changes to Improve Your Health, Wealth, and Happiness
My Book
Aarons, J. (2018, February 3) Single? It's Your Fault
My Book
September 3rd
Shvedsky, L. (2017, March 3) 6 Insane Conspiracy Theories That Actually Turned Out To Be True
https://www.good.is/articles/six-conspiracy-theories-that-are-true
September 4th
NcCrullex (2017, January 8) PEOPLE ARE AMAZING HD 2017
https://youtu.be/fo4rhrTAmo4

People are Awesome (2016, October 29) PEOPLE ARE AWESOME 2016: BEST OF THE MONTH OCTOBER 2016
https://youtu.be/iM_yrugA80o
Gold, A. (2017, May) Miracle of the 1980s: The Talking Car
https://www.autotrader.com/car-news/miracle-of-the-1980s-the-talking-car-265020
The Talking Car app
http://www.talkingcar.com/
IMDB - Duck Tales Nothing to Fear 1987
http://www.imdb.com/title/tt0566947/quotes

September 5th
DePaulo, B. (2017, April 23) More people than ever before are single – and that's a good thing
http://theconversation.com/more-people-than-ever-before-are-single-and-thats-a-good-thing-74658
Wiki - Spinster
https://en.wikipedia.org/wiki/Spinster
Silva, L. (?????) 10 Signs That Your Single Life Is Happy Even Though You Don't Feel Like You Are
https://www.lifehack.org/articles/communication/10-signs-that-your-single-life-happy-even-though-you-dont-feel-like-you-are.html

September 6th
makemegenius (2012, October 13) Germs Movie for Kids Virus & Bacteria Introduction
https://youtu.be/7D0eIsuZC3w
Newman, H. (2013, December 30) BuzzFeed 19 Ways To Tell If You Are A Germaphobe
https://www.buzzfeed.com/hnew92/19-ways-to-tell-if-you-are-a-germaphobe-9qja
Monk
https://en.wikipedia.org/wiki/Monk_(TV_series)
WebMD - Symptom Checker
https://symptomsbeta.webmd.com/#/info
Maserati
https://www.maserati.com/maserati/international/en
Skarnulis, L. (2004, July 4) Cleanliness Rules Germaphobes' Lives
https://www.medicinenet.com/script/main/art.asp?articlekey=46748

September 7th
Konkel, L. (2017, April 25) Scinece News for Students - Concerns explode over new health risks of vaping
https://www.sciencenewsforstudents.org/article/concerns-explode-over-new-health-risks-vaping
Alfaro, D. (2017, February 15) The Spruce - Cooking Oil Smoke Points
https://www.thespruce.com/cooking-oil-smoke-points-995464
Ranker (????) Famous TV Chefs
https://www.ranker.com/list/notable-tv-chef_s)/reference
Disney Definition (2013, July 7) - The Little Mermaid - Les Poissons (HD)
https://youtu.be/Iq-UaXQ1c1M
Wiki – Brave New World
https://en.wikipedia.org/wiki/Brave_New_World

September 9th
Raymond, E. S. and Moen R. (2014, May 21) How to Ask Questions The Smart Way
http://www.catb.org/esr/faqs/smart-questions.html
Martel M. (?????) Life Hack - How to Be Amazingly Good at Asking Questions
https://www.lifehack.org/articles/communication/how-amazingly-good-asking-questions.html

September 11th
Holidays Calendar
http://www.holidayscalendar.com/months/september/

September 12th
Wiki – Manos(Hands) The Hands of Fate
https://en.wikipedia.org/wiki/Manos:_The_Hands_of_Fate
Wiki – Ed Wood
https://en.wikipedia.org/wiki/Ed_Wood

September 14th
NRRArchives (2012, November 30) The Chordettes "Lollipop" & "Mr. Sandman"
https://youtu.be/Fty3Nzc-oiY
Wiki - Tin Foil Hat

https://en.wikipedia.org/wiki/Tin_foil_hat

September 15th

Mashup Math (2017, April 10) 10 Examples of Real World Connections in Math
http://mashupmath.com/blog/2017/4/10/10-examples-of-real-world-connections-in-math
Wiki - Rose (Mathematics)
https://en.wikipedia.org/wiki/Rose_(mathematics)
Bohannon J. (2016, May 17) - Sunflowers show complex Fibonacci sequences
http://www.sciencemag.org/news/2016/05/sunflowers-show-complex-fibonacci-sequences
Kalid (??????) An Intuitive Guide To Exponential Functions & e
https://betterexplained.com/articles/an-intuitive-guide-to-exponential-functions-e/
Poppick, S. (2015, March 9) Money - 3 Simple Equations All Investors Should Know
http://time.com/money/3735703/investing-basic-math-equations/
Math is fun (2014)
https://www.mathsisfun.com/money/budget.html

September 17th

Geek& Sundry
https://geekandsundry.com/shows/tabletop/
Geek & Sundry (2017 Sept 13) TableTop: Wil Wheaton Plays Eldritch Horror
https://youtu.be/87B1Wlz8fMo
Cthulhu Wars - KickStarter
https://www.kickstarter.com/projects/petersengames/cthulhu-wars

September 18th

Prenatal Workouts FitPregnancy -
https://www.fitpregnancy.com/exercise/prenatal-workouts
What to Expect (2015, August 18) 9 Workouts That Get the Green Light During Pregnancy
https://www.whattoexpect.com/pregnancy/exercises-for-pregnant-women
Movieclips Trailer Vault (2012, Janurary 9) Junior Official Trailer #1 - Danny DeVito Movie (1994) HD
https://youtu.be/aNfsJuv0bJU
American Pregnancy Association (2016) September 2 Exercise During Pregnancy
http://americanpregnancy.org/pregnancy-health/exercise-during-pregnancy/

September 19th

Wiki – HomeStar Runner
https://en.wikipedia.org/wiki/Homestar_Runner
HomeStar Runner!
https://homestarrunner.com/
Rooster Teeth
http://roosterteeth.com/show/red-vs-blue
Peters L. (2015, August 6) Bustle - 10 Websites From The Early 2000s You Forgot About, Because Sometimes You Just Need A Little "Badger Badger Badger" In Your Life
https://www.bustle.com/p/21-genius-things-with-a-cult-following-on-amazon-that-cost-less-than-2-8207076

September 21st

Wiki - Gravitron
https://en.wikipedia.org/wiki/Gravitron
Howell, E. (2016, July 23) Space.com - How Fast is the Earth Moving?
https://www.space.com/33527-how-fast-is-earth-moving.html

September 22nd

Wiki - X-Files Pusher
https://en.wikipedia.org/wiki/Pusher_(The_X-Files)
Wiki – Jessica Jones
https://en.wikipedia.org/wiki/Jessica_Jones_(TV_series)
Wiki - Dexter
https://en.wikipedia.org/wiki/Dexter_(TV_series)
Wiki - Mr. Brooks
https://en.wikipedia.org/wiki/Mr._Brooks

September 23rd

Wiki - Sean Astin
https://en.wikipedia.org/wiki/Sean_Astin

Wiki - White Water Summer
https://en.wikipedia.org/wiki/White_Water_Summer
Wiki - Goonies
https://en.wikipedia.org/wiki/The_Goonies
Wiki - Lord of the Rings
https://en.wikipedia.org/wiki/The_Lord_of_the_Rings_(film_series)
Wiki - Stranger Things
https://en.wikipedia.org/wiki/Stranger_Things

September 25th
Independent – Merry, S. (2016, July 4) - Kitty Genovese murder
https://www.independent.co.uk/news/world/americas/kitty-genovese-murder-the-real-story-of-the-woman-killed-in-front-of-38-witnesses-in-queens-in-1964-a7118876.html

September 26th
Men's Fitness - Workout Routines
https://www.mensfitness.com/training/workout-routines
Carlson, C. (2015, March 30) - 4-Week Weight Training Plan for Women
https://www.shape.com/fitness/workouts/4-week-weight-training-plan-women
Schwartz, J. (2017, July 18) LiveStrong - Exercise Plan for the Atkins Diet
https://www.livestrong.com/article/262011-exercise-plan-for-the-atkins-diet/

September 29th
bronx9999 (2007, December 9) Pirates of the Caribbean
https://www.youtube.com/watch?v=SeNDzbFv2f8
Ol' Chumbucket (2018, January 13) International Talk like a Pirate Day WordPress - Good Pirate, Good Reader: Remnants of a Book Found on Blackbeard's Ship
http://talklikeapirate.com/wordpress/
Maritime Connector - Modern Piracy
http://maritime-connector.com/wiki/piracy/
History Channel (2012, September 19) 8 Real-Life Pirates Who Roved the High Seas
http://www.history.com/news/8-real-life-pirates-who-roved-the-high-seas

September 30th
Mcspadden (2015, May 14) Time - You Now Have a Shorter Attention Span Than a Goldfish
http://time.com/3858309/attention-spans-goldfish/

October 4th
Niemann K. (2015, August 8) Pressure wash inside of your car
https://youtu.be/d73K5gMSCHE

October 7th
SNL (2013, September 25) Matt Foley: Van Down By The River - SNL
https://youtu.be/Xv2VIEY9-A8
Westfalia Digital Nomads (2017, November 13) VANLIFERS: Portrait of an Alternative Lifestyle (Subs: EN-FR-ES-DE-IT) Full Movie
https://www.youtube.com/watch?v=gRQamLSFTy0

October 11th
Symington A. (2015, September 13) Cook Sunday for the Whole Week in 6 Easy Steps
https://www.cleaneatingmag.com/meal-plans/cook-sunday-for-the-whole-week-in-6-easy-steps

October 12th
Hammacher Schlemmer The Submarine Sports Car
https://www.hammacher.com/Product/12531
Simona(2013(?), December 2) 2015 Lamborghini Veneno Roadster
https://www.topspeed.com/cars/lamborghini/2015-lamborghini-veneno-roadster-ar159850.html
Zhang, Benjamin (2018, February 1) The 7 most luxurious private jets in the world
http://www.businessinsider.com/most-luxurious-private-jets-in-the-world-photos-details-2018-1

October 14th
United Federation of Planets
http://memory-alpha.wikia.com/wiki/United_Federation_of_Planets

October 16th
Kennedy-Moore E. Ph.D. (2013, January 31) Imaginary Friends
https://www.psychologytoday.com/blog/growing-friendships/201301/imaginary-friends
Amazon - Drop Dead Fred
My Book

Wiki – Little Monsters
https://en.wikipedia.org/wiki/Little_Monsters
Amazon – Flight of the Navigator
My Book
October 18th
TritoxHD (2016, August 8) The Universal Language - Why Did It Fail?
https://youtu.be/079myzI9xj0
Koebler, J. (2016, Apr 22) Why a Universal Language Will Never Be a Thing
https://motherboard.vice.com/en_us/article/ezpvx4/why-humans-dont-have-a-universal-language
October 20th
YESWorksOrg (2013, December 20) Napoleon Dynamite talks about skills
https://youtu.be/XsiiIa6bs9I
October 21st
USHMM - Holocaust Encyclopedia - Book Burning
https://www.ushmm.org/wlc/en/article.php?ModuleId=10005852
Wiki - Book Buring
https://en.wikipedia.org/wiki/Book_burning
October 22nd
Wiki – Divide and Rule
https://en.wikipedia.org/wiki/Divide_and_rule
Penguin Random House - The Master and Margarita Reader's Guide
https://www.penguinrandomhouse.com/books/531360/the-master-and-margarita-by-mikhail-bulgakov-a-newly-revised-translation-by-richard-pevear-and-larissa-volokhonsky-introduction-by-richard-pevear-foreword-by-boris-fishman/9780143108276/readers-guide/
October 23rd
Florio, G. M. (2015, November 16) 5 Signs You're Allergic To Alcohol — Not Just Alcohol Intolerant
https://www.bustle.com/articles/123630-5-signs-youre-allergic-to-alcohol-not-just-alcohol-intolerant
Fulton, W. (2016, February 6) What It's Like to Be Deathly Allergic to Alcohol
https://www.thrillist.com/drink/nation/what-its-like-to-be-deathly-allergic-to-alcohol
UNODC - (2017, June 22) World Drug Report 2017: 29.5 million people globally suffer from drug use disorders, opioids the most harmful
http://www.unodc.org/unodc/en/frontpage/2017/June/world-drug-report-2017_-29-5-million-people-globally-suffer-from-drug-use-disorders--opioids-the-most-harmful.html
October 24th
Wasserstein, R. L. (2017, December 6) A Statistician's View: What Are Your Chances of Winning the Powerball Lottery?
https://www.huffingtonpost.com/ronald-l-wasserstein/chances-of-winning-powerball-lottery_b_3288129.html
Wiki – American Dream
https://en.wikipedia.org/wiki/American_Dream
Lamorghini Veneno
https://www.lamborghini.com/en-en/models/one-off/veneno-roadster
Audi R8
https://www.audiusa.com/models/audi-r8
BMW i8
https://www.bmw.com/en/bmw-models/bmw-i8-coupe.html
October 25th
Coaching Positive Performance (?????) - 17 Essential time management skills
https://www.coachingpositiveperformance.com/17-essential-time-management-skills/
Conrad, B. Dr. (????) Tech Addiction - Computer Game Addiction - Symptoms, Treatment, & FAQs
http://www.techaddiction.ca/computer_game_addiction.html
Pereira, S. (2017, December 26) World Health Organization Says Video Game Addiction Is a Mental Health Disorder—Are They Really That Bad?
http://www.newsweek.com/world-health-organization-says-video-game-addiction-mental-health-disorder-are-759660
October 28th
Ravenscraft, E. (2014, April 2) Does Speeding Really Get You There Any Faster?
https://lifehacker.com/does-speeding-really-get-you-there-any-faster-1556767685
Wiki – 24

https://en.wikipedia.org/wiki/24_(TV_series)

October 29th

Leahy, R. L. Ph.D (2008, May 19) Jealousy Is a Killer: How to Break Free From Your Jealousy
https://www.psychologytoday.com/blog/anxiety-files/200805/jealousy-is-killer-how-break-free-your-jealousy
Good Therapy.org
https://www.goodtherapy.org/learn-about-therapy/issues/jealousy
Wiki - Fear
https://en.wikipedia.org/wiki/Fear_(1996_film)
Wiki – Daddy's Home
https://en.wikipedia.org/wiki/Daddy%27s_Home_(film)

October 31st

Wiki - Prometheus
https://en.wikipedia.org/wiki/Prometheus
Wiki – Lycaon
https://en.wikipedia.org/wiki/Lycaon_(Arcadia)
Wiki – The Labours of Hercules
https://en.wikipedia.org/wiki/Labours_of_Hercules
The Machine Stops
https://en.wikipedia.org/wiki/The_Machine_Stops

November 3rd

Martin, E. (2017, June 7) The Top 10 Ways American's Waste Money
https://www.cnbc.com/2017/06/07/the-top-10-ways-americans-waste-money.html
Food and Agriculture Organization of the United Nations Key facts on food loss and waste you should know!
http://www.fao.org/save-food/resources/keyfindings/en/

November 4th

Wiki - Pirate Radio
https://en.wikipedia.org/wiki/Pirate_radio
Amazon - Pump up the Volume
My Book
Wiki - Radio Shack
https://en.wikipedia.org/wiki/RadioShack

November 6th

Amadeo, K. (2018, March 8) - What Is Average Income in the USA? Family, Household, History
https://www.thebalance.com/what-is-average-income-in-usa-family-household-history-3306189
Rose, J. (2017, May 27) CNBC - Want to be a millionaire? Nowadays it's just not enough
https://www.cnbc.com/2017/05/27/want-to-be-a-millionaire-nowadays-thats-not-enough-to-retire-on.html
Frankle, N. (?????) Can You Retire Now? The Complete Answer
https://wealthpilgrim.com/can-you-retire-now/
Amazon – Throw Momma From the Train
My Book

November 8th

Pandora's Box
https://www.pandorasboxinc.com/
Wiki - Pandora's Box
https://en.wikipedia.org/wiki/Pandora%27s_box
Bullying Statistics – Bullying and Suicide
http://www.bullyingstatistics.org/content/bullying-and-suicide.html

November 9th

Swami, V. (2016, September 13) Women's idealised bodies have changed dramatically over time – but are standards becoming more unattainable?
https://theconversation.com/womens-idealised-bodies-have-changed-dramatically-over-time-but-are-standards-becoming-more-unattainable-64936

November 10th

Prancercise (2012, December 25) Original - Prancercise: A Fitness Workout
https://youtu.be/o-50GjySwew
AwakenWithJP (2017, October 24) Prancercising - Ultra Spiritual Life episode 78

https://youtu.be/MoRMUzljoAA
GOOD MYTHICAL MORNING S7 E74 (2015, April 22) Youtube - The Weirdest Workout Videos Ever
https://youtu.be/eGMcv6KnIyQ
CCMusicFactoryVEVO (2009, October 25) C+C Music Factory - Things That Make You Go Hmmmm.... (Video Version) ft. Freedom Williams
https://youtu.be/XF2ayWcJfxo

November 11th
Napier, N. K. Ph.D. - (2014, May 12) - The Myth of Multitasking
https://www.psychologytoday.com/blog/creativity-without-borders/201405/the-myth-multitasking

November 12th
MCHammerVevo (2009, February 24) MC Hammer - U Can't Touch This
https://www.youtube.com/watch?v=otCpCn0l4Wo

November 13th
Bleiberg, Larry (2018, November 25) - 10 Great places to get lost in a labyrinth
https://www.usatoday.com/story/travel/destinations/10greatplaces/2016/11/25/labyrinth-maze/94316058/

November 15th
Griffiths K. (2016, October 4) The Meaning Of "Always Forward" In 'Luke Cage' Is A Call To Action For Black Viewers
https://www.bustle.com/articles/187494-the-meaning-of-always-forward-in-luke-cage-is-a-call-to-action-for-black-viewers

November 16th
Copple, K. (2016, February 12) If every person on earth was to be given an equal portion of inhabitable land, how much land would each person get?
https://www.quora.com/If-every-person-on-earth-was-to-be-given-an-equal-portion-of-inhabitable-land-how-much-land-would-each-person-get

November 17th
American Heart Association (?????) Portion Size Versus Serving Size
https://healthyforgood.heart.org/eat-smart/articles/portion-size-versus-serving-size

November 20th
UNODC - (2017, June 22) World Drug Report 2017: 29.5 million people globally suffer from drug use disorders, opioids the most harmful
http://www.unodc.org/unodc/en/frontpage/2017/June/world-drug-report-2017_-29-5-million-people-globally-suffer-from-drug-use-disorders--opioids-the-most-harmful.html

November 21st
Glass, J. (2014, January 24) The 11 Manliest Candles on the Market
https://www.thrillist.com/home/best-scented-candles-10-aromatic-candles-to-make-your-place-smell-nice-supercompressor-com
Homesick Candles
https://homesickcandles.com/
One Kings Lane
https://www.onekingslane.com/live-love-home/scented-candles/
CandleJunkies - (2016, September 19) Best Smelling Candles Under $30 2016
http://www.candlejunkies.com/best-smelling-candles-under-30-2016/

November 22nd
BatDad (2017, August 12) BatDad - Compilation August 2017
https://youtu.be/QYWFqMYQIA8
vlogbrothers (2014, October) I Kind of Hate Batman
https://youtu.be/LATPfqT4118

November 23rd
Tassi, P. (2015, August 12) Felicia Day's 'You're Never Weird On The Internet' Is An Emotional Look At Geekhood
https://www.forbes.com/sites/insertcoin/2015/08/12/felicia-days-youre-never-weird-on-the-internet-is-an-emotional-look-at-geekhood/#1d8188547231
Amazon - Felicia Day You're Never Weird on the Internet (Almost): A Memoir
My Book
Mastrapa, G. - (2009, September 29) How Felicia Day Recruited Millions for Her Guild
https://www.wired.com/2009/09/felicia-day-recruits-millions-for-her-guild/

Wiki - Felicia Day
https://en.wikipedia.org/wiki/Felicia_Day
Wiki – Buffy the Vampire Slayer
https://en.wikipedia.org/wiki/Buffy_the_Vampire_Slayer
November 24th
DeMichele, T. (2017, September 23) Machiavelli Said, "the Ends Justify the Means"
http://factmyth.com/factoids/machiavelli-said-the-ends-justify-the-means/
Hudspeth, C. (2016, October 13) 20 Examples Of The Mandela Effect That'll Make You Believe You're In A Parallel Universe
https://www.buzzfeed.com/christopherhudspeth/crazy-examples-of-the-mandela-effect-that-will-make-you-ques
Wiki - False Memory
https://en.wikipedia.org/wiki/False_memory
November 25th
Cruze, R. (?????) 15 Practical Budgeting Tips
https://www.daveramsey.com/blog/the-truth-about-budgeting
Practical Money Skills (?????) Budgeting
https://www.practicalmoneyskills.com/learn/budgeting
Konsko, L. (2014, December 4th) Can I Use One Credit Card to Pay Off Another?
https://www.nerdwallet.com/blog/credit-cards/can-i-use-credit-card-to-pay-another-credit-card/
November 26th
Saunders, E. G. (2017, July 4) A Way to Plan If You're Bad at Planning
https://hbr.org/2017/07/a-way-to-plan-if-youre-bad-at-planning
Amy Landino (2016, September 18) How to Plan Your Day
https://youtu.be/e7QrmHiF2SI
Thomas Frank (2015, February 19) My 3-Tier Planning System for Getting Stuff Done - College Info Geek
https://youtu.be/8nkCt3OF6-8
Amazon – Ashlee Vance - Elon Musk: Tesla, SpaceX, and the Quest for a Fantastic Future
My Book
November 29th
Vicedecanato Claustro IE (2014, March 11) Interview with adjunct professor Guadalupe de la Mata
https://www.youtube.com/watch?v=r34arpC33_4
Guadalupe de la Mata (2014, May 2) The Five Monkeys Experiment: "this is the way things are done here"
http://innovationforsocialchange.org/five-monkeys-experiment/?lang=en
December 1st
Okura L. (2014, February 27) The Real Voices Behind Milli Vanilli Share Their Side Of The Lip Syncing Scandal (VIDEO)
https://www.huffingtonpost.com/2014/02/27/milli-vanilli_n_4860222.html
Wiki - Milli Vanilli
https://en.wikipedia.org/wiki/Milli_Vanilli
December 2nd
Amazon - Animal House
My Book
Amazon – Dazed and Confused
My Book
Amazon – The Hangover
My Book
Amazon – Risky Business
My Book
December 3rd
Adopt A Highway Business - USA
http://www.adoptahighway.com/our-mission/
Adopt A Highway government - Canada
https://www2.gov.bc.ca/gov/content/transportation/transportation-environment/adopt-a-highway
December 5th
Webster (2018, March 14) - Sarcasm
https://www.merriam-webster.com/dictionary/sarcasm

Calvillo, F. (2017 March) Only a Legend Like MacLaine Can Have THE LAST WORD
https://cinapse.co/only-a-legend-like-maclaine-can-have-the-last-word-f9aad5282afe
Lazarus, C. N. Ph.D. (2012, June 26) Think Sarcasm is Funny? Think Again
https://www.psychologytoday.com/us/blog/think-well/201206/think-sarcasm-is-funny-think-again
Wise B. (2016, April 18) Dry Wit and Sarcasm... Be Careful What You Wish For!
https://www.huffingtonpost.com/brooke-wise/dry-wit-sarcasmbe-careful_b_9721700.html
Gino, F. (2015, November 17) - The Surprising Benefits of Sarcasm
https://www.scientificamerican.com/article/the-surprising-benefits-of-sarcasm/
Chin, R. (2011, November 14) - The Science of Sarcasm? Yeah, Right
https://www.smithsonianmag.com/science-nature/the-science-of-sarcasm-yeah-right-25038/

December 6th
Skwarecki B. (2018, January 11) The Life Hacks We Actually Use
https://lifehacker.com/tag/life-hacks
HowStuffWorks
https://www.howstuffworks.com/
Instructables
https://www.instructables.com/
Youtube - DIY Network
https://www.youtube.com/user/DIYNetwork
Youtube - Jordan Page, FunCheapOrFree - Channel
https://www.youtube.com/channel/UCIBM8DAHoehmJ7_LSLDkB3A
Prince, A. (?????) - 25 Killer Sites For Free Online Education
https://www.lifehack.org/articles/money/25-killer-sites-for-free-online-education.html
Robinson, R. (2018, March 15) - The 26 Best Websites for Learning New Skills
https://www.thebalance.com/websites-learn-new-skills-1200627
ConsumerAffairs Research team (2018, January 1) - Best Online Homeschools
https://www.Consumeraffairs.com/education/online-homeschools/#
Udemy - Home Page
https://www.udemy.com/
Martin T. & Priest David (2017, December 18) The complete list of Alexa commands so far
https://www.cnet.com/how-to/amazon-echo-the-complete-list-of-alexa-commands/

December 7th
Westenberg, J. (2016, October 23) - Stop telling each other it's alright. Sometimes, it's just not.
https://medium.com/hi-my-name-is-jon/stop-telling-each-other-its-alright-sometimes-it-s-just-not-7b3180298257

December 9th
Team Empire (2009, August 25) The Greatest Movie Sequels
https://www.empireonline.com/movies/features/50greatestsequels/

December 11th
Wiki – VR
https://en.wikipedia.org/wiki/Virtual_reality#Before_the_1950s
Wiki – Theory of Forms
https://en.wikipedia.org/wiki/Theory_of_forms
Wiki - Hylomorphism
https://en.wikipedia.org/wiki/Hylomorphism

December 12th
Yahoo View – Consumer Probe – Irwin Mainway
https://view.yahoo.com/show/saturday-night-live/clip/50022029/irwin-mainway

December 13th
Marshall, C. (2015, October 27) 11 really stupid things people on the internet still believe
http://metro.co.uk/2015/10/27/11-really-stupid-things-people-on-the-internet-still-believe-5427051/
Niggulis, O. (2017, August 11) 11 Things People Believe – But Shouldn't
https://conversionxl.com/blog/11-things-people-believe-but-shouldnt/

December 14th
Ranker (?????) The Best Black and White Movies Ever Made
https://www.ranker.com/list/best-black-and-white-movies-ever-made
Amazon (?????) Metropolis
My Book
Amazon (?????) The Hustler

My Book
Amazon (?????) What Ever Happened to Baby Jane?
My Book
Amazon (?????) Psycho
My Book
Amazon (?????) Casablanca
My Book
Amazon (?????) It's a Wonderful Life
My Book
Amazon (?????) Laural & Hardy
My Book

December 15th
PaulaAbdulVEVO - (2009, June 16) Paula Abdul, Randy Jackson - Dance Like There's No Tomorrow
https://youtu.be/ygT4sCJIdVo
TBS (2014, July 3) That Ain't Dancing Sally | Seinfeld | TBS
https://youtu.be/B5dogmMj-s0
ANI (2017, August 27) Dance like there's no tomorrow! It can reverse signs of ageing
https://economictimes.indiatimes.com/magazines/panache/dance-like-theres-no-tomorrow-it-can-reverse-signs-of-ageing/articleshow/60240992.cms

December 16th
Don, K. (2015, November 2) I Couldn't Watch Violent TV While Pregnant
https://www.huffingtonpost.com/katherine-don/i-couldnt-watch-violent-tv-while-pregnant_b_7973682.html
Faris, S. (2016, June 17) The exhilarating thrill of watching scary movies alone
http://theweek.com/articles/628500/exhilarating-thrill-watching-scary-movies-alone
Wolcott, J. (2017, February 3) Trump: The Movie, Coming Soon to a Theater Near You (if Theaters Still Exist)
https://www.vanityfair.com/hollywood/2017/02/trump-the-movie-coming-soon-to-a-theater-near-you
Foutch H. (2017, October 29) The Best Horror Movies for Kids (and Scaredy-Cats)
http://collider.com/horror-movies-for-kids/
Heid, M. (2017, October 25) You Asked: Is Watching Scary Movies Good for You?
http://time.com/4995896/scary-movies-burn-calories/

December 17th
Bellis, M. (2017, March 26) The History of Money
https://www.thoughtco.com/history-of-money-1992150
Kusimba, C. (2017, June 19) When – and why – did people first start using money?
https://theconversation.com/when-and-why-did-people-first-start-using-money-78887
Siebold, S. (2014, July 14) The Way Millionaires View Money Is Different From Everyone Else
http://www.businessinsider.com/how-millionaires-think-about-making-money-2014-7
Elkins, K. (2016, October 31) Self-made millionaire: 3 things everyone should know about money
https://www.cnbc.com/2016/10/31/self-made-millionaire-3-things-everyone-should-know-about-money.html
Nesiba, R. F. (2013, September 23) Was money created to overcome barter?
http://neweconomicperspectives.org/2013/09/money-created-overcome-barter.html
Wiki – Wimpy
https://en.wikipedia.org/wiki/J._Wellington_Wimpy
Wiki – Angular Momentum
https://en.wikipedia.org/wiki/Angular_momentum#Conservation_of_angular_momentum

December 19th
Bangell08 - (2018, February 6) The Lion King and Shakespeare's Hamlet: Similarities and Differences
https://owlcation.com/humanities/Similarities-Between-The-Lion-King-and-Hamlet
Mehrotra, A. (2014, December 5) 10 Hollywood Movies That Were Inspired By Bollywood
https://www.scoopwhoop.com/entertainment/hollywood-movies-copied
Tomar, A. (2016, September 24) 10 Hollywood Movies That Are Copied From Asian Cinema
https://www.rvcj.com/10-hollywood-movies-that-are-copied-from-asian-cinema/
Brew, S. (2017, November 29) 126 Movie Remakes and Reboots Currently in the Works
http://www.denofgeek.com/us/movies/reboots/248590/126-movie-remakes-and-reboots-currently-in-the-works
CRACKED Readers (2017, August 2) 21 Terrible Hollywood Reboots And Why They Failed

http://www.cracked.com/pictofacts-755-bad-remakes-side-by-side-with-originals/
Goodyear UK (2016, February 29) - The Goodyear Eagle-360 concept tire
https://youtu.be/oSFYwDDVgac

December 20th
SkyDiveMonroe (2017, February 21) - Winter Skydiving: What to Wear When It's Cold
http://skydivemonroe.com/about/news/winter-skydiving-what-to-wear-when-its-cold/
Skydive Orange - (2018, February 1) Top Tips for Skydiving in Winter
http://www.skydiveorange.com/2018/02/01/top-tips-skydiving-winter/
Amazon (?????) – Along Came Polly
My Book
Wiki – Polar Bear Plunge
https://en.wikipedia.org/wiki/Polar_bear_plunge
Weisberger, M. (2015, December 30) - Everybody Freeze! The Science of the Polar Bear Club
https://www.livescience.com/53226-polar-bear-plunge.html

December 22nd
Breyer, M. (2013, September 12) - 10 things you didn't know about koalas
https://www.mnn.com/earth-matters/animals/stories/10-things-you-didnt-know-about-koalas
Shapiro A. D. (2013, April 25) - Koala chlamydia: The STD threatening an Australian icon
http://www.bbc.com/news/magazine-22207442
Australian Koala Foundation
https://www.savethekoala.com/about-koalas/help-save-koalas
World Wildlife Fund
https://gifts.worldwildlife.org/gift-center/gifts/Species-Adoptions/Koala.aspx
National Wildlife Federation - Ranger Rick
http://kids.nwf.org/Kids/Ranger-Rick.aspx

December 23rd
ABC – NEWS (2017, November 1) Former employees expose inner workings of Russian troll farm
http://abcnews.go.com/International/employees-expose-workings-russian-troll-farm/story?id=50866368
Stein, J. (2016, August 18) How Trolls Are Ruining the Internet
http://time.com/4457110/internet-trolls/
Merrill, B. (2015, June) Here's What Happens When You Confront An Internet Troll Face To Face
https://www.makeuseof.com/tag/heres-happens-confront-internet-troll-face-face/
Chen, A. (2014, December 18) MIT Technology Review - The Troll Hunters
https://www.technologyreview.com/s/533426/the-troll-hunters/

December 24th
Zimmerman, N. (2012, April 19) Why Knowing The Difference Between Colon And Cologne Is Kind Of Important
http://gawker.com/5903384/why-knowing-the-difference-between-colon-and-cologne-is-kind-of-important
Grammarly
https://www.grammarly.com/

December 25th
Hillerbrand, H. J. (2018, February 22) Encyclopaedia Britannica - Christmas
https://www.britannica.com/topic/Christmas

December 26th
St. Jude Children's Hospital
https://www.stjude.org/
Shriner's Hospital For Children
https://www.shrinershospitalsforchildren.org/shc
Dave Thomas - Foundation for Adoption
https://davethomasfoundation.org/

December 27th
Power, C. (2015, November 6) The Telegraph - What the Koran really says about women
http://s.telegraph.co.uk/graphics/projects/koran-carla-power/index.html

December 29th
Bomey, N. (2018, February) U.S. vehicle deaths topped 40,000 in 2017, National Safety Council estimates
https://www.usatoday.com/story/money/cars/2018/02/15/national-safety-council-traffic-deaths/340012002/

Donath, J. (2017, December 22) The Atlantic Driverless Cars Could Make Transportation Free for Everyone—With a Catch
https://www.theatlantic.com/technology/archive/2017/12/self-driving-cars-free-future/548945/
Leefeldt, E. (2018, January 15) CBS NEWS - Florida seniors could hold the future of driverless cars
https://www.cbsnews.com/news/florida-seniors-to-test-self-driving-cars/
Miller, J. (2014, August 19) BBC News - Google's driverless cars designed to exceed speed limit
http://www.bbc.com/news/technology-28851996
Hern, A. (2017, January 16) The Guardian - Tesla allows self-driving cars to break speed limit, again
https://www.theguardian.com/technology/2017/jan/16/tesla-allows-self-driving-cars-to-break-speed-limit-again

Additional Sources I found interesting but have no point of direct reference within this body of work:
https://www.inc.com/amy-morin/mentally-strong-kids-have-parents-who-refuse-to-do-these-13-things.html
https://www.theladders.com/career-advice/10-unmistakable-habits-utterly-authentic-people

www.ingramcontent.com/pod-product-compliance
Lightning Source LLC
LaVergne TN
LVHW041537070426
835507LV00011B/811